American Culinary
Federation
since 1929

American Culir
Federation
since 1929

an Culinary
deration
ce 1929

American Culinary
Federation
since 1929

American Culinary
Federation
since 1929

American Culinary
Federation
since 1929

American Culinary
Federation
since 1929

American Culinary
Federation
since 1929

American Culinary
Federation
since 1929

American Culinary
Federation
since 1929

American Culinary
Federation
since 1929

American Culinary
Federation
since 1929

American Culinary
Federation
since 1929

baking fundamentals

AMERICAN CULINARY FEDERATION

Saint Augustine, Florida

by Noble Masi, CMB, CEPC, AAC, HOF

With Brenda R. Carlos

PEARSON

Prentice
Hall

Upper Saddle River, NJ 07458

Library of Congress Cataloging-in-Publication Data

Masi, Noble.
   American Culinary Federation baking fundamentals / by Noble Masi with Brenda R. Carlos.
      p. cm.
   Includes bibliographical references and index.
   ISBN 0-13-118351-6
   1. Baking. I. Carlos, Brenda R. II. Title.
   TX763.M324 2007
   641.8'15—dc22

2005034709

Editor-in-Chief: Vernon R. Anthony
Senior Acquisitions Editor: William Lawrensen
Director of Publishing & Manufacturing: Bruce Johnson
Managing Production Editor: Mary Carnis
Production Editor: Emily Bush, Carlisle Publishing Services
Production Liaison: Janice Stangel
Manufacturing Manager and Buyer: Ilene Sanford
Executive Marketing Manager: Ryan DeGrote
Senior Marketing Coordinator: Elizabeth Farrell
Marketing Assistant: Les Roberts
Cover Design: Cheryl Asherman
Cover Photograph: Ben Fink, PictureArts Corporation
Interior Design: Brigid Kavanagh
Composition: Carlisle Publishing Services
Printing and Binding: Courier Kendallville

Pearson Education Ltd.
Pearson Education Canada, Ltd.
Pearson Education Australia PTY, Limited
Pearson Educacion de Mexico, S.A. de C.V.

Pearson Education Singapore, Pte. Ltd.
Pearson Education—Japan
Pearson Education North Asia Ltd.
Pearson Education Malaysia, Pte. Ltd.

10 9 8 7 6 5 4 3 2 1
ISBN: 0-13-118351-6

Dedicated to my son, John Noble Masi, and my daughter, Andrea Masi Carlsen, whose love and warmth have fueled my work, and their smiles and hugs filled my dreams. I would like to further dedicate this book to my wife, Robin, for supporting my ambitions with warmth and love and for her careful attention to detail.

Noble Masi

brief contents

contents

The book will be structured around sections and learning units. A section is an organizational device, containing one or more learning units. The following is a list of sections and learning units:

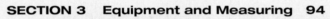

acknowledgments

From Noble Masi

I would like to thank the American Culinary Federation for the opportunity to write this book introducing the principles of baking. My journey began with the love, warmth, respect, and very strong work ethics of my parents, Rosa and Antonio, strengthened by the firm guidance of my mentor and brother, Tony, whose entrepreneurial spirit and baking skills led to the opening of Buzzeo's Bakery on November 15, 1947, with his wife, Marie. Additional support came from my brother, Albert, and my twin sister, Concetta, as well as Dominick Simone, my friend and colleague, during my apprenticeship at Buzzeo's Bakery.

My inspiration for teaching began when I entered Food and Maritime Trades High School and, under the guidance of William Sultan, the author of *Practical Baking,* teaching became a reality. My most challenging and rewarding experience followed with a 35-year tenure at the Culinary Institute of America, working side by side with the finest faculty in the world, sharing knowledge and success with over 30,000 alumni. For this experience, I thank the Culinary Institute of America family and alumni. At the conclusion of my tenure I was appointed Ambassador for the school.

This book became a reality with the help and support of many individuals. First and foremost, I want to thank my wife, Robin, who processed my knowledge into an understandable text; and Brenda Carlos, for her dedication and hard work, her quotes, summaries, and for the life she gave to the text. I wish to acknowledge Mark Huth for his reviews and guidance, Vern Anthony for believing in me, and Richard Embery for his attention to detail with the photography. I would also like to acknowledge the Culinary Institute of America for supporting our photo shoot and support of this textbook with kitchen space, students, and resources.

Noble Masi

From Brenda R. Carlos

It has been over two years since I first received the assignment to work on this book with Chef Noble Masi, and what an experience it has been. We have been in contact on almost a daily basis; and during that time, I have been impressed with Chef Masi's discipline and dedication to this work. Through this experience, I have been able to get a glimpse of his passion and adoration for the baking industry. He is truly revered by his former students and fellow bakers, and I am extremely grateful to Vern Anthony, our Prentice Hall editor, who put us together to work on this project.

I can't go further without thanking Chef Masi's wife, Robin, whose dedicated service has kept this project rolling. She has been an important part of our team. I also must thank Mark Huth, whose wise counsel and advice have steered this project. It was a privilege to work with Richard Embery, our food photographer, whose talents and experience added greatly to this book. To our many reviewers, I offer my sincere thank you. Your comments and suggestions were appreciated. Leaders from the Retailer's Bakery Association have offered their support and assistance, and I am grateful for their involvement. The professionals from the American Culinary Federation, including Michael

Baskette, have been behind this project from the beginning. I appreciate their support throughout the process. To the more than 30 bakers and pastry chefs whose bios appear throughout the text, I offer a sincere thank you. Your stories will surely inspire the students who study this book.

Finally, I must thank my family. Rudy, my beloved husband of over 30 years, I couldn't immerse myself in my work without your undying support. To my sons, Chad and Clint and my daughter-in-law Melissa, I wish to express my love and thanks for your continued belief in my many projects. To my parents, Jean and Perry Langer, I want you to know that you always taught me to have faith in my abilities, and without that foundation I surely couldn't have embraced this opportunity.

Brenda R. Carlos

Reviewers

Michael Baskette, CEC, CCE, AAC
ACF Director of Educational Development

Volker Baumann CMB
Southern Alberta Institute of Technology

Robert W. Beighey, CEC
Sullivan College

Walter Bronowitz, CCC, CCE, AAC
Executive Chef
Children's Hospital
Seattle, WA

Robert Brown
Paul Smith College

Steve Cornelius/Hospitality Management M. Ed, CEC, CCE, FMP
Sinclair Community College

Patricia Curfman CEC, AAC
Chef/Owner Patti Cakes

Vincent Donatelli
A-B Tech

Amy Felder CEPC
College of Culinary Arts
Johnson Wales University

Catherine Hallman, CEPC
Walters State Community College

Chef Melissa L. Karasek CEPC
Le Cordon Bleu / Orlando Culinary Academy

Audrey Langenhop CEPC
York Technical Institute

David McSwane, HSD, REHS, CFSP
Associate Professor Indiana University
School of Public and Environmental Affairs-
Room 4067

David Pantone CEPC, CEC, CCE, AAC
Florida Culinary Institute

George Pastor, CEC, CCE, AAC
Culinary Dean
Hillsborough Community College

Arno Schmidt CEC, author, consultant

Fritz Sonnenschmidt CMC, AAC
Retired Culinary Dean, Culinary Institute
of America

James Taylor, CEC, AAC
Columbus State Community College

Mark Wright, CEC, AAC
Executive Chef, Assistant Professor
Erie Community College

We would like to acknowledge the following people from the Image Resource Center and at Pearson Education:

Melinda Reo, Director, Image Resource Center

Zina Arabia, Manager, Rights and Permissions

Beth Brenzel, Manager, Visual Research

Karen Sanatar, Manager, Cover Visual Research & Permissions

Rita Wenning, Image Cover Coordinator

Fran Teopfer, Image Permissions Coordinator

We would also like to acknowledge the following people from Pearson Imaging Centers:

Rob Handago, Director of Digital Imaging Pearson Imaging Centers

Joe Conti, Site Supervisor USR2

Ron Walko, Technician

Corin Skidds, Color Tech Support

Robert Uibelhoer, Technician

Gregory Harrison, Technician

foreword

As a chef, educator, and mentor to many young culinarians, I am pleased to be able to write this introduction for the newly released American Culinary Federation's *Baking Fundamentals* written by Certified Master Baker and Certified Executive Pastry Chef Noble Masi under ACF's guidance and advice. A textbook of this magnitude has been long overdue.

The ACF has been committed to improving the knowledge and skills of cooks, chefs, and pastry chefs for over 76 years. Founded in 1929 with training and networking as two of its primary purposes, the ACF continues to provide guidance and career advice to thousands of foodservice professionals every year through accreditation, apprenticeship training, and certification.

Chef Masi holds dual certifications with both the Retailer's Bakery Association (RBA) and the ACF, proving his intense educational background and professional achievements. I applaud his detailed precision, but also his insights into the reality of everyday bakery production. Together the art and the science of baking have finally been masterfully recorded.

Baking Fundamentals was designed to offer the basic information needed by both cooking and pastry students as they begin their careers in professional foodservice. All formulas and techniques have been expertly tested by the author himself and/or students under his tutelage. Chef Masi contributed his expertise as a baker, his finesse as an instructor, his talents as a writer, and his dedication to professionalism in every page of the book.

Brenda Carlos, who assisted Chef Masi in compiling this monumental project, is also to be commended for a great job handling the details and precision that is necessary for a book to carry the ACF's name in its title. This indeed is an ACF book, but written specifically by the expertise of two individuals and reviewed and now supported by a thousand others.

Now partnering with the launch of American Culinary Federation's *Culinary Fundamentals* in 2006, Baking *Baking Fundamentals* begins to round out the necessary training for foodservice professionals working in kitchens and bakeshops. If the information doesn't whet your appetite, the baking formulas will.

Enjoy, learn, and bake.

Sincerely,
John Kinsella, CMC, CCE, AAC
ACF National President

about the authors

Chef Noble Masi, CEPC, CMB, AAC, CHE

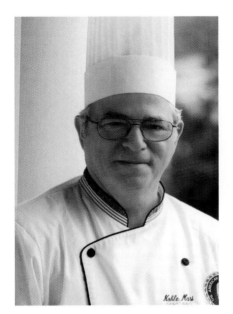

Noble Masi is currently serving as Ambassador for the Culinary Institute of America. He retired in August, 2000, as a professor in baking and pastry arts at The Culinary Institute of America, where he had worked since 1965. During his tenure he served as Chairman of the Baking Department, Coordinator of the Progressive Learning Year System, Director of Continuing Education, as well as Director of Education.

In 1999, Chef Masi was named "Chef of the Year" by the American Culinary Federation. He earned ACF's Professionalism Award in 1996, and was the organization's "Educator of the Year" in 1982. At the conclusion of his tenure, he was appointed Ambassador for the school.

He was introduced to the foodservice industry through his family's bakery and added to his knowledge at the Food & Maritime Trades High School in New York City. He then studied at the American Institute of Baking and became a member of the American Society of Baking Engineers. He holds an associate degree in business and a bachelor of science degree in hotel and restaurant management from the University of New Haven, New Haven, CT.

Chef Masi is a "Hall of Fame" member of the American Academy of Chefs (AAC). He is also a member of the Order of the Golden Toque. He is a Certified Executive Pastry Chef (CEPC), a Certified Master Baker (CMB), and a Certified Hospitality Educator (CHE). He is a certified culinary judge for both the American Culinary Federation (ACF) and the Retail Baker's Association. He has served as Program Administrator for the ACF Master Chef Certification Program and founded the Mid-Hudson Culinary Association, and has served as Chairman of the Board. He has also served two terms as National ACF Treasurer.

Brenda R. Carlos

Brenda Carlos has served as publisher and managing editor for the Hospitality News Group, publishers of *Hospitality News for the Western U.S.* as well as the *International Education Guide.* She has authored countless articles focusing on all aspects of the foodservice industry, event management, and running a business. She also was a contributing editor to "Service at its Best, Waiter-Waitress Training" (Prentice Hall). She is the co-author of "Event Management for Tourism, Cultural, Business and Sporting Events" (Prentice Hall). She is currently under contract working on a number of other food and business textbooks and is a regular contributor to the *National Culinary Review* and *Sizzle* magazines. Ms. Carlos is an enthusiastic and dynamic speaker; she loves to speak to students and professionals about the culinary, hospitality, and event management industries as well as goal setting and lifestyle issues. She is a graduate of Brigham Young University, and she has many years experience in hospitality editing and writing. Ms. Carlos is a member of the International Foodservice Editorial Council.

baking fundamentals

baking's rich history and understanding food safety and sanitation

*For centuries bakers
have provided food for
daily nourishment and
sweet goods for special
occasions. Unit 1 covers
the historical
significance of the
baker's role. It will also
discuss the development
of baking in America and
offer some insight for the
future of the industry.
Unit 2 serves as a review
of the importance of
sanitation and safety
within every bakeshop.*

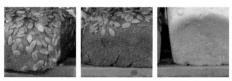

introduction to baking

"[Breadbaking is] one of those almost hypnotic businesses, like a dance from some ancient ceremony. It leaves you filled with one of the world's sweetest smells . . . there is no chiropractic treatment, no Yoga exercise, no hour of meditation in a music-throbbing chapel that will leave you emptier of bad thoughts than this homely ceremony of making bread."

M. F. K. Fisher, *The Art of Eating*

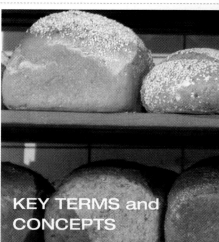

KEY TERMS and CONCEPTS

acid-alkaline reaction

creaming

fermentation

foaming

gluten

leavening

ratio

sequence

temperature

time

yeast

LEARNING Objectives

After you have finished reading this unit, you should be able to:

- **Explain** the historical development of bread baking from the cultivation of grain to milling and baking

- **Describe** the time line of major events that shaped the baking industry

- **Discuss** the development of equipment and ingredients, and the growth of baking in America

- **Describe** the skills and knowledge required to become a successful baker

- **Define** the dynamics of the baking industry

WELCOME TO THE WONDERFUL WORLD OF BAKING! YOU are about to embark on an exciting adventure, exploring one of the oldest and most honored professions. From ancient civilizations until today, bread has remained the cornerstone and building block of the daily diet in many cultures around the world; and bakers continue to be held in high esteem. Today a baker not only concentrates on bread but also a variety of other baked goods including cakes, pastries, cookies, and desserts. Baking challenges a person's body as much as his or her mind. It is a physical job that demands a reliable sense of timing and constant attention to detail as well as a sound understanding of baking methodology. Today, as then, a baking professional is considered an artist.

DEMAND FOR TRAINED BAKERS IS ON THE RISE

More than ever, the baking industry needs technically trained individuals. According to the *Occupational Outlook Handbook*, 2004–05 Edition, approximately 173,000 workers were employed as bakers. The report further indicates that demand will be on the rise by 2010. You will find professional bakers working in wholesale and retail bakeries, catering companies, supermarkets, restaurants, hotels, resorts, cafeterias, and factories.

Whether preparing for a career in baking or studying it as a component to a culinary education, it will be important for the student to understand the principles and theories behind baking. Before beginning, we will start with a brief history.

WORLD HISTORY OF BAKING

It All Started with Bread

"Bread has always accompanied every step of civilization. The simple act of crushing wheat, the first primitive milling was a major step for mankind. Man became sedentary because of the desire to grow wheat and make bread. Fermentation of dough was the start of biotechnology. The first sewing was probably to put skins together as primitive silos. The first gears, teethed wheels, were probably for flour mills, and the first clutch mechanisms, too and the first governors and the first camshafts. The art of mechanics came from the need for bread. It was the quest for bread that engendered industry."

Lionel Poilane, legendary French baker "Smithsonian"
(January, 1995)

Many centuries ago man learned how to sustain himself and his family by planting and harvesting crops. Grasses such as wheat, rye, rice, barley, oats, and later corn were cultivated to produce a bountiful food source. In Eastern civilizations the grain of choice was rice, which continues as the fundamental food source. In the Western world, grains such as wheat, corn, and rye have sustained the masses. Let us take a look at some of the significant, historical baking-related world events as listed in the following time line.
It was supplied by the American Society of Baking and is used here with permission.

BC

c 8000 BC–c 3000 BC

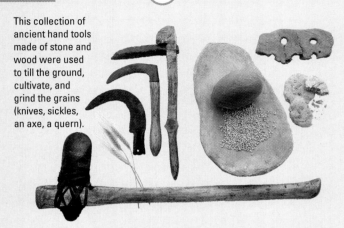

This collection of ancient hand tools made of stone and wood were used to till the ground, cultivate, and grind the grains (knives, sickles, an axe, a quern).

At first grain was crushed by hand with pestle and mortar. In Egypt a simple grinding stone (quern) was developed. All bread was unleavened, there were no raising agents, and bread was made from a mixed variety of grains. Today's equivalents are Indian chapattis and Mexican tortillas.

Egypt developed grain production along the fertile banks of the Nile. Barley, emmer (a type of wheat), corn, flax, and dourah (a type of millet) were common harvests. Grain became a staple food and spread to the Balkans and throughout Europe, eventually being cultivated in Britain.

Tougher wheat varieties were developed, and the baking of bread became a skill in Egypt along with brewing beer. In this warm climate, wild yeasts were attracted to multi-grain flour mixtures and bakers experimented with leavened dough.

The Egyptians invented the closed oven, and bread assumed great significance. Homage was paid to Osiris, the god of grain, and bread was used instead of money; the workers who built the pyramids were paid in bread.

The following satirical quote dates back to the period called The New Kingdom (1150 to 1295 BC)

> The baker kneads incessantly and puts the loaves in the fire. His head is in the middle of the fireplace. His son holds him by his legs. Should they slip out of his hands, the father would fall into the fire.

This gives us a glimpse into the large fireplace ovens used at the time.

This painted model depicts the life of two ancient Egyptian servants. One kneads the dough while the other fans the fire.

c 1000 BC–c 40 BC

Yeast wheat bread became popular in Rome, and by 500 BC a circular quern was developed, which was a circular stone wheel that turned on another fixed stone. This was the basis of all milling until the Industrial Revolution in the 19th century and is still the way stone-ground flour is produced today.

In Greece the watermill was invented, although it was a few centuries before its significance was fully realized.

In Rome the first bakers' guilds were formed, and well-to-do Romans insisted on the more exclusive and expensive white bread—a preference which persists in Europe and English-speaking countries to this day. A Roman invented the first mechanical dough-mixer, powered by horses and donkeys.

Romans invaded Britain where wheat was still being crushed by hand and baked over open fires. More sophisticated techniques were introduced, including watermills.

Bread and politics: In Rome the authorities decreed that bread should be distributed free to all adult males.

Grains could be dried and stored for long periods of time. They could also be easily transported, which increased the mobility of man and the establishment of new communities.

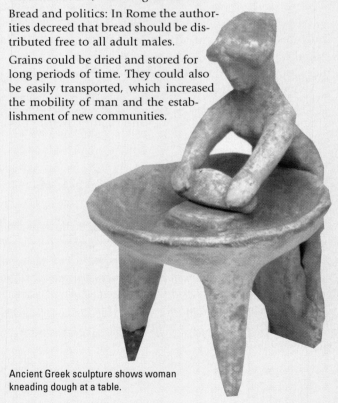

Ancient Greek sculpture shows woman kneading dough at a table.

c 50 AD–c 600 AD

1150 AD–1266 AD

AD

Saxons and Danes settled in Britain and introduced rye, which was well suited to cold northern climates. Dark rye bread became a staple, which lasted to the Middle Ages.

The Persians are said to have invented the windmill. The power generated could drive much heavier stone querns for milling, but it was 600 years before they appeared in Western Europe.

The growth of towns and cities throughout the Middle Ages saw a steady increase in trade, and bakers began to set up in business. Bakers' guilds were introduced to protect the interests of members and to regulate controls governing the price and weight of bread. By Tudor times, Britain was enjoying increased prosperity; and bread had become a real status symbol. The nobility ate small, fine white loaves called manchets; merchants and tradesmen ate wheaten cobs; while the poor had to be satisfied with bran loaves.

Bakers formed guilds to protect them from manorial barons, and in 1155 London bakers formed a brotherhood.

King John introduced the first laws governing the price of bread and the permitted profit.

The Assize of Bread was organized. This body sat to regulate the weight and price of loaves. The first bread subsidy was given—12 pennies for eight bushels of wheat made into bread. (A bushel of wheat is the actual weight of 8 gallons of wheat. This could vary according to the hardness or dryness of the grain.) If a baker broke this law, he could be pilloried and banned from baking for life. (A pillory is a device consisting of a wooden framework on a post, with holes for the head and hands, in which offenders were formerly locked and exposed to public scorn as punishment.)

A community baker's oven was excavated from the ruins of Pompeii, an ancient city that was completely destroyed when Mount Vesuvius erupted in 79 AD.

The Industrial Age
1700 AD–1887 AD

c 1700 AD–1757 AD

In Georgian times the introduction of sieves made of Chinese silk helped to produce finer, whiter flour; and white bread gradually became more widespread. Even today more than 70 percent of the bread we eat is white. Tin from the flourishing mines began to be used to make baking tins. Bread baked in tins could be sliced and toasted, and it was not long before the sandwich was invented. In the early 19th century, life was dramatically changed by the Industrial Revolution. As large numbers of farm workers moved from the country into cities to work in the new factories, less food was produced. When the Corn Laws were passed prohibiting the importation of grain, starvation became a serious problem in Britain.

Wheat began to overtake rye and barley as the chief bread grain.

A new Act superseded the Assize of 1266. Magistrates were empowered to control the type, weight, and price of loaves. Only white, wheaten (wholemeal), and "household" bread (made from low-grade flour) were permitted.

A report accused bakers of adulterating bread by using alum lime, chalk, and powdered bones to keep it very white. Parliament banned alum and all other additives in bread but some bakers ignored the ban.

1822 AD–1826 AD

In London standard weights for loaves were abolished. Bakers had to weigh each loaf in the customer's presence.

Wholemeal bread, eaten by the military, was recommended as being healthier than the white bread eaten by the aristocracy.

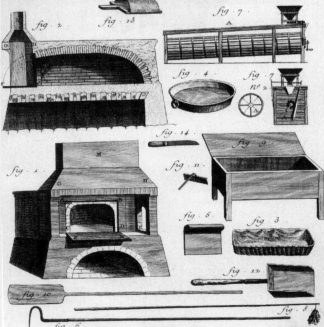

This illustration of a French bakery was published in Diderot's 1751 *Encyclopedia*.

BAKING IN AMERICA

In the vast majority of cases, the early American baker was a man, who shared his techniques with the colonial housewife. Their methods became similar. The brick oven, developed by the Romans, was fired by wood. While waiting for the "arch" of the oven to turn "white," flour was sifted, a **yeast** brew was prepared, coals were removed from the oven, and eventually a sponge dough mixture was **fermented** and transformed into a loaf of bread.

In 1999, the American Society of Baking Engineers celebrated its 75th Annual Technical Conference and presented a video called "Baking in America." The following time line of significant American baking-related events was compiled using that information. It is presented here with permission from the American Society of Baking.

While productivity alone has increased by over 900 percent in the past 40 years, the challenge still remains to produce a superior, nutritional baked product for the constantly changing American diet.

For over 300 years, the undaunted spirit of the American baker has revolutionized an industry. Through ingenuity, passion, and practice, craft has been integrated with science. As a social experiment and as a reflection on our society, the history of baking has no equal.

NOTE: Without thermometers, the baker would judge the readiness of the oven by the color of bricks in the arch. When they turned white, the oven was ready for baking.

1640 AD–1775 AD

In 1640 commercial bakeries began to appear, with the first bakery established in Plymouth, Massachusetts.

By 1650, the price of a loaf was directly related to the cost of wheat. By 1685, authorities fixed bakers' return at four shillings to each quarter of wheat. In return, municipal authorities did protect bakers by recognizing the general rules of apprenticeship and by prohibiting peddlers and middlemen from selling bread products.

By the time of the Revolutionary War, the colonial population had grown to 2.5 million. Boston, with a population of 7,000, had six bakeries. New York and Philadelphia, each with populations around 5,000, reported five bakers each.

This line engraving depicts a colonial American baker during the late 1700s.

1780 AD–1850 AD

As the colonial era came to a close, westward expansion turned trading posts into towns and the baking industry soon benefited. Cincinnati, in 1780, was a struggling outpost with less than 2,000 people and two bakeries. By 1820, the town boasted a population of 12,000 with 15 bakeries.

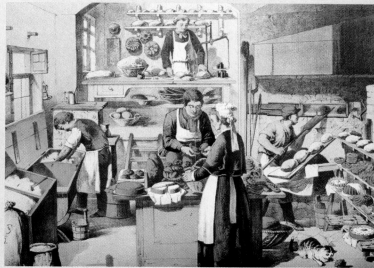

This drawing offers us a glimpse of a busy bakeshop in the mid-1800s. Notice the flour bins and ovens and the variety of products being produced.

By 1850, the Census of Manufacturers reported 2,027 bakeries throughout the United States producing over $13 million in baked goods and employing 6,727 wage earners. Owning a small-scale bakery was gaining a respectable position in the nation's economy. It ranked 19th by value of product sold. By number of plants and employees, it ranked 13th in the nation. Among food processing industries, the baking industry ranked second in value of products, second in number of establishments, and third by wage earners.

In 1850, consumption of wheat flour was 205 pounds per year and was greater than any other food group, up by 35 pounds from 1830.

At this time, the baker had two methods of mixing, "straight dough" and "sponge dough." Although more laborious, the sponge method provided more control over the fermentation and afforded the baker greater variety of yeast-raised products by creating a "master sponge."

1850 AD–1900 AD

Between 1850 and 1900, profound social changes created enormous opportunities for commercial baking. A growing population fueled the demand for baked goods. During that 50-year period, the number of people in America increased from 23 million to over 75 million.

By 1868, Charles Fleischmann revolutionized the baking industry when he began to market compressed yeast.

In the mid-1870s, the first indirect continuous-firing oven was introduced. Prior to that time, the peel oven was a major obstacle in increasing efficiency. (Increased production was not easy to achieve because the oven's basic design prevented continuous baking.) The new indirect oven was created by removing the firebox from the baking chamber and repositioning it either behind or below the chamber. The new oven could do the work of three older units, and the baker had more control over the heat.

By 1893, Simon and Weil Company of Cincinnati, Ohio, manufactured the first gas-fired oven. Three years later Meek Baking Company opened a new plant that featured installed oil burners that provided considerable energy savings.

A third oven introduction, the reel oven made by AJ Fish & Company, had been used extensively in the biscuit and cracker industry. It consisted of a series of horizontal hearths pivoting on a rotating axis in a large baking chamber. The oven was powered by a system of weights and counterweights. Like the rotary oven, loading and unloading was a distinct advantage, as no peel was needed (wooden paddle) to reach the baked goods. The baked goods were easily accessible.

In 1876, Hunter and Sifter Company (predecessors to the JH Day Company) introduced the first mechanical mixer. The capacity of some of these machines ran as high as six barrels of flour or around 1,175 pounds.

The first dough divider was introduced in 1895 by the Dutchess Tool Company. Originally designed for roll production, it was quickly adapted to bread dough.

By 1900, improvements in transportation and the introduction of refrigeration began to alter the American diet. The canning industry brought year-round fruits and vegetables to American tables. Bottled milk was appearing on doorsteps, and the packing industry was providing a consistent and affordable supply of meat.

1904 AD–1929 AD

The Alsop bleaching process was discovered in 1904, permitting flour to be chemically bleached, thereby reducing the naturally occurring process to a few hours. Although the process had no effect on the quality or nutritive content of flour, the issue emerged at a time when there was growing concern about adulteration, mislabeling, and chemical treatment of food. The passage of the Food and Drug Act of 1906 was one result of these concerns.

In the early 1900s, the U.S. Food Administration urged the nation to eat more fruits and vegetables. They also imposed a program for conserving wheat and flour. Mondays and Wednesdays were "Wheatless Days." Because of the bakers' ability to adjust their recipes, formulas, and bread products—and still make a palatable loaf of bread using 75 percent wheat and 25 percent corn, rye, oats, and barley—the Food Administration encouraged everyone to buy baker's bread.

B.H. Kroger, the founder of Kroger Grocery and Baking Company, first conceived of chain store baking in 1901. He began operations with two double-deck drawplate ovens and 14 bakeries to supplement baked products at 42 retail stores.

In a 1929 Census of Manufacturers survey, the industry had grown to 200,000 wage earners working in 20,785 bakeries producing over $1.5 billion of baked goods. By the end of 1929, 50.8 percent of all baked foods were distributed through grocery stores, 3.1 percent were sold to institutions, 11.1 percent were distributed through multiunit retail stores and chain stores, 25 percent were distributed house-to-house, and 10 percent were distributed through retail outlets.

Haggard, impoverished Southern women riot for bread outside the broken windows of a bakery during the Civil War.

1939 AD–1945 AD

Many homemakers in the suburbs preferred to have bread delivered to the door of their homes. This bread man delivered bread, rolls, and sweet goods on a weekly or biweekly route.

Enriched flour was introduced. In 1939, the American Medical Association's Council on Foods and Nutrition recommended the restoration of vitamins and iron in white flour.

The 1940s proved to be a period of unparalleled expansion. The war effort not only increased per capita income but offered countless jobs to women who might otherwise have baked at home. By 1941, incomes were up 43 percent in a 10-year period. Unemployment had declined to 2.7 million, a drop of 70 percent from two years earlier. House-to-house delivery began to expand in the early 1940s.

The War Food Order, issued in January 1943 during WW II, was one of the most important regulations affecting the baking industry. War Food Order #1 provided for the mandatory enrichment of all white bread and eventually rolls. The order also created provisions for the restrictive use of shortenings, milk solids, and sugar because of their shortage and price volatility.

To support the war effort, the American Institute of Baking transformed their Chicago campus into a training center for Bakery Field Officers. Baking was taught under field or battle conditions to the U.S. Army and Marine Officers.

1950 AD–Present

By the midcentury thousands of bakeries were engaged in home delivery.

The early 1950s was a transition period for the baker, from semi-automatic to nearly total automation.

In 1963 numerous film wrapping machines were introduced.

By 1968, the wholesale baking industry sales were up 3.6 percent with profits of 2.3 percent, and multiunit baking was still continuing its struggle. While sales increased 5.7 percent, profits were barely .3 percent.

The 1970s saw a continual rise of ingredient prices. By 1974, the demand for sugar outstripped the supply. Sugar had peaked at $71.95 per hundredweight, nearly 500 percent higher than the previous year. Bakers who had successfully experimented with alternative sweeteners continued to do so after the crisis subsided in 1975.

In the early 1990s Artisan bread gained popularity. This movement returns to the traditional methods of bread baking, which emphasize quality of ingredients, slow fermentation, hand shaping, and baking in small batches. It retreats from mechanized bread and harmonizes with the popularity for all things organic, natural, and health-conscious. Restaurants, local bakeries, and even commercial grocery stores caught on to the irresistible nature of a freshly baked, rustic-style loaf of bread.

By the late 1990s, the baking industry was a highly automated, multisegmented industry, producing over $30 million in traditional baked goods. Technology and applied science continued to impact both production and development. The use of enzymes and dough conditioners extended product shelf-life and added to increased production volume.

By 2004, robotic systems were being used to maximize storage and retrieval functions, and automated order makeup systems became a reality rather than a dream.

LEARNING ACTIVITY 1-1

Write a two- to three-page paper on the development of the baking industry from breads to cakes to cookies and pastries. Include in this report the evolution of equipment, ingredients, and baking products. Students will need to do some research for this outside of class using the library or Internet.

THE EMERGING ROLE OF THE BAKER

In ancient times, after observing the effect of heat on dough, it was concluded that a closed chamber could provide a more efficient method of cooking dough. Larger units of dough could be made, requiring baking only once or twice a week.

The first ovens were shaped like beehives and contained shelves and dampers to control the heat. The ovens were built to serve an entire community. Families throughout the community would bring their home-mixed dough to bake in the community oven. The person assigned to operate the oven was called the baker. The baker was an important member of the community.

Beyond Breads

Over the years, as the market basket of ingredients began to grow and as bakers expanded the principles used in bread baking, additional products were made. For example, holiday breads such as panettone, stollen, and babka and other iced loaves and rolls were made when small quantities of sugar, butter, eggs, and milk were added to basic yeast dough.

With improvements in transportation and fabrication of ingredients, the market basket continued to grow and so did the products being produced by bakers. Lamination of dough brought croissants and puff pastry dough. The understanding of **gluten** development (gluten is the protein part of flour that gives structure to the baked good) brought new recipes for strudel, pies, turnovers, and cookies. Once it was learned that eggs were capable of providing structure and **leavening** (raising or lightening by air, steam, or gas), bakers **foamed** the eggs by whipping them to incorporate air and made cake batters such as sponge cake. Eggs were added to sugar and shortening that was beaten or **creamed** together to make pound cake.

It was discovered that when an alkaline such as baking soda was mixed with an acid like buttermilk, carbon dioxide was released, creating an **acid-alkaline reaction.** The gas created bubbles, which could leaven the batters. This knowledge led to the development of scones, muffins, and quick breads. The combination of baking soda and acid produced a single action. Double-acting baking powder was activated in two stages: the first with moisture and the second with heat. New developments in shortenings and baking powder produced the first high-ratio cakes and single-stage cake mixes.

BECOMING A SUCCESSFUL BAKER

Bakers of today must possess a combination of knowledge, skill, and passion (Figure 1-1). They need to know how to purchase quality ingredients, and understand the proper methods of receiving, storing, and utilizing those products, as well as how to create fresh, convenient, and nutritional baked goods.

In addition, a baker must also be able to complete the following tasks:

- Understand the function of many different ingredients
- Weigh and measure ingredients accurately in large quantities
- Blend the ingredients to prepare dough and batter
- Roll, shape, and cut a variety of dough products and pastries by hand
- Know how to operate production machinery

Figure 1-1 Certified Master Bakers gather for annual meeting. The Retailer's Bakery Association awards the certification to seasoned bakers who have accomplished certain professional goals and passed a rigorous written and practical exam. (For more details, see Unit 21.)

One cannot underestimate the need for passion. It is an important element for a baker's success. One with passion always seeks the highest standards. A true professional will look at the products he or she produced today and try to figure out what can be done to improve the formula for tomorrow (Figure 1-2). Always searching for the latest ingredients, equipment, methods, and presentations, a passionate baker has a drive for excellence and is never satisfied with the status quo. Additionally, he or she will spend time visiting bakeries, restaurants, supermarkets, and local farmer's markets, always looking for new ideas. Because the industry is constantly evolving, his or her thirst for knowledge is never quenched. Joining trade associations and reading periodicals and books helps the passionate baker keep up on the latest news of the industry.

Throughout my 50 years as a professional baker and educator, I have used the following phrase as my motto: clean, utilize, and improve. By incorporating these principles as a personal mantra, students will be on their way to becoming successful bakers.

Observe the Fundamentals of Cleanliness

Cleanliness and sanitation are key elements for success. Be proud of your profession. Always demonstrate your pride by wearing a clean apron and shoes. Keep your workspace organized and neat. Clean and well-maintained tools and equipment not only help to exhibit a professional image, they are safer to use (Figure 1-3).

Utilize Ingredients Properly

Ingredients are a baker's most important resource. They must be respected and handled correctly. The observance of strict temperature control is imperative throughout storage, preparation, and consumption of the product. Always use care and precision when measuring ingredients in order to eliminate waste. Improper handling of foods means lost revenues. For example, when whole

Figure 1-2 Professional baker.

spections of the facility to see if there are any cracks or broken screens that provide an open invitation to pests.

Flies breed on garbage and then land on places around the bakeshop (Figure 2-7). Air curtains installed on exit doors can help to keep flies out of the shop. Inside the bakeshop, keep the garbage covered and remove it every few hours. Outside the shop, garbage containers must be equipped with tight-fitting lids, and refuse storage areas must be kept as tidy as possible.

FOOD SAFETY

According to *Food Safety Fundamentals* by McSwane, Rue, Linton, and Graf Williams (Pearson Education, 2004), food-borne hazards are classified into three categories: biological, chemical, and physical. They can cause illness or injury when consumed with food.

- Biological hazards consist of bacteria, viruses, parasites, and fungi and cause the most incidents of food-borne illness.
- Chemical hazards are toxic substances that may occur naturally or may be added during the processing of food.
- Physical hazards are hard or soft foreign objects in food that can cause illness and injury.

Biological Hazards

BACTERIA

Bacteria are single-celled, living microscopic organisms that can be carried by food, water, human beings, animals, and insects (Figure 2-8). Various species of bacteria are the cause of fermentation and spoilage in food.

Bacteria require moisture and proper temperatures to grow; and commodities such as flour, sugar, legumes, and beans are rarely at risk until they are cooked. Because bacteria can reproduce at amazing speeds (one bacterium can become nearly 10 billion in a day), controlling microorganisms can seem like a daunting task. The good news is that most microorganisms are harmless. But some do cause food-borne illness and food spoilage. The Centers for Disease Control and Prevention (CDC) defines food-borne illness as a situation that happens when two or more people experience the same illness for eating the same food.

NOTE: These microorganisms cannot be detected by smell, taste, or appearance.

Harmful bacteria is no laughing matter; it causes food-borne illness in 76 million people each year with 325,000 individuals being hospitalized and 5,000 Americans dying each year, according to a report issued by the CDC. With proper training and care, foodservice workers can dramatically decrease the risk of food-borne illness.

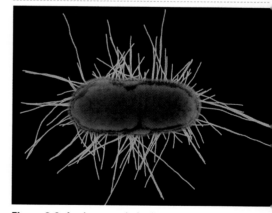

Figure 2-8 A microscopic look at a *Escherichia coli* (*E. coli*) bacterium.

VIRUSES

While viruses do not multiply in foods, they are still considered one of the top cause of food-borne and waterborne diseases in the United States. Viruses are transferred from one contaminated food source to another or from a foodservice worker to the food. Contaminated water can also transfer a virus to a food.

Hepatitis A is the No. 1 food-borne virus associated with food. It can cause serious liver damage. One of the problems with hepatitis A is that a person can have it for up to six weeks before symptoms occur. During that time, an infected foodservice worker can pass it to foods and other workers by spreading fecal material through improper handwashing practices.

Raw seafood is another source of hepatitis A. For those culinarians who work with seafood, it is important to remember that raw foods such as shellfish are stored separate when refrigerated and then cooked to the recommended temperatures before serving them.

PARASITES

Parasitic infections are less common than bacterial or viral food-borne illness, but they still should be examined. Parasites are microscopic organisms that live on or inside another organism including humans. There are a number of parasites that can be transmitted through food. Some are associated with fish or meat, which can be eliminated with proper cooking. Others come from contaminated water, or fresh produce after it has been exposed to fecal material from polluted water or from a contaminated human being. Proper sanitation and personal hygiene can prevent the spread of this type of parasite.

FUNGI

Yeast and mold are types of fungi. They do not lead to food-borne illnesses but should be a concern to bakers. Once a baked food is contaminated by either type of fungi, it is not saleable.

When a food is contaminated by yeast or mold it will produce unappealing sight, smell, and taste characteristics. Yeasts and molds can cause foods to taste and smell spoiled or sour. If mold grows on food for long periods of time it can produce a substance called "mycotoxin," which can cause food-borne illness.

Chemical Hazards

The FDA Food Code lists allergens, ciguatoxins, mycotoxins, scombrotoxin, and shellfish toxins as naturally occurring chemical hazards. Cleaning solutions, food additives, pesticides, and heavy metals such as lead and mercury are derived from man-made chemicals.

The FDA has identified foods that are known to cause allergic reactions. Food allergens for allergen-sensitive people can cause life-threatening reactions. The top food allergens are milk, eggs, wheat proteins, soy, tree nuts, peanuts, fish, and shellfish. Many of these ingredients are important components of baked goods. It is the responsibility of the baker to clearly label food products that contain a common allergen.

Two other common chemical hazards are ciguatoxin found in finfish and scombrotoxin found in fish and Swiss cheese. In both cases the toxin is not eliminated by cooking. The best protection is to purchase fish from a reputable supplier and store them at proper temperatures.

Physical Hazards

Foreign objects that find their way into a food can cause injury or illness. They include items such as fragments of glass, metal shavings, toothpicks, jewelry, adhesive bandages, and human hair. Physical hazards usually occur from accidental contamination or poor food-handling practices that can happen throughout the food chain from the farm to the consumer. All fresh produce and other food ingredients should be thoroughly inspected for signs of foreign objects. Foodservice workers and bakers should not wear jewelry (other than a plain ring) when preparing food.

FOOD HANDLING

Receiving and Storing Foods

Food safety must be adhered to in every step of the food chain. From the time that produce is received and stored to when it is prepared and served, certain steps must be carefully administered. Remember that every time food is handled, there is a chance to preserve or compromise its safety.

Follow these guidelines when receiving foods:
- Always take a minute to check out the conditions of the delivery trucks. Are they clean and free of filth and pests, and are nonfood items kept separate during transport?
- Check the temperature of the truck.
- Check the temperature of the product upon receipt. Do not hesitate to deny receipt of any product that is questionable.
- If foods come with an expiration date, check the date before accepting the delivery.

Adequate storage is imperative for dry goods and refrigerated and frozen foods. Never let foods sit on the dock or in a holding area. Secure proper storage as soon as the products are received. Keep storage areas clean and organized. Have a plan to break down and discard cardboard containers as soon as the goods are received. Keep containers out of storage areas, as they can become breeding grounds for insects and rodents.

Refrigerating/Freezing Foods

Temperature is the most important factor in deterring the growth of bacteria. Bakers must be particularly concerned about the proper handling of shell eggs and all cream and egg-rich desserts. Additional information for specific ingredients is found throughout the book.

LEARNING ACTIVITY 2-1

Place a small pan of fresh berries on a tray and leave it out on a table overnight.

Place a similar pan of covered berries in the refrigerator. Check the condition of both pans of berries after 12 hours. Note the differences between the two pans.

One critical area of food safety is proper storage. Cooked foods that are to be stored must be cooled down to below 41°F (5°C) as soon as possible. The FDA Food Code recommends two-stage cooling:

1. Cooked foods must be cooled from 135°F (57°C) to 70°F (21°C) within 2 hours.
2. The same foods must then have their temperature reduced from 70°F (21°C) to 41°F (5°C) within 6 hours.

There are several methods that can be used to bring hot foods down to safe temperatures including:
- using blast chillers and walk-in coolers
- transferring the product into a shallow pan or into smaller containers
- placing the container of hot food into an ice water bath, and stirring frequently

Figure 2-9 Uniform distribution of refrigerated ingredients will maintain proper temperatures.

- using cooling paddles for rapidly reducing the temperatures of liquid ingredients
- adding ice to cooling liquids or foods if the recipe permits
- spreading pastry creams in a thin layer in a shallow pan to speed up the cooling process

Remember never to combine cooked and uncooked foods in the same container for storing in a refrigerator. Always store cooked foods above the raw foods. Refrigerators and freezers must be kept within the safe temperature range for storing food. The temperature in refrigerators should be between 36° to 40°F (2° to 4°C) (Figure 2-9).

Freezer temperatures should be between −1° and 0°F (−18° to −17°C). In a bakeshop pay particular attention to shell eggs, which should always be kept between 38° to 40°F (3° to 4°C); dairy products 36° to 40°F (2° to 4°C); and most produce at 40° to 45°F (4° to 7°C). There is a new process for pasteurizing the eggs while still inside the shells. Those eggs only can be left out at room temperature for up to 4 hours. (Some produce should be kept at higher temperatures, like tomatoes, potatoes, and bananas.) Make sure thermometers are checked on a regular basis to ensure proper temperature range. These units should be regularly cleaned and properly maintained. Remember to use the FIFO method (first in, first out) when working with refrigerated foods, to ensure that you are moving the stock appropriately.

Freezing does not kill the microorganisms; it slows down or retards the growth. Once foods are thawed, the bacterial growth will begin again.

Thawing Frozen Foods

There are a number of ways to safely thaw foods. Some small items can be cooked without thawing, but most solid foods need to be thawed before cooking. Do not thaw at room temperature. If time permits, allow food to thaw in the refrigerator. This may take several days, depending on the product. Another method is to place the wrapped food in a container under cool running water in a sink. (Make sure the sink is washed and sanitized before and after thawing the food and that the sink is not used for any other purpose during the time the food is being thawed.) The water used to thaw the food should be 70°F (21°C) or below. A microwave oven can also be used to thaw foods, using the defrost setting. It is best to use the microwave for thawing small portions of food that will be cooked immediately upon thawing.

Serving Hot Foods

Always serve hot food as soon as it has been cooked. If a sauce is to be used later, keep it simmering on the stove. Microorganisms prefer temperatures from 41° to 135°F (5° to 57°C). This range is known as the food temperature **danger zone.** It is important to try to keep foods out of the danger zone as much as possible.

Food that is to be held hot before service must be kept at 135°F (57°C) or above. Use reliable holding systems and check the temperatures of the food on a regular basis. When food is to be transported, it also must be held at those temperatures. It is best to serve in small batches and never add fresh product to those batches being held.

THE PRINCIPLES OF HAZARD ANALYSIS CRITICAL CONTROL POINT (HACCP)

Hazard Analysis Critical Control Point (HACCP) is the name of a state-of-the-art food safety program that is being adopted around the country. Those using the HACCP system will need to receive additional instruction in order to properly execute it. In a nutshell, the HACCP system uses a scientific approach that follows the flow of food through the food-service operation and identifies each step in the process where contamination might occur.

The HACCP system is based on the following seven principles:

1. **Conduct a hazard analysis.** Follow the food from the time it arrives in the bakeshop until it is served. Determine which steps along the way are most vulnerable and prepare a process flowchart of the steps. Identify and list all possible hazards that might be introduced into food by people, poor food-handling practices, and/or contaminated equipment. Hazards may be biological, chemical, or physical in nature.

2. **Determine Critical Control Points. Critical control points** (CCPs) are the steps in the food-handling process at which a hazard can be prevented, eliminated, or reduced. At this stage, the critical control points of each step are determined. (The cooking, cooling, and storing steps must all be maintained at proper temperatures and would all be considered critical control points.)

3. **Establish Critical Limits.** Bakers must know the critical limits for the products that they cook, store, and serve. Critical limits are standards that determine the criteria that must be met to ensure that each hazard is under control. Established critical limits include safe holding, cooking, and serving temperatures; time measurements for reheating foods; pH levels; and other measurements that determine the safety of foods.

4. **Establish Monitoring Procedures.** Implement systems to monitor the control status of the identified hazard. Compile data and maintain complete log books at all times.

5. **Establish Corrective Actions.** This is a plan that will determine what will happen when a CCP has gone out of control. Since a plan is already in place, dealing with the out-of-control substance can be done effectively and calmly.

6. **Establish Verification Procedures.** This is the step that verifies if the HACCP plan is working or not.

7. **Establish Documentation.** All procedures and records such as temperatures and holding times must be kept appropriate to the HACCP plan.

BAKESHOP SAFETY

The most common safety concerns in a bakeshop are trips and falls, cuts, and burns. Most workplace accidents are created by simple carelessness. Try to implement the following safety rules:

- Clean up spills as soon as they occur (Figure 2-10).
- Keep floors clean at all times.
- Maintain a "walk, don't run" policy.
- Keep all walking pathways free from obstructions.

Figure 2-10 Since trips and falls are the cause of many kitchen accidents, it is important to clean up all spills immediately.

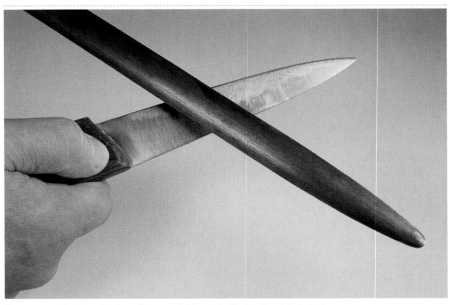

Figure 2-11 A sharp knife will cut quickly and efficiently with little force.

- Keep knives sharpened. (A dull knife is much less safe than a sharp knife (Figure 2-11).
- Use knives and other utensils only for their intended uses.
- Pass knives correctly. (Either lay the knife down on the table or hand it to the person with the handle first.)
- Walk with the blade of the knife pointed toward the ground.
- Do not submerge a knife in a sink of soapy water.
- Do not leave a knife lying close to the edge of a workbench or hidden under a towel.
- Assume that pots are hot and handle them with dry towels. (Do not use wet towels as they will not properly insulate.)
- Be careful to sit pots away from the edge of the work space.
- Do not let the handles protrude beyond the stovetop.
- Warn others that you are walking behind them with a hot substance.
- Remove the lid on a pot of steaming product so that the steam vents away from the face.
- Use a ladder when reaching for something on a high shelf; stacking boxes or climbing on counters or chairs is not a safe practice.
- Use proper lifting techniques by stooping and lifting with your leg muscles rather than using your back.
- Use a cart or get the assistance of a coworker when transporting a heavy load.
- Keep all chemicals clearly marked and safely stored away.
- Have a good first-aid kit.
- Post all pertinent emergency phone numbers near every phone.

Most businesses have made sure that at least one employee is trained in CPR and mouth-to-mouth resuscitation. All employees should know where the emergency numbers and first-aid kits are kept. Also, all employees should be trained on the obstructed airway maneuver for a choking person.

LEARNING ACTIVITY 2-2

Mix 10 lb (4,500 g) of lean dough in a 20-qt (19 liters) mixing bowl. Try mixing it for 1 minute each at 1st, 2nd, and 3rd speed. Note the vibrations within the mixer. What do you think is the safest speed for dough mixing?

CHEF'S TIP: *Equipment is only safe when it is used for its intended purposes. Never try to use one tool or piece of equipment for another purpose.*

Fire Safety

Every business should have a fire-safety plan that includes what to do in case of a fire. Make sure all employees know where fire extinguishers are located and which one should be used depending on the type of fire. Each employee should be trained on how to use the extinguishers. (Figure 2-12).

Grease and electrical fires should never be put out with water. Grease fires will only spread and electrical fires will spread their electric charge through the water to the person trying to put out the fire. Use only appropriately marked fire extinguishers for each type of fire:

- **Class A** extinguishers are for ordinary combustible materials such as paper, wood, cardboard, and most plastics. The numerical rating on these types of extinguishers indicates the amount of water it holds and the amount of fire it can extinguish.

- **Class B** fires involve flammable or combustible liquids such as gasoline, kerosene, grease, and oil. The numerical rating for class B extinguishers indicates the approximate number of square feet of fire it can extinguish.

Figure 2-12 All employees should know where the fire extinguishers are kept and how to use them.

- **Class C** fires involve electrical equipment, such as appliances, wiring, circuit breakers, and outlets. Never use water to extinguish class C fires—the risk of electrical shock is far too great! Class C extinguishers do not have a numerical rating. The C classification means the extinguishing agent is nonconductive.

Have a designated meeting place in case of a catastrophic fire. Make sure all exits are kept clear and open at all times.

Conduct fire-safety checks periodically, looking for frayed or exposed wires and faulty plugs, along with overused outlets and extension cords. Have routine maintenance checks on all stoves and ovens as well as fire-control systems, such as the Ansul system. Carefully maintain equipment that has a heating element or coil such as coffee pots or warmers.

PROFILE

Ed Fraser
Consultant and Past President of RBA
Kelso, Wash.

Ed Fraser recently retired from his family's business, Fraser's Bakery in Kelso, Washington. The bakery had been in the family since 1949, but it was time to move on. Fraser admits that he had mixed emotions about leaving. After all, he had so many happy memories in the bakery.

Since 1971, Fraser has run the bakery doing every task imaginable. "When you own a small business, you get to do whatever needs to be

done, including mopping the floors. Our customers always recognized our uniqueness; we tried to cater to their interests and needs. There was nothing they wanted that we couldn't produce. Sometimes it took research on our part and extra time, but we always thought it was worth the effort," says Fraser.

Fraser attended the Dunwoody Institute to fine-tune the skills that he had garnered from his father's knee. During his time at Dunwoody, he was able to work for three different bakeries before working in a research setting with a large manufacturer. These experiences helped him learn the basics needed in order to take over the family bakery. Now Fraser is doing some consulting work having just served as RBA's president.

SUMMARY

There is much an informed baker can do to prevent food and personnel safety problems in the bakeshop. Cleanliness is the fundamental requirement for food safety. It begins with personal hygiene of each worker. The most critical element in sanitation is keeping your hands clean. Always wash your hands when you change from one task to another, using hot water and antibacterial soap.

Cleaning means removing all the visible food waste and residues from the surface of equipment, prep surfaces, hand tools, utensils, and all other pieces used in food preparation and service. Sanitizing destroys the disease-causing organisms that may be present after cleaning.

Effective pest management can reduce the presence of bacteria since rodents and insects can cross-contaminate products used in the preparation of food. Watch for evidence of pest infestations and take quick and appropriate actions to rectify the situation.

Microorganisms cannot be detected by smell, taste, or appearance, yet they are the cause of food-borne illness among 76 million Americans each year. With proper training and care, foodservice workers can help to decrease those figures.

Secure proper storage for food immediately upon receipt. Temperature is the most important factor in deterring the growth of bacteria. Hot foods must remain hot and cold foods kept cold.

Most workplace accidents are caused by simple carelessness. Always clean up spills as soon as they occur. Use common sense when working with knives or hot substances. Have emergency numbers posted by every phone and develop a fire-safety plan. Keep fire extinguishers handy and make sure that every employee knows how to use them.

Unit Review Questions

SHORT ANSWER

Provide the correct answer for the following questions.

1. What is the proper method for handwashing?
2. Describe the difference between cleaning and sanitizing.
3. What are the two most common types of sanitizers?
4. Once equipment and utensils have been sanitized, how should they be dried?
5. Garbage cans attract undesirable creatures. How should they be handled inside the bakeshop? Outside the shop?
6. What are five ways that bacteria can be carried from one site to another?
7. In general, a bacterium needs moisture and what other conditions to grow?
8. According to statistics from the Centers for Disease Control and Prevention, how many Americans are hospitalized due to a food-borne illness every year?
9. Cooked foods that are to be stored need to be cooled down as soon as possible to what temperature?
10. In what part of the refrigerator should raw foods be stored?
11. What are two of the preferred methods for thawing foods?
12. What temperature range makes up the danger zone?
13. Describe the purpose of the HACCP system.
14. What are the two correct ways to pass a knife?

MULTIPLE CHOICE

Choose the correct answer or answers.

15. Hot foods should be held at or above
    a. 140°F (60°C)
    b. 135°F (57°C)
    c. 150°F (66°F)
    d. below 135°F (57°C)

16. One bacterium can grow to nearly
    _____ in a day.
    a. 1 million
    b. 100,000
    c. 10 billion
    d. 1 billion

17. FIFO stands for
    a. first in, first out
    b. frequent inspection fights organisms
    c. freezing inhibits food-borne outbreaks
    d. fight insulation fires through observation

18. Grease fires should be extinguished using a
    _____ type of extinguisher.
    a. Class A
    b. Class B
    c. Class C
    d. all of the above

ingredients

Gaining an understanding of ingredients is a prerequisite to maximizing their use, to improving purchasing and cost efficiencies, and, in the end, to creating high-quality products. Units 3, 4, and 5 cover the ingredients found in the baker's pantry. Section 2 begins with the basics discussed in Unit 3, progresses through sweeteners, fats and oils, and eggs found in Unit 4, and ends in Unit 5 with the introduction of specialty ingredients, which add variety and flavor.

the basics:
grains, water, salt, and yeast

"As with any craft or trade, be it a carpenter, a mason, an artist or a baker—the end result of one's efforts will only be as good as the quality of the ingredients or mediums that are used, as well as one's understanding of how those ingredients or mediums must be handled or manipulated in order to achieve the desired results. A thorough knowledge of ingredients and their function, especially in baking, is a key to achieve success at any level!"

Joe McKenna CMPC, Executive Chef Bakery
Wegman's Food Markets, Inc.

KEY TERMS and CONCEPTS

ash

baker's pantry

bran

bromates

crumb

crust

enzyme

fermentation

gliadin

glutenin

pH factor

slurry

LEARNING Objectives

After you have finished reading this unit, you should be able to:

- **Evaluate** the qualities of flours milled from hard wheat

- **Assess** the quantity and quality of gluten in hard wheat flours

- **Evaluate** the qualities of flours milled from rye, corn, oats, and rice

- **Discuss** the effect on fermentation and flour absorption from hard or soft water

- **Describe** the functions of salt in baked goods

- **Explain** how to convert quantity of yeast types

- **Define** the functions and types of yeast

JUST AS A MASTER CARPENTER WOULD NEVER CONSIDER using an inferior piece of lumber to create a one-of-a-kind table, so the successful baker understands the importance of using the right ingredients to produce the perfect loaf of bread, chiffon-type cake, and other bakery products, depending on the recipe. We will begin by exploring the basic ingredients found in a **baker's pantry** including flour, water, salt, and yeast. These four ingredients were the first commodities available to bakers. Over the years as more products became obtainable, the baker's pantry grew. As we progress from the simplest of baking recipes to more intricate formulas, additional ingredients will be introduced.

A baker works with a variety of grains such as wheat, rye, oats, corn, and rice. Even though a potato is not a grain, it will be discussed in this section as it is used in much the same way as flour in certain baked goods. Grains are milled to create flour.

GRAINS

Flour is the major ingredient in breads and baked goods. Consistent quality flour is the key to creating superior finished products. The cornerstone of baking is wheat flour, which is set apart from the others by its high gluten content. Gluten gives baked goods their ability to rise. There is a vast array of wheat flours on the market today and they are not all equal. Every recipe is written with specific flour in mind to give the best results. Bread depends on gluten for its structure, cakes to a lesser extent, and cookies almost not at all, which is why it is important to understand the variety of flours available.

Wheat Flour

Although not a native grain to the United States, today wheat is grown on more acres in this country than any other grain (Figure 3-1). Approximately 62 million acres of wheat are harvested each year in the United States. Each wheat berry contains a certain amount of protein, moisture, ash, and fat, which are determined by the type of growing soil, temperature, and rainfall as well as maturity at harvest. These variances affect the flour produced from the wheat berry.

Wheat is classified by growing season (winter or spring); the bran color (red or white); and the kernel texture (hard or soft) (Figure 3-2).

GROWING SEASON

Wheat is either grown in winter or in the spring. *Winter wheat* is grown in the regions of the country where the winters are mild. Winter wheat flours range between 10 and 12 percent protein and have medium gluten strength. *Spring wheat* is planted in the spring and harvested during late summer. Spring wheat flours range between 12 and 14 percent protein and have high gluten strength. Spring wheat is grown primarily in the midsection of the country where the winters are too severe for winter wheat to grow.

BRAN COLOR

The outer shell of a wheat kernel is the **bran,** which is removed during the milling process. Bran is a good source of carbohydrates, calcium, phosphorus, and fiber. It is often added to cereals and baked goods. The second category of wheat type is determined by the color of the bran, which is either *red* or *white.* It is the opinion of some bakers that white winter wheat

Figure 3-1 Wheat on stalks growing in the field.

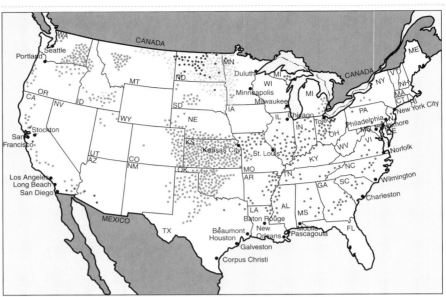

Figure 3-2 This map shows the various growing regions and types of wheat being grown around the country.

The *green areas* primarily grow hard red winter wheat, which is high in protein and strong in gluten. This type of wheat is used for yeast breads and hard rolls.

The *yellow areas* grow hard red spring wheat. Spring wheat is highest in protein and is also used in yeast breads and hard rolls.

The *red sections* grow durum wheat, a type of hard wheat, which is preferred for pasta making.

The *light blue areas* grow soft white winter wheat. This type of wheat is used for artisan flatbreads, cakes, pastries, and crackers.

The *brown regions* grow soft red winter wheat, which is primarily used for cakes, pastries, and crackers.

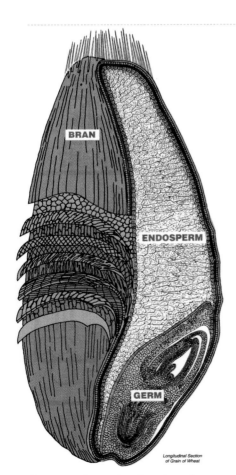

Figure 3-3 Parts of a wheat kernel.

is preferred for bread baking because it allows for better water absorption, which creates a lighter, crispier loaf of bread.

KERNEL TEXTURE

Kernels are classified as being either *hard* or *soft*. Hard wheat is higher in protein than soft wheat, and therefore produces more gluten.

The wheat kernel, which is sometimes called the berry, is the seed from which a wheat plant grows. Each kernel contains three parts, the bran, endosperm, and germ, which are separated during the milling process to produce flour (Figure 3-3). Enriched bread is made from enriched white flour, which is produced from the endosperm of the wheat kernel. Whole wheat bread is made from whole-grain flour or the whole wheat kernel, including the bran, endosperm, and germ. Wheat bread is made from a combination of white and whole-grain flour.

Wheat flour that is milled from hard white or red spring and winter wheat is the primary flour for bread dough, croissants, bagels, puff pastry, and pizza dough. Soft winter wheat is the primary flour for cake batters, cookies, and biscuits. The milling of the grain and sifting process produces different grades of flour based on the quantity and quality of the protein.

FROM KERNEL TO FLOUR

Various steps are used to clean and break up the wheat kernels, which then continue through reducing rollers and sifters (Figure 3-4). The hard wheat is separated into five streams: bran, middlings, clear flour, wheat germ, and patent flour.

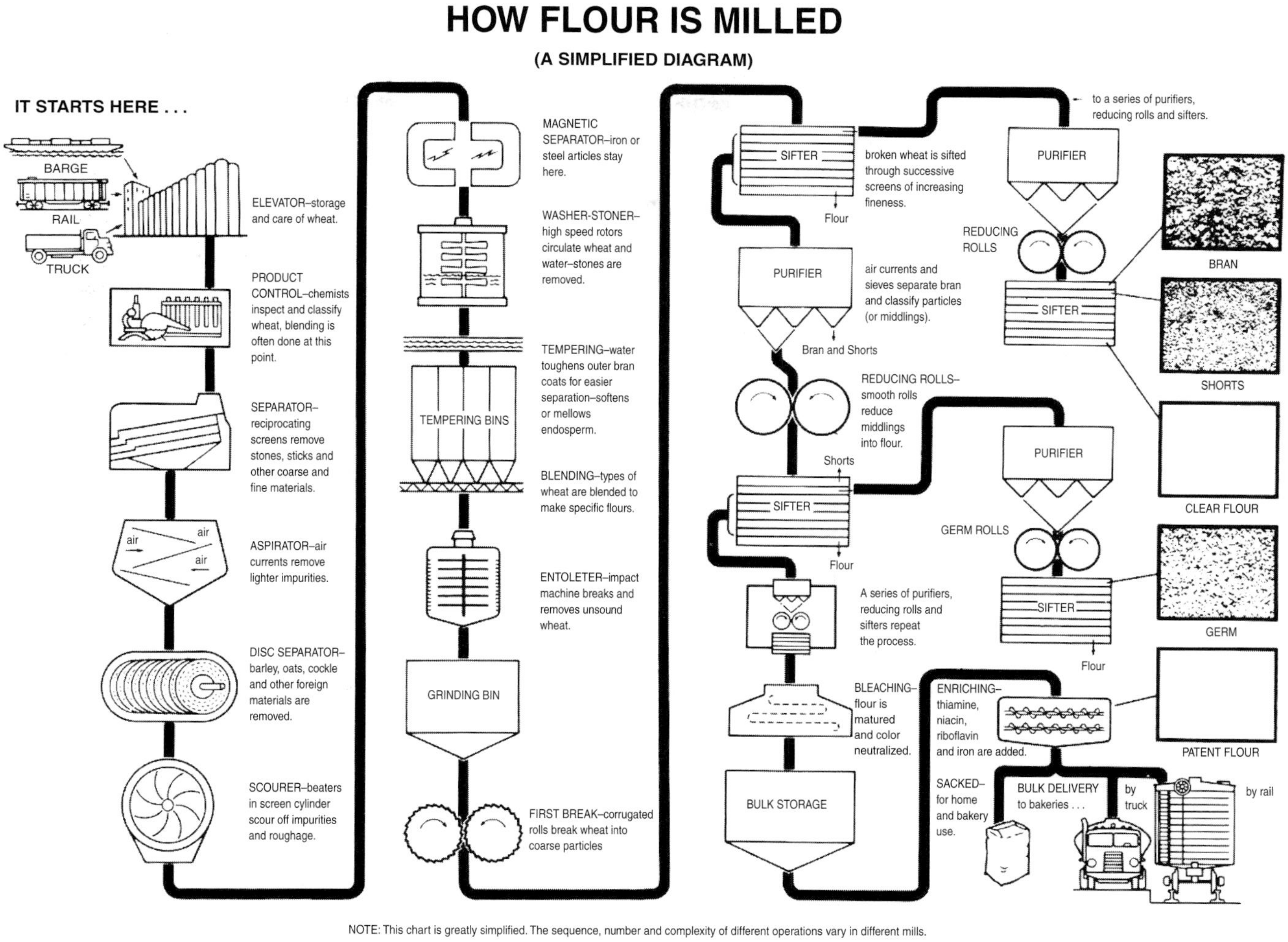

HOW FLOUR IS MILLED

(A SIMPLIFIED DIAGRAM)

IT STARTS HERE . . .

BARGE
RAIL
TRUCK

ELEVATOR–storage and care of wheat.

PRODUCT CONTROL–chemists inspect and classify wheat, blending is often done at this point.

SEPARATOR– reciprocating screens remove stones, sticks and other coarse and fine materials.

ASPIRATOR–air currents remove lighter impurities.
air   air
air   air

DISC SEPARATOR– barley, oats, cockle and other foreign materials are removed.

SCOURER–beaters in screen cylinder scour off impurities and roughage.

MAGNETIC SEPARATOR–iron or steel articles stay here.

WASHER-STONER– high speed rotors circulate wheat and water–stones are removed.

TEMPERING BINS

TEMPERING–water toughens outer bran coats for easier separation–softens or mellows endosperm.

BLENDING–types of wheat are blended to make specific flours.

ENTOLETER–impact machine breaks and removes unsound wheat.

GRINDING BIN

FIRST BREAK–corrugated rolls break wheat into coarse particles

SIFTER
Flour

broken wheat is sifted through successive screens of increasing fineness.

PURIFIER

air currents and sieves separate bran and classify particles (or middlings).

Bran and Shorts

REDUCING ROLLS– smooth rolls reduce middlings into flour.

Shorts

SIFTER
Flour

to a series of purifiers, reducing rolls and sifters.

PURIFIER

REDUCING ROLLS

SIFTER

BRAN

SHORTS

PURIFIER

GERM ROLLS

A series of purifiers, reducing rolls and sifters repeat the process.

SIFTER
Flour

CLEAR FLOUR

GERM

BULK STORAGE

BLEACHING– flour is matured and color neutralized.

ENRICHING– thiamine, niacin, riboflavin and iron are added.

SACKED– for home and bakery use.

BULK DELIVERY to bakeries . . .

by truck

by rail

PATENT FLOUR

NOTE: This chart is greatly simplified. The sequence, number and complexity of different operations vary in different mills.

Figure 3-4 The process of flour milling.

Whole wheat flour goes through the coarse screen during the sifting process; it contains bran and may also contain some wheat germ. Most bakers prefer de-germinated whole wheat as the wheat germ contains fat, which limits the shelf life of the flour. Wheat germ can be purchased separately and added when needed. The fine screen, made of nylon, extracts the smallest particles of flour, which contain a high quality and quantity of gluten. This flour is generally blended into high-gluten and bread flours. Wheat flour is sold by brand or mill name. The flour types are classified as bread, high-gluten, clear, cake, pastry, and cookie flour.

Flour may be chemically or naturally aged to improve the baking performance. The following terms appear on flour sacks and bakers should become acquainted with them.

■ **Enriched Flour**—Following the Great Depression of the 1930s, studies found serious nutritional deficiencies in the U.S. population. In 1941, the U.S. government mandated that wheat-based products such as bread and pasta be enriched with thiamine, riboflavin, niacin, and iron to compensate for the nutritive value lost during processing, and to increase the nutritional value of the product.

NOTE: The additives help replace nutrition lost during milling and to compensate for nutrition lacking from the average American diet.

About every 10 years the enrichment list has been revised, and in 1998 folic acid was added. Enriched flour does not change the color, texture, baking quality, or caloric value of the bread. Enriched bread became known as "The Staff of Life" since 8 ounces of bread, made with enriched flour, provides 50 percent of the USDA recommended daily vitamins and minerals.

NOTE: Enriched flour is only required for pasta and bread.

- **Bleached Flour**—Before Colonial times darker breads were considered an inferior product compared to the white breads. The darker breads were produced for the peasants, and the white bread was reserved for royalty. In America, the flour mills could produce whiter flour using a bleaching process involving chlorine gas, rather than following the natural aging process, which took up to 14 days at most mills. This bleaching process enabled bakers to produce large quantities of white bread at a lower cost than ever before. The bleaching process destroys the flour's natural carotenoid pigments and changes the flavor profile. In recent years, consumers have become more interested in flavor rather than the whiteness of the bread, and they are willing to pay the extra cost to allow for the natural aging process. Many wholesale bakeries, however, continue to use bleached flour to produce sandwich breads and buns.

- **Malted Flour**—Malt is the substance that comes from the conversion of a starch to maltose, a simple sugar. The addition of malted barley flour supplements the naturally occurring enzymes in wheat, converting starch to dextrin and then to fermented sugar (maltose). Yeast can then convert the sugar to carbon dioxide and alcohol. The addition of a small percentage of malted barley flour improves fermentation and crust color as well as the volume of the product.

NOTE: Malted flour is recommended for yeast-leavened dough.

- **Bromated Flour**—The addition of potassium **bromate** or chlorine dioxide to wheat flour chemically ages or cures the flour. Naturally aging the flour takes 10 to 14 days, which adds to the cost of the flour. The natural aging process is achieved through aeration and must take place before the flour is packaged. The addition of bromate reduces the time required for aging. Aged or bromated flour will have a higher yield and greater volume because the pH factor is altered and produces a better gluten development. **The FDA suggests that consumers avoid potassium bromate** and has urged bakers to stop using it on a voluntary basis. It is prohibited in Europe and Asia, and in California Proposition 65 required a warning label on every product containing bromated flour. The warning reads, "This product may contain a chemical deemed by the state of California to cause cancer or birth defects." Bakers who use naturally aged flour, rather than bromated flour, often use ascorbic acid (vitamin C) to improve the flour's yield and volume.

As discussed earlier, each wheat berry contains a certain percentage of protein, **ash** (the powdery residue left after burning a measured amount of milled flour), moisture, and fat, depending on a number of growing conditions. Flour is evaluated by these same components. The following chart shows the approximate percentages for a variety of common hard wheat flours. The baker can use this information to determine the type of flour to use in order to produce the best product. Bakers look for low moisture, low

"How can a nation be great if its bread tastes like Kleenex?"

Julia Child

KEY TERMS and CONCEPTS

caramelization

crystallization

emulsification

fructose

glucose

hydrogenated oil

invertion

lactose

maltose

LEARNING Objectives

After you have finished reading this unit, you should be able to:

- **Discuss** the different types of sugars and their functions

- **Identify** the different levels of sweetness in sugars

- **Describe** the effect of caramelization of sugars

- **Identify** the baking properties of fats and oils in baked goods

- **Select** the best fat or oil to be used in a recipe

- **Describe** how to purchase, store, and use eggs in baked goods

IN ITALY DURING THE NINETEENTH CENTURY, A BAKER

named Tony desired to marry the mayor's daughter. He was told that

in order to win her hand in marriage, he would first have to make a

special loaf of bread. Looking in the pantry, Tony assembled honey,

sugar, milk, butter, eggs, and currants. Adding these ingredients to

the products studied previously, which were flour, water, salt, and

yeast, Tony made a very rich dough that became known as Panet-

tone, Pan di Toni, or Tony's Bread (Figure 4-1). During this same era,

sweet rolls took their place on holiday and special occasion tables.

This unit will focus on sweetening agents such as sugar, as well as fat and oils and eggs. These ingredients will be added to the basic ingredients discussed in the previous unit. Students will gain an understanding of how the addition of these commodities affects the grain, texture, crumb, crust, and flavor of the bread dough. Sugar, fat and oil, and eggs have a major influence in cakes and pastries, which will be discussed in a later section.

SWEETENING AGENTS

Sugar is a carbohydrate that occurs naturally in every fruit and vegetable. It is the major product of photosynthesis, the process by which plants transform the sun's energy into food.

Sugar originally arrived in Europe about A.D. 1300 from Asia. Then Christopher Columbus introduced sugarcane to the Caribbean on his second voyage in A.D. 1493, where it flourished in the tropical climate. Spain dominated sugar production for the next century because they controlled the Caribbean islands where sugar was being produced. By the seventeenth century most European countries were refining sugar based on Caribbean sugarcane. Early attempts to grow cane sugar in Colonial America failed due to the weather and lack of knowledge; but by the eighteenth century, America was able to grow some sugarcane in Florida, Louisiana, and Texas. Cuba was the major source of cane sugar for the United States until 1960. When the United States stopped trading with Cuba, beet sugar production increased dramatically in the United States (Figures 4-2 and 4-3).

The sugar obtained from cane and sugar beets is 99.5 percent pure *sucrose*. These sugars are identical to one another, however, the molasses from beet sugar is darker and more bitter than from cane sugar. Sugar syrup is refined by centrifugal force, a spinning action that allows the lighter sucrose to separate from the heavier molasses.

Granulated and Powdered Sugars

Granulated sugar is refined sucrose that has been **crystallized** (Figure 4-4). There are many different types of granulated sugar. They differ in crystal size and are available in standard, extra-fine, and powdered forms. Regular sugar, as it is known to most consumers, is commonly found in kitchen sugar bowls and is the sugar that is called for in most recipes.

Extra-fine sugar is also known as bar sugar due to its ability to dissolve quickly in cold liquids. It is ideal for angel food cakes and meringues.

Powdered sugar is finer and would dissolve quicker but it contains 3 percent cornstarch to prevent the sugar from lumping (Figure 4-5). When powdered sugar is mixed in cold liquid the cornstarch will make the cold liquid cloudy. Powdered sugar is ground to a smooth powder and then sifted. It is available in different grades of fineness: 4X, 6X, and 10X. The number before the X indicates how fine the sugar is compared to standard granulated sugar; the lower the number, the finer the grain. The 10X

Figure 4-1 Note the panettone's golden interior created with added ingredients from the expanded market basket.

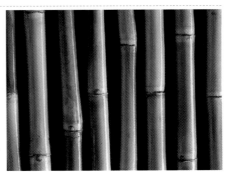

Figure 4-2 Sugar obtained from sugar cane and sugar beets is identical.

Figure 4-3 Sugar is found in both sugar cane and sugar beets from which it is separated for commercial use.

Figure 4-4 Granulated sugar comes in a variety of crystal sizes including standard and extra-fine.

is called confectioners' sugar, 6X is used for icings and frostings, and 4X is used for dusting and glazing of donuts, Danish, and coffee cakes. The powdered sugar found in grocery stores is confectioners' sugar or 10X. The other two types are primarily used by industrial bakers.

Brown Sugar

Light and dark brown sugars are manufactured by spraying sugarcane molasses onto the beet or cane sugar (Figure 4-6). Because the components have been separated and reconstituted it is not considered a natural sugar. For foods to be classified as natural, they must contain all their original components. A natural brown sugar is obtained from sugarcane only, and it contains a small percentage of molasses; the molasses in the beet sugar is bitter. Natural brown sugar is more expensive than standard brown sugars.

Sugar has the ability when heated to sweeten, retain moisture, and develop flavor through a process known as **caramelization** (Figure 4-7). To understand the function of caramelization, conduct the following experiment.

Figure 4-5 Powdered sugar is ground to a fine powder and contains 3 percent cornstarch to prevent it from lumping.

Figure 4-6 Both light and dark brown sugars are available. The light variety is preferred for making butterscotch, condiments, and glazes. Dark brown sugar's rich flavor enhances gingerbread, baked beans, plum pudding, and other full-flavored foods.

LEARNING ACTIVITY 4-1 Caramelization of Sugar

In this learning activity, you will be able to taste and see the affect of heat on sweetness and caramelization of sugar.

1. Measure 8 oz (230 g) cold tap water.
2. Dissolve 4 oz (110 g) of granulated sugar into the tap water.
3. Taste the level of sweetness and make a note of it.
4. Bring the liquid to the boiling point.
5. Let liquid cool, taste and compare its degree of sweetness to the original sugar water.
6. Add 1 teaspoon of lemon juice to the liquid and bring back to a boil.
7. Boil until a light amber color is obtained; the sign that caramelization has begun.
8. The addition of an acid (lemon juice) inverts some of the sucrose to dextrose.

NOTE: Invertion occurs when an acid mixes with a carbohydrate and changes sucrose to dextrose and levulose. This allows the sugar to caramelize and reduces the chance of crystallization.

9. Let the liquid cool and then taste the caramelized syrup and compare it to the previous tastings.

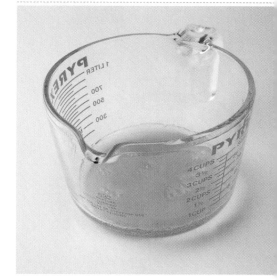

Figure 4-7 A light amber colored carmelized sugar is ready for application.

Other Sugars, Syrups, and Sweeteners

Turbinado sugar is a dark brown, fine-grained, crunchy specialty sugar. It is a completely pure, natural, and chemical-free sugar. Its rich caramel flavor is ideal for rum cakes, brown breads, flans and puddings, treacle biscuits, mincemeat, and other full-flavored foods and savory recipes.

Muscovado sugar is a moist, fine-grained specialty sugar that is brown in color. It performs well with high temperatures and has a reasonably good shelf life. Use muscovado sugar in the same applications as turbinado sugar.

Baker's special sugar is a specialty sugar made for professional bakers. Its fine crystal size is perfect for sugaring doughnuts and for use in cookies, cakes, pastries, meringues, frostings, and glazes. The fine grain blends, mixes, and melts faster and more even than other sugar. It provides a fine crumb texture, creating a smooth end product.

LEARNING ACTIVITY 4-2

Sugar has the ability to retain moisture, which increases the shelf life of cakes and breads.

In the following experiment you will note that plain water evaporates sooner than sugar water.

The Ability to Retain Moisture

1. Measure two units of water, each 8 oz (230 g).
2. Add 2 oz (60 g) of sugar to one of the units.
3. Bring both liquids to a boil in separate pots.
4. Boil for 5 minutes uncovered.
5. Measure how much water evaporated by measuring the liquid remaining and compare it to the amount of liquid that you had at the start of the experiment.

MOLASSES

Molasses has a distinct flavor that can enhance some baked goods (Figure 4-8). Prior to World War I, molasses was the major sweetener used in the United States, because it was less expensive than sugar. After World War I, sugar prices plummeted and molasses took a backseat to sugar as a popular sweetener. Molasses is a by-product of cane sugar refining and is available in three grades:

- *Unsulfured* molasses is the finest quality of molasses and is obtained from the first stage of sugar extraction; it is light and very sweet.
- *Sulfured* molasses is obtained from the second extraction and is darker and not as sweet.
- *Blackstrap* molasses is from the final extraction; it is very dark and is less sweet than the first two grades. Generally blackstrap molasses is used in the manufacture of cattle feed and other industrial uses.

MAPLE SUGAR

Maple sugar is a reduction or concentration of syrup obtained from certain species of maple trees in the Northern New England states, New York, and Quebec, Canada (Figure 4-9). Maple syrup is amber in color and contains about 66 percent sugar (sucrose). It was not readily available in a crystallized form before the 1990s.

HONEY

Honey is a natural invert sugar (**fructose**) produced by bees from flower nectar that has been ingested and then deposited into beehive combs (Figure 4-10). Five gallons of nectar will yield one gallon of honey. The flavor of the honey is dependent upon the nectar source. A general rule of thumb is that light honey is generally milder in flavor, golden honey is richer, and

Figure 4-8 Molasses is a by-product of cane sugar refining.

Figure 4-9 Buckets of maple syrup are being poured into a bin during the Vermont harvest season.

darker honey can be strong flavored. Honey may crystallize at cold temperatures and can easily be liquefied by placing the container in warm water. It is not recommended that you microwave honey.

Because honey is not refined and is natural, it increases the customer's perception of value whenever it is used. Since before recorded history, honey has enhanced man's daily bread; almost every country and culture has contributed a type of honey loaf to the baker's repertoire. When two loaves of bread are offered in a bakery, the honey wheat bread will often sell better than the white sugar loaf and will command a better price. It is recommended that only pasteurized honey is used in a food-service setting. For a formula for Honey Cake, see Appendix VII (The Workbench).

LACTOSE MILK SUGAR

Lactose is a sugar found in milk and milk powder. It has the ability to caramelize at a lower temperature than sugar, and it adds flavor and color (golden-brown) to baked goods. Lactose is not fermentable by yeast, but is important due to its browning or caramelizing action.

Figure 4-10 Honey adds consumer value to baked goods.

LEARNING ACTIVITY 4-3

When milk reaches 180°F (80°C), it will turn an amber color. Lactose found in milk and milk powders caramelizes quicker than sucrose; therefore, cakes and breads that contain milk or milk powder may be baked at a lower temperature. Conduct the following experiment to see how quickly milk caramelizes:

Caramelization of Lactose

1. Put 2 oz (60 g) of milk in a small stainless steel pot.

2. Place the milk on medium heat; do not leave on stove unattended.

3. Observe how quickly it caramelizes.

Figure 4-11 As milk is heated it quickly caramelizes.

MALTOSE

Maltose is a simple sugar obtained from fermented barley and is used as a yeast food in dough. Maltose is barely sweet at all.

CORN SYRUP

Corn syrup is sweet syrup obtained from corn. It is resistant to crystallization and capable of retaining moisture. Corn syrup is the most common form of liquid **glucose** used in baking. Glucose is about half as sweet as fructose or sucrose.

Sugar Substitutes

Saccharin, which is 200 to 700 times sweeter than table sugar, can be used to sweeten either hot or cold foods. Pregnant women are cautioned not to use it.

Aspartame is 160 to 220 times sweeter than table sugar and is not appropriate for recipes that are cooked more than 20 minutes, because the chemical compound breaks down. It is therefore suggested that it be added at the very end of cooking recipes like puddings. People with a rare condition called phenylketonuria (PKU) should avoid aspartame. Otherwise, it is a safe sweetener.

Acesulfame potassium, also known as acesulfame-K, was introduced in 1988. It can be used in baking and cooking because it does not break down when heated. Two hundred times sweeter than table sugar, it is often used with sugar in baking to achieve the desired texture.

Sucralose, which is made from sucrose, was approved in 1998 and is 600 times sweeter than table sugar. It can be used in recipes that require prolonged heating without losing any of its sweetness. It has no reported side effects or restrictions on its use by pregnant women.

BLENDS

The recent trend is to blend sugar with a sugar substitute, creating a product that reduces the calories and carbohydrates but can easily be used in baking. Tests have found that 100 percent sugar produces superior products, achiev-

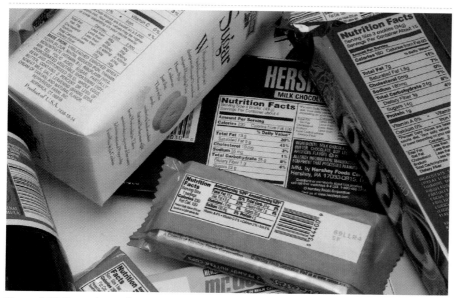

Figure 4-12 Sugar in one form or another is found in many popular packaged snacks.

ing higher volume and better crumb than these blends, but blends are probably the best substitute to use in baking when a decrease in sugar is necessary.

Sweetness and Flavor of Sugar

Sugar intensifies the flavors of the baked good. In evaluating the sweetness of sugar, a scale has been developed giving cane or beet sugar a value of 100. The following chart identifies the level of sweetness in different forms of sugar.

Types of Sugar	Relative Sweetness
Sugar (cane or beet)	100
Invert sugar	130
Corn syrup	60
Lactose	15

Invert sugar and corn syrup are the result of an acid reaction with sucrose or cornstarch, which produces syrup. The inverted sugar becomes sweeter (130) and the corn syrup less sweet (60). The sweetness level for lactose (natural sugar found in milk) is 15; but as it caramelizes at a lower temperature than sugar (see Learning Activity 4–3), it provides a richer flavor and optimum crust color in cake and bread.

Look closely at the processed food labels and soda labels in the accompanying photo (Figure 4-12). What type of sugar is used? Do you understand why? Corn syrup adds bulk, is less expensive than sugar, and keeps the sweetness low. Check the candy labels; what type of sugars are used? Do you understand why? Invert sugar adds a higher level of sweetness with less bulk.

FAT AND OIL

Fat and oil are recognized as essential nutrients in both human and animal diets (Figure 4-13). They provide the most concentrated source of energy of any foodstuff. Fat and oil are sometimes referred to as shortenings. They

Figure 4-13 Fats and oils.

have the ability to shorten protein strands, making baked goods tender. Fat and oil also transfer heat more efficiently; water only heats to 212°F (100°C) before it begins to evaporate and the vapors turn to steam. Some fats and oils can be heated to 400°F (200°C) before they start to smoke and become bitter. Therefore, fat and oil increase the browning qualities in baked goods. Fat and oil also have emulsification properties and retain moisture.

The single most important function is their ability to enhance the flavor of a product. Fat and oil do not perform this function equally, selecting the right fat or oil for the recipe is very important. Fat is solid at room temperature; oil is liquid. Natural fats are of animal origin and natural oils are vegetable, seed, or fruit origin.

In the early 1900s, a process of hydrogenation was discovered for solidifying oil. Semisolid shortenings were produced from vegetable oils. The hydrogenation process prevented rancidity and gave the oil creaming and lamination properties. A solid form was also easier to measure than oil.

It is important to match the melting point of fat to its function in baked goods. For example, when making pound cake, icing, and laminated dough, a low melting point is desired, because the baked goods have a high percent of fat. Butter with a melting point of 86°F (30°C) would be an excellent choice and it also provides an excellent mouth feel. In a pie crust a harder fat is desired in order to prevent absorption by the flour. A blend of butter and shortening or lard will produce a flaky crust. For pies and tarts the filling provides the flavor and the crust the texture. While the pie crust may contain up to 70 percent fat, when the pie is filled and finished, one slice only has 15 percent total fat. Let us take a look at some of the more common choices of fats and oils.

Fats: Animal Origin

LARD

Lard is rendered hog fat. It has a high melting point and may be used for dough and for frying because it has a neutral flavor.

TALLOW

Tallow is rendered beef fat. It is not used in any baked good because of its strong beefy flavor.

BUTTER

Butter is milk fat that is churned from cream. It has a low melting point that gives excellent results in all baked goods, icings, and creams.

Oils: Vegetable Origin

Cooking oils are prepared from vegetable oils that are refined, bleached, deodorized, and sometimes de-waxed or lightly hydrogenated.

COTTONSEED

Cottonseed oil has a neutral flavor; it is clear in color and economical to use. It is also used to make solid shortening.

SOYBEAN

Soybean oil has excellent emulsification properties; it is used to make high-ratio shortening and margarine. Soybean and corn oil are the principal oils used today in modern bakeries.

CORN OIL

Corn oil is golden in color. It is the job of the baker to produce baked goods that appeal to the consumer. Since most of the public is familiar with corn oil, many bakers prefer to use it in their products. The professional baker needs to be aware of consumer preferences and marketability.

PALM OIL

Palm oil is blended with other oils to produce frying shortenings, which are very heat stable. This extends the life of the frying shortening.

SUNFLOWER, SESAME, AND PEANUT

These are specialty oils that are used to impart the specific flavor of their origins. These oils are more expensive than the other oils and are primarily used to finish products. Oils are botanically classified as a fruit, making olive oil the only worldwide oil made from a fruit.

NOTE: Peanut oil must be used with caution and identified to the customer since peanuts and peanut by-products can cause severe allergic reaction in some people.

Hydrogenated Oils

Hydrogenation is a process by which liquid oil is solidified. When the oils are hydrogenated, they are more shelf stable. They also have less of a chance of becoming rancid. This form is sometimes used in the production of laminated dough as well as for creaming.

NOTE: In recent years it has been determined that the bonds that are created when hydrogen is added to vegetable oil (called trans-fatty acid bonds or trans fats) are known to cause health concerns such as lowering of HDL (good) cholesterol and a significant increase in LDL (bad) cholesterol. They can contribute to the clogging of arteries, cause insulin resistance, and are associated with other serious health problems.

There are three major types of **hydrogenated oils,** each with variations:

FRYING SHORTENING

Frying shortening is blended for a high-smoking point. It is a hard shortening with a high-melting point.

PASTRY SHORTENING

Pastry shortening is a blend of vegetable oils that are hydrogenated to remain firm at 80°F (26°C). Pastry shortening is blended for the ability to shorten protein strands in dough and pastry. When the protein strands are shortened, a tender baked good results.

CAKE AND ICING SHORTENING

Cake and icing shortening is blended for the ability to emulsify; it is used in high-sugar products, and is referred to as *high-ratio shortening*. This type of shortening is recommended when the sugar is greater than the flour in a formula. It is not interchangeable with an all-purpose shortening when making pie crust or pâte à choux.

LOW TRANS FAT

All of the previously listed shortenings are now available in a healthier variety. They are being produced with a reduction or elimination of the trans-fatty acids that were traditionally created through the hydrogenation process.

Other Fats

Margarine, which contains low amounts of milk fat, was created to be a less expensive alternative to butter that enjoyed a longer shelf life. It is made by blending fats and/or oils with other ingredients such as water, and/or milk products, suitable edible proteins, salt, flavoring, and coloring materials. The dairy farmers lobbied against manufacturers making margarine the color of butter, thinking they would loose market share. Therefore margarine was originally sold as white shortening with an orange-colored tablet of carotene to change its color for use and service. Finally the government agreed to subsidize the dairy farmers and yellow margarine came to the marketplace.

Baker's margarine contains added emulsifiers, which allow dough and batter to retain more moisture than butter. It is less expensive than butter, but it lacks the flavor profile of real butter.

Properties of Fat and Oil

The next two learning activities will demonstrate the functions of fat and oil.

LEARNING ACTIVITY 4-4 Emulsification

Emulsification is the suspension of a liquid and fat created by agitation, temperature, or the addition of an emulsifying agent, such as lecithin, or an acid during the agitation process. The product will also incorporate air. For this experiment, take heavy cream which contains milk fat and whip it to create an emulsion or suspension. Continued whipping causes a separation.

1. Place 8 oz (230 g) of heavy cream in a bowl.

2. Whip the cream to a soft peak stage.

3. The whipping action makes the milk fat suspend the liquid within the protein and the volume increases.

4. Continue to whip. The emulsion breaks down and the milk fat and liquid separate.

5. The fat becomes butter and the liquid is used to make buttermilk with the addition of a beneficial bacteria.

LEARNING ACTIVITY 4-5 Shortening Ability

Egg whites do not contain fat and will expand six to eight times in volume. When whole eggs are whipped, the volume is considerably reduced due to the presence of fat in the yolk. Fat shortens the protein strands. Test the effect of fat in eggs for yourself by conducting the following experiment:

1. Separate 5 eggs. Place egg whites and egg yolks in separate bowls.

2. Whip up egg whites and note the volume.

3. Whip up egg yolks and note the volume.

4. Take 5 additional whole eggs and whip them up and note the volume.

5. Compare the volume of egg whites, egg yolks, and whole eggs.

6. The egg yolks contain fat; and as we have learned, fat shortens protein structure.

7. In the absence of fat, the egg whites increase in volume 6 to 8 times.

8. The whole eggs only increase 3 to 4 times due to the shortening action of the fat in the egg yolks.

EGGS

One evening on the local news channel, there appeared a "buyer beware" story about eggs. The cameraman filmed a store associate removing Grade A eggs from a refrigerator; the expiration date was past. The associate then proceeded to change the date and return the eggs to the shelf marked Grade A. Were they still Grade A? While that is hardly an ethical practice, the eggs would still remain Grade A under the following provisions: If the eggs had been kept under constant refrigeration below 40°F (5°C) and if the eggs are within four to five weeks of their pack date (refrigerated raw

Figure 4-14 Eggs contain protein and fat.

shell eggs will keep without significant loss of quality for that time). Grading is a classification determined by interior and exterior quality and designated by letters—AA, A, and B, in descending order of quality. An official grade certifies that it has been graded under federal supervision according to USDA standards and regulations. The grading service is not mandatory. Some eggs are packed under state regulations, which must meet or exceed federal standards. Grade quality and size are not related to one another. There is no difference in nutritive value between the different grades.

Eggs contain protein and fats that are important—just as important to cakes as wheat flour is to dough (Figure 4-14). The first cake batters, Pane de Espagna, were made by whipping egg whites and egg yolks with sugar and then folding in sifted flour. Eggs perform the following functions:

- Leaven (by incorporating air into the batter)
- Form emulsions
- Build structure and additional stability
- Tenderize
- Add moisture and nutritive value
- Improve flavor and add color

The baker has many choices when buying eggs.

Fresh Whole Eggs

Many bakers are of the opinion that fresh whole eggs offer the best quality, versatility, and economy. When used in creams, custards, and icings, this is very important. When used in cakes and dough, aged eggs perform better, giving more volume. Fresh eggs have a pH factor of about 7.2. As an egg becomes aged and as it is exposed to temperatures above 45°F (10°C), its pH drops to below 7. A lower pH adds volume. When using fresh egg whites for meringues, bakers often add lemon juice or cream of tarter, which drops the pH and adds better volume. Before 1980, bakers would let eggs come to room temperature overnight; after that date, most county health departments mandated that eggs be kept under refrigeration at all times because they are highly perishable. The change

Figure 4-15 Bakers warm eggs by placing them in water.

was because of their possible contamination with salmonella as a result of modern breeding practices. When making cakes, bakers may place the required amount of eggs needed in warm water (80°F or 30°C) for 30 minutes before cracking them (Figure 4-15).

When using fresh eggs, whisk the egg whites and yolks thoroughly to get uniformity and strain them to avoid egg shells in the baked goods. There is no difference in the egg product due to the color of the egg shell. Egg yolk color and size may vary when using fresh eggs. Some bakers prefer the convenience of shelled, frozen, or fresh egg products.

NOTE: Fresh whole eggs should not be frozen when in the shell. To freeze, remove the shell, blend, strain, and add 3 percent sugar by weight.

Eggs should be kept under proper refrigeration at 40°F (5°C) or below. Eggs will retain their quality for several weeks. Store eggs in their original packaging materials to prevent the loss of moisture and away from foods with strong odors such as fish, onions, and cabbage.

Frozen Egg Products

Frozen egg products are available and sold by the pound (Figure 4-16). They offer convenience and uniformity, require less refrigeration space, and produce less waste (shells). Frozen eggs are pasteurized, making them safe for use in uncooked sauces, dressings, and creams.

Frozen Whole Eggs

Frozen whole eggs are fortified with additional egg yolks. Bakers measure these eggs by weight rather than by individual count. Frozen whole eggs provide uniformity because there is the same ratio of egg whites to egg yolks in each carton. Three percent dextrose (sugar) is added to frozen whole eggs. Dextrose helps to maintain the emulsification properties of the yolk by preventing crystallization of the water.

Frozen Egg Whites

Frozen egg whites give the baker the assurance of a fat-free product. Perhaps the most important reason for using frozen egg whites in the bakeshop is to reduce waste when egg whites are all that are required.

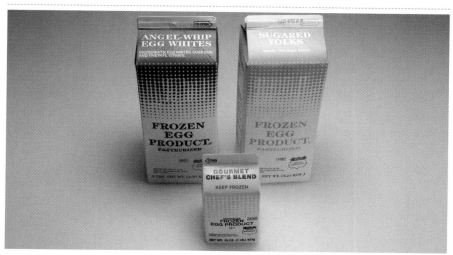

Figure 4-16 Frozen egg products.

Unlike separating shell eggs, where tiny bits of the yolk can slip into the egg whites and greatly reduce the volume, frozen egg whites are pure egg whites and contain no fat from the yolk. When using frozen egg whites, cream of tartar or lemon juice will make the whipped egg whites more stable.

Frozen Egg Yolks

Frozen egg yolks contain 10 percent dextrose (sugar), which is added to prevent water from crystallizing and separating from the fat in the yolks. The dextrose also darkens the egg yolk color.

Frozen egg products should always be defrosted in the refrigerator; defrosting time is two to three days. Removal of each individual carton of egg product from its shipping carton will reduce the defrosting time.

NOTE: Always stir or shake frozen egg products before using.

Powdered Whole Eggs

Powdered whole egg products have a long shelf life; they require no refrigeration and are concentrated, making them ideal for the production and packaging of mixes. Due to the ease of use, the U.S. military also uses this form of eggs.

Powdered Egg Whites

Bakers find that powdered egg whites are convenient for meringues, icing, and angel food cake. The professional baker should understand the characteristics and different uses for egg products.

PROFILES

Janet Carver
Culinary Group Leader
National Starch Food Innovations, Bridgewater, N.J.

Janet Carver's culinary career began when she joined National Starch as a food scientist 15 years ago, a position she held for 12 years. Four years ago Carver returned to school to study culinary arts. While she was working for the company during the day, she attended the Institute of Culinary Education (formerly Peter Kump's) on weekends. "My company was very supportive of me and actually footed the bill for my additional education," says Carver. Upon graduation, she moved into the company's foodservice division. Now she manages two other chefs, and together the team spends much of its time at the baker's bench developing recipes and making culinary products that utilize the company's products.

"Adding the culinary division was a new step for National Starch. Three years ago, when someone from our company made a sales call, they would take a 4-ounce jar of cherry pie filling. Now our culinary division works with them and sends an actual product such as a cherry ginger pie. Our customers can now see how to use our products with a visually appealing example," says Carver. By utilizing the skills of the chefs, National Starch's products have become more marketable.

Carver and her team also spend 60 percent of their time traveling and visiting with many high-profile clients as well as demonstrating products at trade shows throughout the United States and some in Europe. "One of the things I love about my job is that it never gets boring. Every day is new and exciting. I also enjoy working closely with two other creative chefs. We have great synergy. As we travel, we keep our eyes open and continually read cookbooks and culinary magazines. When we're back at our test kitchens we try to recreate some of the foods we have recently seen or tasted in our travels, using our products," adds Carver. Carver's team also does internal training with the company's food scientists helping them to expand their base knowledge of culinary terms so that they can feel comfortable talking with chefs.

Carver appreciates her company's continual support as she broadens her culinary knowledge. "National Starch continues to support my education. I have taken many of the advanced continuing education courses offered by a variety of culinary schools. There's always something else to learn."

For students who may want to work in a research chef position, Carver suggests that they get a basic science foundation in chemistry, biology, or food science with at least an associate's degree. "You must have a thorough knowledge of weights and measures and establishing base controls," she says. Carver also suggests getting at least a two-year culinary degree as well as having hands-on experience in a variety of foodservice settings. "Many manufacturing companies are adding culinary divisions and are in need of chefs who have some food science knowledge. Some might wonder how exciting starch can be, but I find this entire industry intriguing and inviting," she adds.

Robert Colalillo
Territory Manager
General Mills Bakeries and Foodservice, Syosset, N.Y.

As a territory manager, Robert Colalillo spends his time selling and educating his customers about a host of baking products manufactured by General Mills. His customers are primarily distributors who in turn sell to retail bakeries or large wholesale bakeries. In this position, Colalillo is able to couple his passion for the baking industry with his marketing skills. A typical day finds him out in the field calling on customers. For distributors, he works with their sales force and trains them how to use and sell the products. His strong baking background makes him a valuable resource for the customers that he represents. Answering technical baking questions and helping customers to develop signature recipes starting with General Mills mixes or frozen products is common for him.

Colalillo brings credibility to his position. He graduated from New York Institute of Technology with a Bachelor of Science degree in business administration before heading to the Culinary Institute of America. He has spent time working in the industry both in his parent's bakery and other shops. "I love what I'm doing. Every day is a new challenge. There is no repetition, I enjoy meeting people and working with them to help build their business and to make their life easier through our products," says Colalillo.

SUMMARY

When additional ingredients are added to the basic ingredients a myriad of baked goods can be created. This unit focused on sweetening agents such as sugar, as well as fat and oils and eggs.

Sugar is a carbohydrate that occurs naturally in every fruit and vegetable. Sugar not only adds taste to baked goods, it also has the ability to retain moisture, which increases the shelf life of cakes and breads. Besides beet and cane sugars, there are a number of different types of sweeteners used in baking including molasses, maple sugar, honey, lactose milk sugar, maltose, and corn syrup.

Fat and oil are recognized as essential nutrients in our diets. They provide the most concentrated source of energy. They have the ability to shorten protein strands, making baking goods tender. Common types of fat and oil are lard, tallow, and butter as well as cooking oils prepared from a variety of seeds and vegetables, hydrogenated oils, and shortening as well as margarine.

Eggs contain important protein and fats. Eggs perform the following functions: leaven, emulsify, build structure, tenderize, add moisture, and improve the flavor and color of baked goods.

Unit Review Questions

SHORT ANSWER

Provide the correct answer for the following questions.

1. Who introduced sugarcane to the Caribbean?
2. From which two plants is sugar (sucrose) most commonly derived?
3. How does table sugar differ from extra-fine (or bar) sugar? When might you use extra-fine sugar?
4. What ingredient is added to powdered sugar? Why is it added?
5. 10X powdered sugar is also known as _____.

6. Explain how brown sugar is produced. What are the two main classifications of brown sugar?
7. Invertion occurs when an acid mixes with a carbohydrate and changes sucrose to _____ and _____.
8. List and describe the three main classifications of molasses.
9. Why does honey differ in flavor from region to region?
10. What is lactose? What is its function in baked goods?
11. What is maltose? What is its function in baked goods?
12. What is the advantage of using corn syrup in baked goods?
13. _____ is the most common form of glucose.
14. Compare and contrast fats and oils.
15. What is hydrogenation? What are the advantages of the hydrogenation process?
16. List and describe the three main types of hydrogenated oils most often used in the bakeshop.
17. Is it mandatory that eggs be graded? What do the grades indicate?
18. The three egg grades are _____, _____, and _____.
19. List the main functions of eggs in baked goods.
20. How is the pH of eggs affected as they age?
21. Why might you add acid to egg whites that are to be whipped for meringues?
22. Describe proper storage procedures for fresh eggs.
23. What are the advantages to using frozen egg products?
24. What are the three main market forms of frozen eggs?
25. Why do frozen whole eggs and frozen egg yolks contain added dextrose (sugar)?
26. The two main market forms of powdered eggs are _____ and _____.

MULTIPLE CHOICE AND MATCHING

Choose the correct answer or answers.

27. Which of the following is the chemical name of table sugar?
    a. glucose
    b. fructose
    c. maltose
    d. sucrose

28. Match the following sugars to their relative sweetness level:

    a. sugar (cane or beet)   1. 60
    b. invert sugar   2. 130
    c. corn syrup   3. 15
    d. lactose   4. 100

29. Glucose is _____ as sweet as fructose or sucrose.
    a. twice
    b. three times
    c. half
    d. one quarter

30. Match the following fats to their description.

    a. lard   1. Rendered beef fat
    b. tallow   2. Milk fat churned from cream
    c. butter   3. Rendered hog fat

specialty
ingredients

"Variety is the spice of life."

Anonymous

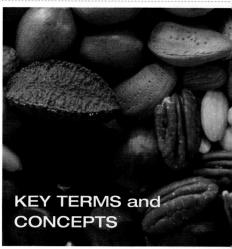

KEY TERMS and CONCEPTS

blanched

emulsions

extracts

flavoring compounds

gums

marzipan

nuts

LEARNING Objectives

After you have finished reading this unit, you should be able to:

- **Evaluate** the qualities of nuts, spices, and dried fruits

- **Describe** how to store nuts, spices, and dried fruits

- **Identify** nuts and spices by color, aroma, and taste

- **Discuss** the market forms of nuts, spices, and dried fruit

- **Describe** how and when to use emulsions and extracts

IN ORDER TO CREATE A VARIETY OF SIGNATURE BAKED

goods, it is important that students understand and learn about ingredients such as nuts, spices, and dried fruits. These specialty ingredients create unique flavor and texture profiles when added to cake, bread, and cookie formulas.

NUTS

Nuts can add texture, taste, and perceived value to most baked goods. Nuts have been defined as a "simple dry fruit with one seed (rarely two) in which the ovary wall or part of it becomes very hard at maturity" (Wikipedia). Nuts are high in protein and have a high oil content making them an excellent source of energy. Nut allergies are common and for those affected, even the smallest amount ingested can cause anaphylactic shock, which can be fatal. It is important to clearly label all baked goods containing nuts, nut oils, or any of their derivatives.

Purchasing and Storing Nuts

Nuts can be purchased in bulk form and are packaged in tin cans or waxed-cardboard boxes. Nuts are available shelled, whole, halved, sliced, chopped, ground, in paste form, and as oils. *Do not* store nuts in paper bags because the bags will absorb the oils from the nuts, which may cause the nuts to become rancid. Nuts should be stored in a cool, dry place or in the freezer packaged in a plastic bag or original container. (Shelled nuts will keep longer if stored in an air-tight container in the refrigerator or freezer.) To bring out the flavor of nuts, toast them *lightly* and cool them before you add them to a formula. Toasting also gives the nuts a golden color and added crunch, and will suspend better in batters than raw nuts for a more even consistency.

CHEF'S TIP: *Toasting nuts is a simple process. Generally, it takes between 8 and 20 minutes to toast nuts in the oven, depending on their size and shape. Nuts are considered roasted when they are golden brown in color. Simply spread the nuts on a baking sheet and bake in the oven at 350°F (180°C).*

Variety of Nuts

ALMOND

For many centuries, almonds (Figure 5-1) have been cultivated in the Mediterranean region and in the Orient. Today, California has become a major almond grower. The almond is available in many forms including whole, **blanched,** sliced, slivered, ground, flour, and paste. Almond flour is used in creams, custards, and cakes; almond paste can also be used in these products. Almond paste contains equal parts of sugar and ground almonds; the paste is used to make **marzipan** and is used in pastry making and confectionary work to cover cakes and pastries and as a key ingredient in almond cookies. *Macaroon paste,* a less expensive paste made with apricot, peach, and almond kernels, is sometimes substituted. When peanuts are added to this mixture, it is sold as almond-flavored kernel paste and is the least expensive alternative. Almond oil and extract round out the versatility of this nut. Almonds are a good source of calcium, fiber, folic acid, magnesium, potassium, riboflavin, and vitamin E.

BRAZIL NUT

Botanically, the Brazil nut (Figure 5-2) is not a true nut—it is the seed of a globular fruit made up of many hard-shelled segments arranged like orange segments. The tree grows wild in the tropics. Large-scale commercial production has not been successful in the United States. Brazil nuts are available blanched and unblanched; they can be used to garnish pastries and cakes. A few years ago, a food-science professor at Rutgers University did a study of foods that were high in nutrient density. He cited the Brazil nut as one of two nuts that contain the most vitamins and minerals (*Nutrition for the Culinary Arts,* 2005, Pearson Education).

Unit Review Questions

SHORT ANSWER

1. Gums are extracts from _____ that have the ability to suspend oil and water mixtures.
2. Describe the proper procedure for storing nuts.
3. Why is it sometimes recommended that nuts be lightly toasted and cooled prior to being added to a formula?
4. Almond paste contains equal parts of _____ and _____.
5. What is marzipan?
6. What is macaroon paste?
7. What is almond-flavored kernel paste?
8. What is the primary use for Brazil nuts in the bakeshop?
9. Explain the method for roasting chestnuts.
10. Hazelnuts are also known as _____.
11. The paste that is made from hazelnuts is called _____ paste.
12. Describe one method for removing the husks from hazelnuts.
13. Four market forms of pecans are _____, _____, _____, and _____.
14. Which variety of pine nut is preferred in bakery formulas?
15. Walnuts are graded by _____ and _____.
16. The two main varieties of walnuts are _____ and _____.
17. Describe the proper storage procedure for spices.
18. How do you determine if spices are fresh?
19. What is allspice?
20. Which spice is used in rye bread?
21. How is cardamom most often used in the bakeshop?
22. True cinnamon is derived from _____.
23. In addition to Ceylon cinnamon, the USDA recognizes what other product as "cinnamon"?
24. Which type of cinnamon is more commonly known and available?
25. What are the most common uses for sesame seeds in the bakeshop?
26. What are extracts?
27. What does the term "fold" refer to when discussing vanilla extract?
28. What is vanillin?
29. When are emulsions preferred over extracts?
30. What are the two main methods of preserving fruits by drying?
31. What are candied fruits?

MULTIPLE CHOICE AND MATCHING

32. Which is *not* a market form of almonds?
    a. blanched
    b. slivered
    c. halved
    d. ground
33. Chestnut flour may be added to bread formulas up to what percent?
    a. 5%
    b. 10%
    c. 15%
    d. 20%
34. Which of the following famous tortes has hazelnuts as a main ingredient?
    a. Linzer Torte
    b. Sacher Torte
    c. Tarte Tatin
    d. Dobos Torte
35. Which of the following nuts has the highest fat content?
    a. almond
    b. peanut
    c. walnut
    d. macadamia
36. Which of the following nuts is most likely to cause a serious allergic reaction?
    a. hazelnut
    b. peanut
    c. walnut
    d. almond
37. As a rule of thumb, whole spices such as cinnamon sticks will stay fresh up to
    a. 6 months
    b. 1 year
    c. 2 years
    d. 3 years
38. As a rule of thumb, ground spices will stay fresh up to
    a. 6 months
    b. 1 year
    c. 2 years
    d. 3 years
39. Which spice has a licorice flavor?
    a. allspice
    b. cardamom
    c. mace
    d. anise
40. Which two spices are derived from the same fruit?
    a. allspice/nutmeg
    b. cloves/allspice
    c. nutmeg/mace
    d. allspice/mace

equipment
and measuring

The selection of proper equipment and tools is essential for production efficiency and cost control, which is covered in Unit 6. Unit 7 includes a discussion on measuring ingredients and changing yields to meet production requirements.

tools of the trade

"An apprentice carpenter may want only a hammer and saw, but a master craftsman employs many precision tools."

Robert L. Kruse

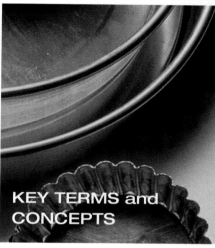

convection oven

depositing

dough hook

paddle

proofer

rotary oven

rotary rack convection oven

sheeter

small-deck oven

spiral mixers

"swab the deck"

vertical mixers

LEARNING Objectives

After you have finished reading this unit, you should be able to:

- **Select** oven types and fuel for a variety of baked goods

- **Discuss** mechanical mixing and rolling equipment

- **Gain** a competency for the care and use of the baker's bench

- **Understand** the principles of bakery refrigeration and freezing equipment

- **Determine** how to care for racks and pans

- **Identify** and know how to care for the hand tools used in baking

THE FOUR BASIC INGREDIENTS FOR BAKING BREAD— grains, water, salt, and yeast—were introduced in Unit 3. Later in that section, we ventured deeper into the baker's pantry and discussed sugars, fats and oils, eggs, and numerous specialty ingredients. A few centuries ago these ingredients were mixed by hand and baked in community ovens, using charcoal, wood, and coal. In this section, we discuss the basic equipment and tools of the modern bakery, such as ovens, mechanical mixing equipment, refrigeration, and small hand tools.

The world of commercial baking requires sophisticated equipment and tools for bakers to cope with the complexity of applications. Only practice with these tools will build skill in their use. Students must first become familiar with the equipment and tools needed to become a successful baker; then, with practice, the baking process can begin.

There's no doubt that having the proper equipment is essential to the success of any bakery. From aiding in food preparation to minimizing labor and energy costs to ultimately maintaining the quality of the food products that keep customers coming back, equipment is one of the key capital expenditures foodservice operators make.

OVENS AND PROOFERS

Traditionally, bread ovens were made out of clay or adobe, stone, brick, or concrete—materials that could withstand the high heat from the fire inside the oven. The community bread oven (Figure 6-1) was often found in the center of towns and villages. Villagers would bring their raw dough to the village bakeshop on a daily basis to be baked by the skillful baker. The baker was kept busy keeping the oven fires going, providing a needed service, and bartering for fresh produce, chickens, eggs, milk, or any other items that the baker could use.

In today's baking operations, the bread oven (Figure 6-2) is the largest and most expensive oven to operate. These ovens are designed for volume bread production; they are fueled by either gas or electricity. In some cases, the same oven offers the option of either gas or electricity. Bread ovens take up a lot of square feet of floor space (some bread ovens can be over 120 feet long). Since floor space costs money, the size of these ovens creates a large, fixed expenditure. Smaller models of bread ovens (with footprints approximately 20 ft by 30 ft or 6 M by 9 M) are available for retail shops. For these smaller ovens to be cost effective, the shop must bake 500 to 1,000 pounds (200 kg to 400 kg) of dough daily (oven capacity varies by model). Many models of bread ovens have the ability to inject moisture in the form of low-pressure steam during the baking cycle.

Gas ovens provide indirect heat to the baking chamber; they heat more quickly and recover faster than do electric versions. Electric ovens have top and bottom heat plates that heat the baking chamber; this allows the baker to control top and bottom heat separately. These ovens take longer to heat

Figure 6-1 This mosaic shows how bread was baked in ancient Rome. The common stone oven served the entire community.

and recover during the baking cycle than do gas ovens. Electric and gas ovens have been the industry standard for many years. Recent developments in oven technology have moved the heat-producing elements outside of the oven, allowing the heating of a thermal liquid to be piped in the top and bottom decks of the baking chamber. The thermal fluid can transfer heat more effectively, allowing for better heat control. By placing the heating chamber outside, the oven is easier to repair, reduces ventilation in the shop, and conserves shop space. This type of oven can be repaired on the outside, so there is little downtime when repairs are needed. Traditional ovens must be shut down and cooled before repairs can be made. Some bakers prefer to use an oven with multiple fuel choices—each deck can be heated by either gas or electricity. When the gas is down due to a clogged pilot light or some other malfunction, the baking can continue using electricity. In areas where gas is not readily available, oil may be used as a fuel.

Bread ovens feature a stone hearth that also retains moisture. The phrase **"swab the deck"** was a term given to the oven attendant before steam injection ovens were available. The oven attendant would swab the deck (a shelf in the oven) with a wet mop; the stone would absorb the water and release moisture during the baking cycle. The moisture improved oven spring and crust formation of the bread.

A typical bread oven is large, but the doors to the decks are small to prevent heat and moisture loss; it is critical to have solid oven heat during the

Figure 6-2 Modern bread oven.

Figure 6-3 Rotary oven.

baking process. When there is a drop in temperature, the leavening and color of the baked product may be affected.

Students often ask if it is true that they should not open the oven door until the product is almost done. The answer is "yes" if you are using a home oven. Home ovens can lose up to 75 percent of their heat in 2 minutes. However, this is not true for commercial ovens because their doors are smaller. When you select the fuel type for these large ovens, you have to balance cost and convenience. Gas and electricity require no storage and burn clean. Oil is less expensive but requires storage.

There are a number of bread ovens on the market today. You can learn more about the many oven options by attending bakery trade shows.

Rotary or Reel Ovens

Rotary ovens (Figure 6-3), which are sometimes called reel ovens, are ideal for large productions that bake up to 3,000 pieces of baked goods per day. This conventional oven is moderate in size and has a capacity of 12 to 36 pans. The pans are placed on shelves that rotate like a ferris wheel. There are models available with steam for bread baking. Because the product rotates in a large, heated chamber, it bakes evenly. When loading this type of oven, be sure the pans are properly aligned on the shelves or equipment damage and possible injury to the operator could result. Typically, there is less heating loss during loading and unloading of product because the door is open for a shorter time compared to that for convection ovens.

Small-Deck or Pizza Oven

The **small-deck oven** (Figure 6-4), or pizza oven, is used in retail operations because it affords the baker multiple temperature options and uses limited floor space (approximately 64 to 72 sq ft or 6 to 7 square meters) and may have two to four decks. It is ideal for bakeries that produce between 800 and 1,000 pieces of baked goods on a daily basis. Each deck has a two-pan capacity, and the deck is generally made of steel or stone. Decks have individual temperature zones so a number of products can be baked

Figure 6-4 Small-deck oven.

The baker uses a refrigerator for perishable ingredients, dough, and batter and a freezer for long-term storage. The baker's refrigerator provides more moisture than do conventional refrigeration units, so that the products retain moisture and the dough does not develop a crust.

Additional specialty items such as doughnut fryers, storage bins, baking pans and forms, racks, and hand tools are often added to the baker's arsenal of important tools of the trade.

The operation of equipment and the use of hand tools require practice. To gain efficiency and productivity from the equipment and tools, read and follow all posted instructions found on most pieces of equipment or the accompanying manufacturer's manual. Failure to follow safety instruction may result in injury.

Unit Review Questions

SHORT ANSWER

1. What are the advantages of gas ovens versus electric ovens?
2. What are the advantages of electric ovens versus gas ovens?
3. What are thermal ovens?
4. What are the advantages of thermal ovens?
5. Describe a rotary or reel oven.
6. What are the advantages of a small-deck oven, or pizza oven?
7. Due to the air circulation, convection ovens bake about _____ percent faster than nonconvection ovens.
8. What is a proofer?
9. The temperature range of a proofer is _____ °F. The humidity range is _____ percent.
10. Which type of dough is proofed at a *lower* temperature—lean or rich?
11. List and describe the two main types of conventional mechanical batch mixers.
12. What are the three main attachments used on a vertical mixer?
13. Describe the proper care of a laminated, hardwood baker's bench.
14. How does a baker's refrigerator differ from a conventional refrigerator?
15. Today, most baking pans are made of _____.
16. Describe how to season a metal pan.
17. Why is it important to cool bread on a bread-cooling rack?
18. In the bakeshop, what does the term "deposit" mean?

MULTIPLE CHOICE AND MATCHING

19. Which type of oven is most efficient in terms of floor space?
    a. small-deck or pizza
    b. convection
    c. rotary or reel
    d. bread
20. A convection oven is usually considered to be how much hotter than a standard oven?
    a. 5–10 percent
    b. 10–15 percent
    c. 25–50 percent
    d. 55–70 percent
21. Convection ovens are not recommended for which of the following items?
    a. cookies
    b. cakes
    c. breads
    d. pizza
22. When using the whip attachment on a 20-quart mixing bowl, what is the recommended capacity for each of the following items that are to be whipped?
    a. egg whites   1. 6 quarts
    b. whole eggs   2. 2 quarts
    c. heavy cream   3. 4 quarts
23. Many health departments will allow laminated, hardwood work tables if they are free from scratches and cracks and if they have a moisture content of less than
    a. 1/2 percent
    b. 1 percent
    c. 1 1/2 percent
    d. 10 percent
24. The standard commercial size sheet pan has an inside measurement of
    a. 9 inches × 13 inches
    b. 12 1/4 inches × 18 inches
    c. 14 1/4 inches × 22 inches
    d. 16 1/2 inches × 24 1/2 inches
25. Match the following hand tools to their use:
    a. bench scraper   1. for spreading batters and icings
    b. spatula
    c. serrated knife   2. trims small ingredients
    d. paring knife   3. cuts bulk dough
    e. bench brush   4. removes excess flour from bench and dough
                          5. slices cake and bread

measuring ingredients and changing formula yields

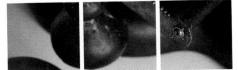

"*Correct measurements are absolutely necessary to ensure the best results.*"

Fannie Farmer, *The Boston Cooking School Cookbook,* 1918

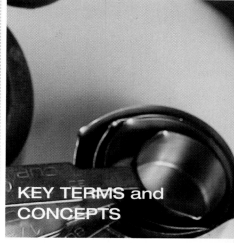

KEY TERMS and CONCEPTS

balance beam scale

liquid measures

production yield

yield

LEARNING Objectives

After you have finished reading this unit, you should be able to:

- **Select** the proper measuring equipment for liquids and dry ingredients

- **Describe** how to change a formula yield using a baker's percentage

- **Discuss** how to determine a formula yield

- **Demonstrate** how to change a formula yield based on production requirements

UNLIKE OTHER COOKERY, WHERE INTUITION SOMETIMES creates delicious dishes, baking is a science. As ingredients are mixed together, chemistry is created. Precise measurements ensure that the flour, leaveners, fats, and liquids combine to create a balance. Too much flour will make the bread dry and crumbly. Too much salt will ruin the muffin. Too little baking soda will destroy the cake. Bakers learn to carefully weigh all of the ingredients—after all, the success of the recipe depends on it.

If a cook forgets to add salt when preparing chowder, he or she can add it after it has cooked, just prior to serving. It won't change the outcome of the product. This is not so in the bakeshop. A baker who forgets to add salt to rye dough, for example, cannot add the salt after the bread is baked and the quality of the bread will most certainly be jeopardized.

MEASURING DRY INGREDIENTS

Dry ingredients are measured by weight using electronic digital scales or the old standard, the baker's balance beam scale.

The **balance beam scale** has two balanced platforms and a graduated bar with either standard or metric measurements (Figure 7-1). The bar measures

ingredients in small increments—less than 1 lb—and the right balance platform measures greater amounts. The left platform holds the ingredients to
be weighed. The right platform counterbalances the weight of the container
that holds the ingredients (tare the scale) and adds additional standard or
metric weights depending on the amount of ingredients being weighed. The
items are weighed properly when the scale returns to a balanced position
with equal weight on both platforms, plus the bar (up to 1 lb). Digital scales
are also available that automatically weigh the ingredients (Figure 7-2).

The baker's balance beam scale is a favorite of many bakers; it needs no
electricity and has no springs. Using a spring scale for weighing baking
soda, baking powder, or spices is not recommended because it is less accurate than the balance beam scale. Small errors in quantities can affect the
final outcome of the formula.

Using a Baker's Balance Beam Scale

1. Place the scale on a level table that is free of obstructions (Figure 7-3).
2. Place a scoop or container on the left platform where the product will
   eventually be placed (Figure 7-4). (**Note:** Make sure you place this
   container on the left platform and not the right. If it is placed on the
   right platform, the ounce bar cannot be used.) Balance the scoop or
   container with a counterweight placed on the right platform.
3. Set the scale for weighing by placing the correct amount of pounds on
   the right platform and ounces on the ounce bar (Figure 7-5). When
   using the ounce bar to counterweight your container, add the total
   amount needed to the ounces already used. For example, if 3 oz (90 g)
   are used to balance the container and 8 oz (680 g) of ingredient are
   needed, set the ounce bar at 11 oz (310 g).
4. Add your desired ingredient until the scale balances (Figure 7-6).
   When all 16 oz on the bar are used, add a 1 lb weight to the right
   platform and return the ounce measure to zero, so it may be used
   again.

Figure 7-1 Balance beam.

Figure 7-2 Digital scales.

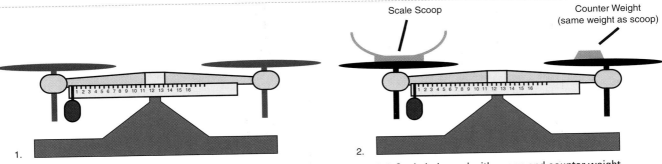

Figure 7-3 Balanced scale.

Figure 7-4 Scale balanced with scoop and counter weight.

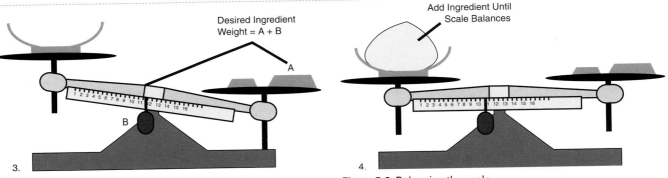

Figure 7-5 Scale with the desired weight.

Figure 7-6 Balancing the scale.

LEARNING ACTIVITY 7-1

Balance the bakers balance beam scale and weigh these quantities of sugar in sequence, then add the total weight of the sugar

Step 1:   Measure 1 lb-14 oz

Step 2:   Add 2 lb-9 oz

Step 3:   Add 7 1/2 oz

Step 4:   Add 14 oz

Step 5:   Add 23 oz

After all 5 steps have been completed see how many lb are on the right platform and how many oz are on the bar.

_____ lb _____ oz

4. Change the ingredients in the following chart to ounces and then multiply by 1.35.

Flaky Pie Crust

Ingredients	Original Amounts	Adjustments Needed	New Formula Amounts
Pastry flour	3 lb 6 oz = 54 oz	54 × 1.35	73 oz (2,070 g)
Shortening	2 lb 8 oz = 40 oz	40 × 1.35	53 oz (1,500 g)
Salt	2 oz	2 × 1.35	2½ oz (70 g)
Water	1 lb 6 oz = 22 oz	22 × 1.35	30 oz (850 g)
Original yield: (118 oz) 7 lb 6 oz (3,350 g)			New yield: (158 1/2 oz) 9 lb 14 1/2 oz (4,475 g)

Blueberry Filling
Blueberry Pie Filling (original formula)

Ingredients	Lb	Oz	Metric
Water	2		900 g
Sugar	2	4	1,020 g
Blueberries		4	110 g
Water		4	110 g
Cornstarch		4½	130 g
Sugar		1	30 g
Blueberries	3		1,360 g

Yield: 8 lb 1 1/2 oz (Four 10-inch pies) (3,670 g)
Serving size: 6 oz (170 g)

Production requirement: Eight 10-in. blueberry pies containing 2 lb of filling each
Follow these steps to change the yield:

1. Determine the quantity of pie filling needed to complete the production requirement.

   2 lb × 16 = 32 × 8 = 256 oz (RQ)

2. The original formula yields 8 lb 1 1/2 oz or 129.5 oz (OQ).

3. Divide the required quantity (RQ) 256 oz by the original formula yield (OQ) 129.5 = 1.98.

   It will take 1.98 times the original formula to fulfill the production requirements.

4. Change the ingredients in the following chart to ounces and then multiply by 1.98. (In this situation we will round up 1.98 to 2 and double the formula.)

Blueberry Pie Filling

Ingredients	Original Amounts	Adjustments Needed	New Formula Amounts
Water	2 lb = 32 oz	32 × 2	64 oz (1,810 g)
Sugar	2 lb 4 oz = 40 oz	40 × 2	80 oz (2,270 g)
Blueberries	4 oz	4 × 2	8 oz (230 g)
Water	4 oz	4 × 2	8 oz (230 g)
Cornstarch	4.5 oz	4.5 × 2	9 oz (260 g)
Sugar	1 oz	1 × 2	2 oz (60 g)
Blueberries	3 lb = 48 oz	48 × 2	96 oz (2,720 g)
Original yield: (129.5 oz) 8 lb 1½ oz (3,670 g) (3.67 kg)			New yield: (267 oz) 16 lb 11 oz (7,570 g)

Corn Bread/Muffins (original formula)

% Ratio	Ingredients	Lb	Oz	Metric
50	Corn meal		12	340 g
100	Milk	1	8	680 g
75	Sugar	1	2	510 g
42	Corn oil		10	280 g
1	Salt		1	30 g
8	Eggs		8	230 g
2	Baking powder		2	60 g
100	Pastry flour	1	8	680 g

Yield: 6 lb 3 oz (2,810 g)
Serving size: 3 oz (90 g)

Production requirement: 12 dozen corn muffins at 3 oz each
   Follow these steps to change the yield:

1. Determine the quantity of batter needed to complete the production requirement.
   12 dozen × 12 = 144 × 3 oz = 432 oz (RQ)
2. The original corn muffin mix yields 6 lb × 16 = 96 + 3 = 99 oz (OQ).
3. Divide the required quantity by the original formula yield: 432 oz (RQ) ÷ 99 oz (OQ) = 4.36.
   It will take 4.36 times the original formula to fulfill the production requirements.
4. Change the ingredients in the following chart to ounces and then multiply by 4.36.

Corn Bread/Muffins

Ingredients	Original Amounts	Adjustments Needed	New Formula Amounts
Corn meal	12 oz	12 × 4.36	52 oz (1,470 g)
Milk	1 lb 8 oz = 24 oz	24 × 4.36	105 oz (2,980 g)
Sugar	1 lb 2 oz = 18 oz	18 × 4.36	79 oz (2,240 g)
Corn oil	10 oz	10 × 4.36	44 oz (1,250 g)
Salt	1 oz	1 × 4.36	4 oz (110 g)
Eggs	8 oz	8 × 4.36	2 oz (60 g)
Baking powder	2 oz	2 × 4.36	8.5 oz (240 g)
Pastry flour	1 lb 8 oz = 24 oz	24 × 4.36	105 oz (2,980 g)
Original yield: (99 oz) 6 lb 3 oz (2,810 g)			New yield: (399.5 oz) 25 lb (11,330 g)

Sugar Cookie (original formula)

% Ratio	Ingredients	Lb	Oz	Metric
50	Sugar	1		450 g
37½	Butter		12	340 g
¾	Salt		¼	5 g
25	Eggs		8	230 g
12½	Milk		4	110 g
100	Pastry flour	2		900 g
3	Baking powder		1	30 g
1½	Vanilla		½	10 g

Yield: 4 lb 9 ¾ oz (2,090 g), 60 cookies
Serving size: 2 oz (60 g)

Production requirement: 18 dozen sugar cookies at 2 oz each
Follow these steps to change the yield:

1. Determine the quantity of dough needed to complete the production requirement.

   18 dz × 12 = 216 × 2 oz = 432 oz (RQ)

2. The original cookie dough yield is 4 lb × 16 = 64 + 9¾ oz = 73.75 (OQ).

3. Divide the required quantity yield, 432 oz (RQ), by the original quantity (OQ) yield, 73.75 = 5.86.

   It will take 5.86 times the original formula to fulfill the production requirements.

4. Change the ingredients in the following chart to ounces and then multiply by 5.86.

Sugar Cookie

Ingredients	Original Amounts	Adjustments Needed	New Formula Amounts
Sugar	1 lb = 16 oz	16 × 5.86	94 oz (2,660 g)
Butter	12 oz	12 × 5.86	70 oz (1,985 g)
Salt	¼ oz	.25 × 5.86	1½ oz (40 g)
Eggs	8 oz	8 × 5.86	47 oz (1,330 g)
Milk	4 oz	4 × 5.86	23 oz (650 g)
Pastry flour	2 lb = 32 oz	32 × 5.86	188 oz (5,330 g)
Baking powder	1 oz	1 × 5.86	5½ oz (160 g)
Vanilla	½ oz	.5 × 5.86	3 oz (90 g)
Original yield: (73.75 oz) 4 lb 9¾ oz (2,090 g)			New yield: (432 oz) 27 lb (12,250 g)

Hi-Ratio Yellow Cake (original formula)

% Ratio	Ingredients	Lb	Oz	Metric
100	Sugar	2	8	1,130 g
2½	Salt		1	30 g
48	Cake shortening	1	3	540 g
5	Baking powder		2	60 g
100	Cake flour	2	8	1,130 g
20	Milk		8	230 g
40	Eggs	1		450 g
10	Egg yolks		4	110 g
20	Milk		8	230 g

Yield: 8 lb 10 oz (3,910 g)

Serving size: 2 oz (60 g)

Production requirement: 30, 8-in. cake layers, 14 oz each
   Follow these steps to change the yield:

1. Determine the quantity of batter needed to complete the production requirement.

   30 × 14 oz = 420 oz (RQ)

2. The original cake batter yield was 8 lb × 16 = 128 + 10 = 138 oz (OQ).

3. Divide the required quantity yield, 420 oz (RQ), by the original quantity yield, 138 oz (OQ) = 3.

   It will take three times the original formula to fulfill the production requirements.

4. Change the ingredients in the following chart to ounces and then multiply by 3.

Hi-Ratio Yellow Cake

Ingredients	Original Amounts	Adjustments Needed	New Formula Amounts
Sugar	2 lb 8 oz = 40 oz	40 × 3	120 oz (3,400 g)
Salt	1 oz	1 × 3	3 oz (90 g)
Cake shortening	1 lb 3 oz = 19 oz	19 × 3	57 oz (1,620 g)
Baking powder	2 oz	2 × 3	6 oz (170 g)
Cake flour	2 lb 8 oz = 40 oz	40 × 3	120 oz (3,400 g)
Milk	8 oz	8 × 3	24 oz (680 g)
Eggs	1 lb = 16 oz	16 × 3	48 oz (1,360 g)
Egg yolks	4 oz	4 × 3	12 oz (340 g)
Milk	8 oz	8 × 3	24 oz (680 g)
Original yield: (138 oz) 8 lb 10 oz (3,910 g)			New yield: (414 oz) 25 lb 14 oz (11,560 g)

LEARNING ACTIVITY 7-3

Determine the quantity of dough or batter in pounds and ounces needed to produce the following. Record your answer next to each problem.

1. 20 dz rolls @ 1.5 oz _____ lb _____ oz

2. 15 loafs of bread @ 1 lb-14 oz _____ lb _____ oz

3. 6 dz rolls @ 2 oz and 6 breads @ 14 oz _____ lb _____ oz

4. 6 8" cake rounds @ 15 oz _____ lb _____ oz

5. 8 loaf cakes @ 1 lb-6 oz _____ lb _____ oz

PROFILES

Jackie Scott, CMB
President
Scott's Pastry Shoppe, Middleton, Wis.

Jackie Scott is busy wearing two hats these days. She is president of her own 22-year-old bakery and is currently serving as the past president of the Retailer's Bakery Association. "One of the benefits of owning your own business is that it allows you the opportunity to be involved in your community. I sit on numerous boards and have always been an active member of our local Chamber of Commerce. I'm always sad when I hear small-business owners who say they don't have time for such things. To me, it has helped our business to grow and has given me an outlet, which has helped me to get a break from the business at times. I've always believed that you should join your professional organizations. My membership in RBA has been very beneficial," says Scott.

With her daughter and son-in-law now working full-time at the busy shop, Scott has been able to give back to the RBA by serving as its president and now as its past president. She spends a lot of time on the road, attending meetings and speaking at trade shows and conventions on behalf of the RBA.

Scott was married at age 17. Both she and her young husband began supporting their family by working in bakeries. In 1982 they opened up Scott's Pastry Shoppe, which has developed a loyal following over the years and has grown to three retail outlets with over 40 employees. "I have always tried to learn as much as I could from people who were already in the business. I didn't have the opportunity to go to school, so I had to learn from those around me. Getting my CMB, (Certified Master Baker) was a big step for me (see Unit 21 for information on the RBA and CMB certification). I had to study and work really hard to earn it. This has not been a job—it's a life. As we think of turning our business over to the next generation in the next few years, we can say that we've had a great life," says Scott.

Bill Reynolds
Provost
Washburne Culinary Institute, Chicago, Ill.

Bill Reynolds began his career as a minister and Latin teacher. Having helped out in his aunt and uncle's restaurant, he realized that his heart was in the foodservice industry. He headed to the Culinary Institute of America and fell in love with the school, so much so that he didn't want to leave. He spent 25 years there, first as a student, then as a part-time instructor. Eventually he worked his way to vice-president. Three years ago he began consulting for Washburne Culinary Institute and eventually accepted the position as provost. Washburne is the oldest, continually running culinary program in the country. Ninety percent of its students are African American, which is something that initially attracted Reynolds to the program. "I have always felt that not enough was being done to attract African Americans to the foodservice industry. This has been an exciting opportunity for me to help change their perception of the industry," says Reynolds. Washburne currently has 100 students but is in the midst of a major facility renovation that will enable the school to grow to 500 students.

Reynold's major responsibilities include staff development and overseeing the cooking and pastry programs. He is also in charge of overseeing the current renovation. "Once that is complete, we will also be adding two restaurants and a catering company. Our facility will truly be a world-class operation. It has been tremendously rewarding to see the program grow and expand. I wasn't looking for a change, but when this opportunity came I simply couldn't pass it up," says Reynolds.

SUMMARY

Accurate measurements are critical in the bakeshop. Dry ingredients are measured by weight using either an electronic digital scale or a baker's balance beam scale. Liquids are measured by volume and then converted to weight.

A baker must be able to change yields according to the production requirement. This process requires taking the basic formula and changing it to produce more or less product, depending on the production needs. It is important that you fully understand the process involved in changing yields.

Unit Review Questions

SHORT ANSWER

1. The left platform on a balance beam scale is used to
   _____ _____.

2. The right platform is used to _____
   and for _____.

3. The bar on a balance beam scale is used for
   _____.

4. Why is a balance beam scale preferred over a spring
   scale for measuring baking soda, baking powder, and
   spices?

5. Which ingredient is always calculated at 100 percent
   when using baker's percentage?

6. Why is it recommended that weight be converted
   entirely to ounces for recalculating recipes?

7. When changing the yields of a formula, carry out the
   math two decimal points and round down at .50 for
   _____ and _____
   and round up for _____.

8. Convert the following to ounces.
   a. 2 lb 5 oz
   b. 4 lb 3 oz
   c. 6 lb 15 oz
   d. 8 lb 2½ oz

9. Convert the following into pounds and ounces.
   a. 22 oz
   b. 49 oz
   c. 96 oz
   d. 185 oz

10. Calculate the percentages for the following formula:
    1 lb 4 oz bread flour
    10 oz water
    2 oz yeast
    1/2 oz salt

MULTIPLE CHOICE AND MATCHING

11. If from one bread formula you need to produce 12
    dozen rolls at 1.5 oz each and 4 loaves of bread at 1
    lb 8 oz each, how much dough will you need to make?
    a. 18 lb 12 oz
    b. 19 lb 5 oz
    c. 19 lb 8 oz
    d. 7 lb 2 oz

12. What is the total yield of the following recipe?

    2 lb 6 oz bread flour   a. 4 lb 5 oz
    1 lb 12 oz water   b. 4 lb 8 oz
    2 oz sugar   c. 4 lb 3 oz
    3 oz yeast   d. 4 lb 10 oz
    1 oz salt

13. The original formula for croissant dough yields 9 lb
    and you need to make 12 dozen croissants scaled at
    3 oz each. How many times the original formula
    must you make?
    a. 2.25 times
    b. 2.75 times
    c. 4.5 times
    d. 3 times

14. If the amount of flour in a recipe is 2 lb and the
    amount of milk is 3 lb, what is the percentage of the
    milk (using baker's percentages)?
    a. 67%
    b. 100%
    c. 150%
    d. 167%

15. If your cake formula produces 30 cakes scaled at 12 oz
    each and you now must make 27 cakes scaled at 10 oz
    each, by what amount will you multiply each
    ingredient in the recipe?
    a. .75
    b. 1.33
    c. 1.5
    d. .25

yeast dough mixing and baking

Good breadmaking skills are based on the correct use of ratio, sequence, time, and temperature. Units 8 and 9 discuss those issues and introduce the student to mixing methods, fermentation, proofing, and baking procedures for yeast breads. A variety of bread formulas are presented in Unit 9.

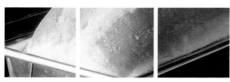

baking principles
for yeast dough

"Good bread is the most fundamentally satisfying of all foods; and good bread with fresh butter is the greatest of all feasts."

James Beard

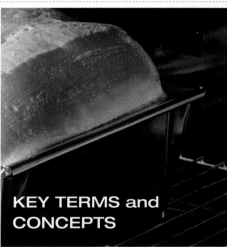

KEY TERMS and CONCEPTS

LEARNING Objectives

After you have finished reading this unit, you should be able to:

- **Discuss** the difference between stabilizers and tenderizers

- **Identify** dough types by ratio

- **Discuss** the sequence in yeast dough mixing

- **Describe** the effects of time and temperature on dough

- **Describe** the principles of organic (yeast) leavening and mechanical (steam) leavening

- **Determine** the effect of temperature on leavening during the mixing and baking process

fold-over

lean dough

oven spring

rich dough

sponge method

stabilizers

straight-dough method

tenderizers

NOTHING WHETS THE APPETITE LIKE THE AROMA AND taste of freshly baked yeast bread. According to the Wheat Foods Council, the average American eats 53 pounds of bread a year. Bread is certainly "the staff of life" for Western civilizations and plays a large role in diets around the world. Learning to bake a consistent and delicious loaf of bread becomes a rewarding experience for the baker with each and every batch.

This section explores the methods and procedures needed to produce quality baked bread and rolls. To become a successful baker, the student must understand the baking principles introduced here.

FUNCTIONS OF YEAST DOUGH INGREDIENTS

Ingredients (Figure 8-1) can be classified by their reaction to the baking process.

Stabilizers

Ingredients that bind liquids and become firm during baking are called **stabilizers.** The proteins and starches found in eggs and flour are stabilizers. Once heat is applied, stabilizers bind the liquefiers and form the structure for dough and batter. The application of heat causes the starches to absorb the liquid (gelatinize) and the proteins to become firm (coagulate).

Tenderizers

Ingredients that affect the stabilization of dough and batter are called **tenderizers;** they provide moisture and tenderness or softness to the grain and texture of the baked good. Sugar, fat, oil, and liquids are tenderizers. The following information describes how each of these ingredients works as a tenderizer:

Sugar delays and softens the gelatinization of starch by blocking the absorption of the liquid from the starch and preventing the starch from swelling.

Fats and *oils* soften gelatinization and shorten the protein strands.

Liquids such as water, milk, and juice soften and tenderize the dough or batter by thinning the effects of coagulation and gelatinization.

Dough versus Batter

It's important for bakers to understand the difference between dough and batter, as it will determine the mixing and leavening method needed to produce the best-quality product. To determine whether a formula is dough or batter, add the weight of the stabilizers and tenderizers separately and compare the ratio. If the weight of the stabilizers is greater than the weight of the tenderizers, the formula is dough. Dough is a heavy mass and requires more time to leaven. If the weight of the tenderizers is greater than the weight of the stabilizers, the formula is batter. Batters are leavened by creaming, foaming, or adding chemical leaveners.

The leavener used for yeast dough is the yeast itself. Yeast is capable of sustained growth over long periods of time. The yeast activity, called *fermentation,* leavens and flavors the dough. Batters can be leavened mechanically by steam or chemically by creaming or foaming, or they can be leavened by adding baking powder or soda because batters are more fluid than dough. We will learn more about chemical and mechanical batter leavening in Unit 14.

DOUGH RATIOS

All baking formulas are based on percentages, as was discussed in Unit 7. Flour is always 100 percent, and the other ingredients are balanced to the weight of the flour.

Example: The amount of flour called for in a recipe is 5 lb. So, 5 lb equal 100 percent. The water in that recipe needs to be 3 lb, which is 60 percent when compared to the weight of the flour.

There are three dough ratios that affect mixing and dough-handling procedures:

1. **Lean dough: Lean dough** contains less than 10 percent* shortening and sugar (French bread or Italian-style loaf).
2. **Rich dough: Rich dough** contains more than 10 percent* shortening and sugar, but less than 30 percent (American sandwich loaf or brioche).
3. **Laminated dough:** When shortening exceeds 30 percent*, the dough is considered to be laminated (Puff pastry, Danish and croissants).

*NOTE: To a baker, the term "shortening" identifies the function of fat and oil—the term refers to all oils and fats that shorten dough structure. The baker has many shortening choices including butter, margarine, oil, hydrogenated oil, and lard. When shortening exceeds 30 percent, the dough is laminated (layers of dough and shortening). An in-depth study of laminated dough will follow in Unit 10.

Figure 8-1 Ingredients can be identified by the way they react to the baking process.

DOUGH SEQUENCE

When baking with yeast you must use the ingredients in certain proportions to one another and add them at the proper time. Otherwise, problems can occur. For lean dough, the **straight-dough method** is often used. This method combines all of the ingredients in the mixing bowl. To obtain maximum volume, the gluten must be properly developed. Best results are obtained by mixing the ingredients at slow speed; high speeds tend to tear gluten, which results in dough that is slack and has lost its ability to bond with water. The proper sequence of adding ingredients in the straight-dough mixing method is liquid, yeast, flour, and salt, in that order (Figure 8-2).

For rich dough, a two-step mixing method is used to give the yeast action a head start; this is referred to as the **sponge method** (Figure 8-3). The two-step mixing method contains a higher percentage of sugars and fats, so the yeast will develop more strength if the sugars and fats are added in a second step.

Fermentation

The dough requires several time and temperature steps prior to baking. The first step is fermentation. Fermentation is a period of yeast activity controlled by time and the temperature of the dough and its environment. At room temperature, 72°F (22°C), dough will double in size every 20 to 30 minutes; warmer environments and dough temperatures cause the dough to develop faster. We can retard (slow down) the activity by dividing the dough into small units and refrigerating them. We can speed up the activity by placing the dough into a proofer as described in Unit 6.

Figure 8-2 Sequence is important. For the straight-dough method, always add the liquid first, followed by yeast, then flour, and finally salt.

Figure 8-3 In the sponge-mixing method, add the sugar and fat during the second step for rich dough.

There are four fermentation periods in the straight-dough method (see stages 2–4 that follow), and there are five fermentation periods in the sponge-dough method. The sponge dough has an additional fermentation period before mixing the final dough (see stages 1–5 below).

NOTE: As a living organism, yeast must be treated in a specific way to ensure proper results. The baker must understand the growth and death patterns of living yeast and follow specific instructions for ensuring their proper function.

STAGES OF FERMENTATION

Stage 1: Pre-ferment when mixing sponge dough (Figure 8-4).

Stage 2: After mixing, allow the dough to rest in a warm area of the shop (Figure 8-5). Cover it with a cloth to prevent crusting. This period lasts about 30 minutes, and the dough will double in size. During this stage, the yeast converts carbohydrates to carbon dioxide and alcohol. Remove these gases by folding the dough over itself and returning the dough to the original size. It is important to remove the gases by **fold-over** (punching) to equalize the dough temperature, introduce fresh air, and redistribute the yeast to feed on fresh or new food. This process also helps to distribute the flavor produced by the yeast.

Figure 8-4 First stage.

Figure 8-5 Second stage.

Figure 8-6 Third stage.

Figure 8-7 Fourth stage.

Stage 3: The yeast activity continues as the dough is divided and shaped (Figure 8-6). If this process takes longer than 40 minutes, the dough should be retarded by chilling. If not, it will become old, the yeast will not perform as well, and it will bake poorly. The finished product will lack volume and color.

Stage 4: This fermentation takes place in the proofer (Figure 8-7). The temperature is adjusted as specified in the formula and the yeast activity is accelerated; this begins the leavening of the dough. The first two fermentations condition and flavor the dough; conditioning mellows the gluten and allows the dough to be shaped. During this fermentation stage the leavening activity begins, the dough becomes fragile, and you must take care not to deflate the dough. (The term *leavening* is the act of making light or causing to ferment by means of yeast activity.)

Stage 5: This fermentation activity takes place during the first stage of the baking process. It is a very lively period of yeast activity as the dough temperature increases. We refer to this as **oven spring**—the rapid rise of dough during the first phase of baking; a time when the yeast is very active. The yeast activity terminates at an internal dough temperature of 138°F (60°C).

Mixing Procedures

As mentioned earlier, there are two different methods for mixing yeast dough: the straight-dough method and the sponge-dough method. The correct dough temperature is very important and is easily achieved if you monitor the temperature of the water used in the dough. Following is the method for calculating the water temperature.

STRAIGHT-DOUGH MIXING METHOD
Water Temperature
For this method of baking the maximum dough temperature should be 80°F (27°C). To reach this desired dough temperature, multiple factors have to be taken into consideration: the temperature of the flour, the room, and the amount of heat generated through friction while the machine turns the dough using a hook or paddle. To determine the proper temperature of ingredients to ensure a dough of 80°F (27°C) multiply 80 by 3

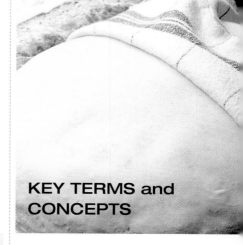

"It is a mysterious business, this making of bread, and once you are hooked by the miracle of yeast, you'll be a breadmaker for life."

James Beard

KEY TERMS and CONCEPTS

kaiser rolls

pumpernickel

rope

sour dough starter

LEARNING Objectives

After you have finished reading this unit, you should be able to:

- **Describe** the ratios of yeast-dough formulation by percentage

- **Demonstrate** how to control dough temperature

- **Shape** a variety of bread and rolls

- **Describe** typical bread and roll variations such as whole wheat, oat, rye, milk, and egg bread

- **Discuss** how to mix, condition, shape, and bake a variety of rye bread and rolls

- **Describe** common breadmaking problems and offer suggestions to overcome them

TO CREATE SIGNATURE YEAST-DOUGH PRODUCTS, YOU must understand formula ratios and the proper sequence to use during the mixing procedure. Maximum flour absorption, optimal dough temperature, proper gluten formation, and full flavor development throughout the fermentation process are the direct result of using proper formula ratios and sequence.

This unit explains the sequence of steps best suited to create quality bread and rolls. Calculations to achieve proper dough temperatures for yeast control are also explained. This unit will end with a variety of yeast bread and roll formulas.

UNDERSTANDING DOUGH RATIOS

Creating signature breads and rolls begins with understanding how to combine ingredients into different ratios. Water, yeast, salt, and hard flour (high-gluten bread flour) are the key ingredients in forming lean dough.

Lean dough produces breads and rolls that have a crispy crust and a light crumb (the crumb is the texture of the interior of the bread or roll) (Figure 9-1). This bread develops full flavor with proper mixing and fermentation. The use of steam during baking is an aid to develop a light, crispy loaf of bread. You will find that most professional bakeries have steam-injection ovens. The moisture introduced at the beginning of the baking cycle allows the bread to expand and the starches to gelatinize, forming a thin crust.

When you are baking lean dough with steam, set the oven between 400° to 450°F (200° to 230°C). Hearth baking produces the best-quality breads because the stones retain moisture. There are many professional stone, brick, and adobe ovens with steam injection available on the market today.

Lean-dough breads and rolls are best if baked no longer than 3 to 4 hours before service, as they have a poor shelf-life and can quickly become dry.

Ingredients

The key ingredients of yeast dough are flour, liquid, yeast, salt, sugar, and oil/shortening. Although each ingredient was discussed at length in Unit 3, the information here will serve as a quick review and offer insight into working with different types of dough.

FLOUR

Several types of flour can be blended to create texture and flavor. For proper gluten development, 60 percent of the flour should be from hard wheat flour. High-gluten flour gives elasticity to the dough and improves the volume.

LIQUID

Water is the liquid of choice for making lean dough. In some cases egg whites are added which contain a high percentage of water and are an excellent source of protein. However, only egg whites are used in lean dough as whole eggs contain a high amount of fat in the yolk. When making lean dough and using egg whites, don't let the egg whites represent more than 10 percent of the total volume of liquid used.

When egg whites are used in lean dough formulas, bakers prefer to use either hotel or restaurant flours (commonly referred to as all-purpose flours). These types of flours are fairly low in protein, compared to other hard, or high gluten bread flours, allowing the proteins in the egg whites to expand properly and become more elastic.

YEAST

When making bread and rolls, a baker has a choice of yeast. Each type of yeast—fresh, active dry, and instant—must be handled properly to assure uniform results. Refer back to Unit 3 where the various types of yeasts were discussed in detail.

NOTE: Lean dough requires less yeast than does rich dough.

SALT

Salt is essential to yeast dough—it prevents rapid yeast activity in the dough and prevents the formation of **rope,** which is a type of bacteria. Because the

Figure 9-1 Lean dough produces light, crispy full-flavored bread and rolls.

bacterium is not destroyed in the baking process, rope causes bread to become moldy within a few hours of baking. Salt also strengthens gluten development. If you are making salt-free bread, replace the salt with an equal amount of vinegar.

NOTE: Flour, water, yeast, and salt will produce lean dough, made light and flavorful through fermentation and hearth baking.

The following ingredients can be added to increase the flavor, moisture, and richness.

SUGAR

Sugar adds moisture, softness, sweetness, and flavor. It also improves crust color through carmelization. For most lean bread and roll dough formulas, the sugar content should be kept below 10 percent of the flour. Brown sugar, honey, and maple sugar (not maple syrup) can be used in place of granulated sugar.

SHORTENING/OIL

Hydrogenated oil, which contains trans-fatty acids, is no longer recommended for bread dough. In recent years, various health concerns have raised questions about the use of this type of oil. From a report published on July 10, 2002, The Food and Nutrition Board of the Institute of Medicine of the National Academics stated the following: ". . . therefore due to the increased risk of cardiovascular heart disease, the Food and Nutrition Board recommends that trans-fatty acid consumption be as low as possible." Instead of hydrogenated oil, bakers can use vegetable oils, such as soy, corn, and cottonseed, which are all good choices for dough. Creaming properties associated with butters and shortenings are not important to bread dough, so vegetable oil works fine.

In the past, vegetable oils sometimes became rancid; better packaging and regular product rotation have eliminated that problem. Shortening and oil shorten the gluten strands, which adds tenderness to crumb moisture. Sweet dough, which will be discussed later, utilizes emulsified shortening, margarine, or butter.

The Basic Formula:
Dough Ratios

Percent Ratio	Ingredients	Lb	Oz	Metric
100	Flour (60% from hard wheat)	5		2,270 g
60–65	Liquid (water and up to 10% egg whites)	3		1,360 g
2–4	Salt		1 1/2–3	40 g–90 g
3–5	Yeast (fresh)		2 1/2–4	70 g–110 g
3–5	Water		2 1/2–4	70 g–110 g
0–10	Sugar (granulated, brown, maple, or honey)		0–8	0 g–230 g
0–10	Shortening (vegetable oil is preferred)		0–8	0 g–230 g

When bakers increase the percentage of sugar, shortening, and milk, the dough becomes richer and softer, and the baked product will have an increased shelf-life. After you have prepared several batches of this lean-dough formula, you will be able to write your own formulas by adjusting the percentages to produce signature bread and rolls.

YEAST-DOUGH FORMULAS

The following collection of formulas represents a variety of lean and rich doughs. Read through each formula and compare the ingredients, ratios, and mixing methods with the other formulas listed.

NOTE: All formulas in this book are designed to use fresh yeast. (Refer to Unit 3 for a yeast conversion chart if you are using any other type of yeast.)

Refer to the mixing methods, if needed, in Unit 8.

LEARNING ACTIVITY 9-1

Mix one formula of 100 percent whole-wheat bread (page 169) and one formula of wheaten bread, 50 percent whole wheat (page 169). After the bread is baked, evaluate the two loaves and note the effect of the increased bran found in the 100 percent whole-wheat bread. Look at the volume, crumb, crust, and flavor. Record your findings in the following chart.

Evaluating the Effect of Bran

Factors	100% Whole-Wheat Bread	Wheaten Bread (50% whole wheat)
Volume		
Crumb		
Crust		
Flavor		

Throughout this text you will find benchmark formulas. These formulas teach fundamental techniques. The following dinner roll formula will teach you how to mix and scale a variety of rolls. Typical dinner rolls weigh between 1 1/2 oz and 2 1/2 oz (40 g to 70 g). To determine the yields, the rolls in the following list weigh 2 oz (60 g).

dinner rolls *Yield: 9 lb 13 1/2 oz (4,465 g)*

% Ratio	Ingredients	Lb	Oz	Metric	Procedures
100	Bread flour	5		2,270 g	Use 75 percent of the water to dissolve the sugar, salt, and milk powder.
60	Water	3		1,360 g	
10	Eggs		8	220 g	
3	Yeast		2 1/2	70 g	
2 1/2	Salt		2	60 g	Place the flour on top and let hydrate for 30 minutes.
10	Sugar		8	220 g	
5	Milk powder		4	110 g	
6	Shortening		5	140 g	

Dissolve the yeast in the remaining water and add to the flour mixture.

Mix until flour is thoroughly incorporated and add shortening. Adjust dough consistency to create soft, elastic dough that does not stick to the dough hook when mixed. Flour absorption is variable and is affected by the temperature of the liquid.

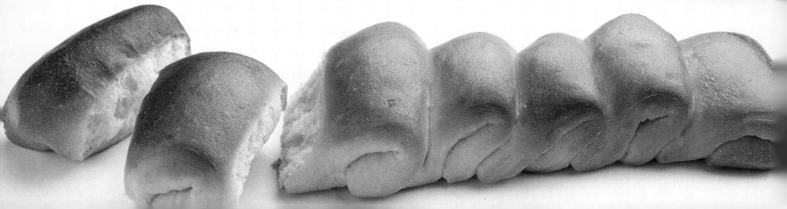

shaping rolls

This dinner roll formula can be used for a variety of rolls. Following are directions on how to form Parker House, clover leaf, and knotted rolls. These rolls can be made with a variety of dough formulas.

Use straight-dough mixing method: Scale 3 lb (1,360 g). Press and shape into 1 oz Parker House, Clover Leaf, or Single Knot. Proof. Bake at 400°F (200°C) until golden brown.

Parker House Rolls

Parker House rolls are made by first scaling the dough and dividing the dough into units. Take one unit and roll into a ball, then flatten so that it is approximately 1/4 in. thick. Make an off-center crease and fold it in half so that the top overlaps slightly, forming two lips. Press the folded edge. Pan close together.

Clover Leaf Rolls

After scaling and dividing the dough into units, take one unit and divide it into thirds. Create three, equal-sized 1-in. balls. Pull the edges under and smooth the top. Place the three balls into a greased muffin tin, with the smooth side of each ball facing up. Clover leaf rolls are often topped with a coarse salt before baking.

Single Knot

Single knot rolls are made by taking a 6-in. dough string and knotting it in the middle. Pull on the ends, and flatten each end to ensure a good finished shape.

Double Knot

Create a pencil-sized string of dough, approximately 8 in. long. Form a loop with one end extending beyond the other. Take that outside end and create a knot by putting it through the center hole from the left-hand side. Twist the oval-shaped knot in the opposite direction and repeat the process, making a knot from the right-hand side. After you make the knot, there should be one opening; put the final end in that bottom loop. Fold the roll if you desire.

NUTRITIONAL INFORMATION PER 2 OZ (60 G) SERVING: 161 Calories; 5 g Fat (26.0% calories from fat); 4 g Protein; 25 g Carbohydrate; trace Dietary Fiber; 2 mg Cholesterol; 284 mg Sodium. Exchanges: 1 1/2 Grain (Starch); 0 Lean Meat; 0 Non-Fat Milk; 1 Fat; 0 Other Carbohydrates.

Mediterranean lean dough
Yield: 8 lb 4 1/2 oz (3,760 g)

% Ratio	Ingredients	Lb	Oz	Metric	Procedures
50	Bread flour	2	8	1,130 g	Use straight-dough mixing method: Breads—12 to 14 oz (340 g to 400 g); rolls—1 1/2 to 2 oz (40 g to 60 g); subs—6 oz (170 g). Proof. Bake at 425°F (220°C).
50	High-gluten flour	2	8	1,130 g	
60	Water	3		1,360 g	
2 1/2	Salt		2	60 g	
3	Yeast		2 1/2	70 g	

SHAPING THE BREAD
Mediterranean lean dough can be scaled into 12 to 14 oz (340 g to 400 g) round loaves. Rolls are made the same way with smaller units of dough. For sub rolls, scale 6 oz (170 g) units and taper the ends so that each one looks like a small football.

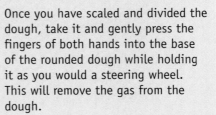

Once you have scaled and divided the dough, take it and gently press the fingers of both hands into the base of the rounded dough while holding it as you would a steering wheel. This will remove the gas from the dough.

Now shape the dough into a round loaf using the palms of your hands, gently rolling the dough back and forth.

Pinch together the base of rounded white dough while shaping a round loaf. Turn the loaf over and bake with seam on the bottom.

NOTE: You can apply bread glazes to give the crust a shine. See the Bread Glaze section in Unit 16 for further instructions on bread glazes.
NUTRITIONAL INFORMATION PER 2 OZ (60 G) SERVING:
128 Calories; 1 g Fat (3.6% calories from fat); 4 g Protein; 26 g Carbohydrate; 1 g Dietary Fiber; 0 mg Cholesterol; 334 mg Sodium. Exchanges: 1 1/2 Grain (Starch); 0 Lean Meat.

hard roll dough (Kaiser rolls)* *Yield: 8 lbs 4 1/2 oz (3,760 g)*

% Ratio	Ingredients	Lb	Oz	Metric	Procedures
100	Bread flour	5		2,270 g	Use straight-dough mixing method: Kaiser and Vienna rolls 4 1/2 lb (2,040 g)—press. Proof. Bake at 425°F (220°C).
58	Water	2	14 1/2	1,320 g	
2	Yeast		1 1/2	40 g	Kaiser rolls were originally created in honor of a former German Kaiser whose crown had five points. These rolls also have five points. You can make Kaiser rolls by using a folding method or by handstamping them with a Kaiser roll stamp. A braided method that gives you five points and a button is also presented here. Depending on the bakery that prodcues them, Kaiser rolls weigh between 2 oz and 4 oz (60 g to 120 g).
1	Sugar		1	30 g	
2	Salt		1 1/2	40 g	
1	Shortening		1	30 g	

Shaping Kaiser Rolls by Hand
To shape and fold Kaiser rolls by hand, scale and divide the dough into equal units. Roll into individual balls by using a rolling pin or your hands. Flatten the ball like a pancake. Place your thumb in the middle of the dough and fold the dough in half over your thumb. Make the first crown by sealing it with the opposite hand in a chopping motion. Repeat that step four more times, each time adding a fold. Remove your thumb with the final fold and stick the remaining fold into the center of the dough to replace your thumb. This seals the roll.

Using a Stamp
Take a small ball and press down on the ball with a Kaiser roll stamp (center the stamp in the middle of the circle). Dip the stamp into oil every three or four rolls. The oil will keep the folds separated during baking.

Braided Kaiser Rolls
Take a 10-in piece of dough and roll it into a dough string. Form a loop; weave the end in and out of the loop five times to create the five crowns. Push the end piece of the dough up through the center to create a button.

NUTRITIONAL INFORMATION PER 2 OZ (60 G) SERVING: 132 Calories; 1 g Fat (7.2% calories from fat); 4 g Protein; 26 g Carbohydrate; trace Dietary Fiber; 0 mg Cholesterol; 251 mg Sodium. Exchanges: 1 1/2 Grain (Starch); 0 Lean Meat; 0 Fat; 0 Other Carbohydrates.
* This dough can be used for thin-crust pizza.

braided egg bread *Yield: 9 lb 12 1/2 oz (4,440 g)*

% Ratio	Ingredients	Lb	Oz	Metric	Procedures
100	Bread flour	5		2,270 g	Use straight-dough mixing method: Braided bread and twists—12 oz-1 lb (340 g to 450 g). Proof. Bake at 375°F (190°C).
60	Water	3		1,360 g	
3	Yeast		2 1/2	70 g	**BRAIDING BREAD**
2.5	Salt		2	60 g	The preceding formula can be braided a variety of ways. The most common braid style is the three-strand braid, which is made by dividing the dough (12 oz to 1 lb or 340 g to 450 g) into three equal balls. Follow these steps:
7	Sugar		6	170 g	
7	Vegetable oil		6	170 g	
7	Egg yolks		6	170 g	
7	Eggs		6	170 g	

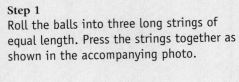

Step 1
Roll the balls into three long strings of equal length. Press the strings together as shown in the accompanying photo.

Step 2
Lift the left string and cross over the center string. Then lift the right string and cross over the new center string. Continue until all the strings are braided.

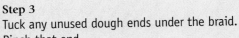
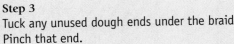

Step 3
Tuck any unused dough ends under the braid. Pinch that end.

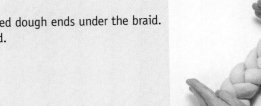

NUTRITIONAL INFORMATION PER 2 OZ (60 G) SERVING: 146 Calories; 4 g Fat (22.2% calories from fat); 4 g Protein; 24 g Carbohydrate; trace Dietary Fiber; 36 mg Cholesterol; 287 mg Sodium. Exchanges: 1 1/2 Grain (Starch); 0 Lean Meat; 1/2 Fat; 0 Other Carbohydrates.

Four-Strand Braided Bread

white pan bread *Yield: 9 lb 1 oz (4,110 g)*

% Ratio	Ingredients	Lb	Oz	Metric	Procedures
100	Bread flour	5		2,270 g	Use straight-dough mixing method: Scale into 1 lb 2 oz per loaf (510 g). Shape and pan. Serving size after slicing is 2 oz. Proof. Bake at 430°F (220°C).
64	Water	3	4	1,470 g	
2 1/2	Yeast		2	60 g	
2 1/2	Salt		2	60 g	
5	Sugar		4	110 g	
3	Milk powder		2 1/2	70 g	
3	Shortening		2 1/2	70 g	

SHAPING AND PANNING BREAD
After you have divided and weighed the dough into units, it's time to shape it into loaves in preparation for pan baking. Follow these steps:

Step 1
Take the scale dough unit and flatten it into a rectangle. Keeping it in a round shape, take one end of the dough and fold it into the center of the circle.

Step 2
Use the thumbs of both hands to create an indentation in the center of the dough, folding one half over the other. Remove the gas within the dough with uniform pressure as you roll the dough into a tight roll or tube.

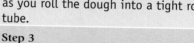

Step 3
Seal the seam of the rolled dough by gently pressing down on the final edge of dough.

Step 4
To pan the dough, take the dough roll and with the seam side up, fold over the ends so that the dough is the length of the bread pan.

Step 5
Place the dough into a bread pan, making sure the folded ends are tucked underneath.

NUTRITIONAL INFORMATION PER 2 OZ (60 G) SERVING: 136 Calories; 2 g Fat (12.1% calories from fat); 4 g Protein; 25 g Carbohydrate; trace Dietary Fiber; 1 mg Cholesterol; 311 mg Sodium. Exchanges: 1 1/2 Grain (Starch); 0 Lean Meat; 0 Nonfat Milk; 1/2 Fat; 0 Other Carbohydrates.

milk hearth bread *Yield: 9 lb 2 1/2 oz (4,160 g)*

% Ratio	Ingredients	Lb	Oz	Metric	Procedures
100	Bread flour	5		2,270 g	Use straight-dough mixing method: Scale into 14 oz units. Mold in oblong shape with square ends. Top with Holland Dutch Topping brushed on top (see recipe below). Proof. Bake on hearth. Bake at 390°F (200°C).
60	Water	3		1,360 g	
2 1/2	Salt		2	60 g	
2 1/2	Yeast		2	60 g	
5	Powdered milk		4	110 g	
3	Butter		2 1/2	70 g	
5	Sweetened condensed milk		4	110 g	
5	Egg whites		4	110 g	

NUTRITIONAL INFORMATION PER 2 OZ (60 G) SERVING (WITHOUT HOLLAND DUTCH TOPPING): 145 Calories; 2 g Fat (12.8% calories from fat); 5 g Protein; 26 g Carbohydrate; trace Dietary Fiber; 4 mg Cholesterol; 345 mg Sodium. Exchanges: 1 1/2 Grain (Starch); 0 Lean Meat; 0 Nonfat Milk; 1/2 Fat; 0 Other Carbohydrates.

Holland Dutch topping for milk hearth bread *Yield: 1 lb 12 1/2 oz (810 g)*

Ingredients	Lb	Oz	Metric	Procedures
Rice flour		10	80 g	Mix all ingredients except melted butter. Add butter last.
Sugar		1 1/2	40 g	
Salt		1/2	10 g	
Melted butter		3	90 g	
Yeast		1 1/2	40 g	
Water		12	340 g	

NUTRITIONAL INFORMATION PER SERVING (2 OZ (60 G) MILK HEARTH BREAD WITH HOLLAND DUTCH TOPPING): 173 Calories; 3 g Fat (16.4% calories from fat); 6 g Protein; 30 g Carbohydrate; 1 g Dietary Fiber; 7 mg Cholesterol; 436 mg Sodium. Exchanges: 2 Grain (Starch); 0 Lean Meat; 0 Nonfat Milk; 1/2 Fat; 0 Other Carbohydrates.

covered wagon bread *Yield: 8 lb 14 oz (4,030 g)*

% Ratio	Ingredients	Lb	Oz	Metric	Procedures
100	Bread flour	5		2,270 g	Use straight-dough mixing method: Boil potatoes in water. Drain. Save cool water for dough. Mash potatoes; add with shortening. Pan bread 1 lb 4 oz. Dust with snowflake topping (page 168) after proofing. Bake at 390°F (200°C).
60	Water	3		1,360 g	
2 1/2	Salt		2	60 g	
2 1/2	Sugar		2	60 g	
2 1/2	Shortening		2	60 g	
10	Peeled potatoes		8	230 g	

NUTRITIONAL INFORMATION PER 2 OZ (60 G) SERVING: 128 Calories; 1 g Fat (9.5% calories from fat); 4 g Protein; 25 g Carbohydrate; trace Dietary Fiber; 0 mg Cholesterol; 311 mg Sodium. Exchanges: 1 1/2 Grain (Starch); 0 Fat; 0 Other Carbohydrates.

snowflake rolls *Yield: 10 lbs 15 oz (4,960 g)*

% Ratio	Ingredients	Lb	Oz	Metric	Procedures
100	Bread flour	5		2,270 g	Use straight-dough mixing method: Boil potatoes in water. Drain. Save and cool for dough. Mash potatoes; add with shortening. Rolls scale 3 lbs 12 oz (1,700 g). Press. Dust with snowflake topping (See formula for topping on next page.) Proof. Bake at 375°F (190°C).
54	Water	3	10	1,640 g	
3	Yeast		2 1/2	70 g	
3	Salt		2 1/2	70 g	
10	Sugar		8	230 g	
5	Milk powder		4	110 g	
10	Shortening		8	230 g	
15	Peeled potatoes*		12	340 g	

NUTRITIONAL INFORMATION PER 2 OZ (60 G) SERVING (WITHOUT SNOWFLAKE TOPPING): 139 Calories; 3 g Fat (22.3% calories from fat); 4 g Protein; 23 g Carbohydrate; trace Dietary Fiber; 1 mg Cholesterol; 322 mg Sodium. Exchanges: 1 1/2 Grain (Starch); 0 Lean Meat; 0 Nonfat Milk; 1/2 Fat; 0 Other Carbohydrates.

*NOTE: To prevent potatoes from turning dark before or during cooking, peel and cut only what is required at the time, soaking cut pieces in water if necessary so oxidation does not occur before cooking, and cook in a stainless steel pot. Cooking potatoes in either tin-lined or aluminum pots can cause the color of the cooked potatoes to grey and become unappealing.

snowflake topping *Yield: 3 lb 4 oz (1,470 g)*

Ingredients	Lb	Oz	Metric
Bread flour	1		450 g
Rye flour	1		450 g
Potato flour	1		450 g
Salt		4	110 g

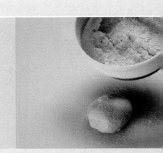

NUTRITIONAL INFORMATION PER SERVING (2 OZ SERVING OF SNOW FLAKE ROLLS WITH SNOW FLAKE TOPPING): 195 Calories; 4 g Fat (16.9% calories from fat); 5 g Protein; 35 g Carbohydrate; 1 g Dietary Fiber; 1 mg Cholesterol; 830 mg Sodium. Exchanges: 2 Grain (Starch); 0 Lean Meat; 0 Nonfat Milk; 1/2 Fat; 0 Other Carbohydrates.

oat-n-honey bread *Yield: 11 lb 13 1/2 oz (5,370 g)*

% Ratio	Ingredients	Lb	Oz	Metric	Procedures
100	High-gluten flour	5		2,270 g	Use straight-dough mixing method: Add oat-n-honey mixture at the end with shortening. Scale into 1 lb 4 oz units and shape into a loaf. Bake in bread pan. Proof. Bake at 400°F (200°C).
64	Water	3	4	1,470 g	
3	Yeast		2 1/2	70 g	
3	Salt		2 1/2	70 g	
3	Sugar		2 1/2	70 g	
4	Milk powder		3	90 g	
4	Shortening		3	90 g	

OAT-N-HONEY MIXTURE

	Ingredients	Lb	Oz	Metric	
	Rolled oats	1	4	570 g	Soak ingredients for 2 hours; use cool water. Then add to the above formula with the shortening.
	Water	1		450 g	
	Honey		8	230 g	

NUTRITIONAL INFORMATION PER 2 OZ (60 G) SERVING: 178 Calories; 2 g Fat (11.9% calories from fat); 5 g Protein; 34 g Carbohydrate; 2 g Dietary Fiber; 1 mg Cholesterol; 388 mg Sodium. Exchanges: 2 Grain (Starch); 0 Lean Meat; 0 Nonfat Milk; 1/2 Fat; 0 Other Carbohydrates.

100% whole-wheat bread   *Yield: 9 lb 7 oz (4,250 g)*

% Ratio	Ingredients	Lb	Oz	Metric	Procedures
100	Whole-wheat flour	5		2,270 g	Use straight-dough mixing method: Make up same as White Pan bread. Proof. Bake at 420°F (220°C).
68	Water	3	7	1,560 g	
3	Yeast		2 1/2	70 g	
3	Salt		2 1/2	70 g	
3	Shortening		2 1/2	70 g	
6	Sugar		5	140 g	
3	Milk powder		2 1/2	70 g	

NUTRITIONAL INFORMATION PER 2 OZ (60 G) SERVING: 126 Calories; 2 g Fat (12.2% calories from fat); 5 g Protein; 25 g Carbohydrate; 4 g Dietary Fiber; 1 mg Cholesterol; 372 mg Sodium. Exchanges: 1 1/2 Grain (Starch); 0 Lean Meat; 0 Nonfat Milk; 1/2 Fat; 0 Other Carbohydrates.

wheaten bread 50% whole wheat   *Yield: 9 lb 6 oz (4,250 g)*

% Ratio	Ingredients	Lb	Oz	Metric	Procedures
50	Whole-wheat flour	2	8	1,130 g	Use straight-dough mixing method: Make up same as White Pan bread. Proof. Bake at 425°F (220°C).
50	High-gluten flour	2	8	1,130 g	
67	Water	3	6	1,530 g	
3	Yeast		2 1/2	70 g	
3	Salt		2 1/2	70 g	
3	Shortening		2 1/2	70 g	
6	Sugar		5	140 g	
3	Milk powder		2 1/2	70 g	

NUTRITIONAL INFORMATION PER 2 OZ (60 G) SERVING: 129 Calories; 2g Fat (11.3% calories from fat); 4 g Protein; 25 g Carbohydrate; 3 g Dietary Fiber; 1 mg Cholesterol; 372 mg Sodium. Exchanges: 1 1/2 Grain (Starch); 0 Lean Meat; 0 Nonfat Milk; 1/2 Fat; 0 Other Carbohydrates.

Rye Flour Yeast Dough

Bread made from crushed or ground whole rye kernels, without any wheat flour, such as **pumpernickel,** is dark, tough, and coarse-textured. Many people prefer a lighter textured and colored rye, which is made from mixture of rye flour (with bran removed) and wheat flour. Caramel coloring is often added to make a darker rye bread. Most rye bread is flavored with caraway seeds.

soft rye rolls   *Yield: 9 lb 11 oz (4,390 g)*

% Ratio	Ingredients	Lb	Oz	Metric	Procedures
25	Rye flour	1	4	570 g	Use straight-dough mixing method: Scale 3 lb. Press. Round into rolls. 1 press = 36 rolls. Proof. Bake at 390°F (200°C).
75	Clear flour	3	12	1,700 g	
56	Water	2	13	1,280 g	
4	Yeast		3	90 g	
2 1/2	Salt		2	60 g	
12	Sugar		10	280 g	
12	Shortening		10	280 g	
5	Milk powder		4	110 g	
1	Malt		1	30 g	
1/4	Ground caraway		1/4	10 g	

NOTE: To get the flavor of the caraway seeds without adding the seeds to the dough, boil a cup of water with seeds; strain the liquid and use as part of the water.

NUTRITIONAL INFORMATION PER 2 OZ (60 G) SERVING: 173 Calories; 5 g Fat (24.5% calories from fat); 4 g Protein; 29 g Carbohydrate; 1 g Dietary Fiber; 2 mg Cholesterol; 309 mg Sodium. Exchanges: 1 1/2 Grain (Starch); 0 Lean Meat; 0 Vegetable; 0 Nonfat Milk; 1 Fat; 1/2 Other Carbohydrates.

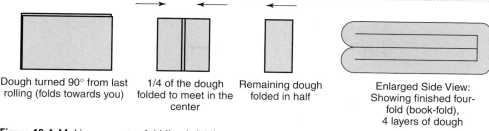

| Dough turned 90° from last rolling (folds towards you) | 1/4 of the dough folded to meet in the center | Remaining dough folded in half | Enlarged Side View: Showing finished four-fold (book-fold), 4 layers of dough |

Figure 10-4 Making a quarter-fold (book-fold).

Dusting Flour

To keep the dough from sticking to the baker's bench where the folding takes place, spread a light sprinkling of bread flour over the bench (Figure 10-5). Excessive use of this dusting flour will create an imbalance of the formula. Use just enough flour to avoid sticking and brush off the remainder. Proper dusting will result in the successful formation of the laminated dough.

Thickness

Dough must be rolled to a uniform thickness throughout the entire sheet. Bakers take a great deal of care in weighing their ingredients so that their formulas are not out of balance; they should use just as much caution in watching uniformity when rolling laminated dough.

LEARNING ACTIVITY 10-1

Mix two formulas of croissant dough (page 190). Roll in butter in one formula and roll in baker's margarine in the second formula. Evaluate the results in handling and shaping the dough. Which roll-in was easier? After baking, evaluate the volume, texture, and flavor.

Evaluation Criteria	Dough Made with Butter	Dough Made with Baker's Margarine
Volume		
Texture		
Flavor		

Figure 10-5 A student should practice grabbing just the right amount of flour to cover the bench with one spray.

Croissant dough is leaner than Danish dough; it contains no eggs and a smaller percentage of sugar. Croissant dough uses water as the liquid while Danish uses milk—it is the milk that makes Danish dough richer and sweeter. The make-up procedure for croissant dough is the same as it is for Danish dough. The buttery croissant may be served plain, filled, or coated with various toppings. Fruit, cream, chocolate, and nuts make excellent fillings and/or toppings to apply to croissants, creating an endless amount of varieties. The croissant also does well with savory fillings, such as ham, cheese, and other variations of sandwich fillings.

croissant dough formula   *Yield: 6 lb 15 oz (3,150 g)*

% Ratio	Ingredients	Lb	Oz	Metric	Procedures
57	Milk	1	8	680 g	Use straight-dough method for mixing. **PROCEDURE FOR LAMINATING CROISSANT DOUGH:** 1. Place dough on floured, parchment-lined pan; refrigerate for 30 minutes.
7	Yeast		3	90 g	
2	Salt		1	30 g	
7	Sugar		3	90 g	
9	Butter (soft)		4	110 g	
100	Bread flour	2	10	1,190 g	

ROLL-IN

% Ratio	Ingredients	Lb	Oz	Metric	Procedures
72	Butter	2		900 g	2. Knead roll-in butter, baker's margarine, or a combination of the two until pliable; spread on parchment paper 1/2" in. (1 cm) thick.
4	Bread flour		2	60 g	

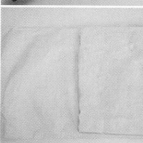

3. Lock-in the butter by rolling the dough into a rectangle that is 1/3 larger than the roll-in fat layer. Place the fat on 2/3 of the dough surface. Make a tri-fold and roll the dough and fat together into one single dough representing five alternating layers of fat and dough.

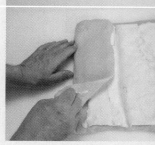

4. Rest the dough for 30 minutes between the rolling and folding procedures and refrigerate; do not allow dough to become warm during this process, or too cold, which may cause the butter to crack.

Procedures

5. After the folding process is complete, rest the dough 12 to 24 hours before makeup.

6. Roll out the dough and trim the edges to create an even rectangle. Using a pastry wheel or specially-designed croissant cutter, divide the dough into even triangles. The trimmings should be saved and reworked.

7. Cut a 1/2-in. (1.2 cm) notch in the center of the short end or the triangle base.

8. Place any filling just above the notch and roll up the dough, beginning with the filled end. Roll up to the pointed end of the dough. Place it so that pointed end is under the croissant for baking.

Croissants should be proofed until they double in size. Proof croissants at temperatures no higher than 85°F (30°C) to prevent the butter from melting. Bake at 375°F (190°C) until golden brown. **Note:** Temperatures may need to be adjusted for different types of ovens.

NUTRITIONAL INFORMATION PER 2 OZ (60 G) SERVING: 233 Calories; 16 g Fat (60.9% calories from fat); 4 g Protein; 19 g Carbohydrate; 1 g Dietary Fiber; 42 mg Cholesterol; 360 mg Sodium. Exchanges: 1 Grain (Starch); 0 Lean Meat; 0 Nonfat Milk; 3 Fat; 0 Other Carbohydrates.

Figure 10-6 Products made with Danish dough.

DANISH DOUGH

Danish dough contains yeast which aids in the leavening process. The dough's taste, flakiness, tenderness and volume are influenced by the lamination. Baked Danish products (often referred to as simply "Danish") contain a variety of fillings including fruit, cream cheese, almond paste, nuts, and raisins. Danish dough can be configured in a number of shapes as seen in the varieties (Figure 10-6) listed on pages 194–196. The Danish which is a very rich dough, has a higher percentage of yeast as compared to the croissant dough. Compare the two formulas and note any other differences.

Danish dough formula   *Yield: 7 lb 4 oz (3,290 g)*

% Ratio	Ingredients	Lb	Oz	Metric	Procedures
44	Milk (cold)	1		450 g	Place milk, egg yolks, and yeast in bowl.
11	Yeast		4	110 g	
22	Egg yolks		8	230 g	
14	Sugar		5	140 g	Stir and add balance of ingredients, except roll-in. Mix at first speed until flour is incorporated and at the second speed for 6 to 7 minutes.
2	Salt		1/2	10 g	
4	Butter (soft)		4	110 g	The laminating procedure for Danish is the same as that for croissant dough.
35	Pastry flour		12	340 g	

% Ratio	Ingredients	Lb	Oz	Metric	Procedures
65	Bread flour	1	8	680 g	
	Cardamon		1/8	5 g	

ROLL-IN

% Ratio	Ingredients	Lb	Oz	Metric	Procedures
76	Butter, baker's margarine, or combination	1	8	680 g	**PROCEDURE FOR LAMINATING THE DANISH DOUGH**

PROCEDURE FOR LAMINATING THE DANISH DOUGH

1. Place dough on floured parchment-lined pan; refrigerate for 30 minutes.
2. Knead roll-in butter, baker's margarine, or a combination of the two with flour until pliable; spread on parchment paper 1/2" (1 cm) thick.

3. Lock-in the butter by rolling dough into a rectangle that is 1/3 larger than roll-in fat layer. Spread the butter over two-thirds of the prepared dough.

4. Fold the dough in thirds. Rest the dough for 30 minutes between the rolling and folding procedure and refrigerate; do not allow dough to become warm during this process, or too cold.

5. Roll dough to three times its original size.

6. Fold the dough into thirds and rest it for 30 minutes before make up.

7. Danish dough can be rolled, filled, and cut to create a variety of shapes. (See some examples on the next page.)

NUTRITIONAL INFORMATION PER 2 OZ (60 G) SERVING: (prior to filling): 112 Calories; 3 g Fat (27.3% calories from fat); 4 g Protein; 17 g Carbohydrate; 1 g Dietary Fiber; 55 mg Cholesterol; 118 mg Sodium. Exchanges: 1 Grain (Starch); 0 Lean Meat; 0 Nonfat Milk; 1/2 Fat; 0 Other Carbohydrates.

NOTE: Total flour consists of 65 percent bread flour and 35 percent pastry flour, equaling 100 percent. Total liquid is 44 percent milk and 22 percent egg yolks, equaling 66 percent. The Danish, which is a very rich dough, has a higher percentage of yeast as compared to the croissant dough. Compare the two formulas and note any other differences.

Varieties

Variations of Danish pastries include double snail, elephant ears, basket, bowtie, schneken, almond horn, diamond-shaped pocket, closed pocket, bear claw, butterfly, nut twist, and snail (Figure 10-7).

STRING VARIETIES

By starting with a string of dough, you can shape Danish dough into a variety of shapes including single knots, snails, figure eights, and eye-glasses. Always start by rolling out an 8-in. by 6-in. rectangle that is 1/4 in. thick. Fill it with almond filling (formula is given later in this unit) or cinnamon sugar, fold in half, and roll out again to the original size (Figure 10-8). Cut the dough in 1-in. strips without cutting all the way through. Twist the

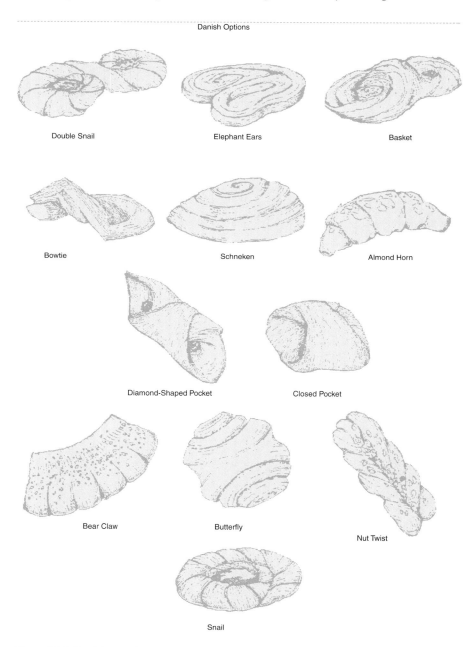

Danish Options

Double Snail   Elephant Ears   Basket

Bowtie   Schneken   Almond Horn

Diamond-Shaped Pocket   Closed Pocket

Bear Claw   Butterfly   Nut Twist

Snail

Figure 10-7 Danish pastries.

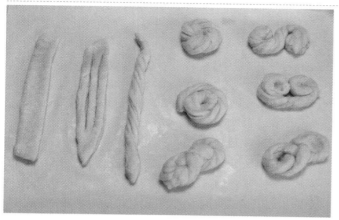

Figure 10-8 String varieties.

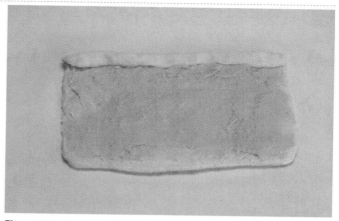

Figure 10-9 A piece of Danish dough is rolled out and filled prior to being rolled into a long tube.

dough into a string. Once the product has been proofed, garnish with fruit or cheese filling. Add glaze or icing after it has been baked.

ROLLED VARIETIES

Rolled up Danish can be used to make cinnamon rolls, palm leafs, elephant ears, and a host of other popular baked goods (Figure 10-9).

Roll out an 8-in. by 6-in. rectangle that is 1/4 in. thick. Spread a thin layer of almond filling (formula is given later in this unit) or cinnamon sugar on the top of the dough. Roll up the dough like a jelly roll. Seal the edge and turn it so that the edge is on the bottom.

The rolled-up Danish can be used to create a variety of shapes (Figure 10-10).

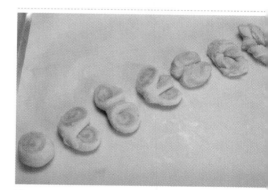

POCKET VARIETIES

Roll out dough to create 4-in. squares. Drop a round dollop of filling (1 oz or 30 g.). This photo shows the various placements of the dollop depending on the type of pocket you are creating (Figure 10-11).

Shape as desired. Notice the different shape options (full pocket, half pocket, log, or turnover) (Figure 10-12).

Figure 10-10 Finished Danish, rolled up.

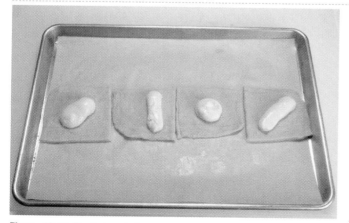

Figure 10-11 Pocket varieties.

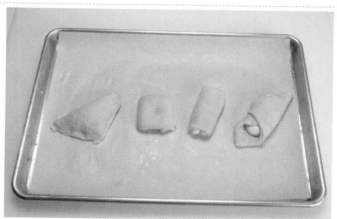

Figure 10-12 Pockets folded.

22. Which is *not* an advantage of baker's margarine in laminated dough?
    a. less expensive than butter
    b. better flavor
    c. easier to work with
    d. higher melting point

23. Danish and croissant doughs are generally given three tri-folds after the addition of fat; this equals how many layers?
    a. 75
    b. 135
    c. 180
    d. 225

24. At what temperature should cream puff dough be baked?
    a. 325°F
    b. 350°F
    c. 375°F
    d. 400°F

the stove-top
and oven

The stove top is the site for cooking many types of creams, custards, and fruit fillings for pies, cakes, and tarts. Unit 11 includes additional formulas that require baking. Unit 12 covers the important elements of mixing, rolling, and baking pie crust and short dough.

creams
and custards

"The proof of the pudding is in the eating."

Miguel de Cervantes, Spanish author (1547–1616),
Don Quixote de la Mancha

KEY TERMS and CONCEPTS

balloon whip

bloom

chinois

fluid milk

homogenized milk

liaison

nappe

pasteurized milk

standardization

stiff peaks

tempering

LEARNING Objectives

After you have finished reading this unit, you should be able to:

- **Define** important sanitation and handling procedures related to creams and custards

- **Evaluate** fluid milk products

- **Describe** the cooking principles for creams and custards

- **List** the steps for cooking pudding and custards

WHILE DOUGH IS GENERALLY ASSOCIATED WITH BREAD

baking and batters are used primarily for cakes, creams, custards, puddings, and pie fillings form a third category of mixtures. This book refers to this third category as "stove-top" cookery. Also included in this category are cake frosting, meringue, icing, and fudge, which will be covered in Unit 16.

FOOD SAFETY PRECAUTIONS

Creams custards, milk custards, and cream fillings must always be made and handled carefully (Figure 11-1). In many instances, food-borne illnesses have been traced back to various bakery cream products. These unfortunate situations are not only detrimental to the public, but also to the individual baker involved as well as the entire baking industry. Check your state and local food and health laws and protect yourself by following such laws. If the laws are difficult to follow, it is definitely to your advantage to discontinue the sale of cream products during extremely hot weather. You may want to refer back to Unit 2 for a review of sanitation and safe food handling procedures. Follow these rules when you prepare cream products:

1. It is important that all employees handling creams are clean, tidy, and careful about their personal hygiene.
2. Use only stainless steel containers that have been thoroughly cleaned and sanitized for preparation and cooking.
3. Use sterile shallow pans and refrigerate immediately to quick-cool.
4. Discard any leftover cream custard and day-old or leftover finished products that contain pastry cream.

5. Day-old creams may still have a pleasant, sweet, palatable taste, but this does not mean that they are safe to eat—various harmful bacteria do not always impart an unpleasant or distinguishable taste to the cream.

6. Do not use your hands for stirring. Hands must never come in contact with cream custard.

Unlike dough and batter, which must be baked to produce a finished product, the majority of creams are not baked at all. Due to their large proportion of liquefiers and low flour content, creams do not contain gluten in significant amounts. Thus, the high, dry oven heat, which helps gluten produce a rigid structure in breads and cakes, is not required to make creams. Instead, most creams are merely warmed, simmered, or briefly boiled. This is because the main stabilizer in cream mixture is not flour, but eggs, which need lower temperature to perform their function of binding a recipe's liquefiers. Indeed, when creams are prepared by baking (like caramel custard), they rest in a water bath to moderate the effect of the oven's high temperatures and prevent the egg proteins in the mixture from cooling too quickly, lumping together, and separating from the milk or cream, creating a scrambled or curdling effect. Water baths are made by placing the pan or ramekins of custard mixture into a shallow steam table pan filled 1/3 of the way with water.

DAIRY PRODUCTS

A variety of dairy products are used to create creams and custards (Figure 11-2).

Whole Milk

Fluid milk is the whole-milk product normally served as a beverage and utilized in the preparation of certain foods. Although legal standards vary, most states require that whole milk must contain at least 3.25 percent butterfat. In the labeling and identification of fluid milk, the terms *pasteurized, homogenized, standardized,* and *vitamin D* milk are used.

CHEF'S TIP: *Lightly sprinkle granulated sugar on top of the cooked pudding to prevent a skin from forming or cover with plastic wrap.*

BAVARIAN CREAM

Bavarian cream is a cool, smooth, creamy, and delicate dessert. This cooked custard contains unflavored, dissolved gelatin. Whipped cream is folded in the cooled custard, which is then poured into a mold prior to chilling and serving. Bavarian cream is also used as a cake filling.

Bavarian cream *Yield: 5 lb 10 1/2 oz (2,550 g)*

Ingredients	Lb	Oz	Metric	Procedures
Milk	1		450 g	Heat the milk and cream with the sugar.
Heavy cream	1		450 g	
Sugar		4	110 g	
Egg yolks		9	260 g	Combine the egg yolks with the balance of the sugar; temper with hot milk mixture. Cook slowly to 180°F (82°C). Do not boil.
Sugar		4	110 g	
Vanilla		1/2	10 g	Add to the above mixture.
Gelatin sheets		1	30 g	Bloom the gelatin in cold water and add it to the above mixture. (See instructions for blooming on page 228.)
Cold water		8	230 g	
Heavy cream	2		900 g	Cool the mixture to 80°F (27°C). Whip the heavy cream and fold into the cooled mixture.

NUTRITIONAL INFORMATION PER 4 OZ (110 G) SERVING: 310 Calories; 27 g Fat (77.8% calories from fat); 4 g Protein; 14 g Carbohydrate; 0 g Dietary Fiber; 236 mg Cholesterol; 39 mg Sodium. Exchanges: 0 Lean Meat; 1/2 Nonfat Milk; 5 Fat; 1/2 Other Carbohydrates.

Gelatin

One of the key ingredients in Bavarian cream is gelatin. There are two kinds of gelatin commonly used in baking: powder gelatin and sheet, or leaf, gelatin. Powder gelatin has a slight smell and aftertaste that does not exist in sheet or leaf gelatin. It comes in 100, 200, or 300 **blooms,** which is the measurement of its strength (the higher number being stronger). Powder gelatin holds food together.

Sheet or leaf gelatin must be soaked in cold water. The excess water should be squeezed out of the regenerated gelatin leaves. Seven sheets of gelatin equal 1 oz (30 g) of powdered gelatin.

To thicken 2 qt of liquid, use 1 oz (30 g) of gelatin. To bring 1 oz (30 g) of gelatin to bloom, use 8 oz (230 g) of cold water. To bloom, sprinkle the gelatin on top of the water in a large, steel bowl. Let stand approximately 5 minutes. (If using gelatin in a cold base such as a mousse or cheese cake, bring it to 110°F (45°C), melting it over a double boiler.)

DESSERT SAUCES

Sauces are thickened liquids. They are lighter than creams and custards and are used to accent and enhance many different types of desserts by adding flavor, color, and texture. They are often used as an effective way to decorate plated desserts, contributing to the overall presentation.

Sauces vary greatly—there are fruit purees and chocolate-, caramel-, coffee- and liqueur-based sauces. When you use sauces with baked goods, it is important to carefully select a sauce that complements but doesn't overpower the product.

This rum sauce formula is a good example of a starch-thickened sauce. Fruit, wine, and other alcohol-based sauces are often thickened with starches such as cornstarch or arrowroot. No eggs or dairy products are used, so it is a shelf-stable sauce which does not require refrigeration.

rum sauce   *Yield: 1 lb 2 oz (510 g)*

Ingredients	Lb	Oz	Metric	Procedures
Sugar		2	60 g	Bring the first five ingredients to a boil.
Water		8	230 g	
Corn syrup		4	110 g	
Dark rum		2	60 g	
Vanilla		1/2	10 g	
Cornstarch		1/2	10 g	Make a slurry with the cornstarch and water and add it to the above ingredients. Bring it to a boil. Remove from heat and cool.
Water		1	30 g	

NUTRITIONAL INFORMATION PER 1 OZ (30 G) SERVING: 40 Calories; trace Fat (0.0% calories from fat); trace Protein; 9 g Carbohydrate; trace Dietary Fiber; 0 mg Cholesterol; 8 mg Sodium. Exchanges: 0 Grain Starch); 1/2 Other Carbohydrates.

This caramel sauce formula produces a thick, rich, golden sauce. Because caramel sauces thicken as they cool, they are almost always served hot or warm. The addition of corn syrup prevents the sugar from crystallizing.

The second formula on this page is orange sauce. It is made by thinning marmalade with a simple syrup made from the sugar and juice, and is an example of a preserved-based sauce. The orange juice cuts the sweetness of the marmalade.

caramel sauce *Yield: 4 lb 2 oz (1,870 g)*

Ingredients	Lb	Oz	Metric	Procedures
Heavy cream	2		900 g	Heat the cream to a boil and then turn off the flame (set aside).
Sugar	1	2	510 g	Cook the sugar and corn syrup slowly to a golden caramel color.
Corn syrup		13	370 g	
Butter		3	90 g	Stir in the butter and then carefully stir in the hot cream.

NUTRITIONAL INFORMATION PER 1 OZ (30 G) SERVING: 108 Calories; 6 g Fat (49.7% calories from fat); trace Protein; 14 g Carbohydrate; 0 g Dietary Fiber; 22 mg Cholesterol; 16 mg Sodium. Exchanges: 0 Nonfat Milk; 1 Fat; 1 Other Carbohydrates.

orange sauce *Yield: 14 1/4 oz (400 g)*

Ingredients	Lb	Oz	Metric	Procedures
Apricot marmalade		7	200 g	Combine all ingredients except the liquor. Simmer for 2 minutes; strain.
Sugar		2 3/4	80 g	
Orange zest		1	30 g	
Orange juice		3 1/2	100 g	
Grand Marnier or apricot liquor		1	30 g	Add the liquor to taste. Let it cool and then serve.

NUTRITIONAL INFORMATION PER 1 OZ (30 G) SERVING: 68 Calories; trace Fat (0.6% calories from fat); trace Protein; 17 g Carbohydrate; trace Dietary Fiber; 0 mg Cholesterol; 6 mg Sodium. Exchanges: 0 Fruit; 1 Other Carbohydrates.

This chocolate sauce can be served either hot or cold and is an example of a cream-based chocolate syrup. Commercially prepared, syrup-based chocolate sauces are also popular but they are made with a sugar syrup and contain no cream.

chocolate sauce *Yield: 1 lb 12 1/4 oz*

Ingredients	Lb	Oz	Metric	Procedures
Heavy cream	1		450 g	Heat the cream, sugar, and butter over medium heat to dissolve the sugar. Bring the cream mixture to a boil and remove from heat.
Sugar		6	170 g	
Butter		1	30 g	
Unsweetened chocolate		4	110 g	Add the chopped chocolate, stirring with a whip until smooth.
Vanilla		1/4	5 g	Add the vanilla when the above mixture is cooled to 50°F (10°C).

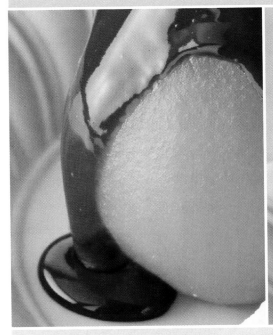
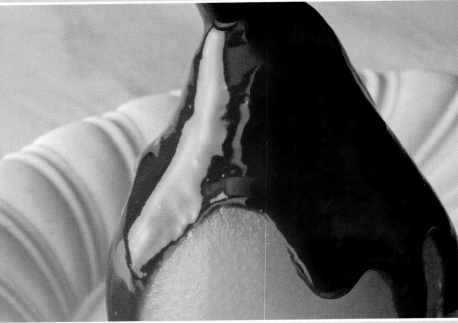

NUTRITIONAL INFORMATION PER 1 OZ (30 G) SERVING: 111 Calories; 9 g Fat (71.1% calories from fat); 1 g Protein; 8 g Carbohydrate; 1 g Dietary Fiber; 26 mg Cholesterol; 15 mg Sodium. Exchanges: 0 Grain (Starch); 0 Lean Meat; 0 Nonfat Milk; 2 Fat; 1/2 Other Carbohydrates.

NOTE: Chocolate sauce, like the other sauces presented in this section, is versatile. It can be used in numerous applications. The photo shows it poured over a cooked pear, for Pear Helene.

Lemon curd is a tart, soft, thick, cooked cream. It differs from a lemon filling or a custard because it contains more lemon juice and zest, which give it a sharper flavor. It also contains butter, which provides a smooth and creamy texture. Lemon curd is often used as a topping, similar to a sauce, for scones, cakes or tarts.

lemon curd *Yield: 8 lb 3 oz (3,720 g)*

Ingredients	Lb	Oz	Metric	Procedures
Gelatin leaves		1	30 g	Bloom the gelatin in cold water.*
Lemon juice, fresh-squeezed	2		900 g	Heat the lemon juice, lemon zest, and half the sugar.
Lemon zest, grated		4	110 g	
Sugar	3		1,360 g	
Eggs	1	8	680 g	Mix in the remaining sugar, eggs, and egg yolks and temper in the lemon juice. Continue to cook, whisking continuously until the mixture reaches 195°F (90°C). Remove from heat; add the butter and bloomed gelatin leaves. Strain into a hotel pan and cover the surface with plastic wrap to prevent a skin. Chill.
Egg yolks		6	170 g	
Butter, melted		1	30 g	

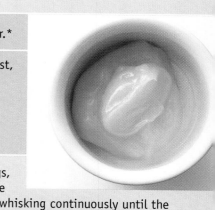

NUTRITIONAL INFORMATION PER 1 OZ (30 G) SERVING: (excluding unknown items): 54 Calories; 1 g Fat (13.6% calories from fat); 1 g Protein; 11 g Carbohydrate; trace Dietary Fiber; 35 mg Cholesterol; 6 mg Sodium. Exchanges: 0 Lean Meat; 0 Fruit; 0 Fat; 1/2 Other Carbohydrates.

*NOTE: Instructions for blooming gelatin were given on page 228 under the Gelatin section.
NOTE: Use only a stainless steel pot to prepare lemon curd, as the curd may turn gray in an aluminum pan.

vanilla soufflé *Yield: 10 soufflés*

Ingredients	Lb	Oz	Metric	Procedures
Butter		8	230 g	Mix the flour and butter.
Bread flour		8	230 g	
Milk	2		900 g	Bring the milk and vanilla to a boil; add to the flour mixture. Mix well; cool to 180°F (82°C).
Vanilla extract		1	30 g	
Egg yolks		10 each	200 g	Add the egg yolks slowly.
Egg whites		10 each	300 g	Whip the egg whites to soft peaks; add sugar gradually. Fold into the first stage and pour into buttered and sugared molds.
Sugar		10	280 g	Bake at 350°F (180°C) for 15 minutes for 6 oz size. Serve warm with the sauce of your choice.

NUTRITIONAL INFORMATION PER 6 OZ (170 G) SERVING: 486 Calories; 27 g Fat (49.5% calories from fat); 12 g Protein; 50 g Carbohydrate; trace Dietary Fiber; 275 mg Cholesterol; 294 mg Sodium. Exchanges: 1 Grain (Starch); 1/2 Lean Meat; 1/2 Nonfat Milk; 5 Fat; 2 Other Carbohydrates.

NOTE: The chef can add powdered sugar to the finished soufflé. Notice how the soufflé dish in the photo was wrapped in aluminum foil to raise the sides. This is an optional technique.

The soufflé is another custard-based dish. This French delicacy is generally lightened with whipped egg whites. The mixture is then molded and baked. During the baking process, the whipped egg whites make the dish puff. Both sweet and savory soufflés are popular today.

cheese soufflé *Yield: 10 soufflés*

Ingredients	Lb	Oz	Metric	Procedures
Butter		8	230 g	Mix the flour and butter.
Bread flour		8	230 g	
Milk	2		900 g	Bring the milk to a boil. Add the butter/flour mixture. Mix well. Cool to 180°F (80°C).
Egg yolks		12 each	240 g	Add the egg yolks slowly to above mixture.
Egg whites		12 each	360 g	Whip the egg whites and fold into the mixture.

Ingredients	Lb	Oz	Metric	Procedures
				Butter the molds.
				Fill the buttered molds half-full.
Gruyere cheese		8	230 g	Add the grated cheese to the mixture in the molds.
Salt		1/4 oz	5 g	
Pepper		1/8 oz	2.5 g	
				Add the balance of the mixture.
				Salt and pepper to taste. Bake at 350°F (180°C) for 15 minutes.

NUTRITIONAL INFORMATION PER 6 OZ (170 G) SERVING: 485 Calories; 35 g Fat (65.5% calories from fat); 20 g Protein; 22 g Carbohydrate; trace Dietary Fiber; 342 mg Cholesterol; 383 mg Sodium. Exchanges: 1 Grain (Starch); 2 Lean Meat; 1/2 Nonfat Milk; 6 Fat.

fruit soufflé *Yield: 2lb 8 oz (570 g)*

Ingredients	Lb	Oz	Metric	Procedures
Fruit juice or purée		14	400 g	Mix the fruit juice with sugar and cook on the stove top to 240°F (120°C).
Sugar	1	2	510 g	
Egg whites		8	230 g	Pour the mixture into egg whites that have been whipped to medium peaks. Pour into buttered and sugared ramekins. Bake at 350°F (180°C) for 12 to 15 minutes, depending on the size of the ramekin. If desired, add a spoonful of the purée to the top of the hot soufflé.

NUTRITIONAL INFORMATION PER 5 OZ (170 G) SERVING: 261 Calories; 0 g Fat (0.0% calories from fat); 3 g Protein; 64 g Carbohydrate; 0 g Dietary Fiber; 0 mg Cholesterol; 47 mg Sodium. Exchanges: 1/2 Lean Meat; 4 1/2 Other Carbohydrates.

PROFILE

Charlie Edwards
Bakery Manager
Sam's Club, Clarksville, Ind.

Charlie Edwards has found that working for a large corporation such as Sam's Club has its benefits. "Not only do I appreciate the good benefits and pay scale, I also like having access to a lot of resources. The company also gives me many opportunities to sharpen my work skills with added training. I also enjoy the hours, something my friends who own their own businesses can't experience," says Edwards. As the bakery manager, he oversees a staff of 10 in the bakery and 7 in the foodservice deli area. He is involved in the day-to-day operations and production as well as the deli operation and admits that he finds something new and challenging in his job each and every day.

Edwards started in the industry in 1967, following in his father's footsteps. He continues, "My father was a great teacher. From him I learned to have respect for the equipment and the ingredients. I saw him working long, hard hours. I never had the opportunity to get a formal education, but I have always looked for ways to gain more knowledge. I'm sure that I wouldn't be where I am today if I hadn't been active in both my local ACF chef's association and the RBA as well as the Kentucky Baker's Association. The workshops and seminars that I have attended over the years have helped me to keep up with new technologies and products available in the industry."

SUMMARY

Most custards and creams are made on the stove top and often in kettles. The high, dry oven heat, which helps gluten produce rigid structures in breads and cakes, is not required for making creams. Instead, most creams are merely warmed, simmered, or briefly boiled. This is because the main stabilizer in a cream mixture is not flour, but eggs, which need lower temperatures to perform their function of binding the recipe's liquefiers. The formulas for creams and custards are not flour based, so the percent ratio found in dough and batter does not apply to these formulas.

One of the most commonly used sauces is the English sauce (sauce anglaise or vanilla sauce). It is a simple mixture of heated milk, sugar, and egg yolks with some vanilla flavoring added. It is used as a dessert sauce or it can be baked in the oven, becoming caramel custard.

Pastry cream is a thicker cream with a pudding-like consistency that makes it suitable for use as a filling in a variety of cakes and pastries. Pastry cream is thickened by the swelling of its starch granules.

Bavarian cream is a cool, smooth, creamy, and delicate dessert. This cooked custard contains unflavored, dissolved gelatin. A soufflé is another custard-based dish. It is generally lightened with whipped egg whites. The mixture is molded and baked. During the baking process the whipped egg whites make the dish puff.

Unit Review Questions

SHORT ANSWER

1. List six rules for the safe handling of cream products.
2. The main stabilizer in creams is
   _____.
3. What is pasteurization?
4. What is homogenized milk?
5. What is "standardization" as it refers to milk? Why is this process important?
6. The higher the fat content of the whipping cream, the more _____ the emulsion. (stable/unstable)
7. The higher the fat content of the whipping cream, the _____ the volume. (higher/lower)
8. Why is chilling the bowl, whip, and cream important in preparing whipped cream?
9. When should sugar be added in making whipped cream?
10. What is the recommended usage of low-heat, nonfat dry milk?
11. What is the recommended usage of high-heat, nonfat dry milk?
12. By what other names is English sauce known?
13. Describe the basic preparation of English sauce.
14. What does the term "nappe" mean?
15. What happens to eggs if you mix sugar in and allow it to stand for a length of time?
16. Explain the tempering process used in making English sauce. Why is this process used?
17. When flavoring English sauce with extracts, when are they added? Why?
18. How does pastry cream differ from English sauce?
19. Why should converted rice *not* be used in rice pudding?
20. What are the two types of tapioca?
21. List two methods to prevent the formation of a skin on a pudding or cream.
22. What causes the separation of a custard?
23. What are the advantages of using modified cornstarch?
24. What is a mousse?
25. What is Bavarian cream?

MULTIPLE CHOICE AND MATCHING

26. Although legal standards vary, most states require that whole milk must contain what percentage of butterfat?
    a. 2.5 percent
    b. 3.25 percent
    c. 5.25 percent
    d. 10.5 percent
27. Match the type of milk to its fat content:
    a. non-fat milk   1. less than 1 percent
    b. skim milk   2. less than 2 percent
    c. lowfat milk   3. less than 0.1 percent
28. Match the type of cream to its fat content:
    a. whipping cream   1. 32–36 percent
    b. light cream   2. 28–32 percent
    c. Half & Half   3. 40 percent
    d. heavy cream   4. 10–12 percent
    e. medium cream   5. 16–20 percent
    f. extra-heavy cream 6. 20–25 percent

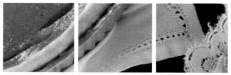 # pies and tarts

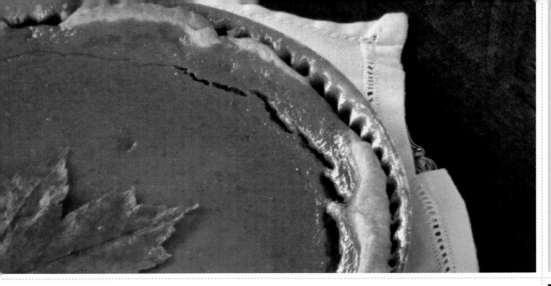

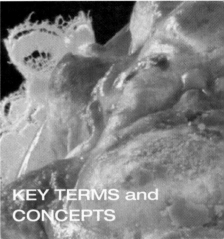

"But I, when I undress me each night upon my knees, will ask the Lord to bless me, with apple pie and cheese."

Eugene Field

LEARNING Objectives

After you have finished reading this unit, you should be able to:

- **Explain** how fat distribution causes flaky and mealy pie crusts

- **Discuss** how to use pie crust and short dough to make shells and envelope-filled products

- **List** the steps for cooking pie filling

- **Describe** starch functions

amylopectin

amylose

blind baked

cutting or cut

flaky

gelatinization

IQF

Linzer tart

mealy

pasting

short dough

zest

WE'VE ALL HEARD THE PHRASE "AS AMERICAN AS APPLE pie." It's no wonder that pies have become a symbol for this country because pie is American in design. A pie can be sweet or savory and is one type of baked good that is served directly from its pan. The dough is used to line single-crust, custard-type pies; double-crust, fruit-filled pies; and turnovers. Pie crust has a high percentage of fat. The melting of the distributed fat makes pie crust flaky and tender; however, there is no leavening. Short dough contains a high percentage of fat and sugar and is used to line flan and tart pans.

PIE CRUST AND SHORT DOUGH

It is important that you use the correct, high-quality ingredients when you make pie crust. Most formulas for pie crust use only three ingredients: flour, fat or shortening, and water or milk. The term "**short dough**" refers to tart crusts that have been "shortened" with fat. The result is a tender, sweetened product.

Flour

Medium soft-wheat flour such as pastry or all-purpose flour yields excellent results with minimum shrinkage. Very soft flour (cake) produces a more mealy crust. You should increase the fat by 10 to 15 percent if you use stronger (bread) flour. Gluten production in the pie crust is not desired, so bakers often prefer pastry flour because it has less protein, yielding less gluten. Less gluten results in a tender crust; this is preferred for pie crust.

Shortening (Fat)

The type of shortening used in pie crust has a direct effect on the flavor of the baked product. Flakiness and tenderness are influenced more by the consistency than by the percentage or type of fat.

Lard is sometimes preferred in pie crust because it is the proper consistency at room temperature. Due to its high melting point, hard fat such as lard makes a flaky pie crust. Fat shortens the gluten strands. When more fat is used, the texture of the dough will be crumbly and less elastic. Shortening that is too soft will become absorbed by the flour, preventing proper water absorption and making a mealy crust. Butter, when used in pastry dough, aids in caramelization and browning. The caramelization builds good flavor into the crust and also provides flakiness.

Liquids

Water or milk can be used for the liquid. The liquid must be cold, with temperatures around 45°F to 50°F (7°C to 10°C).

Mixing

To obtain the correct type of crust for your pie and pastry products it is very important that you mix the dough properly. Three pie crust formulas will be presented in this unit: standard, mealy, and flaky. The standard pie crust formula can be used for all-purpose applications and is generally a cross between a mealy and a flaky crust. A **flaky** pie crust is achieved by distributing larger particles of fat; this results from **cutting** the ingredients rather than mixing. In a **mealy** pie crust, the fat is distributed in smaller pieces due to continued mixing. Note that all of the formulas use the same ingredients, but each is mixed in a unique sequence. The standard formula can be used for pie tops and reworked with trimmings for the bottom crust. Make pie tops first—the reworked trimmings are best suited for the bottom crust when you use the standard formula.

Pie crust is used to form shells for tarts and pies and envelopes for turnovers and pocket-style pastries that are filled with fruits and creams. Understanding the principles of making standard pie crust forms the foundation for the production of flaky, mealy, and short dough.

standard pie crust   *Yield: 6 lb 5 oz (2,860 g)*

% Ratio	Ingredients	Lb	Oz	Metric	Procedures
100	Pastry flour	3		1,360 g	Cut the shortening into the flour with a bowl scraper.
66	Shortening	2		900 g	
2	Salt		1	30 g	Add salt to the water.
41	Water (cold)	1	4	570 g	
					Mix into the above ingredients until the dough holds together and forms a ball.

NUTRITIONAL INFORMATION PER 1 OZ (30 G) SERVING: 128 Calories; 9 g Fat (64.5% calories from fat); 2 g Protein; 10 g Carbohydrate; trace Dietary Fiber; 0 mg Cholesterol; 109 mg Sodium. Exchanges: 1/2 Grain (Starch); 2 Fat.

blueberry filling
Yield: 8 lb 1/2 oz (3,670 g); four 10-in. (250 cm) pies

Ingredients	Lb	Oz	Metric	Procedures
Water	2		900 g	Bring the first water, sugar, and a small quantity of blueberries to a boil.
Sugar	2	4	1,020 g	
Blueberries		4	110 g	
Water		4	110 g	Combine the second water, cornstarch, and remaining sugar. Add this solution to the boiling liquid, stirring constantly.
Cornstarch		4 1/2	120 g	
Sugar		1	30 g	
Blueberries	3		1,360 g	Pour the mixture into a stainless steel bowl and gently fold in the remaining blueberries.

NUTRITIONAL INFORMATION PER 4 OZ (110 G) SERVING (filling only): 168 Calories; trace Fat (0.9% calories from fat); trace Protein; 43 g Carbohydrate; 1 g Dietary Fiber; 0 mg Cholesterol; 4 mg Sodium. Exchanges: 0 Grain (Starch); 1/2 Fruit; 2 Other Carbohydrates. This formula and procedure work for all fresh or IQF (individually quick frozen) berries. Do not thaw the frozen berries prior to use.

pineapple filling
Yield: 7 lb (3,180 g); 4 10-in (250 cm) pies

Ingredients	Lb	Oz	Metric	Procedures
Pineapple*	3		1,360 g	Bring pineapple, water, and first sugar to a boil.
Water	2		900 g	
Sugar	1	4	570 g	
Cornstarch		6	170 g	Make a solution with cornstarch, remaining sugar and water. Add it to boiling liquid, stirring constantly, until it returns to a boil.
Sugar		2	60 g	
Water		4	110 g	

NUTRITIONAL INFORMATION PER 4 OZ (110 G) SERVING (filling only): 121 Calories; trace Fat (0.3% calories from fat); trace Protein; 31 g Carbohydrate; trace Dietary Fiber; 0mg Cholesterol; 2 mg Sodium. Exchanges: 1/2 Grain (Starch); 1/2 Fruit; 1 1/2 Other Carbohydrates. *Crushed, canned pineapple is preferred. Fresh pineapple must be blanched first because its high acid levels will prevent the starch from gelatinizing.

pecan filling
Yield: 4 lb 3 1/2 oz (1,910 g); three 10-in. (250 cm) pies

Ingredients	Lb	Oz	Metric	Procedures
Pastry flour		2	60 g	Blend the sugar and flour.
Sugar		2	60 g	
Dark corn syrup	3		1,360 g	Add the corn syrup and eggs.
Eggs	1		450 g	
Vanilla extract		1/2	10 g	
Butter (melted)	3		1,360 g	Add the melted butter and vanilla.
Pecans		12	340 g	Distribute the pecans evenly on the bottom of the pie shell. Fill the pie shell with the custard and bake. Bake at 400°F (204°C) 45 to 50 minutes.

NUTRITIONAL INFORMATION PER 4 OZ (110 G) SERVING (filling only): 705 Calories; 67 g Fat (70.3% calories from fat); 4 g Protein; 51 g Carbohydrate; 1 g Dietary Fiber; 193 mg Cholesterol; 577 mg Sodium. Exchanges: 1/2 Grain (Starch); 1/2 Lean Meat; 11 Fat; 3 Other Carbohydrates.

pumpkin filling

Yield: 10 lb 8oz (4,760 g); four 10-in. (250 cm) pies

Ingredients	Lb	Oz	Metric	Procedures
Sugar		8	230 g	Combine all of the dry ingredients and sift twice.
Brown sugar		8	230 g	
Pastry flour		2	60 g	
Salt		1/2	10 g	
Cinnamon		1/2	10 g	
Ginger		1/2	10 g	
Nutmeg		1/2	10 g	
Pumpkin purée	3	8	1,590 g	Add the pumpkin, corn syrup, and molasses. Mix until blended.
Light corn syrup		8	230 g	
Molasses		4	110 g	
Milk	4		1,810 g	Add the milk and eggs. Pour the mixture into a pie shell. Bake at 400°F (204°C) for 30 to 35 minutes until the filling is set.
Eggs	1		450 g	

NUTRITIONAL INFORMATION PER 4 OZ (110 G) SERVING (filling only): 165 Calories; 3 g Fat (18.2% calories from fat); 4 g Protein; 31 g Carbohydrate; 2 g Dietary Fiber; 59 mg Cholesterol; 230 mg Sodium. Exchanges: 0 Grain (Starch); 0 Lean Meat; 1 Vegetable; 0 Nonfat Milk; 1/2 Fat; 1 1/2 Other Carbohydrates.

Additional Formulas

The following filling and pie formulas appear in Appendix G, *The Workbench:*

Lemon pie filling

Mincemeat

Italian cheese pie

German chocolate pie

PROFILES

Janet Lightizer
Pastry Chef Instructor
Leominster Center for Technical Education, Leominster, Mass.

Leominster is a public vocational school for students in 9th through 12th grades. Janet Lightizer not only teaches all aspects of the baking industry to her students, she also oversees the baking production for a retail bakery and restaurant housed on the campus and run entirely by the students.

Back when she was in school earning an associate's degree in culinary arts and, later, a bachelor's degree in business management, Lightizer never dreamed that she would spend her time teaching. After graduation she worked in a number of restaurants and bakeries. Six years ago she accepted a teaching position at Leominster and now she can't imagine doing anything else. "I love working with our students. It has become a very rewarding career. There's nothing better than sharing my love for baking with our students," says Lightizer.

Terry Wagner, CMB
Owner
Olde Tyme Pastries, two locations: Turlock and Modesto, Calif.

Olde Tyme is a full-line bakery featuring fancy tortes, cookies, Danish, cakes, and artisan breads. Terry Wagner is living out his dream as owner of a successful bakery. "My father was a baker, and I learned a lot of what I know from him. He always told me to learn from everyone you meet. Over the years, I have tried to improve my knowledge and skills by taking classes, being an active member of the RBA and attending conventions and seminars whenever possible," says Wagner, who founded Olde Tyme 23 years ago. Wagner starts his day at 5:30 A.M., when he oversees the heavy production. Then it's time to check his email and focus on paper work. By mid-morning he is out front getting ready for the lunch crowd or working in production, depending on where he is most needed. His day ends around 4:00 P.M. As owner, he oversees a staff of 72 employees and often toggles between the two retail stores. He adds, "Watching my business grow and get better each year has been very enjoyable."

SUMMARY

Pie crust is used to line single-crust, custard-type pies; double, fruit-filled pies; and turnovers. It has a high percentage of fat. The melting of the distributed fat makes the pie crust flaky and tender. Most formulas use only three ingredients: flour, fat or shortening, and water or milk. Short dough contains a high percentage of fat and sugar and is used for flans and tarts.

Starch cookery is used to make most pie fillings and custards. As starch cells swell when heated in a liquid, gelatinization occurs and thickens the ingredients. Cornstarch is often used as the primary starch in starch cookery; however, it is better to use pastry flour rather than cornstarch when making custard. Pastry flour completes its gelatinization at a lower temperature. Cornstarch must be cooked at higher temperatures, causing the eggs in the custard to curdle.

Unit Review Questions

SHORT ANSWER

1. What type of flour is recommended for pie dough?
2. Is gluten development desired in pie dough? Why or why not?
3. What does the term "cutting" mean in making pie dough?
4. What happens to pie dough if the shortening is too soft?
5. What are the advantages of using butter in pie dough?
6. Why is lard sometimes preferred in pie dough?
7. The three main pie dough formulas are:
   _____, _____, and _____.
8. Which pie dough formula is recommended for bottom and single-crust pies?

9. Which pie dough formula is recommended for the top crust of pies?

10. Why is sugar not recommended in pie dough formulas?

11. Why use shortening in pie dough formulas? Why is it recommended that milk powder be added?

12. What might cause pie dough to shrink during baking?

13. How do tarts differ from pies?

14. What type of dough is recommended for tarts?

15. The two types of granules that make up starch include _____ and _____.

16. List three factors that affect starch cookery.

MULTIPLE CHOICE AND MATCHING

17. If a stronger flour is used in making pie dough, fat should be increased by
    a. 5–10%.
    b. 10–15%.
    c. 15–25%.
    d. 25–30%.

18. The liquid used when making pie dough should be
    a. room temperature.
    b. lukewarm.
    c. hot.
    d. cold.

19. A rule of thumb is to use _____ of pastry dough for each inch of pie pan diameter.
    a. 1/2 oz
    b. 1 oz
    c. 2 oz
    d. 2 1/4 oz

cookies

Unit 13 presents cookies
made in a variety of
methods, including
spritzing, rolling,
panning, and baking. It
also introduces the
mixing methods used for
cookie making. Common
cookie baking problems
are discussed along with
the solutions to
overcome them.

cookie variations

"A balanced diet is a cookie in each hand."

Unknown

KEY TERMS and CONCEPTS

bar cookies

biscotti

dropped cookies

icebox

refrigerated cookies

rolled cookies

sheet cookies

spritz

LEARNING Objectives

After you have finished reading this unit, you should be able to:

- **Define** the mixing, rolling, and cutting methods of rolled cookie variations

- **Describe** the mixing, piping, and garnishing of spritz cookies

- **Demonstrate** mixing, dropping, and panning of dropped cookies

- **Discuss** how to mix, shape, pan, and cut bar cookies and biscotti

- **Define** the mixing, panning, and cutting of sheet cookies

- **Describe** the mixing, shaping, refrigerating, and cutting of refrigerated cookies

- **Explain** common cookie baking problems and how to overcome them

COOKIES ARE THE ALL-TIME FAVORITE COMFORT FOOD FOR
people around the world. From English shortbread to French sables;
from Polish thumbprints to Indian Coconut Chews; from Mexican
wedding cakes to Israeli rugelach and Chinese almond cookies, almost every culture has its own beloved cookie recipe. The English
name for "cookie" comes from the Dutch word "koekje," meaning
"little cakes." Many years ago, bakers made small test cakes to check
out their oven temperature before they placed larger cakes in the
oven. Those "little cakes" date back to seventh-century Persia.

Cookies were purchased in Paris in the late 1300s. Renaissance cookbooks included cookie recipes, and by the seventeenth century, cookies
were commonplace. The chocolate chip cookie has its roots in the United
States. Ruth Wakefield, the innkeeper for the Massachusetts Toll House Inn,
was baking her favorite cookie recipe in 1930. When she realized that she
ran out of nuts, Mrs. Wakefield searched her cupboards and found a bar of
baking chocolate. She broke it into little pieces and created the first chocolate chip cookie.

By 2004, the U.S. cookie market had sales of $4.7 billion according to
The Market Research Report. We all have purchased cookies from time to
time, and many of us share memories of making and baking cookies for
special occasions and holidays.

Cookies require little or no leavening, and many are mixed in one
stage. They can be made in many different shapes with a variety of gar-

nishes. Cookies have a long shelf-life and are easy to package and ship, whether to students at college or our military overseas. Together with a letter and photo, cookies bring back memories of the warmth and love of home. Many bakers have opened successful businesses with high-quality cookie lines.

There are hundreds of formulas and variations of cookies. In this section, you will be introduced to at least two variations of each of the basic types of cookies. Once you understand ratios and sequence, you will be able to bake any formula and create your own signature cookies.

Cookies are most often prepared by creaming the sugar, butter or shortening, salt, and spices; adding eggs; and, finally, folding in the sifted flour (Figure 13-1). Some formulas, however, are made by simply mixing all of the ingredients together in one step. Cookie dough is generally made with a higher percentage of stabilizers compared to tenderizers, creating a stiff mixture. Because most cookies are cut or piped into size and shape rather than being poured into molds or pans like cake batter, cookie batter needs a thicker consistency. In some formulas, additional tenderness is provided by the action produced by chemical leavenors such as baking soda or baking powder.

Cookie production requires a minimal amount of capital and equipment, and cookies are easy to market.

Now, it's time to bake a batch of cookies!

MIXING METHODS

Creaming Method

Place the sugar, butter or shortening, salt, and spices in a mixing bowl and cream them together (Figure 13-2). Ingredients must be at room temperature to cream properly (Figure 13-3). Add the eggs slowly (Figure 13-4) and fold in the sifted flour (Figure 13-5); be careful not to overmix.

Figure 13-1 The creaming process begins with butter and sugar.

Figure 13-2 Cream the sugar, butter or shortening, and spices together until light and fluffy.

One-Stage Method

Another mixing method is to place all of the ingredients in a mechanical mixing bowl and mix for 2 to 3 minutes at low speed until the batter is smooth. The six basic methods for shaping these mixtures gives the cookies their names: rolled, spritz, dropped, bar, sheet, and refrigerated.

HAND-CUT OR ROLLED COOKIES

Roll out the stiff dough for hand-cut and other types of rolled cookies with a rolling pin to a thickness of 1/8 in. (.6 cm). Use cookie cutters to cut pieces to the desired shape and size, and place them on parchment-lined sheet pans for baking.

Figure 13-3 Ingredients should be at room temperature.

LEARNING ACTIVITY 13-1

Mix one formula of sugar cookies (page 265). Roll 1/3 of the dough on a canvas cloth dusted with bread flour. Roll another 1/3 of the dough onto a wooden baker's bench dusted with bread flour. Roll the remaining dough on a stainless steel bench dusted with bread flour. Evaluate the surfaces. Which is the easiest to use for dough-rolling? Record your evaluation in the following chart.

Procedure	Evaluation
Rolled on canvas cloth	
Rolled on wooden baker's bench	
Rolled on stainless steel bench	

Figure 13-4 Adding the eggs.

Figure 13-5 Sift the flour before folding it into the creamed mixture.

Hand-cut the sugar cookie dough after you have rolled it flat with a rolling pin. Making a batch or two will help you to develop mixing and rolling skills. By changing the consistency of the sugar cookie dough, you can make a variety of different types of cookies, from plain round to complex gingerbread houses. You can also change the shape of your cookies by using different shaped cutters. Dust with a variety of toppings to create a wide range of recipes. Rolled cookies are an important addition to any baker's repertoire.

sugar cookies   *Yield: 4 lb 9 3/4 oz (2,090 g); 60 cookies*

% Ratio	Ingredients	Lb	Oz	Metric	Procedures
50	Sugar	1		450 g	Combine the sugar, butter, and salt. Cream until smooth.
37 1/2	Butter		12	340 g	
3/4	Salt		1/4	5 g	
25	Eggs		8	230 g	To this mixture, slowly add the eggs and milk.
12 1/2	Milk		4	110 g	
100	Pastry flour	2		900 g	
3	Baking powder		1	30 g	
1 1/2	Vanilla		1/2	10 g	

Add the flour, baking powder, and vanilla. Mix until smooth.

Roll out the dough with a rolling pin and cut with cookie cutters to desired shape.

Place on parchment-lined sheet pans for baking. Bake at 375° to 400°F (191° to 204°C). Baking time will vary with shape and size of cookie.

NUTRITIONAL INFORMATION PER 2 OZ (60 G) SERVING: 219 Calories; 9 g Fat (34.9% calories from fat); 3 g Protein; 33 g Carbohydrate; trace Dietary Fiber; 44 mg Cholesterol; 247 mg Sodium. Exchanges: 1 1/2 Grain (Starch); 0 Lean Meat; 0 Nonfat Milk; 1 1/2 Fat; 1 Other Carbohydrates.
NOTE: Once the cookies are cooled, you can ice and decorate them as desired.

hazel nut cookie Yield: 5 lb 11 1/2 oz (2,590 g); 90 cookies

% Ratio	Ingredients	Lb	Oz	Metric	Procedures
86	Butter	1	8	680 g	Combine the butter and sugar; cream lightly.
64	Sugar	1	2	510 g	
1 1/2	Vanilla		1/2	10 g	Add the eggs and vanilla.
21	Eggs		6	170 g	
100	Cake flour	1	14	850 g	Sift the flour, cinnamon, and baking powder. Add the sifted ingredients to the creamed mixture. When the flour is incorporated, add the toasted nuts.
1 1/2	Cinnamon		1/2	10 g	
1 1/2	Baking powder		1/2	10 g	Roll out and cut with cookie cutters to desired shape.
43	Toasted hazelnuts, ground		12	340 g	Place on parchment-lined sheet pans for baking. Bake at 375° to 400°F (191° to 204°C) for 12 to 15 minutes.

NUTRITIONAL INFORMATION PER 2 OZ (60 G) SERVING: Per Serving: 281 Calories; 15 g Fat (47.6% calories from fat); 3 g Protein; 34 g Carbohydrate; 1 g Dietary Fiber; 47 mg Cholesterol; 163 mg Sodium. Exchanges: 1 1/2 Grain (Starch); 0 Lean Meat; 3 Fat; 1 Other Carbohydrates.

NOTE: For Linzer cookies, sandwich raspberry jam between two cookies. If desired dust the tops, before layering, with powdered sugar.

gingerbread *Yield: 6 lb 4 oz (2,830 g)*

% Ratio	Ingredients	Lb	Oz	Metric	Procedures
39	Light-brown sugar		14	400 g	Cream together the sugars, shortening, baking soda, and salt.
61	Sugar	1	6	620 g	
33	Shortening		12	340 g	
1 1/2	Baking soda		1/2	10 g	
1 1/2	Salt		1/2	10 g	
8	Molasses		3	90 g	Slowly add the molasses and eggs.
33	Eggs		12	340 g	
3/4	Ginger		1/4	5 g	Sift the flour with spices; combine with the above ingredients until mixed. Chill the dough at least 4 to 6 hours.
3/4	Cinnamon		1/4	5 g	
100	Cake flour	2	4	1,020 g	Roll out and cut with cookie cutter to desired shape. Place on parchment-lined sheet pans for baking. Bake at 375° to 400°F (191° to 204°C) for 20 minutes or less depending on size of cut out.

NUTRITIONAL INFORMATION PER 2 OZ (60 G) SERVING: 226 Calories; 8 g Fat (29.9% calories from fat); 2 g Protein; 38 g Carbohydrate; trace Dietary Fiber; 25 mg Cholesterol; 199 mg Sodium. Exchanges: 1 Grain (Starch); 0 Lean Meat; 1 1/2 Fat; 1 1/2 Other Carbohydrates.

Gingerbread Decorations

Gingerbread dough is often used for making holiday decorations including gingerbread people, trains, cars, boxes, churches, and houses.

PROCEDURE FOR MAKING A GINGERBREAD HOUSE

1. Prepare a template by drawing and cutting out the desired design. Cardboard bakery boxes work well for the templates (Figures 13-6–13-12).
2. Roll the dough evenly on a flour-dusted canvas cloth. Make a track using two 1/4-in wood slats (a ruler or cake board will also work for the track). Using the slats, create a frame on both sides of the dough. Then roll the rolling pin over the two tracks; this will ensure that the dough is rolled evenly (even dough is essential to creating professional-looking gingerbread pieces).
3. Place the template on the dough and cut around it. Move the cut-out dough figure onto a parchment-papered pan by sliding the template under the dough. (Use the template as a sort of spatula to move the dough. Once the dough is in place, slide the template out and remove.)
4. Bake at 375°F (190°C) for 20 minutes or until the gingerbread is dry to the touch. When all parts are cool, put the house together and decorate with royal icing (see formula in Unit 16) (Figures 13-13–13-14 show assembly. Figure 13-15 shows the finished decorated house.)

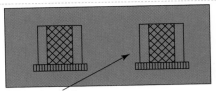

Use cut outs from
window for shutters

Figure 13-6 Left side—use cut-outs from
windows for shutters.

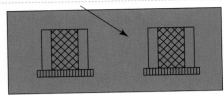

Figure 13-7 Right side.

Figure 13-8 Left side of roof.

Figure 13-9 Right side of roof.

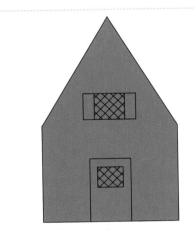

Figure 13-10 Front of house.

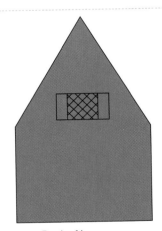

Figure 13-11 Back of house.

Figure 13-12 Chimney pieces.

Figure 13-13 Side view.

Figure 13-14 Front/side views.

Figure 13-15 Decorate gingerbread house with frosting or candies.

LEARNING ACTIVITY 13-2

Mix one formula of gingerbread dough and divide the dough into three units. Roll each unit on a canvas cloth or baker's bench that has been dusted with a different type of flour. Use bread flour, pastry flour, and cake flour. Which flour provides the best lubrication and least absorption?

Record your findings in the following chart.

Procedure	Evaluation
Using bread flour	
Using pastry flour	
Using cake flour	

SPRITZ OR BAGGED COOKIES

Spritz or "bagged" are the terms given to cookies that are formed by forcing a stiff batter through a pastry bag fitted with a variety of different tips (tubes) (Figure 13-16). The mixture is shaped by fitting the bag with either a round or a star tip of the desired size and squeezing the batter directly onto the sheet pan for baking. Because it can be difficult to pipe out a mixture filled with solid ingredients like nuts and candied fruit, these cookies are usually garnished after they are formed and before baking. To garnish, lightly press bits of nuts or candied fruits on each cookie.

Spritz or bagged baked cookies can be used to make sandwich cookies by filling with jam, sandwiching two cookies together, and dipping into chocolate fondant or coating (Figure 13-17–Figure 13-18). (See Unit 17 for more information about chocolate coating.)

Figure 13-16 Spritz-style cookies.

Spritz cookies are light and delicate. They are made that way from lightly creaming the butter and sugar and folding in the sifted flour **by hand.**

butter spritz cookies
Yield: 6 lb 5 1/2 oz (2,880 g); 200 cookies

% Ratio	Ingredients	Lb	Oz	Metric	Procedures
45	Sugar	1	2	510 g	Cream the sugar, butter, vanilla, and salt.
80	Butter	2		900 g	
3/4	Vanilla		1/4	5 g	
3/4	Salt		1/4	5 g	
12 1/2	Eggs		5	140 g	Slowly add the eggs and milk to the mixture.
12 1/2	Milk		5	140 g	
75	Pastry flour	1	14	850 g	
25	Bread flour		10	280 g	
2 1/2	Milk powder		1	30 g	Sift the flours and milk powder. Fold the sifted ingredients into the mixture; do not overmix.

Fill a pastry bag that has been fitted with a #4 French tip with the batter, and pipe out desired shapes onto parchment-lined sheet pans. Bake 12 minutes at 375° to 400°F (190° to 200°C).

NUTRITIONAL INFORMATION PER 2 OZ (60 G) SERVING: 255 Calories; 15 g Fat (53.0% calories from fat); 3 g Protein; 27 g Carbohydrate; trace Dietary Fiber; 50 mg Cholesterol; 208 mg Sodium. Exchanges: 1 Grain (Starch); 0 Lean Meat; 0 Nonfat Milk; 3 Fat; 1/2 Other Carbohydrates.

almond butter spritz   *Yield: 5 lb 2 oz (2,320 g); 165 cookies*

% Ratio	Ingredients	Lb	Oz	Metric	Procedures
18	Almond paste		6	170 g	Mix the sugar and almond paste.
37 1/2	Sugar		12	340 g	
75	Butter, softened	1	8	680 g	Add the butter and cream until smooth.
25	Egg whites		8	230 g	Slowly add the egg whites.
100	Bread flour	2		900 g	Sift the flour and fold in by hand. Fill a pastry bag with dough and form into desired shape. Deposit shapes onto parchment-lined sheet pans for baking. Bake 12 minutes at 375° to 400°F (191° to 204°C). If desired, add a drop of jam to the center of each cookie prior to baking.

NUTRITIONAL INFORMATION PER 2 OZ (60 G) SERVING: 253 Calories; 15 g Fat (52.8% calories from fat); 4 g Protein; 26 g Carbohydrate; trace Dietary Fiber; 36 mg Cholesterol; 147 mg Sodium. Exchanges: 1 Grain (Starch); 0 Lean Meat; 3 Fat; 1/2 Other Carbohydrates.

lemon spritz cookies   *Yield: 3 lb 3 oz (1,450); 60 cookies*

% Ratio	Ingredients	Lb	Oz	Metric	Procedures
75	Butter		12	340 g	Cream the butter and sugar.
62 1/2	Powdered sugar		10	280 g	
75	Egg yolks		12	340 g	Add the egg yolks and lemon zest to the creamed mixture.
6	Lemon zest		1	30 g	
100	Pastry flour	1		450 g	Fold sifted pastry flour into the mixture. Fill a pastry bag with dough and form into desired shape. Deposit shapes onto parchment-lined sheet pans for baking. Bake 12 minutes at 375° to 400°F (190° to 200°C).

NUTRITIONAL INFORMATION PER 2 OZ (60 G) SERVING: 257 Calories; 15 g Fat (53.8% calories from fat); 4 g Protein; 26 g Carbohydrate; trace Dietary Fiber; 204 mg Cholesterol; 119 mg Sodium. Exchanges: 1 Grain (Starch); 0 Lean Meat; 0 Fruit; 3 Fat; 1 Other Carbohydrates.

sandwich cookies
Yield: 3 lb 12 1/4 oz (1,710); 60 cookies

% Ratio	Ingredients	Lb	Oz	Metric	Procedures
70	Sugar		14	400 g	Cream the butter and sugar.
70	Butter		14	400 g	
40	Eggs		8	230 g	Add the eggs, orange juice, and zest to the creamed mixture.
1/2	Orange juice		1/2	10 g	
1	Orange zest		2	60 g	
100	Cake flour	1	5	600 g	Sift the flour and baking powder; fold into the mixture and mix until smooth.
1/4	Baking powder		1/4	5 g	Fill a pastry bag with dough and form into desired shape. Deposit shapes onto parchment-lined sheet pans for baking. Refer to Figures 13-17 and 13-18 for sandwich assembly instructions.
					Bake at 375° to 400°F (191° to 204°C) for 12 minutes.

NUTRITIONAL INFORMATION PER 2 OZ (60 G) SERVING: 230 Calories; 12 g Fat (44.9% calories from fat); 3 g Protein; 29 g Carbohydrate; trace Dietary Fiber; 56 mg Cholesterol; 143 mg Sodium. Exchanges: 1 Grain (Starch); 0 Lean Meat; 0 Fruit; 2 Fat; 1 Other Carbohydrates.

Figure 13-17 To create the sandwich, spread filling lightly on the cookie and put two together.

Figure 13-18 Once the sandwich cookies are filled, they can be dipped in chocolate.

DROPPED COOKIES

You can make **dropped** cookies by scooping out a portion of the thick mixture with a spoon or portion scoop and dropping it onto the sheet pan prior to baking (Figure 13-19). Sometimes the raw cookie mounds are flattened out with a spatula to shape them. In many cases, the formulas for this type of cookie have a high percentage of fat, which melts during baking to give the cookie its finished shape. Remember to space the dropped pieces farther apart than usual so that they do not run into each other as the butter melts and they spread during baking. The garnishes for these cookies, such as chocolate chips and nuts, are usually mixed right in with the batter.

Figure 13-19 Dropped cookie varieties.

chocolate chip cookies *Yield: 4 lb 4 1/2 oz (1,930 g); 50 cookies*

% Ratio	Ingredients	Lb	Oz	Metric	Procedures
66	Butter		12	340 g	Combine the butter and sugar; cream lightly.
39	Brown sugar		7	200 g	
61	Sugar		11	310 g	
33	Eggs		6	170 g	Add the eggs.
1/4	Salt		1/4	5 g	Add the salt and baking soda to the mixture.
1/4	Baking soda		1/4	5 g	Sift the flour and add.
100	Pastry flour	1	2	510 g	When the flour is incorporated, add the chocolate chips. Drop the cookies with a spoon or scoop onto parchment-lined sheet pans for baking. (Allow room for cookies to spread during baking.)
77	Chocolate chips		14	400 g	Bake at 375° to 400°F (191° to 204°C) for 15 to 17 minutes.

NUTRITIONAL INFORMATION PER 2 OZ (60 G) SERVING: (excluding unknown items): 246 Calories; 12 g Fat (42.9% calories from fat); 2 g Protein; 34 g Carbohydrate; 1 g Dietary Fiber; 40 mg Cholesterol; 230 mg Sodium. Exchanges: 1 Grain (Starch); 0 Lean Meat; 2 1/2 Fat; 1 1/2 Other Carbohydrates.

LEARNING ACTIVITY 13-3

Mix one formula of chocolate chip cookies. Deposit one dozen cookies on a pan that has been lined with parchment paper; deposit another dozen cookies onto a pan sprayed with nonstick spray; deposit the third batch on a pan brushed with shortening and dusted with flour; and, finally, bake the last batch on an untreated pan. How does pan preparation affect the baking of the cookies? Record your findings in the following chart.

Procedure	Evaluation
Pan with parchment	
Pan sprayed with nonstick spray	
Pan brushed with shortening and dusted with flour	
Pan left untreated	

peanut butter cookies Yield: 6 lb 5 oz (2,860 g)

% Ratio	Ingredients	Lb	Oz	Metric	Procedures
80	Brown sugar	1		450 g	Lightly cream sugars, shortening, salt, and baking soda.
80	Sugar	1		450 g	
80	Shortening	1		450 g	
2 1/2	Salt		1/2	10 g	
2 1/2	Baking soda		1/2	10 g	
40	Eggs		8	230 g	Add eggs gradually.
120	Peanut butter	1	8	230 g	Add peanut butter.
100	All-purpose flour	1	4	120 g	Add sifted flour and scrape bowl and mix for 5 minutes on slow speed. Drop the cookies with a spoon or scoop onto parchment-lined sheet pans for baking. (Allow room for cookies to spread during baking.) Flatten the cookie with a fork; turn and flatten again to create lattice-like markings. Bake at 350° to 400°F (190° to 205° C) for 15 to 17 minutes.

NUTRITIONAL INFORMATION PER 2 OZ (60 G) SERVING: 274 Calories; 16 g Fat; 5 g Protein; 29 g Carbohydrate; 1 g Dietary Fiber; 17 mg Cholesterol; 257 mg Sodium.

Figure 13-20 Biscotti are a type of bar cookie.

BAR COOKIES

Bar cookies are made from a thick batter. Biscotti are a type of bar cookie that is baked in large rectangular bars, which are cut into 1/2 pieces, placed on their side, and baked a second time (Figure 13-20). Bar cookies should always be cooled before they are cut.

double chocolate biscotti *Yield: 4 lb 10 oz (2,100 g); 72 biscotti*

% Ratio	Ingredients	Lb	Oz	Metric	Procedures
40	Butter		8	230 g	Lightly cream the butter and sugar.
90	Sugar	1	2	510 g	
45	Eggs		9	269 g	Add the eggs in three additions to the creamed mixture.
20	Cocoa		4	115 g	Sift the cocoa, pastry flour, and baking powder twice. Add the sifted ingredients to creamed mixture.
100	Pastry flour	1	4	570 g	
5	Baking powder		1	30 g	
30	Whole almonds		6	170 g	Add almonds and chocolate chips and mix for three minutes. Form into bars. Place on parchment-lined sheet pans for baking. Bake at 375° to 400°F (191° to 204°C) for 20 to 22 minutes. When the baked bars are cooled, slice into 1/2- in (1.3 cm) biscotti and lay flat on a sheet pan. Once cut, return the bars to the oven at 375° to 400°F (191° to 204°C) and bake until lightly toasted.
40	Chocolate chips		8	230 g	

NUTRITIONAL INFORMATION PER 2 OZ (60 G) SERVING: 225 Calories; 10 g Fat (39.0% calories from fat); 4 g Protein; 32 g Carbohydrate; 2 g Dietary Fiber; 38 mg Cholesterol; 142 mg Sodium. Exchanges: 1 Grain (Starch); 0 Lean Meat; 2 Fat; 1 Other Carbohydrates.

Figure 14-1 Baking soda and baking powder are the key leavenors used in quick bread formulas.

Figure 14-2 Scones are delicious plain or split in half with jam and cream.

Figure 14-3 A variety of American-style muffins.

Irish soda bread formula *Yield: 5 lb 1 3/4 oz (2,180 g)*

% Ratio	Ingredients	Lb	Oz	Metric	Procedures
50	Pastry flour	1	4	570 g	Sift together all of the dry ingredients.
50	Whole-wheat flour	1	4	570 g	
7 1/2	Baking powder		3	90 g	
2	Salt		3/4	20 g	
15	Shortening		6	170 g	Add the shortening and milk to the dry ingredients; mix with a standard mixer for 5 minutes on low speed.
55	Milk	1	6	620 g	
10	Raisins		4	110 g	Add the raisins and mix for 3 minutes. Form into individual 2-oz units. Using a bench scraper, score the dough with an "X." Bake at 360°F (180°C) for approximately 22 to 25 minutes.
Optional	Caraway seeds		1	30 g	

NUTRITIONAL INFORMATION PER 2 OZ (60 G) SERVING: 155 Calories; 5 g Fat (29.0% calories from fat); 4 g Protein; 25 g Carbohydrate; 2 g Dietary Fiber; 2 mg Cholesterol; 430 mg Sodium. Exchanges: 1 1/2 Grain (Starch); 0 Vegetable; 0 Fruit; 0 Nonfat Milk; 1 Fat; 0 Other Carbohydrates.

Figure 14-4 Blueberry, lemon poppyseed, and cranberry nut muffins baked in seasoned muffin pans.

Panning and Baking

The formulas that follow can be baked as a quick bread in parchment-lined loaf pans or as muffins in seasoned muffin pans (Figure 14-4). Muffin and loaf pans vary in size. These batters will double in size when baked.

To determine the correct weight of the batter you need, fill the pan with water halfway and weigh the water. The weight of the water is equal to the amount of batter needed to fill the pan before baking. To achieve a **crown** (protrusion above the pan line) on your product, increase the weight of the batter by 10 percent. Quick breads are baked at 350°F (180°C) and the muffins at 380°F (190°C). If you desire a split in the quick-bread loaf, increase the baking temperature by 30°F (3°C).

Take note of the changes in the formulas in this unit. Compare them with the ratios that we have studied thus far. The ratio of sugar and fats has increased, and the ratio of liquid to flour has changed, creating a more fluid mix. We now have to bake in a form. The ingredient sequence and mixing or blending have also changed. We need additional ingredients such as chemical leavenors, baking soda, and baking powder.

Variations

You can create signature breads and muffins by adding a variety of ingredients:
- Blueberry muffins: Add 1 lb (450 g) of blueberries and 1 oz (30 g) of lemon juice (Figure 14-5).
- Apple walnut muffins: Add 12 oz (340 g) of apples, 4 oz (110 g) of walnuts, and 1 oz (30 g) of maple syrup.
- Cranberry orange muffins: Add 8 oz (230 g) of cranberries and 1 oz (30 g) of orange zest.
- Chocolate chip tea loaf: Add 12 oz of chocolate chips (340 g) and 1 oz (30 g) of vanilla.
- Dundee tea loaf: Add 12 oz (340 g) of diced candied fruit.
- Black and white drop cake: Add 6 oz (170 g) of flour and deposit on sheet pan with a #20 scoop. After baking, ice one-half of the cake with vanilla fondant and the other half with chocolate fondant.

Figure 14-5 Blueberry muffins baked in oven-proof cups.

The tea bread or muffin formula is a chemically leavened batter. The creaming method of mixing is used. With quick breads, the method of mixing changes to a single stage mixing method, due to the higher percentage of liquids. These formulas are balanced to support added ingredients such as nuts and fruit.

master tea bread/muffin   Yield: 6 lb 14 oz (3,260 g)

% Ratio	Ingredients	Lb	Oz	Metric	Procedures
66	Sugar	1	8	680 g	Cream the sugar, shortening, butter, and salt.
22	Shortening		8	230 g	
22	Butter		8	230 g	
2	Salt		1/2	10 g	
44	Eggs	1		450 g	Add the eggs in three stages to the creamed mixture.
3	Baking powder		1 1/2	40 g	Sift the baking powder and flour. Add the sifted ingredients to the creamed mixture, alternating with the milk. Pour into pans or tins. Bread: Bake at 350°F (180°C) for approximately 30 minutes. Muffins: Bake at 380°F (193°C) for approximately 20 minutes.
100	Pastry flour	2	4	1,020 g	
44	Milk	1		450 g	

NUTRITIONAL INFORMATION PER 3 OZ (90 G) SERVING: 301 Calories; 13 g Fat (39.1% calories from fat); 4 g Protein; 42 g Carbohydrate; trace Dietary Fiber; 61 mg Cholesterol; 350 mg Sodium. Exchanges: 1 1/2 Grain (Starch); 0 Lean Meat; 0 Nonfat Milk; 2 1/2 Fat; 1 1/2 Other Carbohydrates.

CHEF'S TIP: *Do not overbake quick breads. To determine whether or not your bread is done, look for visual clues. Quick breads should have a golden-brown top and they will pull away from the sides of the pans when they are done. The quick bread or muffin should also have a slight resistance to finger pressure. You can use a cake tester (a rigid stainless steel wire with a loop handle) to see if your bread is done.*

zucchini bread   Yield: 8 lb 9 3/4 oz (3,910 g)

% Ratio	Ingredients	Lb	Oz	Metric	Procedures
142	Zucchini (grated)	2	8	1,130 g	Peel the zucchini (peel 50 percent, leaving it striped like a zebra). Split the zucchini, remove seeds, and grate. Combine all ingredients in one stage. Whip for five minutes with a standard mixer at medium speed.
128	Sugar	2	4	1,020 g	
43	Eggs		12	340 g	Pour into pans or tins. Bread: Bake at 350°F (177°C) for approximately 30 minutes.
1	Baking soda		1/4	5 g	
2	Salt		1/2	10 g	Muffins: Bake at 380°F (193°C) for approximately 20 minutes.
43	Vegetable oil		12	340 g	
1	Ground clove		1/4	5 g	
1	Ground cinnamon		1/4	5 g	
2	Baking powder		1/2	10 g	
100	Bread flour	1	12	790 g	
28	Pecans or walnuts		8	230 g	

NUTRITIONAL INFORMATION PER 3 OZ (90 G) SERVING: 266 Calories; 12 g Fat (39.6% calories from fat); 4 g Protein; 37 g Carbohydrate; 1 g Dietary Fiber; 27 mg Cholesterol; 208 mg Sodium. Exchanges: 1 Grain (Starch); 0 Lean Meat; 0 Vegetable; 2 Fat; 1 1/2 Other Carbohydrates.

LEARNING ACTIVITY 14-1

Mix one formula of banana nut bread (page 298) with very ripe, brown bananas and one formula with fresh yellow bananas. Which type of banana produces the best bread? Record your observations in the following chart.

Type of Bananas	Evaluation
Very ripe, brown bananas	
Very fresh, yellow bananas	

CHEF'S TIP: *To ripen bananas quickly, place them in the refrigerator overnight.*

pumpkin bread   *Yield: 9 lb 2 oz (4,140 g)*

% Ratio	Ingredients	Lb	Oz	Metric	Procedures
100	Pumpkin, canned	1	12	790 g	Combine the pumpkin with the sugar, eggs, baking soda, salt, and spices. Mix with a standard mixer for 5 minutes with paddle attachment.
128	Sugar	2	4	1,020 g	
43	Eggs		12	340 g	
1	Baking soda		1/4	5 g	
2	Salt		1/2	10 g	
1	Ground clove		1/4	5 g	
1	Ground cinnamon		1/4	5 g	
43	Vegetable oil		12	340 g	Gradually add the oil, flour, and baking powder, which have been sifted together.
100	Bread flour	1	12	790 g	
2	Baking powder		1/2	15 g	
57	Raisins	1		450 g	Add the water and raisins. Pour into pans or tins. Bread: Bake at 350°F (180°C) for approximately 30 minutes. Muffins: Bake at 380°F (190°C) for approximately 20 minutes.
43	Water		12	340 g	

NUTRITIONAL INFORMATION PER 3 OZ (90 G) SERVING: 250 Calories; 8 g Fat (28.4% calories from fat); 3 g Protein; 43 g Carbohydrate; 1 g Dietary Fiber; 26 mg Cholesterol; 166 mg Sodium. Exchanges: 1 Grain (Starch); 0 Lean Meat; 1/2 Vegetable; 1/2 Fruit; 1 1/2 Fat; 1 1/2 Other Carbohydrates.

banana nut bread *Yield: 11 lb 9 oz (5,240 g)*

% Ratio	Ingredients	Lb	Oz	Metric	Procedures
100	Cake flour	2	8	1,130 g	Combine the sifted flour and shortening.
50	Shortening	1	4	570 g	
1	Orange zest		1/2	10 g	Add the mashed bananas and orange zest and mix until smooth.
100	Bananas	2	8	1,130 g	
100	Sugar	2	8	1,130 g	Add the sugar, milk powder, salt, and baking powder. Mix with a standard mixer for 3 minutes.
12	Milk powder		5	140 g	
2	Salt		1	30 g	
3	Baking powder		1 1/2	40 g	
50	Eggs	1	4	570 g	Add the eggs in two stages.
20	Honey		8	230 g	Add the honey, pecans, and vanilla. Mix 5 minutes at medium speed with paddle attachment. Pour into pans or tins. Bread: Bake at 350°F (180°C) for approximately 30 minutes. Muffins: Bake at 380°F (190°C) for approximately 20 minutes.
20	Pecans or walnuts		8	230 g	
2	Vanilla		1	30 g	

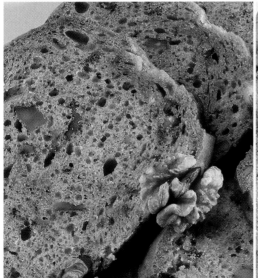

NUTRITIONAL INFORMATION PER 3 OZ (90 G) SERVING: 294 Calories; 13 g Fat (40.4% calories from fat); 4 g Protein; 41 g Carbohydrate; 1 g Dietary Fiber; 36 mg Cholesterol; 273 mg Sodium. Exchanges: 1 Grain (Starch); 0 Lean Meat; 0 Fruit; 0 Nonfat Milk; 2 1/2 Fat; 1 1/2 Other Carbohydrates.

cornbread/muffins
Yield: 6 lb 3 oz (2,810 g)

% Ratio	Ingredients	Lb	Oz	Metric	Procedures
50	Cornmeal		12	340 g	Hydrate the cornmeal by soaking it in the milk overnight.
100	Milk	1	8	680 g	
75	Sugar	1	2	510 g	Blend the sugar, corn oil, salt, and eggs.
42	Corn oil		10	280 g	
1	Salt		1	30 g	
8	Eggs		8	230 g	
2	Baking powder		2	60 g	Sift the baking powder and the flour. Add it to the blended mixture. Add the cornmeal and milk. Mix with a standard mixer only until blended. Pour into pans, tins, or molds. Bread: Bake at 350°F (180°C) for approximately 30 minutes. Muffins: Bake at 380°F (190°C) for approximately 20 minutes.
100	Pastry flour	1	8	680 g	

NUTRITIONAL INFORMATION PER 3 OZ (90 G) SERVING: 270 Calories; 10 g Fat (33.8% calories from fat); 4 g Protein; 41 g Carbohydrate; 1 g Dietary Fiber; 28 mg Cholesterol; 533 mg Sodium. Exchanges: 1 1/2 Grain (Starch); 0 Lean Meat; 0 Nonfat Milk; 2 Fat; 1 Other Carbohydrates.
NOTE: For corn bread, reduce the sugar by 50 percent and add 10 percent more corn oil.
Overmixing reduces the leavening and makes the muffins tough.

DOUGHNUTS

Many consider the doughnut as a truly American morning delicacy (Figure 14-6). The truth is, the doughnut originated as a Dutch refreshment in the late 1800s. In every culture, bakers have had to deal with leftover bits of dough. The Dutch twisted their leftovers, creating knots of dough, which they fried in hot oil. When the treat was brought to the United States, it didn't take long before a fan, who didn't like the doughy centers, thought of a way to improve the product by inventing the hole. The **doughnut** of today can be described as a round cake, usually with a center hole, made of yeast or baking powder dough and cooked in hot deep fat.

Many doughnut shops use special equipment to produce high-volume, high-quality doughnuts. The following formulas are hand-cut and can be made in a typical bakery without the use of specialized equipment. They will add variety to your breakfast menu. Unit 6 describes the equipment you will

Figure 14-6 Powdered sugar is sprinkled over freshly cooked doughnuts.

yeast doughnuts *Yield: 6 lb 7 oz (2,920 g)*

Ingredients	Lb	Oz	Metric	Procedures
Sugar		4	110 g	Cream the first five ingredients.
Salt		1/2	10 g	
Milk powder		1 1/2	40 g	
Shortening		3	90 g	
Eggs		4	110 g	
Yeast		2	60 g	Dissolve the yeast in water.
Water	2		900 g	
Bread flour	3	8	1,590 g	Add the flour to the creamed ingredients, followed by the yeast solution. Develop the dough for 10 minutes at first speed. Ferment at room temperature for 40 minutes before make-up.

Make-up procedure
1. Roll rested dough into 1/2-in-thick rectangular shapes.
2. Cut with a doughnut cutter.
3. Place on flour-dusted canvas cloth and proof in a dry proof box at 90°F (30°C) for 20 to 30 minutes until the dough is almost doubled in size.
4. Transfer to a frying screen if using a commercial fryer. Place screen into the hot oil.
5. Fry at 360°F (180°C); when the bottom is light-brown, flip to fry the top, being careful to get even color on both sides.

Total frying time is approximately 5 minutes.
Glaze with icing or dust with powdered sugar if desired.

NUTRITIONAL INFORMATION PER 1 1/2 OZ (40 G) SERVING (before frying): 109 Calories; 2 g Fat (16.5% calories from fat); 3 g Protein; 19 g Carbohydrate; trace Dietary Fiber; 7 mg Cholesterol; 86 mg Sodium. Exchanges: 1 Grain (Starch); 0 Lean Meat; 0 Nonfat Milk; 1/2 Fat; 0 Other Carbohydrates.
NOTE: Round yeast doughnuts, without a hole, can be filled with jelly to become a **Berliner.** Traditionally they were served on New Year's Day and also contained a prize.

NUTS AND FRUITS

A variety of nuts and dried fruit can be added to heavier batters such as pound cake, wine cakes, and muffin batters. More information on nuts and fruits can be found in Unit 5.

BALANCING CAKE FORMULAS

Although cakes are produced in varieties limited only by the imagination and ingenuity of the baker, there are, in reality, just two basic types of cakes—those that do not contain shortening and those with shortening.

Angel food and sponge cake fall within the first class; pound cakes, layer cakes, and hi-ratio cakes fall within the second. Cake consists of relatively few ingredients, but all must be of high quality and balanced in the formula to produce top-notch cakes. There are times when a baker must balance a formula. For example, let's say you are working at a resort that is 20 miles from town. An inventory error leaves you with a 10 percent shortage on the amount of sugar you will need for a cake formula. Since sugar is considered a tenderizer, it should be balanced against the stabilizers in the formula by the same percentage. So in this example the flour and egg whites would need to be reduced by 10 percent. Read on to get a further understanding.

The major ingredients in cake formulas are:

1. Sugar
2. Flour
3. Eggs
4. Shortening (except angel food and sponge cake types)
5. Water/milk
6. Leavenors

Salt and added flavors are also important to the finished cake, but they are only incidental in balancing a formula. Balancing the formula has four aspects:

1. It is necessary to form a stable structure capable of retaining gas generated by the leavening agents.
2. Ingredients that are stabilizers are balanced against those that impart tenderness.
3. Ingredients that impart moisture must be balanced against ingredients that absorb moisture.
4. Creaming, foaming, and chemical leavening must be balanced to provide sufficient leavening of the cake.

Sugar in all its forms, shortening, egg yolk, and leavening agents are considered tenderizers. Flour, milk solids, and egg white are stabilizers. Sugar, liquids, and eggs are moisteners or moisture retainers, and flour absorbs moisture. Any good cake formula must strike a balance between stabilizers and tenderizers, and moisture and dryness; at the same time, the formula should produce a suitable emulsion. Thus, sugar is balanced against flour; shortening against eggs; and, if milk is used, the total weight of the eggs and the milk is balanced against the sugar. When milk is introduced to a formula, a chemical leavenor must be added. Eggs are natural leavenors, but milk is not.

Figure 15-5 Angel food cake.

Balance in a cake cannot be stated as a mathematical equation because each of the major ingredients allows a range of tolerance within which the skillful baker can exercise his or her knowledge and art. This principle is what allows the baker to create a large variety of cakes.

Now let's compare the basic types of cakes.

ANGEL FOOD/SPONGE/GENOISE CAKES

This class of cake contains little or no additional fat. The leavening is accomplished by foaming a sugar and egg mixture and lightly folding in the sifted flour. The angel food cake is baked in clean, ungreased tube pans; the tube adds support to the center of the cake, allowing for more height and leavening (Figure 15–5). The angel food cake gets supported by clinging to the pan sides and center support tube. Teflon pans should not be used because they cause the batter to slip.

Sponge cakes are light, rich cakes made with egg whites. They can be baked in several different forms. When baked in flat sheet pans, it can be used to make jelly rolls or **roulades,** which are sponge cakes that are filled with creams or jams and rolled. When sponge cake is baked in cake pans, it is the base for cream-filled cakes.

Genoise is a sponge cake with melted butter folded in at the last stage. Genoise cakes should be baked in either flat sheet pans or cake rounds.

basic angel food cake formula   *Yield: 4 lb 9 1/4 oz (2,080 g)*

% Ratio	Ingredients	Lb	Oz	Metric	Procedures
94	Egg whites	1		450 g	Whip the egg whites to a **soft peak.**
23	Sugar		4	110 g	Add the sugar and cream of tartar to the whipped egg whites.
1/2	Cream of tartar		1/4	5 g	
100	Cake flour	1	1	480 g	Continue to whip; sift the second sugar and the flour, and fold in by hand.
211	Sugar	2	4	1,020 g	Bake at 350°F to 375°F (180° to 190°C), depending on the pan size, for approximately 20 minutes for each pound of batter. Test doneness by lightly pressing on the cake top. It should feel springy to the touch. The cake will also pull away from the sides of the pan when it is done. After removing the cake from the oven, invert the pan to cool. After the cake is cool; use a sharp crack on the bench to release it from the pan.

NUTRITIONAL INFORMATION PER 2 OZ (60 G) SERVING SIZE:
177 Calories; trace Fat (0.6% calories from fat); 2 g Protein; 42 g Carbohydrate; trace Dietary Fiber; 0 mg Cholesterol; 21 mg Sodium. Exchanges: 1/2 Grain (Starch); 0 Lean Meat; 0 Fruit; 2 Other Carbohydrates.

Angel Food Cake Ratios

1. The weight of sugar equals the weight of the egg whites.
2. The weight of flour is approximately one-third the weight of the sugar and eggs.

Sponge Cake/Foaming Mixing Methods

Sponge cakes contain little or no shortening, resulting in a "sponge" or "spring-like" texture. Three basic methods can be used for mixing sponge cakes: (1) the cold-foaming method; (2) the warm-foaming method; and (3) the separation-foaming method. Most formulas will designate the preferred mixing method.

COLD-FOAMING METHOD (FIGURE 15-6)

1. Place the eggs and the sugar in a mixing bowl; whip on medium speed for 35 to 45 minutes.
2. Sift all dry ingredients two or three times to incorporate maximum air.
3. Fold the sifted, dry ingredients into the egg mixture.
4. Fold in the melted butter or milk.
5. Portion into cake pans.
6. Bake at 400°F (200°C) for approximately 35 minutes.

WARM-FOAMING METHOD (FIGURE 15-7)

1. Combine the eggs and the sugar in a mixing bowl; place over a double boiler and lightly whip the eggs until the mixture has reached 110°F (43°C).
2. Whip the egg mixture at high speed. (**Note:** Once the eggs reach their full volume, continue whipping at high speed until they recede or drop in volume.)
3. Reduce the speed of the mixer to low; whip for an additional 10 minutes. (**Note:** The mixture can be left at this stage if necessary.)
4. Sift all of the dry ingredients two or three times to incorporate maximum air.
5. Fold the sifted, dry ingredients into the egg mixture.
6. Fold in the melted butter with a liaison of the whipped egg mixture.
7. Portion into cake pans.
8. Bake at high heat, 400°F (200°C), for approximately 35 minutes.

Figure 15-6 Cold-foaming method.

Figure 15-7 Warm-foaming method.

The sponge cake formula introduces the use of egg foams as a leavening agent for cake batters. Clean equipment, proper foaming of the egg-sugar mixture, and double sifting of the flour are the key steps in this formula. Once you have mastered this formula, you can produce many variations.

sponge cake/yellow sponge (genoise) *Yield: 7 lb 6 oz (3,350 g)*

% Ratio	Ingredients	Lb	Oz	Metric	Procedures
160	Eggs	3		1,360 g	The cornstarch plus the flour equal 100 percent for formula balancing. The warm-foaming method is the recommended mixing procedure for this formula.
100	Sugar	1	14	850 g	Combine the eggs and sugar in a mixing bowl.
64	Cake flour	1	6	620 g	Place over a double boiler (bain marie); lightly whip the eggs until the mixture reaches 110°F (43°C).
36	Cornstarch		8	230 g	
33	Melted butter		10	280 g	

Whip the egg mixture at high speed. Once the eggs reach their full volume, continue whipping at high speed until they **recede** or drop in volume. Reduce the speed of mixer to low; whip for an additional 10 minutes.

Sift all of the dry ingredients two or three times to incorporate maximum air.

Fold the sifted, dry ingredients into the egg mixture.

Melt the butter in a saucepan, and fold it into the mixture.

Portion into cake pans.
Bake at 375° to 390°F (190° to 200°C), depending on pan size, for approximately 35 minutes.

Using your index finger, touch the cake lightly in the center. If the cake feels springy and indentation fills up when you remove your finger, the cake is done.

NUTRITIONAL INFORMATION PER 2 OZ (60 G) SERVING: 141 Calories; 2 g Fat (15.6% calories from fat); 3 g Protein; 26 g Carbohydrate; trace Dietary Fiber; 84 mg Cholesterol; 29 mg Sodium. Exchanges: 1 Grain (Starch); 1/2 Lean Meat; 1/2 Fat; 1 Other Carbohydrates

Figure 15-8 Eggs are first separated before starting the separation-foaming method.

SEPARATION-FOAMING METHOD (FIGURE 15-8)

1. Separate the eggs; put the yolks in one mixing bowl and the whites in another.
2. Put 1/3 of the sugar with the yolks and whip until doubled in size.
3. Put the remaining 2/3 of the sugar in with the whites; heat to 110°F (43°C) over a water bath. Whip on high speed to the soft-peak stage.
4. Sift the dry ingredients two or three times.
5. Fold the egg yolk foam and the egg white foam together.
6. Fold in the sifted, dry ingredients.
7. Fold in the melted butter.
8. Bake at high heat, 400°F (200°C), for approximately 35 minutes.

Sponge Cake Ratios

1. The weight of the sugar equals, or exceeds, the weight of the eggs.
2. The total weight of the liquids, including the eggs, exceeds the weight of the sugar.
3. The weight of the sugar or the eggs exceeds the weight of the flour.
4. The total weight of the eggs and the flour exceeds the total weight of the sugar and the liquids.
5. This ratio is for American sponge cakes. The European genoise ratio contains less sugar.

Yellow Sponge for Jelly Rolls/Roulade

Jelly rolls or roulades are made by using the sponge cake formula and the separation mixing method. The butter is eliminated. (See Unit 19, "Specialty Cakes and Tortes," for the make-up instructions for roulades.)

Trouble-Shooting Sponge Cake

Problem	Solution
Cake is tough	Add more sugar; don't overmix the batter; lower the oven temperature
Cake is heavy with sticky layer on the bottom	Beat the eggs properly; fully mix the eggs with the other ingredients; add the milk and butter at room temperature, not hotter
Cracks in the crust	Don't overbeat the eggs; reduce the amount of sugar; decrease oven temperature.
Sticky crust	Decrease the amount of sugar; bake longer
Poor volume	Avoid overmixing; use the smaller pan; increase baking time; use a clean mixing bowl that is free of grease
Lumps in the cake	Dissolve the sugar completely; sift the flour

NOTE: When mixing sponge cake, create a liaison of beaten eggs and melted butter before adding the flour. This will prevent the formation of flour lumps caused by contact with melted butter.

chocolate sponge cake *Yield: 7 lb 1 1/2 oz (3,220 g)*

% Ratio	Ingredients	Lb	Oz	Metric	Procedures
160	Eggs	3		1,360 g	The cornstarch, cocoa, and flour equal 100 percent for formula balancing. Since all are stabilizers, the warm-foaming method is the recommended mixing procedure for this formula.
100	Sugar	1	14	850 g	
54	Cake flour	1		450 g	Bake at 375° to 390°F (190° to 200°C) depending on pan size. Bake for approximately 35 minutes. Sponge cakes will spring back when tested with a fork.
30	Cornstarch		9	260 g	
16	Cocoa		5	140 g	
1/2	Baking soda		1/2	15 g	
16	Melted butter		5	140 g	

NUTRITIONAL INFORMATION PER 2 OZ (60 G) SERVING: 160 Calories; 5 g Fat (24.7% calories from fat); 4 g Protein; 27 g Carbohydrate; 1 g Dietary Fiber; 93 mg Cholesterol; 117 mg Sodium. Exchanges: 1 Grain (Starch); 1/2 Lean Meat; 1/2 Fat; 1 Other Carbohydrates.

American sponge cake *Yield 10 lb 2 1/2 oz (4,600 g)*

% Ratio	Ingredients	Lb	Oz	Metric	Procedures
100	Sugar	3		1,360 g	The cold-foaming method is the recommended mixing procedure for this formula.
84	Eggs	2	8	1,130 g	
100	Cake flour	3		1,360 g	Pour the batter into any type of pan that is lined with parchment paper or sprayed with a pan release.
5	Baking powder		2 1/2	70 g	
50	Milk	1	8	680 g	

Bake at 375° to 390°F (190° to 200°C), depending on pan size, for approximately 35 minutes.

NUTRITIONAL INFORMATION PER 2 OZ (60 G) SERVING: 144 Calories; 1 g Fat (8.3% calories from fat); 3 g Protein; 30 g Carbohydrate; trace Dietary Fiber; 51 mg Cholesterol; 108 mg Sodium. Exchanges: 1 Grain (Starch); 0 Lean Meat; 0 Fat; 1 Other Carbohydrates.

POUND CAKE AND LAYER CAKE

This class of cakes uses another mixing method—the creaming method, which was previously introduced in Unit 13 with the discussion on cookies. The term "pound cake" comes from the original formula in which 1 pound of each ingredient was used—1 pound of sugar, 1 pound of butter, 1 pound of eggs, and 1 pound of flour. Modern formulas include liquids such as milk as well as a chemical leavenor (Figure 15-9). Pound cakes, or layer cakes, are generally baked in loaf form or tube pan and can support added ingredients such as raisins, nuts, and chocolate chips.

Creaming Mixing Method

Air is introduced during the creaming, or first step, of this method. Sugar contains thousands of small crystals that dissolve and are absorbed by the shortening, leaving thousands of tiny air pockets to fill the void where the crystals were, and expand in the oven while heated. As the batter is heated, these air cells expand to leaven the item.

1. Cream the fat and the sugar together (Figure 15-10).
2. Add the flavorings; mix well.
3. Gradually add the eggs, which should be tempered to room temperature.
4. Add the liquid. (If adding a large amount of liquid, alternate with flour.)
5. Add the sifted flour.
6. Mix until smooth (do not overmix).

Mixing Precautions

ADDING EGGS

Always add eggs slowly, in three stages. After adding the first stage, continue beating until the egg disappears into the mass before adding the additional stages. Continue beating until the egg disappears into the mass in a perfect blending before adding another egg.

ADDING LIQUIDS

Be very careful not to let the batter curdle, which is the separation of the fat and liquid. This is more likely to occur in warm weather. Using hi-ratio shortening will alleviate this problem. If not, add part of the required measurement of flour and beat until the curdling disappears before adding any more ingredients. The flour will absorb the excess moisture and pro-

Figure 15-9 Pound cake.   **Figure 15-10** Creaming.

mote normal creaming. Curdling may come from the heat on the shortening or from adding the eggs too rapidly.

BEATING

Avoid over-beating after adding the flour and milk. If the previous blending has been done correctly and the total possible volume has been secured, the last ingredients require only enough mixing to make a smooth batter. Overmixing can stir out part of the air already incorporated and overdevelop the gluten, which can spoil the final texture.

Mixing Temperature

Temperature plays an important part in the quality of the cake. The best batter is mixed at 70°F (20°C) throughout the entire mixing process. This means that all ingredients should be at room temperature before mixing begins. Avoid adding eggs or milk right from the refrigerator. Follow the previous advice on how to safely bring them to room temperature.

Pound Cake/Layer Cake Ratios

1. The weight of the sugar equals or exceeds the weight of the flour.
2. The weight of the eggs equals or exceeds the weight of the shortening.
3. The weight of the eggs and other liquids equals or exceeds the weight of the sugar.

almond pound cake   *Yield: 4 lb 2 1/4 oz (1,900 g)*

% Ratio	Ingredients	Lb	Oz	Metric	Procedures
100	Sugar	1		450 g	Mix the sugar, almond paste, and flour.
13	Almond paste		2	60 g	
13	Cake flour		2	60 g	
88	Butter		14	400 g	Cream these ingredients with butter.
50	Eggs		8	230 g	Blend the eggs, egg yolks, and milk and add slowly to the creamed ingredients.
50	Egg yolks		8	230 g	
13	Milk		2	60 g	
50	Cake flour		8	230 g	Sift the flours with baking powder; then fold into the mixture. Bake at 325° to 340°F (160° to 170°C), depending on pan size, for approximately 35 minutes.
37	Bread flour		6	170 g	
1/2	Baking powder		1/4	5 g	

NUTRITIONAL INFORMATION PER 2 OZ (60 G) SERVING: 232 Calories; 13 g Fat (50.6% calories from fat); 4 g Protein; 25 g Carbohydrate; trace Dietary Fiber; 139 mg Cholesterol; 134 mg Sodium. Exchanges: 1 Grain (Starch); 0 Lean Meat; 0 Nonfat Milk; 2 1/2 Fat; 1 Other Carbohydrates.

This pound cake formula contains equal amounts of sugar, butter, eggs, and flour. When properly creamed, it is the hallmark of this class of cakes. Pound cakes contain a high percentage of fat, which makes them moist, flavorful, and shelf-stable.

old-fashioned pound cake *Yield: 4 lb (1,800 g)*

% Ratio	Ingredients	Lb	Oz	Metric	Procedures
100	Sugar	1		450 g	The creaming method is the recommended mixing procedure for this formula. Cream the fat and sugar together. Add the flavorings; mix well.
100	Butter	1		450 g	
100	Eggs	1		450 g	
100	Bread flour	1		450 g	

Gradually add the eggs. (All ingredients should be at room temperature.)

Add the liquid. (If adding a large amount of liquid, alternate with the addition of the flour.)

Add the flour.

Mix until smooth (do not overmix).

Bake at 275° to 300°F (140° to 150°C), depending on pan size, for approximately 35 minutes. Cooled cakes should be removed from the pan and dusted with powdered sugar if desired.

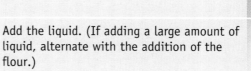

NUTRITIONAL INFORMATION PER 2 OZ (60 G) SERVING: 226 Calories; 13 g Fat (51.0% calories from fat); 3 g Protein; 25 g Carbohydrate; trace Dietary Fiber; 82 mg Cholesterol; 133 mg Sodium. Exchanges: 1/2 Grain (Starch); 0 Lean Meat; 2 1/2 Fat; 1 Other Carbohydrates.

yellow layer cake *Yield: 11 lb (5,060 g)*

% Ratio	Ingredients	Lb	Oz	Metric	Procedures
125	Sugar	3	2	1,410 g	The creaming method is the recommended mixing procedure for this formula.
63	Butter	1	9	700 g	
60	Eggs	1	8	680 g	Bake at 360° to 385°F (180° to 200°C), depending on pan size, for approximately 35 minutes.
100	Cake flour	2	8	1,130 g	
3	Baking powder		1 1/4	35 g	
1	Salt		1/2	10 g	
95	Skim milk	2	6	1,090 g	

NUTRITIONAL INFORMATION PER 2 OZ (60 G) SERVING: 181 Calories; 7 g Fat (36.0% calories from fat); 2 g Protein; 27 g Carbohydrate; trace Dietary Fiber; 46 mg Cholesterol; 187 mg Sodium. Exchanges: 1/2 Grain (Starch); 0 Lean Meat; 0 Nonfat Milk; 1 1/2 Fat; 1 Other Carbohydrates.

NOTE: To make a chocolate layer cake, fold in 14 oz. (400 g) of melted baker's chocolate to the yellow layer cake formula.

yellow loaf cake formula *Yield: 6 lb 8 oz (2,950 g)*

% Ratio	Ingredients	Lb	Oz	Metric	Procedures
117	Sugar	1	12	800 g	The creaming method is the recommended mixing procedure for this formula.
66	Butter	1		450 g	
1	Salt		1/2	10 g	This formula is excellent for loaf and tube cake forms.
1	Orange extract		1/2	10 g	
1	Lemon extract		1/2	10 g	Bake at 360° to 385°F (180° to 200°C), depending on pan size, for approximately 35 minutes.
46	Egg yolks		11	310 g	
46	Eggs		11	310 g	
100	Cake flour	1	8	680 g	
3	Baking powder		3/4	20 g	
50	Milk		12	340 g	

NUTRITIONAL INFORMATION PER 2 OZ (60 G) SERVING: 204 Calories; 10 g Fat (43.1% calories from fat); 3 g Protein; 26 g Carbohydrate; trace Dietary Fiber; 118 mg Cholesterol; 234 mg Sodium. Exchanges: 1/2 Grain (Starch); 0 Lean Meat; 0 Nonfat Milk; 2 Fat; 1 Other Carbohydrates.

HI-RATIO CAKES

In the 1930s, shortening manufacturers introduced new cake shortenings. These shortenings allowed for greater amounts of sugar and liquid in formulations, producing lighter, moister, and more tender cakes. The higher percentage of sugar changed the mixing sequence. Ingredients were mixed in two stages: the first stage combined the dry ingredients mixed with one-third of the liquids; the second stage added the balance of the liquids. The term "hi-ratio" indicates that the sugar is greater than the flour. This two-stage mixing process made possible the development of pre-scaled box mixes. Pre-scaled signature box mixes allow the baker to obtain uniformity by eliminating scaling errors and reducing ingredient inventory. The baker can develop quality hi-ratio cake formulas after reviewing the hi-ratio cake ratios. These cakes do not rely on the foaming or creaming methods because they are leavened with baking powder. To get uniform results, keep the mixing time under 10 minutes. Overmixing can cause the cake to have an open-grain texture. The amount of air incorporated during mixing can be determined by measuring the specific gravity of the batter.

Measuring Specific Gravity of Batter

Specific gravity is the weight of the batter divided by the weight of an equal volume of water. To measure specific gravity, fill a 10 oz (280 g) cup with batter taken from the first stage after 3 minutes of mixing (Figure 15-11). Weigh the batter from the cup and divide it by 10. In this case the water is 10 oz. The answer equals the specific gravity of the batter. The more air that is mixed into the batter, the lower the specific gravity number. Most bakers feel that 9.5 is the ideal specific gravity for the best results in hi-ratio cakes. Hi-ratio cake formulas are used for sheet cakes, loaf cakes, and layer cakes; and they make excellent cupcakes. The importance of measuring specific gravity is to control the amount of air incorporated during the mixing of the batter. The best result is obtained when the specific gravity is measured.

Hi-Ratio Cake Ratios

1. The weight of sugar is equal to or greater than the weight of flour.
2. The weight of liquid is equal to or greater than the weight of sugar.
3. The weight of shortening is less than the weight of eggs.
4. The leavening is 3/4 oz (20 g) per pound (450 g) of flour.
5. Tenderizers are equal to or greater than the stabilizers.
6. The term "greater than" is 50 percent or less of the total weight of the original ingredients.

TWO-STAGE MIXING METHOD

1. Mix all of the dry ingredients, shortening, and 1/3 of the blended liquid (eggs and milk); mix for 4 minutes at medium speed.
2. Add the balance of the liquid in two stages; mix for an additional 4 minutes at medium speed.
3. Scrape down the sides, bottom, and paddle of the bowl with each addition of liquids.

Figure 15-11 To measure the specific gravity of batter weigh an equal amount by volume of batter and water and divide the weight of the batter by the weight of the water.

This benchmark formula introduces the two-stage mixing method and the use of emulsified shortening. The emulsified shortening allows for a higher percentage of liquid and sugar. Note that the term "high" or "hi ratio" indicates that these formulas have a higher percentage of sugar than flour.

hi-ratio cake *Yield: 8 lb 10 oz (3,910 g)*

% Ratio	Ingredients	Lb	Oz	Metric	Procedures
100	Sugar	2	8	1,130 g	Use the two-stage mixing method. Mix all of the dry ingredients.
2 1/2	Salt		1	30 g	
48	Cake shortening	1	3	540 g	
5	Baking powder		2	60 g	
100	Cake flour	2	8	1,130 g	
20	Milk		8	230 g	Add the shortening and 1/3 of the blended liquid (eggs and milk); mix for 4 minutes at medium speed.
40	Eggs	1		450 g	Add the balance of the liquid in two stages. Mix for an additional 4 minutes at medium speed.
10	Egg yolks		4	110 g	
20	Milk		8	230 g	Scrape down the sides, bottom, and paddle of the bowl with each addition of liquids.

Bake at 375° to 390°F (190° to 200°C), depending on pan size, for approximately 35 minutes.

NUTRITIONAL INFORMATION PER 2 OZ (60 G) SERVING: 211 Calories; 9 g Fat (39.1% calories from fat); 3 g Protein; 30 g Carbohydrate; trace Dietary Fiber; 46 mg Cholesterol; 258 mg Sodium. Exchanges: 1 Grain (Starch); 0 Lean Meat; 0 Nonfat Milk; 1 1/2 Fat; 1 Other Carbohydrates.

hi-ratio chocolate cake
Yield: 10 lb 7 1/2 oz (4,750g)

% Ratio	Ingredients	Lb	Oz	Metric	Procedures
140	Sugar	3	8	1,590 g	Use the two-stage mixing method.
80	Cake flour	2		900 g	
20	Cocoa		8	230 g	The cocoa and cake flour combined make up 100% of the formula. Sift all of the dry ingredients to blend the cocoa. Dissolve the baking soda in the milk before adding it to the mix.
4	Salt		1 1/2	40 g	
40	Cake ~~flour~~ *SHORTENING*	1		450 g	
4	Baking powder		1 1/2	40 g	
70	Skim milk	1	12	790 g	Bake at 375° to 390°F (190° to 200°C), depending on pan size, for approximately 35 minutes.
1	Baking soda		1/2	10 g	
60	Eggs	1	8	680 g	

NUTRITIONAL INFORMATION PER 2 OZ (60 G) SERVING: 154 Calories; 1 g Fat (6.9% calories from fat); 3 g Protein; 34 g Carbohydrate; 1 g Dietary Fiber; 30 mg Cholesterol; 314 mg Sodium. Exchanges: 1 Grain (Starch); 0 Lean Meat; 0 Nonfat Milk; 0 Fat; 1 1/2 Other Carbohydrates.

hi-ratio white cake
Yield: 12 lb 2 1/2 oz (5,510 g)

% Ratio	Ingredients	Lb	Oz	Metric	Procedures
116	Sugar	3	8	1,590 g	Use the two-stage mixing method.
100	Cake flour	3		1,360 g	
46	Cake shortening	1	6	620 g	Bake at 375° to 390°F (190° to 200°C), depending on pan size, for approximately 35 minutes.
3	Salt		1 1/2	40 g	
6	Baking powder		3	90 g	
66	Milk	2		900 g	
50	Egg whites	1	8	680 g	
16	Eggs		8	230 g	

NUTRITIONAL INFORMATION PER 2 OZ (60 G) SERVING: 184 Calories; 7 g Fat (34.3% calories from fat); 2 g Protein; 28 g Carbohydrate; trace Dietary Fiber; 10 mg Cholesterol; 282 mg Sodium. Exchanges: 1 Grain (Starch); 0 Lean Meat; 0 Nonfat Milk; 1 1/2 Fat; 1 Other Carbohydrates.

Chiffon Cake-Mixing Methods

1. Blend together all of the dry ingredients except the sugar for the meringue.
2. Add oil, whole eggs, and water slowly; mix for 3 minutes on slow speed. Do not overmix.
3. In a separate bowl, beat the egg whites and the cream of tartar to form a soft peak; add the sugar and whip until stiff.
4. Fold the beaten egg whites into the batter.

COMBINATION CAKES (CHIFFON CAKES)

Chiffon cakes are a type of sponge cake. They combine the standard cake-mixing method and the foam method of mixing (Figure 15-12). Chiffon cakes are made with oil; they do not use melted butter or shortening. Chiffon cakes are light and moist. The whipped egg whites are folded in with a spatula and produce the cake's volume. Baking forms are not greased. The baked cake is inverted and cooled; always allow the cakes to cool thoroughly before removing from the pan.

Figure 15-12 Chiffon cake.

Chiffon Cake Formulas

golden chiffon cake   *Yield: 4 lb 8 3/4 oz (2,060g)*

% Ratio	Ingredients	Lb	Oz	Metric	Procedures
100	Cake flour		14	400 g	Use the two-stage mixing method. In a separate bowl, beat the egg whites and the cream of tartar to form a soft peak; add the sugar and whip until stiff. Fold the beaten egg whites into the batter.
1/2	Baking powder		1/2	10 g	
	Salt		1/4	5 g	
86	Sugar		12	340 g	Bake at 375° to 390°F (190° to 200°C), depending on pan size, for approximately 35 minutes.
50	Oil		7	200 g	
50	Egg yolks		7	200 g	
72	Water		10	280 g	
115	Egg whites	1		450 g	
	Cream of tartar				
42	Sugar		6	170 g	

NUTRITIONAL INFORMATION PER 2 OZ (60 G) SERVING: 170 Calories; 7 g Fat (38.4% calories from fat); 3 g Protein; 23 g Carbohydrate; trace Dietary Fiber; 71 mg Cholesterol; 142 mg Sodium. Exchanges: 1/2 Grain(Starch); 1/2 Lean Meat; 0 Fruit; 1 1/2 Fat; 1 Other Carbohydrates.

cocoa chiffon cake
Yield: 4 lb 10 3/4 oz (2,120 g)

% Ratio	Ingredients	Lb	Oz	Metric	Procedures
86	Cake flour		12	340 g	Use the combination mixing method for this formula.
14	Cocoa		2	60 g	The cocoa and flour combined make up 100%.
	Salt		1/4	5 g	In a separate bowl, beat the egg whites and the cream of tartar to form a soft peak; add the sugar and whip until stiff. Fold the beaten egg whites into the batter.
1/2	Baking powder		1/2	10 g	
100	Sugar		14	400 g	Bake at 375° to 390°F (190° to 200°C), depending on pan size, for approximately 35 minutes.
64	Egg yolks		9	260 g	
50	Oil		7	200 g	
72	Water		10	280 g	
100	Egg whites		14	400 g	
	Cream of tarter				
42	Sugar		6	170 g	

NUTRITIONAL INFORMATION PER 2 OZ (60 G) SERVING: 174 Calories; 8 g Fat (39.2% calories from fat); 3 g Protein; 24 g Carbohydrate; 1 g Dietary Fiber; 88 mg Cholesterol; 136 mg Sodium. Exchanges: 1/2 Grain(Starch); 1/2 Lean Meat; 0 Fruit; 1 1/2 Fat; 1 Other Carbohydrates.

LEARNING ACTIVITY 14-2

After baking several cake formulas, study the ratios for Sponge Cake (page 320), Pound Cake, (page 323), and Hi-ratio Cake (page 326) and write your own signature formula for each type of cake.

Ingredients	Sponge Cake	Pound Cake	Hi-ratio Cake
Flour			
Sugar			
Eggs			
Milk			
Shortening			
Baking powder			
Stabilizers			
Tenderizers			

HIGH-ALTITUDE BAKING

If you live in an area of high altitude, you must give special consideration to the amount of leavening agents. Less chemical leavenors are required. At ordinary altitudes, the amount of baking powder needed is between 1 and 5 percent, based on the flour weight. Too much baking powder will produce a cake that is coarse-grained. Too little baking powder will result in a dense cake that has a tendency to pull away from the pan corners during baking. You will need to experiment to determine the exact amount of baking powder for use in higher altitudes; however, the following is a good guideline.

Feet Above Sea Level	Baking Powder Ounces Per Pound of Flour (450 g)
3,001–6,000	1/2 oz (10 g)
6,001–10,000	1/4 oz (5 g)
Above 10,000	1/8 oz (2 1/2 g)

You must also consider other changes in cake ingredients, baking time, and temperature to get the best results. Emulsified shortening gives better results than butter, because it has a higher water tolerance. Increase baking temperature of 5° for each 3,000 feet above sea level. In extremely high altitudes, the baking time is lengthened slightly because of slower heat penetration. The rule of thumb is to lengthen the baking time 10 percent for every 5,000 feet.

Additional Formulas

The following bread and roll formulas appear in Appendix G, *The Workbench:*
Honey cake (found in the section on Ingredients)
Angel food cake
Carrot cake
Apple cake
Sour cream pound cake
Hi-ratio white cake
Rum cake
Hi-ratio chocolate cake
Reduced sugar apple puree cake

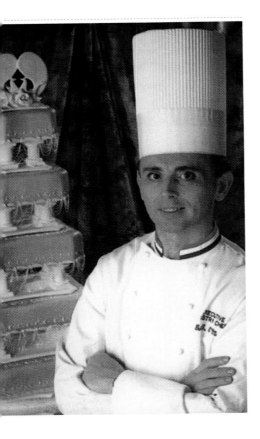

PROFILE

Gale O'Malley, CEPC, AAC
Executive Pastry Chef
Pachacom, Inc., Torrance, Calif.

Gale O'Malley has recently embarked on a new venture. After spending most of his professional life working in top-notch hotels, he accepted the position as the executive pastry chef in charge of research and development for Pachacom, Inc., the makers of all organic, high-end pastries. "Every ingredient must be certified organic, which presents some interesting challenges. From chocolate to glucose and berries to hazelnuts, we search continuously to find the organic version. In my role, I've taken exquisite desserts that were previously successful in other venues and worked them into this new niche. It's challenging but exciting," says O'Malley.

Over the years, O'Malley has been active in ACF culinary competitions including being a member of a Culinary Olympic team. He was the first American-born and -trained pastry chef to receive the Medal of the French Government as the Grand Prize for Pastry, of the Societe Culinaire Philanthropique, New York City. Participating in competitions has helped O'Malley to further develop his skills. A CIA graduate, O'Malley has had the opportunity to serve as mentor to many young people studying pastry arts. "I am proud of those students that I have worked with over the years. I always tell them that they can learn a lot from their teachers and employers if they know the right questions to ask. Be curious, hunger after knowledge and you will advance in your career," says O'Malley.

SUMMARY

The balance of ingredients determines the quality of a cake. A successful formula is balanced so that the ingredients that tenderize do not overpower those that create structure, resulting in a sweetened, light, tender, and moist cake. Like bread dough, cake formulas are balanced using the flour as 100 percent, and all remaining ingredients are balanced against the flour.

Cake batter uses a variety of methods for leavening. Typically, cake formulas will use chemical leavenors such as baking powder or baking soda. Leavening may also be accomplished by aeration and by chemical reaction of alkaline and acid in the presence of a liquid, which produces carbon dioxide.

Although cakes are produced in varieties limited only by the imagination and ingenuity of the baker, there are, in reality, just two basic types of cakes—those that contain shortening and those that do not.

There are three basic mixing methods used for making sponge cakes: the cold-foaming method, the warm-foaming method, and the separation-foaming method. Pound and layer cakes use the creaming method.

With the introduction of cake shortenings came the invention of the hi-ratio cake. These shortenings allowed for greater amounts of sugar and liquid in formulations, producing lighter, moister, and more tender cakes. The term "hi-ratio" indicates that the amount of sugar is greater than the amount of flour. A two-stage mixing process is necessary with this type of cake. This process brought about the development of pre-scaled box mixes. Pre-scaled signature box mixes allow the baker to obtain uniformity by eliminating scaling errors and reducing ingredient inventory.

Chiffon cakes are a type of sponge cake. They combine the standard cake-mixing method and the foam method of mixing. They are made with oil instead of melted butter or shortening. Chiffon cakes are light and moist.

Special consideration must be given in figuring the amount of leavening for those working in high-altitude areas. Less baking powder is required because of the decrease in air pressure. The exact amount to use depends on the specific altitude. Other changes in cake ingredients, baking time, and temperature must be considered to get the best results.

Unit Review Questions

SHORT ANSWER

1. How does the higher percentage of starch in cake flour benefit cake formulas?
2. What are the functions of sugar in cake formulas?
3. Describe how fats function as both moisturizers and tenderizers in cake formulas.
4. Discuss the functions of eggs in cake formulas.
5. Explain why milk is the preferred liquid for making cake formulas.
6. Eggs can suspend _____ their weight in sugar and flour.
7. Foaming is _____ .
8. Explain how creaming differs from foaming.
9. When using baking soda, an _____ is needed in the formula to create the reaction.
10. What are extracts?
11. What are emulsions?
12. What is the advantage of using emulsions versus extracts?
13. When using cocoa with less than 22 percent cocoa butter, the cake is classified as _____ .
14. Explain how to incorporate melted chocolate into a batter.
15. Describe how Dutch cocoa differs from regular cocoa.
16. Explain how cocoa should be incorporated into a batter.
17. Angel food, sponge, and genoise have little or no additional _____ .
18. Why is a tube pan used for making angel food cakes?
19. How does genoise differ from sponge cake?
20. List the three basic mixing methods used for sponge cakes.
21. What types of cakes utilize the creaming mixing method?
22. Describe the steps in the creaming mixing method.
23. What does the term "hi-ratio" mean in reference to cake formulas?
24. Describe the two-stage mixing method used for hi-ratio cakes.
25. Explain how to measure the specific gravity of a cake batter.
26. Describe chiffon cakes.

MULTIPLE CHOICE AND MATCHING

27. Simple sugars or syrups, such as corn syrup and honey, may be used to retain moisture but should be limited to _____ percent of batter weight.
    a. 1
    b. 2 1/2
    c. 5
    d. 7 1/2
28. What is the optimal temperature for cake-making ingredients?
    a. warm
    b. very cold
    c. moderately chilled
    d. room temperature
29. Match the type of egg to its approximate volume increase.
    a. egg yolks   1. 8:1
    b. egg whites   2. 4:1
    c. whole eggs   3. 2:1
30. The percentage of cocoa butter in cocoa is:
    a. 10–12%
    b. 14–16%
    c. 18–20%
    d. 22–24%

enrobing
and garnishing
cakes and pastries

Icings, frostings, and glazes add variety to cakes and pastries. They come in a number of varieties—thick and thin; cooked and uncooked. The basics are covered in Unit 16; Unit 17 explores the wonderful world of chocolate.

icings, frostings, and glazes

"While an expertly decorated cake is one that will sell icings and frostings also keep cakes moist and contribute their distinctive flavor."

Labensky, Van Damme, Martel, Tenbergen, CBM "On Baking"

KEY TERMS and CONCEPTS

buttercream

enrobing

fondant

glaze

melting point

meringue

royal icing

LEARNING Objectives

After you have finished reading this unit, you should be able to:

- **List** the selection of sugars used for icings and frosting

- **Describe** how to control aeration and the melting point of icings and frostings

- **Identify** the effect of temperature on sugar crystallization

- **Describe** how to control consistency of icings and frostings

- **Explain** how to make meringue and creamed frostings

WHILE EACH CATEGORY OF ICINGS, FROSTINGS, AND glazes has a specific application, they all share certain functions when properly prepared and applied. They add attractiveness, volume, sweetness, moisture, and flavor; in addition, they provide a protective coating against air and heat, which can cause cakes to become dry and stale. The filling, enrobing, and decorating of cakes and pastries create a variety of flavors and appearances that add to customer appeal. The quality of the flavor and the shade of the colors used in making the icing or frosting are of utmost importance. A first glance at a product triggers the customer's perception of flavor. In addition, the frosting or icing is the first part of the product that the customer will taste.

FUNCTION OF ICINGS, FROSTINGS, MERINGUES, AND GLAZES

Icings and frostings are used to fill, enrobe, and garnish cakes and pastries. **Enrobing** is simply the act of covering a cake with frosting or icing. Icings are not aerated and they are generally made from sugar and water (Figure 16-1). Frostings differ in that they contain shortening or butter and egg product, which enable them to be aerated.

Icing and frosting should be chosen to add texture and harmony of flavors to the dessert being frosted. Unit 5 profiled several flavor options. Al-

Figure 16-9 Glaze.

Figure 16-10 Glazed fruit tart.

GLAZES

When an icing is applied in a very thin layer and is transparent, it is referred to as a **glaze** (Figure 16-9). Glazes are applied to doughnuts, fruit tarts, Danish, sweet dough, and fruit cake to seal moisture and add a gloss to the product, making it more eye-appealing. Glazes are applied to baked goods after baking or frying while they are hot. If the product is cool, the glaze must be hot (Figure 16-10).

doughnut glaze *Yield: 4 lb 7 1/4 oz (2,020 g)*

Ingredients	Lb	Oz	Metric	Procedures
Powdered sugar	3	8	1,590 g	Place the sugar and honey in a 4-q bowl.
Honey		3	90 g	
Water		12	340 g	Heat the water and gelatin to 160°F (71°C); add to sugar mixture. Mix until smooth. Apply to warm doughnuts by dipping them into the glaze, then place doughnuts on a towel and then onto a screen to dry.
Gelatin		1/3	10 g	

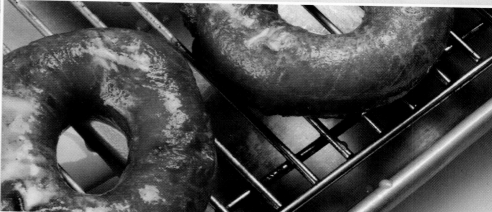

NUTRITIONAL INFORMATION PER 1 OZ (30 G) SERVING: 91 Calories; trace Fat (0.2% calories from fat); trace Protein; 23 g Carbohydrate; trace Dietary Fiber; 0 mg Cholesterol; trace Sodium. Exchanges: 1 1/2 Other Carbohydrates.

sweet glaze (used for Danish, fruit tarts, sweet dough products)
Yield: 2 lb 1/2 oz (920 g)

Ingredients	Lb	Oz	Metric	Procedures
Water		8	230 g	Dissolve the gelatin in water; heat to 160°F (71°C).
Gelatin		1/2	10 g	
Corn syrup	1	8	680 g	Add the corn syrup and bring to a boil.

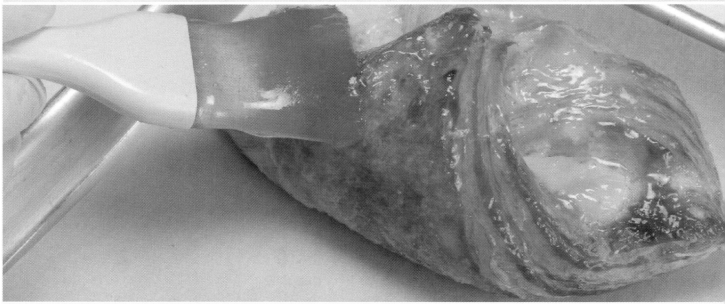

NUTRITIONAL INFORMATION PER 1 OZ (30 G) SERVING: 60 Calories; 0 g Fat (0.0% calories from fat); trace Protein; 16 g Carbohydrate; 0 g Dietary Fiber; 0 mg Cholesterol; 26 mg Sodium. Exchanges: 1 Other Carbohydrates.

CHEF'S TIP: *A few drops of yellow food coloring added to the sweet glaze will bring out the natural colors of baked goods and fruit.*

Bread Glaze

Dissolve 1 ounce (30 g) of cornstarch in 1 quart of water (900 g/mL); bring it to a boil and apply to bread products as you remove them from the oven. This will give the crust a shine (Figures 16-11 and 16-12). For additional flavor, you may add 1/2 ounce (10 g) of salt to this glaze.

CONCLUSION

This unit demonstrates the variety of formulas available for frostings, icings, and glazes. Each formula will add variety, texture, appearance, and a protective wrap to seal in moisture and maintain freshness. There are many types of fully prepared icings, glazes, and frostings available that only have to be heated or whipped prior to application. Evaluate the quality of the ready-made products very carefully. In Learning Activity 16-3, we will make a comparison of Swiss buttercream and a ready-made frosting.

Figure 16-11 Bread without glaze.

Figure 16-12 Bread with glaze.

LEARNING ACTIVITY 16-3

Make a half batch of Swiss buttercream (page 344). Obtain an equal amount of commercial frosting. Taste 1 teaspoon of each product. Which one melts in your mouth? The one that melts in your mouth contains a fat with a lower **melting point**; this is great for flavor and taste but more difficult to work with, particularly in warm weather. Which one tastes the best? Bakers weigh the ease of preparation with the taste and ease of use of the product to determine which one is best for the job at hand.

Record your findings in the following chart:

Swiss Buttercream versus Commercially Prepared Frosting

Type of Frosting	Lower Melting Point	Taste
Swiss buttercream		
Commercially prepared frosting		

Additional Formulas

The following frosting formula appears in Appendix G, *The Workbench:* French buttercream

PROFILES

Stephen James, CMB
Executive Pastry Chef
The BALSAMS Grand Resort Hotel
Dixville Notch, NH

The Balsams is a magnificent, 15,000-acre resort located high in the White Mountains and deep in the Great North Woods of New Hampshire. Executive Pastry Chef Stephen James sees to it that his staff of nine produces the highest-quality breads and pastries. He often gives public demonstrations and participates in radio and television spots. "Much of my job is hands on. In fact, I spend 95 percent of my time producing baked goods and only 5 percent on paperwork. I love that ratio! It is such a pleasure to work in an environment where the best is always expected. We produce centerpieces made of pulled sugar and chocolate and provide hand-made chocolate candies in addition to the finest baked goods and pastries for our guests. Everyday we have an opportunity to strive to do better than yesterday," says Chef James. He is active in Culinary Competitions and has won numerous ACF gold medals for his work, which he credits for helping him stay on top of his craft.

James admits that one of the privileges of his position is to work with and teach the young pastry chefs who come to work under his tutelage. "I expect a lot, and these professionals deliver. I hire for attitude and train for skill. We seem to attract the brightest and best our industry has to offer. I am so proud of the culinarians I have been able to teach," adds Chef James.

James, a graduate of Johnson & Wales University, College of Culinary Arts, perfected his skills working under several executive and master pastry chefs around the country. He has just completed his twentieth year at the Balsams and says, "These have been very rewarding years. I am most proud to pass my knowledge on to others." Chef James also owns a culinary consulting company.

Andrew Comey
Executive Pastry Chef
Mohonk Mountain House, New Paltz, N.Y.

The Mohonk has been in business since 1869 and is listed as a National Historic Landmark. This full-service resort has 261 guest rooms and is a popular family getaway, a meeting and convention location, and a cherished site for weddings. The resort's executive pastry chef, Andrew Comely, is in charge of all phases of the bakery production. "Along with my staff of nine employees, we make all the dinner rolls, bread, finished desserts, cakes, pies, and cookies for daily consumption at the resort. Over 3,000 meals are served daily in the busy summer months. During the holidays we do a lot of showpieces, which is always a lot of fun," says Comey.

A typical day for Comey consists of arriving at 5:00 A.M. to turn on the ovens and get ready for his crew's arrival at 6:00 A.M. Production for the day begins soon after their arrival and continues until it's time to set up the lunch desserts. From there, they move on to the dinner desserts. "We make everything from scratch. Each day's production is different, depending on the needs of our guests. We always work as a team. There's no specialization, where some employees bake the bread, or others decorate all the cakes. Here we all work on every product as needed. I look at our kitchen as a teaching facility. We always have a number of interns working with us, and I enjoy demonstrating throughout the day and working right along with them. I love to teach in this type of environment and give back a little to the industry by sharing my knowledge with the next generation of pastry chefs," says Comey. His workday ends between 3:00 P.M. and 5:00 P.M., and he enjoys having nights with his family.

Comey believes it is important to carefully choose where you are going to work. "This place is fabulous. I enjoy my surroundings. The management is supportive and allows me the freedom to be creative. I like to stay challenged. We have over 30 different baked goods or desserts on our menu, so the work never gets boring," he says.

Comey graduated from CIA and has worked in a casino and a number of restaurants and hotels. For a time he owned his own bakery but quickly found out that it was too much work and took too much time away from his family. Comey has been at the Mohonk Mountain House for 3 years and says he is there to stay.

SUMMARY

Icings and frostings are used to fill, enrobe, and garnish cakes and pastries. They are generally made from sugar and water. Icings differ from frostings because they are not aerated. They are applied to the product by pouring, brushing, dipping, or by using a pastry bag. When icing is applied in a thin layer and is transparent, it is referred to as a glaze. Frostings are aerated and applied with a spatula and may also be used for decorating by piping a pastry bag with decorating tips.

Icings and frostings add attractiveness, volume, sweetness, and flavor. Along with glazes, they also provide a protective coating to maintain the freshness of the baked good by sealing in moisture.

Types of icings and frostings include the following: simple icing, fondant (made by cooking sugar, corn syrup and water); royal icing (a combination of egg whites and powdered sugar); meringues (egg whites and sugar). Fudge icings are not as light and fluffy and are applied to the cake by using a spatula or with a pastry bag.

True buttercream is made with 100 percent butter. In warm weather the addition of 10 percent shortening is acceptable.

Unit Review Questions

SHORT ANSWER

1. What are the main functions of icings and frostings?
2. Explain how icings, frostings, and glazes differ.
3. Why is butter preferred for buttercream frosting?
4. Describe how a simple icing is made and used.
5. What are the advantages and disadvantages of simple icings?
6. Explain how fondant is made.
7. How does fondant differ from simple icing?
8. What is royal icing and how is it used?
9. Why should royal icing be kept covered during use?
10. List the four main factors in obtaining a desirable meringue.
11. What is likely to happen to a meringue if the sugar is added too early?
12. When and in what manner should the sugar be added to a meringue?

13. What are the two main purposes for adding acid to a meringue?
14. Which acid is most preferred when making meringues?
15. Explain how to prepare a Swiss meringue.
16. Explain how to prepare an Italian meringue.
17. Sweet butter is also known as _____ butter.
18. Explain how to prepare both Swiss and Italian buttercream.
19. How does fudge icing differ from creamed or meringue-type buttercream? How is it most often used?
20. What are the two main functions of a glaze?
21. What is the basic ratio of bread glaze? How is it made and applied?

MULTIPLE CHOICE AND MATCHING

22. While true butterecream should be made with 100 percent butter, in warm weather it is acceptable to add up to _____ percent shortening.
    a. 1
    b. 10
    c. 25
    d. 50

23. For the best appearance, at what temperature should fondant be applied?
    a. 85–90°F
    b. 95–105°F
    c. 105–115°F
    d. 120–130°F

24. What is the ratio of sugar to egg white for a soft meringue?
    a. 2:1
    b. 3:1
    c. 1:2
    d. 1:3

25. When meringue is made properly, it will increase in volume approximately _____ times the original volume.
    a. 2
    b. 4
    c. 8
    d. 10

chocolate

"Forget love. . . I'd rather fall in chocolate!"

Anonymous

KEY TERMS and CONCEPTS

LEARNING Objectives

After you have finished reading this unit, you should be able to:

- **Define** the manufacturing process for chocolate

- **Describe** the standards for chocolate products

- **Demonstrate** how to purchase, store, and use chocolate

- **Explain** how to temper chocolate

- **Discuss** ways to enrobe and decorate with chocolate

- **Describe** various types of ganache

baker's chocolate

bittersweet chocolate

cacao

chocolate

chocolate liquor

cocoa butter

compound/coating

conching

couverture

fat bloom

ganache

milk chocolate

nibs

roasting

semi-sweet chocolate

white chocolate

CHOCOLATE LOVERS AROUND THE WORLD OWE A DEBT OF gratitude to the Spanish conquistador, Hernando Cortés, who was introduced to this important commodity by the Aztec Emperor Montezuma II in 1527. Cortés quickly became a fan of the popular Aztec chocolate drink and filled his ship with cocao beans before returning to Spain. He described the beverage as, *"The divine drink which builds up resistance and fights fatigue. A cup of this precious drink permits man to walk for a whole day without food."* Cortés was also responsible for the planting of cacao trees in many countries in the Caribbean, West African islands, and Trinidad. Cacao beans were so valuable that the people of early MesoAmerica used them as currency.

You would be hard-pressed to find another ingredient as beloved and revered as chocolate. Most people's eyes light up in anticipation of eating a chocolate truffle or a chocolate dessert or drinking a cup of hot chocolate. Children and adults alike, around the world, not only love chocolate, but crave it.

CHOCOLATE ORIGINS

Chocolate comes from the fruit of the **cacao** tree. These trees, which were native to South America, are now grown around the globe in the regions that are 20° north and south of the equator. Chocolate-growing countries include Bolivia, Brazil, Colombia, Costa Rica, Dominican Republic, Ecuador, Mexico, Peru, and Venezuela in South and Central America; as well as Equatorial Guinea, Gabon, Sao Thomè, Sierra Leone, Nigeria, Cameroon, Togo, Democratic Republic of Congo (Zaire), Ivory Coast, and Ghana in Africa. Chocolate is also grown in the Caribbean countries of Grenada, Cuba, Trinidad, and Haiti; and in the Southeast Asian countries of Indonesia, Malaysia, Papua New Guinea, and the Philippines and in Sri Lanka in Southern Asia.

CHOCOLATE MANUFACTURING

Harvesting

The fruit of the cocao tree is called cacao. The cacao seeds are encased in a large pod, which looks like a long squash. Each pod contains pulp that surrounds 20 to 40 cacao beans (Figure 17-1). Pods are produced throughout the year, but most growers rely on two major harvests. The major harvest runs from October to March and the mid-crop harvest runs from May through August. Workers reap cacao by hand, cutting the pods off the trees using long poles with sharp, hooked blades (Figure 17-2). Other workers follow the cutters and gather up the pods, which are cut open with a machete. The seeds are scooped out of the husks and placed into boxes where they are covered with banana leaves prior to the fermentation period.

Figure 17-1 Each cacao pod contains between 20 and 40 beans.

Figure 17-2 Cacao pod cut in half exposing the cacao seeds.

Fermentation

The banana leaf creates a sort of warm chamber where the enzymes of the cacao bean are activated and fermentation takes place. The process is complete when the white seeds turn a dark, rich brown. Depending on the weather, the fermentation process takes anywhere from a few days to a week and a half.

Drying

The fermented beans are spread out in the sun for the drying process (Figure 17-3), which shrinks the bean to about half its original size. In some cases, modern technology is used to dry the beans mechanically. At this point, the workers pack the dried beans into burlap sacks.

Figure 17-3 West Indies woman drying cacao beans in the sun.

Roasting

Next, buyers purchase the dried beans and **roast** them (Figure 17-4). The roasting temperatures and the amount of roast time both affect the flavor and the color of the processed bean, much like the process for roasting coffee.

Grinding

Next the shells are removed from the roasted bean in a process called winnowing. The beans, now called **nibs,** are ground and rolled until a rich, thick liquid comes out. This liquid is the basis of all chocolate. The grinding process varies according to the kind of chocolate desired.

Refining

In the refining process, all of the particles in the liquid chocolate are ground together. The result produces an even, smooth texture that is free of grit.

Conching

Conching is the long process of intense mixing, agitating, and aerating of heated, liquid chocolate. During this process, various off-flavored, bitter substances and acids are removed and the moisture is reduced. The long, intense mixing action assures complete coating of every solid particle with cocoa butter, giving the chocolate a well-developed and delicious flavor and texture.

Figure 17-4 Three roasted cacao beans or nibs exposed from their dry, brown shells.

The Term "Chocolate"

"Chocolate" refers to bar chocolate or bitter chocolate, sometimes called **liquor,** a term often used by professional bakers. **Semi-sweet chocolate** products, sometimes referred to as **couvertures, compounds,** and **coating** chocolates, are available in today's market. Cocoa powder is made by removing most of the cocoa butter from the chocolate liquor.

Because of government regulations regarding chocolate, no product may be so named unless it actually is made with a certain percentage of **cocoa butter.** If cocoa is substituted, a coined name is permissible, such as fudge, devil's food, or chocolate flavored. The reverse is also true if a product is made with chocolate; it should not be called cocoa.

Legally, the name "chocolate" applies only to one product—that which results from grinding roasted and cleaned cacao nibs to fine "liquor." This product is known also as baking chocolate and bitter chocolate. Sweet chocolate is sweetened with sugars, again ground or milled to a smooth consistency and pressed into bars. It may be thinned out with cocoa butter to facilitate its application as a coating for other foods.

Government standards are specific in their definition of the various types of chocolate. For example, milk chocolate must contain no less than 12 percent milk solids, and chocolate liquor must contain no less than 50 percent cocoa fat.

NOTE: CHOCOLATE AND COCOA: Chocolate and chocolate-flavored cakes are made with chocolate and cocoa. When a cake contains less than 22 percent cocoa butter, it is classified as chocolate flavored, according to the USDA. When it has more than 22 percent cocoa butter, it can be called a chocolate cake. Adding chocolate and cocoa to a cake batter requires rebalancing the formula, and special handling is necessary to incorporate the chocolate into the batter.

Figure 17-5 The cocoa on the left is Dutch-process cocoa powder, which has a higher pH than the American style of nonalkalinized cocoa powder, as shown on the right. The higher pH makes the Dutch cocoa powder darker.

CHOCOLATE PRODUCTS

Baker's Cocoa

Baker's cocoa comes in a powdered form (Figure 17-5). There are two types of cocoa—regular and Dutch. Both contain 22 to 24 percent cocoa fat. Dutch cocoa is treated with an alkaline (baking soda), which raises the pH, making it darker in color. Cocoa should be sifted with sugar or flour before adding it to a batter. When cocoa is blended with milk or milk products, it becomes lighter in color. The color of chocolate cake can be influenced by the choice of leavenors that are selected.

Perform the following learning activity to help you understand the effect of various types of leavenors on cocoa.

LEARNING ACTIVITY 17-1

Fill three clear glasses with 6 oz (170 g) of cold water. Dissolve 1/2 oz (15 g) of cocoa in each glass; then add to the first glass 1 tablespoon (10 g) of baking soda (an alkaline). To the second glass, add 1 tablespoon (10 g) of cream of tartar (an acid). In the third glass, add 1 tablespoon (10 g) of double-acting baking powder. Observe the change in colors. Record your observations in the following chart.

Type of Leavenor	Observations
Baking soda	
Cream of tartar	
Double-acting baking powder	

NOTE: The baking powder, which is a blend of acid and alkaline, will separate, showing two different colors.

Baker's or Unsweetened Chocolate

Baker's chocolate comes in a solid block (Figure 17-6). It is unsweetened and it should be added to a batter after it is melted.

Figure 17-6 Block of chocolate.

Figure 17-7 Melting chocolate in a double boiler.

MELTING UNSWEETENED CHOCOLATE

Begin the melting process by chopping the chocolate into small pieces. Put them in a double-boiler pan (Figure 17-7). Stir often during the melting process. Be very careful not to let water come in contact with the chocolate because the chocolate will solidify.

You can also use the microwave to melt chocolate. It typically takes about one-third to one-fourth less time to microwave chocolate compared with using a double boiler. To microwave, place the chocolate in a glass bowl in the microwave. Set it on high power for about 1 to 3 minutes, depending upon the amount of chocolate you are melting. Stir often.

If you are using chocolate in a formula, mix the fluid chocolate with the vegetable oil or melted fat called for in the formula before incorporating it into the batter. Make sure that the batter is at room temperature before you add the melted chocolate/fat mixture.

Cocoa Butter

Cocoa butter comes from the fat that is extruded from the pressed block cocoa (Figure 17-8). It is used to adjust the consistency of couverture and for various confection fillings, as well as for coating marzipan.

Couverture

Couverture is the European term for a type of chocolate that consists of cocoa mass, sugar, and cocoa butter (Figure 17-9). You can find couverture with varying ratios and percentages of these three ingredients. Usually, it contains 30 to 40 percent cocoa butter. The more cocoa butter in a couverture, the thinner its viscosity will be and the more expensive it will be.

Couverture is used in the production of numerous products including pralines, fillings, creams, and tortes. It is also used for garnishing, decorating, and molding. To obtain the best results, couverture must be tempered to stabilize the cocoa butter. Never substitute couverture when a formula asks for semi-sweet or **bittersweet chocolate**—the additional cocoa butter will alter the formula.

Figure 17-8 Cocoa butter.

Figure 17-9 Couverture.

Figure 17-10 Milk chocolate.

Milk Chocolate

Milk chocolate is composed of cocoa mass, sugar, and cocoa butter with the addition of a minimum of 12 percent milk solid (Figure 17-10). Milk chocolate can replace couverture in many products.

White Chocolate

White chocolate consists of cocoa butter, sugar, and milk solids (Figure 17-11). White chocolate can be used the same way as milk chocolate or couverture. Because white chocolate has no cocoa solids from the chocolate liquor, the FDA does not classify it as chocolate.

Chocolate Coating/Compound

Chocolate coatings or compounds are also referred to as chocolate glaze (Figure 17-12). They are similar to couverture except they have a lower cocoa butter content—some of the cocoa butter has been removed and is replaced with another type of fat, usually vegetable oil. Coatings are a less-expensive alternative to couverture and provide a simpler method of preparation because they do not have to be tempered. Chocolate coating can replace couverture in most instances. Although they are less expensive and easier to use, chocolate coatings are less flavorful than true couverture.

MELTING, TEMPERING, AND STORING SWEETENED CHOCOLATE

To achieve an end product with a high-gloss finish and an appetizing appeal, you need to follow a few basic rules when you bake with chocolate. Always cut up chocolate and couverture into small pieces with a chef's knife before you begin the melting process (Figure 17-13). By cutting the chocolate up into small-sized pieces, a collectively larger surface area is exposed to the heat source, which hastens melting.

LEARNING ACTIVITY 17-2

Melt 1 oz (30 g) of unsweetened chocolate; add 1/2 oz (10 g) of hot water. Observe the reaction of the melted chocolate to the hot water. What happens when you add hot water to melted unsweetened chocolate? Record your observations.

Figure 17-11 White chocolate.

Figure 17-12 Solidified chocolate compound or glaze.

Melting

To melt chocolate:

- Use equipment that is clean and dry.
- Melt chocolate in a water bath, using a bowl that forms a tight seal on the double boiler.
- The water temperature should be about 120°F (50°C) to 130°F (55°C). (Chocolate actually melts better and faster at lower temperatures.)
- No moisture of any kind (steam, water, condensation) should ever come in contact with chocolate. This will cause the chocolate to become thick and grainy and render it useless for tempering.
- Don't leave chocolate unattended while it is on the heat. Stir it gently, or "massage" it as it melts. Avoid vigorous mixing or stirring—this generates undesirable air pockets in the chocolate.
- Once the chocolate has melted, remove it from the heat source.

NOTE: If the formula calls for melting chocolate with cream, remember to heat the cream first and then add the chopped chocolate. Problems arise when moisture is added during the melting process.

Figure 17-13 Cut chocolate into small pieces before melting or tempering.

Tempering

Chocolate used for dipping, coating, or molding should be tempered first. Chocolate that has been properly tempered will have a smooth and shiny finish. Tempering is achieved via a process of heating, cooling, and then reheating as follows (Figure 17-14):

- Grate or chop the chocolate and then place it in a double boiler.
- Heat the chocolate over hot—not boiling—water. Stir constantly until the temperature of the chocolate reaches 115°F (50°C).
- Remove the chocolate from the double boiler. Cool to 78° to 80°F (25° to 30°C). Stir it in the pan or work it on a marble slab. This process redistributes the cocoa butter.
- Warm the chocolate up to 87° to 90°F (30° to 35°C) before you use it. If the chocolate scorches or becomes grainy, discard it.

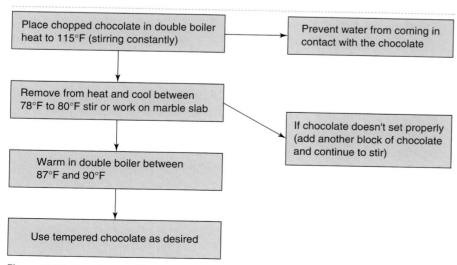

Figure 17-14 Flowchart and instructions on how to temper chocolate.

CHEF'S TIP: *Never heat the chocolate above 130°F (50°C) as it may scorch. Do not allow any moisture or liquid to get into the chocolate during the tempering phase. This will cause clumping. If whitish streaks appear in the finished product, it means that the chocolate was not tempered to the proper temperature.*

Storing

Store chocolate in a cool, dry, dark place that is free of any strong odors. The storage area should have a moderate relative humidity of around 55 to 60 percent and a cool temperature of 65° to 68°F (18° to 20°C). Always keep chocolate well covered or wrapped to protect it from odors, moisture, and light. Do not refrigerate chocolate. Most chocolate will have an average shelf-life of six to eight months if it is wrapped well and kept under proper conditions. Darker chocolate will keep longer.

Sometimes blooms (white or gray streaks) will appear on the surface of chocolate. This is a sign that the cocoa butter has separated. This doesn't affect the quality of the chocolate and there is no problem with using it.

LEARNING ACTIVITY 17-3

The following learning activity will help students to understand the effects of heat and moisture on chocolate's flavor and appearance:

1. Heat 4 oz (110 g) of chocolate to 160°F (70°C) in a double boiler.

2. Pour the melted chocolate into a small pan lined with parchment paper.

3. Place the chocolate in the refrigerator for 15 minutes to cool.

4. Make notes of the appearance and flavor of the chocolate.

5. Compare this to a small piece of the original chocolate.

Record your observations:

Type of Chocolate	Appearance	Flavor
Chocolate that has been melted and cooled		
Original chocolate		

Special Requirements for Couverture

Couverture contains a higher percentage of chocolate liquor and cocoa fat and therefore requires a slightly different handling procedure than that of chocolate compound coatings.

- Do not melt couverture above 122°F (50°C).
- When melting in a water bath, do not let the couverture come in contact with the steam. The ideal water temperature is 140°F (60°C).
- After melting, stir the couverture well. It is very important that you do not beat the couverture; this will cause it to become foamy.
- Once the chocolate is cooled, reheat it to temperatures between 83°F and 86°F (28°C to 30°C), depending on the amount of cocoa butter in the couverture. Check with the manufacturer for specific temperatures.
- Always work with and store couverture at room temperature, about 68°F (20°C).

- When enrobing baked goods with couverture, make sure the goods are room temperature.
- Always store couverture in an airtight container; couverture absorbs moisture easily and gets grainy. When this happens, it cannot be completely melted again. Couverture is also sensitive to foreign odors.
- In most cases, vegetable fats do not combine with couverture and have negative influences on its shine, causing **fat blooming.**

TROUBLE-SHOOTING CHOCOLATE AND COUVERTURE

If you are using chocolate and it is too thick, don't thin it with water. The chocolate will immediately become firm. Add vegetable oil instead. Besides adding water to chocolate, a number of additional factors can cause chocolate or couverture to become too thick:

- Influence of steam
- Influence of moisture when chopping (moisture on knife or board)
- Temperatures too low when tempering the chocolate or couverture
- As a rule, the influence of moisture or steam on chocolate cannot be corrected. If this happens you can use this chocolate or couverture to make fillings or sauces.
- If the chocolate or couverture is too cool, repeat the tempering process (see melting and tempering instructions).
- Couverture or chocolate that has been improperly stored in an area with too much humidity may develop small lumps (sugar crystals). If this happens you can use this chocolate or couverture to make fillings or sauces.

Figure 17-15 Ganache will thicken as it cools.

GANACHE

The following combinations of chocolate, heavy cream, and sweeteners are used in a variety of applications. The **ganache** formulas are used as fillings, icings, and glazes (Figure 17-15). Notice that the ratios of heavy cream to chocolate change in each application.

basic ganache for icing *Yield: 5 lb (2,270 g)*

Ingredients	Lb	Oz	Metric	Procedures
Heavy cream	2		900 g	Bring the cream to a boil; remove from heat. Add the cream to the chocolate and stir constantly until melted.
Dark chocolate (fine chop)	3		1,360 g	

NUTRITIONAL INFORMATION PER 1 OZ (30 G) SERVING: 125 Calories; 10 g Fat (66.5% calories from fat); 1 g Protein; 10 g Carbohydrate; 1 g Dietary Fiber; 16 mg Cholesterol; 7 mg Sodium. Exchanges: 0 Nonfat Milk; 2 Fat; 1/2 Other Carbohydrates.

ganache for glazing *Yield: 2 lb 10 oz (1,190 g)*

Ingredients	Lb	Oz	Metric	Procedures
Heavy cream	1		450 g	Bring the cream and corn syrup to a boil. Pour the cream mixture over the chopped chocolate, stirring constantly until melted.
Corn syrup		2	60 g	
Dark chocolate (chopped)	1	8	680 g	

NUTRITIONAL INFORMATION PER 1 OZ (30 G) SERVING: 118 Calories; 9 g Fat (61.9% calories from fat); 1 g Protein; 11 g Carbohydrate; 1 g Dietary Fiber; 15 mg Cholesterol; 7 mg Sodium. Exchanges: 0 Nonfat Milk; 2 Fat; 1/2 Other Carbohydrates.

ganache for cake filling *Yield: 2 lb 12 oz (1,250 g)*

Ingredients	Lb	Oz	Metric	Procedures
Heavy cream		9	260 g	Chop the chocolate into small pieces. Bring the cream to a boil. Pour the cream mixture over the chopped chocolate, stirring constantly until it cools to 98°F (37°C). Whisk in the butter. Add the liquor (raspberry, orange, and almond are the popular flavors for ganache cake filling).
Chocolate, bittersweet (chopped)	1		450 g	
Butter, softened	1		450 g	
Liquor of choice		3	90 g	

NUTRITIONAL INFORMATION PER 1 OZ (30 G) SERVING: 148 Calories; 16 g Fat (89.3% calories from fat); 1 g Protein; 3 g Carbohydrate; 2 g Dietary Fiber; 31 mg Cholesterol; 89 mg Sodium. Exchanges: 0 Grain (Starch); 0 Lean Meat; 0 Nonfat Milk; 3 Fat.

soft ganache for whipping *Yield: 3 lb 6 oz (1,530 g)*

Ingredients	Lb	Oz	Metric	Procedures
Heavy cream	1	8	680 g	Bring the cream and milk to a boil. Add the butter. Pour the cream mixture over the chopped chocolate, stirring until the chocolate is melted. Strain and cool in an ice bath.
Milk		8	230 g	
Butter		2	60 g	
Chocolate, dark (chopped)	1	4	570 g	

NUTRITIONAL INFORMATION PER 1 OZ (30 G) SERVING: 104 Calories; 9 g Fat (71.5% calories from fat); 1 g Protein; 7 g Carbohydrate; 1 g Dietary Fiber; 20 mg Cholesterol; 17 mg Sodium. Exchanges: 0 Nonfat Milk; 2 Fat; 1/2 Other Carbohydrates.
NOTE: Store for 24 hours in refrigerator before whipping.

chocolate ganache glazed torte (Sacher style)

Ingredients	Volume	Oz	Metric	Procedures
One 10-inch chocolate brownie layer (no nuts)				Cover the top and sides of the chocolate brownie layer with jam. Chill for 1 hour; ice with the glazing ganache (page 366). Chill for 15 minutes. Score the cake for 16 servings. Garnish each serving with a chocolate curl.
Apricot jam		6	170 g	
Glazing ganache		12	340 g	

NUTRITIONAL INFORMATION PER 6 OZ (180 G) SERVING: 713 Calories; 36 g Fat; 5 g Protein; 102 g Carbohydrate; 4 g Dietary Fiber; 65 mg Cholesterol; 133 mg Sodium.

CHOCOLATE DESSERTS

Boston Cream Pie

The Boston cream pie is another famous recipe that uses chocolate glaze. The Parker House Hotel (now the Omni Parker House Hotel) claims to have served Boston cream pies since its opening in 1856. French Chef Sanzian, who was hired for the opening of the hotel, is credited with creating Boston cream pie. This cake was originally served at the hotel with the name Chocolate cream pie or Parker House chocolate cream pie. At that time, sponge cakes were often filled with jam or pastry cream. All Sanzian did was top a cream-filled sponge cake with a chocolate glaze. It was the chocolate, which was expensive in 1871, that made this a special dessert, one that continues to be served at the Parker House as well as many other restaurants and bakeries today.

Boston cream pie *Yield: 1 10-inch pie*

Ingredients	Volume	Oz	Metric	Procedures
One 10-inch (250 cm) sponge cake layer				Slice the cake in half (horizontally); place the cake on a cake circle, top-side down. Leave the flat surface of the bottom crust for the chocolate glazing. Fill the cake with pastry cream. Place on top of the pastry cream and glaze the top.
Pastry cream	1 pt		470 ml	
Chocolate glaze		6	170 g	

NUTRITIONAL INFORMATION PER 6 OZ (180 G) SERVING: 479 Calories; 19 g Fat; 11 g Protein; 70 g Carbohydrate; 2 g Dietary Fiber; 195 mg Cholesterol; 114 mg Sodium.

CHOCOLATE DECORATIONS

Properly tempered chocolate can be piped into decorations, molded into shapes, and used to glaze cakes, tortes, and candies. The following directions will help you to create a host of beautiful, tempting chocolate decorations.

Delicate Shapes

Fill a parchment cone with tempered chocolate and pipe delicate shapes onto parchment paper (Figure 17-16). Once the shapes dry, lift them carefully with a spatula and place them on your cake or dessert.

Figure 17-16 Piping chocolate decorations using a paper cone and chocolate glaze.

Chocolate Leaves

Wash and dry a shiny leaf (lemon leaves work well). Use a pastry brush to paint the vein side of the leaf with tempered chocolate couverture (Figure 17-17). Place the leaf on a rack to dry. Once the chocolate is set, simply peel it off the leaf (Figure 17-18). Use to garnish desserts.

Chocolate Curls

To make chocolate curls, begin with a bar of chocolate that is at room temperature (72°F or 20°C). Hold a chef's knife at a 45° angle, and pull the knife on top of the block of chocolate back toward yourself. This creates a long curl (Figure 17-19).

Chocolate Cigarettes

Spread a thin layer of tempered couverture over a marble slab. Let it set until it is firm to the touch. Using a metal scraper, push it forward approximately 1 in. (2.5 cm). A curl will appear that is about the size of a cigarette (Figure 17-20).

Figure 17-17 Chocolate leaves.

Figure 17-18 Finished leaf.

Figure 17-19 Making chocolate curls.

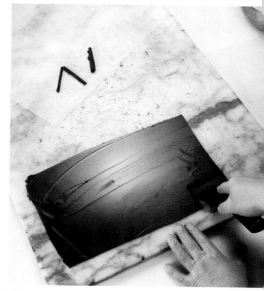

Figure 17-20 Making chocolate cigarettes.

CHOCOLATE CONFECTIONS

Two popular chocolate confections are chocolate truffles and chocolate-covered cherries. They can be served as an accompaniment to most plated desserts and can be made in advance.

chocolate truffles *Yield: 3 lb 4 oz (1,470 g)*

Ingredients	Lb	Oz	Metric	Procedures
Heavy cream	1		450 g	Combine the cream, sugar, and butter. Bring the mixture to a boil. Remove from the heat source and add finely chopped chocolate, stirring until melted. Chill overnight before shaping the truffles.
Sugar		2	60 g	
Butter		2	60 g	
Semi-sweet chocolate	2		900 g	**To shape:** Using a melon baller, scoop out a ball of the chilled chocolate truffle. Coat each ball with cocoa powder. Using a small spoon, dip each truffle ball into tempered chocolate and allow to dry on a baking sheet.

NUTRITIONAL INFORMATION PER 1 OZ (30 G) SERVING: 125 Calories; 9 g Fat (61.1% calories from fat); 1 g Protein; 12 g Carbohydrate; 0 g Dietary Fiber; 14 mg Cholesterol; 14 mg Sodium. Exchanges: 0 Nonfat Milk; 2 Fat; 1 Other Carbohydrates.

chocolate-covered cherries *Yield: 24 chocolate covered cherries*

Ingredients	Lb	Oz	Metric	Procedures
Fondant	1		450 g	Drain and dry the cherries. Heat the fondant (see Unit 16 for formula) to 120°F (50°C) and dip the cherries into the fondant. After the fondant dries, dip the cherries into the chocolate coating; set in a cool place overnight. The fondant will melt inside the chocolate shell, creating the syrup. At this point, the cherry stem can be removed since it is no longer needed.
Maraschino cherries each with stem (24)				
Chocolate coating	1		450 g	

NUTRITIONAL INFORMATION PER 2 EACH SERVING: 370 Calories; 11 g Fat; 2 g Protein; 73 g Carbohydrate; 4 g Dietary Fiber; 0 mg Cholesterol; 6 mg Sodium.

CHOCOLATE MOLDING

Clean and properly conditioned molds are essential for molding chocolate. Molds made from tin must also be kept free of rust. Many newer molds are made of plastic compounds (Figure 17-21). Condition molds by washing them in warm water with a mild, scent-free detergent. Rinse them thoroughly, let them air dry, and then buff them with a nonabrasive cloth. The molds should be scratch-free; never use any abrasive material to clean or dry them. Molds should be at room temperature before you use them (72°F or 20°C).

After the molds have been prepared, fill with tempered chocolate, working in a cool room that is between 65°F to 70°F (18° to 21°C). Let chocolate set up until firm between 5 and 15 minutes, depending on the size of the mold. Do not put the filled molds in the refrigerator as the chocolate will turn white. The chocolate shapes will easily pop out of the molds (Figure 17-22).

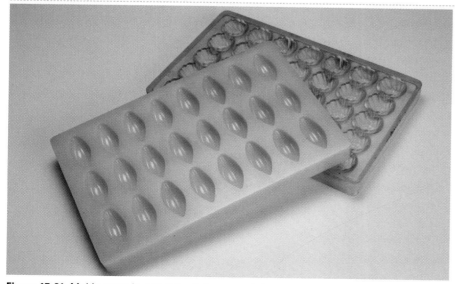

Figure 17-21 Molds come in a variety of shapes and sizes.

Figure 17-22 Fancy molded chocolates are quick and easy to make if the molds are conditioned properly.

PROFILE

Joseph Decker, CMPC
Pastry Chef/Culinary Instructor
Schoolcraft College, Livonia, Mich.

Decker finds himself at school soon after 5:30 A.M. when he gets ready for a busy day of teaching. Class begins at 6:00 A.M., and Decker's responsibilities include giving a variety of theoretical lectures and leading lab sessions. "I enjoy interacting with the students and love to see the light go on in their minds as they learn new techniques. If I can influence my students to develop an appetite for knowledge, then I have succeeded," says Decker. In recent years, Decker has also been heavily involved with the design and construction of a new state-of-the-art facility at Schoolcraft.

Decker started in the industry at age 16 when he began working with a friend of the family, who happened to be a pastry chef. "On my first day the chef asked me to straighten 600 cookies into perfect rows. From there he went on to teach me many valuable lessons about baking and life in general. I spent three years working with him and consider those years as the start of a wonderful career. That pastry chef steered me to work in a busy restaurant. By the age of 25, I was hired as an executive pastry chef and had a staff of 14 people working under me," remembers Decker.

Through the years, he worked in a variety of retail shops and eventually served as the director of research and development for a large bakery manufacturer. One day Schoolcraft offered him a teaching job; he has spent the past 15 years of his career there. "I have always felt very fortunate to have this position and try to give back whatever I can to the school." Decker encourages his students to get good grades as well as to develop business skills, computer skills, and people skills. "To truly succeed in this business, you need to be much more than just a craftsman," he adds.

SUMMARY

Chocolate comes from the cacao bean, which is fermented, dried, and roasted before grinding. It is during the grinding process that the rich chocolate liquor comes out, which is the basis of all chocolate.

There are a variety of chocolate products available, each with its own applications. Bakers who use chocolate must adhere to a few basic rules to achieve an end product with a high-gloss finish and appetizing appeal. Chocolate should always be cut up into small pieces before melting. No moisture of any kind should ever come in contact with the chocolate. Never leave chocolate unattended while on the heat source. It should be gently stirred until it has melted. The term "tempering" means bringing the chocolate to a suitable condition and ready for use in baking. Properly tempered chocolate can be piped into decorations, molded into shapes, and used to glaze cakes, tortes, and candies.

Chocolate should be stored in a cool, dry, dark place that is free from odors. Keep it covered or wrapped and never refrigerate it.

Unit Review Questions

SHORT ANSWER

1. The two main types of cocoa are
   _____ and
   _____.

2. The percentage of cocoa fat in baker's cocoa is
   _____percent.

3. Explain how cocoa should be incorporated into batters.
4. Explain how baker's or unsweetened chocolate should be incorporated into batters.
5. The more cocoa butter a couverture has, the _____ (thinner/thicker) its viscosity will be and the _____ (more/less) expensive it will be.
6. Explain how chocolate coating/compound differs from couverture.
7. What are the advantages and disadvantages of using chocolate coatings/compounds?
8. When using cocoa with less than 22 percent cocoa butter, the cake is classified as _____.
9. Explain why chocolate should be cut up into small pieces prior to melting.
10. Describe the process for tempering chocolate.
11. What is the indicator that chocolate was not tempered properly?
12. Explain how moisture affects couverture.
13. Describe how chocolate molds should be conditioned.
14. Explain the proper storage procedures for chocolate.

MULTIPLE CHOICE AND MATCHING

15. According to government standards, milk chocolate cannot contain less than _____ percent of milk solids.
    a. 7
    b. 12
    c. 21
    d. 30

16. Which explorer is credited with bringing cocoa beans from the Americas to Europe?
    a. Columbus
    b. Montezuma
    c. Cortés
    d. Desoto
17. Match the chocolate product to its description.
    a. milk chocolate
    b. white chocolate
    c. couverture solids

    1. cocoa butter, sugar, milk solids
    2. cocoa mass, sugar, cocoa butter
    3. cocoa mass, sugar, cocoa butter, milk
18. The range of cocoa butter in couverture is generally
    a. 10–20 percent
    b. 20–30 percent
    c. 30–40 percent
    d. 40–50 percent
19. Couverture should not be melted above
    a. 100°F.
    b. 112°F.
    c. 120°F.
    d. 122°F.
20. Chocolate molds should be tempered to _____ before using.
    a. 72°F
    b. 80°F
    c. 85°F
    d. 92°F

principles of cake decorating; specialty cakes and pastries

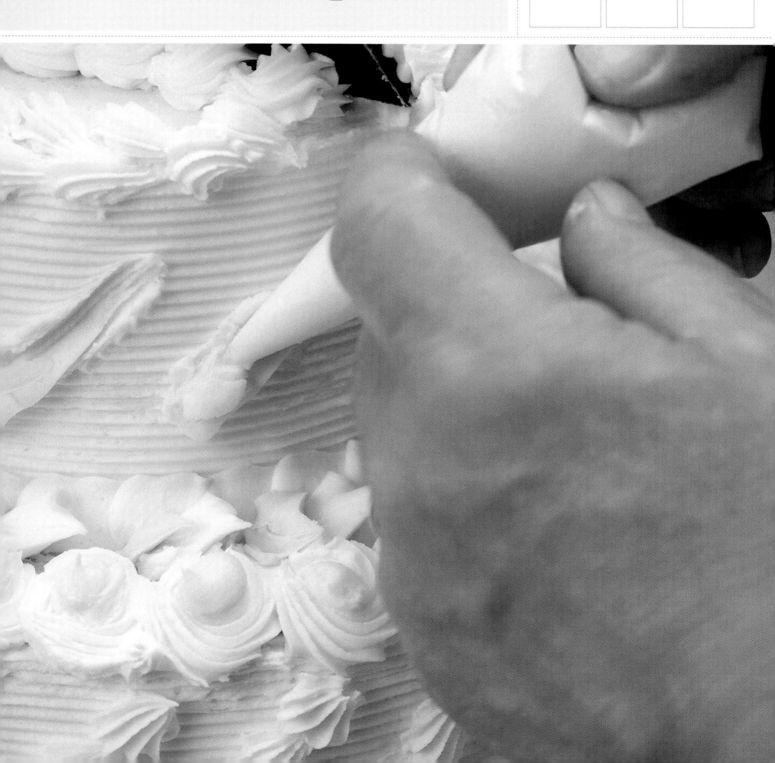

Unit 18 covers the techniques of proper cake assembly and enrobing. Special-occasion cakes and wedding cakes are discussed in Unit 19. Unit 20 introduces students to international cakes, tortes, pastries, and plating techniques.

cake assembly and decorating

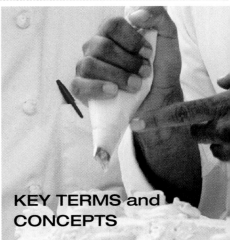

"We can't put the entire world on an 8-inch cake."

Icing on the Cake, a bakery in Los Gatos, CA

KEY TERMS and CONCEPTS

decorating tips

enrobing

pastry bag

piping gel

simple syrup

turntable

LEARNING Objectives

After you have finished reading this unit, you should be able to:

- **Slice and cut** cake layers evenly in preparation for enrobing and decorating

- **Use** a pastry bag for filling and decorating

- **Make** a pastry bag from parchment paper triangles

- **Apply** syrup and fillings to cakes

- **Assemble** tiered cakes

- **Enrobe** filled cakes with frostings or icings

- **Select** the correct decorating tips

DECORATED CAKES CAN BE REWARDING FOR BOTH THE baker and the recipient. This unit covers the assembly and decorating of cakes and will build upon the skills taught in previous units. Cake layers are filled with many different fillings, including creams, fruits, and frostings; they are then enrobed with icings and frostings and decorated. Many bakers find that they enjoy the craft of cake-making, and the resulting aesthetics bring them much satisfaction.

New tools will be introduced in this unit including turntables, icing spatulas, decorating tips, and pastry bags. Disposable pastry bags are readily available and are becoming a popular option because they are sanitary and convenient. Many cake decorators prefer to make pastry bags from parchment paper.

PREPARING THE CAKE

Properly baked cake layers are flat on top. Occasionally, hot spots in the oven will cause a cake to form a dome or may cause the layers to bake unevenly. Level the cake layers by slicing off the dome (Figure 18-1), if one exists, and place the cake layer on a **turntable,** a round revolving platform, with the bottom side up (Figure 18-2).

NOTE: It is recommended that you wear plastic gloves when slicing cake to protect the foods from harmful bacteria.

Slicing

When slicing the layers horizontally, score the cake first. To score the cake, first place your hand on top of the layer and place a serrated knife in the middle of the layer. Score the circumference of the layer by rotating it on the turntable with your other hand (Figure 18-3). Score 2 inches deep, stop turning, and slice through the layer (Figure 18-4).

CHEF'S TIP: *The optimum height for each slice is between 3/4-inch and 1-inch. So a 3-inch cake layer would be cut into thirds and a 2-inch cake layer should be cut in half. When stacked all filled layers or tiers should be the same height. Consistency is the key.*

FILLING CAKES

To create the proper texture, mouth feel, and flavor, the amount and type of filling and frosting need to be balanced with the type of cake.

Sponge Cakes

Sponge cakes are light and dry. A light frosting such as whipped heavy cream and meringue-type frostings (Swiss and Italian buttercreams) make an excellent choice for **enrobing** (process of covering a cake with frosting) a sponge cake. Moist fruit fillings or pastry creams are perfect for the filling.

LEARNING ACTIVITY 18-2

Execute the following work order:

Your Bakery
888 Main Street
Anytown, USA 03039
Date
Order Taker

Customer Name	Jodi Beck
Phone #	800.234.1111
Pick-up date	9-2
Time of pick-up	4:30 P.M.
Cake size	10-inch round
Cake	Chocolate sponge cake
Filling	Raspberry pastry cream
Frosting	Italian buttercream
Inscription	Happy Anniversary to Al and Fran (done in chocolate piping gel)
Flowers	Spray of buttercream yellow and orange roses
Borders	Shell border done in light orange

PROFILE

Karl W. Riesterer, CMB
CEO
Riesterer's Bakery & Café, *West Hempstead, N.Y.*

Riesterer's is the oldest retail bakery on Long Island. Today, the company has two locations and offers a full line of baked goods and serves breakfast and lunch. "My father started the business 74 years ago. I grew up helping around the shop doing all kinds of odd jobs, things like placing cherries on top of cookies or sweeping the floor. I always knew that one day I would work full time in the bakery. In high school I took my first cake decorating course. Over the years I have jumped at every opportunity to attend seminars, workshops, and conventions. Becoming president of RBA and the New York State Baker's Association has certainly helped me to keep up on all the new advances in the industry. Our family has met so many other great baking families through those organizations. Much of our social life is centered on the activities of those groups. My fellow bakers have become my family," says Riesterer.

He continues, "You've heard people say that they have wine in their blood. For us it's flour. Two of my three children attended the CIA, and now all three are working in the business. Every day is a new challenge. It's never boring; we're constantly focusing on a new holiday or on a new product."

Sue Martin
Plymouth South Regional High School
Baking Pastry Instructor

Sue Martin graduated with a culinary degree from the Culinary Institute of America at a time when it didn't offer a baking degree. "I knew that I wanted more baking experience, so I immediately took a job in a bakery and loved it," says Martin.

Later she spent time working as a pastry chef in several luxury hotels including the Four Seasons, Boston, and the Boston Harbor Hotel. From there she worked at a cake shop and gained some retail experience. Her current position as a baking instructor at Plymouth South Regional High School fell into her lap. An acquaintance heard about the opening and called Sue to see if she would be interested in applying. That was 12 years ago, and Martin has no desire to leave at this point. "I went into teaching for myself; the benefits seemed good. I keep on teaching for the students. They keep me learning and energized," says Martin.

As a busy mother of two young sons (ages 9 1/2 and 7), teaching has its advantages. "I'm able to be home with my children during vacations and snow days. Having summers off is a tremendous benefit to me and my family," says Martin, whose husband is also a chef.

At the school, Martin teaches baking and admits that her favorite unit to teach is cake decorating. The students not only study baking; they also produce all the baked goods to supply the school's retail bakery and restaurant, which is a popular spot for local residents. Martin emphasizes good work habits and ethics to her students, which she believes can translate into any professional setting. "I tell my students who want to further their culinary or baking education, that culinary arts is a generous profession. I have never been out of work and have always been able to make a nice living," adds Martin.

SUMMARY

Cakes must be prepared before they are frosted. The first task is to level the cake top by slicing off the dome, if one exists. Place the leveled cake layer on a turntable with the bottom side as the top of the cake. Always score the cake first, before slicing it horizontally.

Fillings are traditionally used between layers. The amount and type of filling or frosting required will vary depending on the type of cake. There are several methods of enrobing a cake with frosting; any will do—pick the method that is most comfortable for you. When you enrobe a cake with fondant or ganache, you must first seal the cake with royal icing, white frosting, marzipan, or a fruit glaze.

The first step in decorating a cake is to know what your customer wants. Special-occasion cakes usually require a written message on the top of the cake. The border is the frame for the decorated cake. By placing it on the outer edge, the cake will appear larger. Piped themes such as floral, clowns, and love birds will often increase the value of the decorated cake and are piped directly onto the cake. Piping gel decals are made on parchment paper and then transferred to cake tops. Emblems, logos, and popular cartoon characters can be duplicated using this method.

Unit Review Questions

SHORT ANSWER

1. What are the advantages of disposable pastry bags?
2. Define the term "enrobing" as it refers to cake assembly and decoration.
3. Explain how and why a cake is scored before slicing it horizontally into layers.
4. To create the proper texture, mouth feel, and flavor, the amount and type of filling and frosting needs to be balanced with the type of _____.
5. What is simple syrup?
6. Explain how and why you seal a filling in a layer cake.
7. Describe how to create a checkerboard design in a filling.
8. What type of icing might be used on a pound cake?
9. Why are angel and chiffon cakes not usually filled or enrobed?

10. When enrobing a cake with icing such as fondant or ganache, the cake must first be _____ with royal icing, white frosting, marzipan, or fruit glaze.

11. Why are bold colors harder to achieve in frostings than in gels and icings?

12. The first step in decorating a cake is _____.

13. List at least eight things you would expect to be listed on a standard cake-order form.

14. When writing on a child's cake, what type of lettering should you use? Why?

15. What type of frosting should be used for creating flowers and sprays?

16. Briefly explain how piping gel decals are made and applied to cakes.

MULTIPLE CHOICE AND MATCHING

17. What is the recommended finished height for a cake that is 6 to 10 inches in diameter?
    a. 2 1/2"
    b. 3"
    c. 3 1/2"
    d. 4"

18. What is the recommended finished height for a cake that is 12 to 16 inches in diameter?
    a. 3 1/2"
    b. 4"
    c. 4 1/2"
    d. 5"

19. It is important to maintain a balance between diameter and height of a finished cake. Match the recommended layer height of the cake with the cake's diameter.
    a. 6 to 10"   1. 3" layers
    b. 12 to 16"   2. 2" layers
    c. tiered   3. 2 1/2" layers

20. Which type of cake should you brush with simple syrup before filling?
    a. sponge cake
    b. hi-ratio cake
    c. pound cake
    d. angel food cake

specialty cakes
and tortes

"The most dangerous food is wedding cake."

James Thurber

KEY TERMS and CONCEPTS

cake stand

garnish

lattice

nesselrode

style

syrup

torte

LEARNING Objectives

After you have finished reading this unit, you should be able to:

- **Discuss** how to make European-style tortes

- **Describe** methods for producing American layer cakes

- **Identify** cakes by their components and flavor

- **Explain** how to garnish and decorate cakes and tortes

- **Discuss** different types of short dough to be used as a base for tarts

- **Demonstrate** how to assemble and decorate tiered cakes (wedding and anniversary)

DESPITE THURBER'S WARNING, THE WEDDING CAKE continues to be an important component of wedding celebrations. Over the years, the wedding cake has remained the center of attention at wedding receptions. It stands as a symbolic reminder of the union between two individuals who are committed to each other and want to begin a new life together. The modern wedding cake, as it is known in Western cultures, is likely a direct descendent of the cakes of early Roman celebrations in which the cake was broken over the bride's head as a symbol of fruitfulness, plenty, and good fortune. Guests scrambled for fragments, hoping to secure such good luck for themselves.

While the wedding cake is the most recognized specialty cake, a host of other creations are included in this unit. The cakes presented on the following pages represent the American style of cakes and tortes.

SPECIALTY DESSERTS

Many of the original cakes were regional specialties. They combined seasonal fruits and nuts that were available in a particular area. Over the last century, with improvements in processing, packaging, and transportation, the majority of these products are available worldwide. To satisfy the American palette and utilize local ingredients, substitutions may occur; it is acceptable to create your own version of many different traditional cakes and tortes. Let's look at an example: The Black Forest cake was traditionally made with sour cherries, Kirschwasser (brandy made from sour cherries), rich chocolate cake, whipped heavy cream, and chocolate shavings. A contemporary style of Black Forest cake uses dark, sweet Bing cherries.

After you have completed this unit, create your own combination of cake, filling, and icing or frosting and select a name and description for your creation. Here is an example of one created for a very special person.

Andrea Torte

A baker created the Andrea Torte for his daughter; it is a light, sweet, creamy torte that reflected her charm and personality. The vanilla and chocolate cream is layered between rum syrup-laced sponge cake; the rum represents her spirit. The Andrea torte was first served on Valentine's Day 1980 aboard the S.S. *Rotterdam* on a world cruise.

Andrea torte   *Yield: 1 10-inch cake; 12 servings*

Ingredients	Volume	Oz	Metric	Procedures
Two 10-inch (25 cm) yellow sponge cakes				When all items are chilled, split the two 10-inch (25 cm) layers and place one layer on a cake board.
Rum syrup		4	110 g	Sprinkle the rum **syrup** over the first layer.
Vanilla pastry cream	1 pt	16	470 ml	Spread the layer with vanilla pastry cream and top with nesselrode.
Nesselrode		2	60 g	
Chocolate pastry cream	1 pt	16	470 ml	Place the second layer on top of the first layer and sprinkle it with the rum syrup. Spread it with chocolate pastry cream and top with nesselrode.
Heavy cream, whipped	1 qt	32	950 ml	Place the third layer on top of the second layer, sprinkle it with rum syrup, and spread it with whipped heavy cream. Top with nesselrode.
Toasted, sliced almonds		1	30 g	Place the final layer on top and sprinkle it with the remaining rum syrup. Frost the sides and top of the cake with heavy whipped cream. Sprinkle the sliced, toasted almonds on the sides and place a border of 12 whipped cream rosettes on top. (Use #4 star tip to make the rosettes.)
Dark-chocolate shavings		2	60 g	Cover the center with the dark-chocolate shavings.

NOTE: Nesselrode is chestnut purée containing candied fruits, currants, raisins, and maraschino liqueur. Nesselrode is available from most bakery suppliers.
NUTRITIONAL INFORMATION PER 6 OZ (180 G) SERVING: 459 Calories; 26 g Fat; 9 g Protein; 43 g Carbohydrate; 1 g Dietary Fiber; 199 mg Cholesterol; 103 mg Sodium.

The remainder of this unit will focus on common specialty cakes and **tortes.**

Hi-Ratio Specialty Cakes and Tortes

lemon pinwheel
Yield: 1 10-inch cake; 12 servings

Ingredients	Volume	Oz	Metric	Procedures
Two 10-inch (25 cm) hi-ratio cakes				Slice the hi-ratio cake layers in half horizontally. Place the first layer on a cake board circle.
Lemon pie filling	1 pt	16	470 ml	Fill two pastry bags—one with lemon pie filling and the other with buttercream. Pipe a pinwheel on the bottom layer with buttercream and fill the pinwheel in with lemon pie filling. Repeat this process for the next two layers. Enrobe the cake with buttercream. Finish the top with a pinwheel design of lemon and buttercream.
Swiss buttercream		28	790 g	
Sweetened, shredded coconut		2	60 g	Sprinkle the sides with coconut.

NUTRITIONAL INFORMATION PER 6 OZ (180 G) SERVING: 732 Calories; 45 g Fat; 6 g Protein; 82 g Carbohydrate; 0 g Dietary Fiber; 104 mg Cholesterol; 528 mg Sodium.

triple chocolate layer cake
Yield: 1 10-inch cake; 12 servings

Ingredients	Volume	Oz	Metric	Procedures
Two 10-inch (25 cm) hi-ratio chocolate cake layers				Split the cake and place one of the layers on a cake circle, crust side down.
Chocolate American buttercream		28	790 g	Fill the sliced layer with chocolate buttercream and stack the next layer on top. Enrobe with chocolate American buttercream and chill.
Chocolate fondant		8	230 g	Temper the chocolate fondant. With a pastry bag, pour the chocolate down the sides of the cake, creating uneven columns and a thin border on the top edge.
Milk-chocolate shavings		2	60 g	Fill the center with milk-chocolate shavings.

NOTE: To make Chocolate American buttercream, add 2 oz (60 g) of Dutch cocoa to 1 lb (450 g) of American buttercream.
NUTRITIONAL INFORMATION PER 4 OZ (120 G) SERVING: 816 Calories; 39 g Fat; 5 g Protein; 120 g Carbohydrate; 3 g Dietary Fiber; 75 mg Cholesterol; 395 mg Sodium.

chocolate fudge cake   *Yield: 1 10-inch cake; 12 servings*

Ingredients	Volume	Lb	Metric	Procedures
Two 10-inch (25 cm) yellow hi-ratio cakes cut in half horizontally				Trim the top of the cake layers so they are level; do not split the layers. Stack the layer with a thin layer of chocolate fudge.
Chocolate fudge icing		2	900 g	Enrobe the cake with fudge icing. Decorate on a turntable.

NUTRITIONAL INFORMATION PER 6 OZ (180 G) SERVING: 608 Calories; 9 g Fat; 4 g Protein; 99 g Carbohydrate; 0 g Dietary Fiber; 40 mg Cholesterol; 424 mg Sodium.

black and white lattice top cake   *Yield: 1 10-inch cake; 12 servings*

Ingredients	Volume	Oz	Metric	Procedures
One 10-inch (25 cm) chocolate hi-ratio cake and one 10-inch yellow hi-ratio cake				Split each cake in half and use three out of the four layers (alternating flavors).
Italian buttercream		32	910 g	Fill and stack the layers with the Italian buttercream.
Chocolate fondant		8	230 g	Enrobe the cake. Decorate with a **lattice** design.

NUTRITIONAL INFORMATION PER 6 OZ (180 G) SERVING: 710 Calories; 45 g Fat; 7 g Protein; 77 g Carbohydrate; 1 g Dietary Fiber; 124 mg Cholesterol; 588 mg Sodium.

SPECIALTY CAKES MADE FROM SPONGE CAKE FORMULAS

Cake Rolls (Roulade)

Roulades are made with only two components: a thin sheet of yellow or chocolate sponge cake that is rolled around a thin layer of filling such as

Figure 19-1 Applying a thin layer of filling.

Figure 19-2 Rolling the sponge cake.

creams, jams, or frostings. (See Unit 15 for the formula for baking a roulade or sponge cake sheet.)

BASIC PROCEDURE:

1. Cut the sponge cake sheet in half. This will yield two pieces approximately 12 in × 16 in (30 cm × 40 cm).

NOTE: Always cut the sponge cake sheet in half vertically before rolling it. Roll each half separately to increase the yield.

2. Place each half on a sheet of lightly sugar-dusted parchment paper.

3. Apply a thin layer of filling (Figure 19-1).

NOTE: Taper the filling by placing more filling at the back edge and use less filling as you work toward the front edge. This will prevent the filling from oozing out the end when it is rolled.

4. Fold over the top edge and pull down to roll the sponge cake (Figure 19-2). Keep a firm grip on the cake as you roll (Figure 19-3).

5. Squeeze tightly and refrigerate the cake overnight.

    You can cover roulade with frosting, jam, or powdered sugar; **garnish** with coconut or chopped nuts (Figure 19-4).

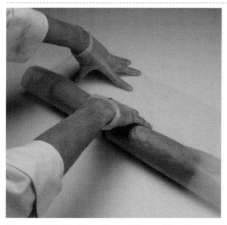

Figure 19-3 Tighten the roll by pulling the parchment paper with a firm grip.

Figure 19-4 Roulades are also used to make the Christmas Yule log.

strawberry whipped cream cake   *Yield: 1 10-inch cake; 12 servings*

Ingredients	Volume	Oz	Metric	Procedures
Two 10-inch (25 cm) yellow sponge cakes				Split the cake layers and place one layer on a cake circle. (You will use only three of the four layers.)
Vanilla pastry cream	1 pt	16	470 g	Pipe a border of whipped cream and fill the center with pastry cream.
Strawberries—washed, sliced, and hulled (save six whole berries for garnish)	1 qt	32	950 g	Place the sliced strawberries on top of the pastry cream. Repeat the filling procedure for the next layers.
Heavy cream, whipped	1 qt	32	950 g	Enrobe the cake with whipped cream. Score the top of the cake for 12 servings and place 12 rosettes of whipped cream (one for each slice) near the edge of the cake and a strawberry half on each slice on the rosette.
Vanilla cake crumbs, fine		2	60 g	Place the crumbs on the bottom edge of the cake going up the sides about 1/2 inch. Crumbs can be gathered when the cakes are split or trimmed.

NOTE: Follow the same procedure using other berries for variety.

NUTRITIONAL INFORMATION PER 6 OZ (180 G) SERVING: 354 Calories; 22 g Fat; 6 g Protein; 35 g Carbohydrate; 3 g Dietary Fiber; 153 mg Cholesterol; 83 mg Sodium.

Black Forest style chocolate cherry cake   *Yield: 1 10-inch cake; 12 servings*

Ingredients	Volume	Oz	Metric	Procedures
Two 10-inch (25 cm) chocolate sponge cakes				Split the cake layers; place the first layer on a cake board circle, crust side down using three of the four split layers.
Kirsch flavored syrup		4	110 g	Brush 1 oz of the Kirsch syrup on each layer.
Heavy cream, whipped	1 qt	32	950 g	Pipe a border of whipped cream and three circles on the inside of the cake. Fill the
Bing cherries, canned (drained)	1 qt	32	950 g	circles with cherries. Place the next layer on top. Spread a thin layer of whipped cream and some chopped cherries. Save six whole cherries for the garnish. Enrobe the cake with whipped cream. Score the top for 12 servings and garnish with whipped cream and a cherry half.
Dark-chocolate shavings		2	60 g	Fill the center with shaved dark chocolate.
Chocolate cake crumbs		2	60 g	Place a thin layer of chocolate cake crumbs on the bottom edge of the cake, coming up the sides approximately 1/2 inch.

NUTRITIONAL INFORMATION PER 6 OZ (180 G) SERVING: 401 Calories; 22 g Fat; 5 g Protein; 49 g Carbohydrate; 3 g Dietary Fiber; 140 mg Cholesterol; 116 mg Sodium.

chocolate mousse dome
Yield: 1 10-inch cake; 12 servings

Ingredients	Volume	Oz	Metric	Procedures
One 10-inch (25-cm) chocolate sponge cake				Cut the chocolate sponge cakes into thin layers approx. 1/4 inch thick. Line 2-quart stainless steel bowl or mold with the larger 10-inch cake pieces.
Chocolate mousse		20	570 g	Fill with half of the chocolate mousse and place the raspberries on top.
Fresh raspberries	1/2 pt	8	230 g	
8-inch (20-cm) chocolate sponge cake				Place the 8-inch layers on the top and brush with simple syrup. Fill with the remaining chocolate mousse. Place a thin, 8-inch layer on top and brush with simple syrup. Wrap and chill for at least 8 hours.
Simple syrup		6	170 g	
Heavy cream, whipped	1 pt	16	450 g	Unmold and enrobe the cake with whipped cream.
		2	60 g	

NUTRITIONAL INFORMATION PER 6 OZ (180 G) SERVING: 456 Calories; 26 g Fat; 7 g Protein; 55 g Carbohydrate; 4 g Dietary Fiber; 203 mg Cholesterol; 125 mg Sodium.

NOTE: Mousse domes can be made in individual servings as shown here. This dome was unmolded and covered by chocolate ganache and topped with a white chocolate curl.

Napoleon torte *Yield: 1 1/4 sheet torte; 12 servings*

Ingredients	Volume	Oz	Metric	Procedures
Three 10-inch (25 cm) discs sheets of baked puff pastry dough				Place one puff pastry sheet on a cake board circle and brush with melted raspberry jam.
Raspberry jam		4	110 g	
10-inch square of yellow sponge cake				Place a thin layer of the yellow sponge cake on the puff pastry sheet.
Vanilla pastry cream	1 qt	32	950 g	Spread half of the pastry cream onto the cake. Place the second sheet on top of the pastry cream and spread the balance of the pastry cream and half of the whipped cream on top of that sheet. Place the third layer of puff pastry on top.
Whipped cream	1 pt	16	470 g	
Fondant		8	230 g	Temper the white and chocolate fondant. Place the chocolate fondant in a pastry bag. Spread the white fondant on top and pipe a pin-wheel with chocolate fondant. Score a spider web design. Finish the sides with whipped cream and toasted sliced almonds.
Chocolate fondant		2	60 g	
Toasted almonds, sliced		2	60 g	

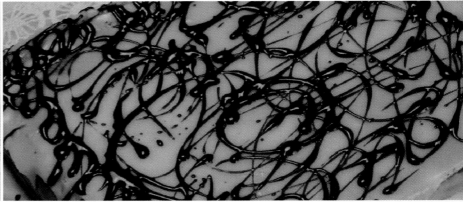

NOTE: Serve this torte within 4 to 6 hours for peak texture and freshness. It must be kept cold as it is very perishable.

NUTRITIONAL INFORMATION PER 6 OZ (180 G) SERVING: 407 Calories; 20 g Fat; 8 g Protein; 51 g Carbohydrate; 0 g Dietary Fiber; 153 mg Cholesterol; 91 mg Sodium.

CHEESECAKES

The rich, creamy texture of the following cheese cake defines it as a cake, but in reality it is a form of baked custard. There are many styles and variations using different types of cheese; the most popular are made with cream cheese and garnished with fresh fruit, fruit toppings, creams and icings (Figures 19-5 and 19-6). Cheesecakes require a pre-baked bottom crust made from graham cracker crumbs, short dough, or a thin slice of cake.

fruit mousse *Yield: 3 lb 9 3/4 oz (1,640 g)*

Ingredients	Lb	Oz	Metric	Procedures
Fruit purée		12	340 g	Bloom the gelatin in the fruit purée.
Gelatin		3/4	20 g	
Egg whites		9	260 g	Make a Swiss meringue (see Unit 16). Fold the gelatin mixture into the warm meringue.
Sugar		4	110 g	
Heavy cream	2		900 g	Whip the heavy cream to a soft peak. Fold the cream into the mixture; chill overnight.

NUTRITIONAL INFORMATION PER 4 OZ (110 G) SERVING (using strawberry fruit purée): 265 Calories; 24 g Fat (79.9% calories from fat); 3 g Protein; 10 g Carbohydrate; 0 g Dietary Fiber; 89 mg Cholesterol; 55 mg Sodium. Exchanges: 1/2 Lean Meat; 0 Nonfat Milk; 5 Fat; 1/2 Other Carbohydrates.
NOTE: Any fruit puree can be used in this recipe, such as mango, passion fruit, raspberry, and strawberry. Some exotic fruits, such as pineapple, mango, and kiwi, must be boiled to inactivate certain enzymes that will inhibit gelatin formation.

WEDDING CAKES

In early times, the line between breads and cake was blurred; the first "wedding cake" was actually a thin loaf that resembled bread more than a confection. In many cultures (Greek and Ukraine, for instance), the wedding cake was baked in symbolic shapes of birds or grains. During the Middle Ages, it became customary for the bride and groom to kiss over a pile of small cakes.

Later, a clever baker surprised a happy couple by creating the traditional, tiered wedding cake we know today (Figure 19-7). European tradition holds that the wedding cake be monochrome white as a symbol of purity. Wedding cakes in other cultures are often much more colorful.

Although the shape, substance, and presentation rituals have changed over the centuries, all wedding cakes share two elements regardless of their historic era: First, the cake is communal—a shared experience symbolizing good fortune; and second, it is made of the very finest ingredients, representing the "best" of its time (Figure 19-8).

Wedding Cake Style

Wedding cake **styles** range from the traditional—with garlands and lace-decorated buttercream flowers and borders—to the more modern, elaborate cakes that feature pulled sugar, rolled fondant, and pastillage (Figure 19-9). Bakers need many years of practice before they can create elaborate wedding cakes (Figure 19-10). In traditional wedding cakes, all tiers contain the same type of cake and filling. Today's customers may request several varieties of cake and filling for their wedding cake.

Figure 19-7 Wedding cake.

Figure 19-8 Wedding cakes are made with the finest of ingredients.

Figure 19-9 Wedding cakes come in all shapes, flavors, and designs.

Figure 19-10 Wedding cakes can be decorated from the simple to the elaborate.

White cake is the "traditional" flavor selection. However, the current trend is to select from a variety of flavors. Anything from chocolate to carrot cake is acceptable. Cake toppers can be traditional—bride and groom figurines, wedding bells, hearts, and love birds, themed with (nonpoisonous) floral décor. Some brides prefer to use sentimental items as cake toppers.

A variety of **cake stands** are used to separate and stack cake layers. They can be simple or elaborate with fountains and moving parts, depending on the tastes of the client.

To get started, we will design a wedding cake that builds on the skills you have learned thus far. Buttercream will be used as the frosting. We will concentrate on uniformity and symmetry in the design and balance in the colors and decorations.

DETERMINING THE SIZE

Before deciding what size cake will work for each wedding, consult with the client directly on some very specific details. It is important to know how many people are expected to attend. What other food will be served at the reception? If the cake is served after a sit-down dinner, the client may opt for smaller pieces. If it is to be the focal point of the reception and the primary refreshment, larger pieces may be required. Is the cake rich or light? Richer cakes are served in smaller portions than lighter, less rich cakes. Once these questions have been answered, the following process can be implemented.

As a rule of thumb, the average piece of wedding cake is the size of an index finger—about 2 inches by 2 1/2 inches by 3 inches high. (Again, that depends on the answers to the previous questions.)

Begin by determining the size and number of tiers required to serve the number of guests. Use the following formula to determine the size of cake you will need. Take the diameter of the cake and divide by 2, then multiply that answer by itself. This number will equal the number of servings.

Example: A 14-inch square cake has a diameter of 14. 14 divided by 2 = 7 × 7 (itself) = 49 servings (2 inch by 2 1/2 inch by 3 inches high). For a round cake, subtract four servings; this represents the four corners.

CHEF'S TIP: *A new tradition has emerged in this modern age of freezers— the top tier of the wedding cake is sometimes removed and carefully packed and frozen for the couple to share on their first anniversary. Always find out* *if the top layer is to be saved for the bride and groom. If so, don't add that cake into the calculations.*

WEATHER CONSIDERATIONS

It is important that you consider a few factors before you decide what type and design of cake to use. First, is the reception going to be indoors or out? What will the weather be like on the day of the wedding? (Make an educated guess, depending on the season of the year.) A pure buttercream frosting may not work on a hot summer day. Any cake with a whipped cream frosting or filling should not be left out for long, especially on a hot day. Is there a good chance of rain? Will that be an issue when you transport the cake from the van to the reception hall? Once the baker considers the possible weather conditions, he or she can offer suggestions to the client.

Procedure for Making the Wedding Cake

Begin three days prior to the date needed.

Day #1: Bake and chill the cake layers and prepare the filling or fillings.

Day #2: Fill the cake layers (Sealing the filling with a piped edge of buttercream.), prepare the frosting, and enrobe the tiers (Figures 19-11, 19-12).

Figure 19-11 Bottom cake layer circled with icing and filled with jam.

Figure 19-12 Enrobe individual layers with buttercream icing.

Figure 19-13 The metal plate will give cake added strength.

Day #3: Decorate and chill the cake before delivery. When stacking one layer on top of another, make sure it is centered on the larger layer. Most bakers allow 3 to 4 inches between each layer. So, if a 14-inch layer was to be topped with a 10-inch layer, it should be centered with a 2-inch border around it. If tiers are to be added, use a metal plate to give added strength (Figure 19-13).

Before adding the garlands, the cake's circumference should be divided and the garland placement planned around the cake. Many bakers use a cookie cutter that is the appropriate size to score the garlands evenly around the cake. The key is to plan the placement. Winging it will generally cause uneven distribution.

Cake Set-up

Large cakes with numerous tiers (more than two or three) generally need support from wooden dowels, which are inserted into the layers. Each additional layer is placed on the dowels (Figure 19-14).

Many wedding cakes have spacers that give the cake added height and create an area for decorating. In most cases, wood, plastic, or metal spacers are used. One of the drawbacks of using the spacers is that they are often lost during the reception clean-up. Many bakeries charge a rental fee and expect these parts to be returned after the reception.

Another option is to use glasses as your tiers. First, place a metal plate (the bottom of a tart pan will work) on top of the layer where the separation will occur. The metal plate will prevent the glasses from sinking into the cake. Ice the top of the metal plate. Place an odd number of glasses upside down on the metal plate, then place the next layer on top of the glasses, using the glasses as the columns or separators (Figure 19-15).

Always consider the type of cake topper that is to be used. Some heavier tops will need to be anchored down into the cake.

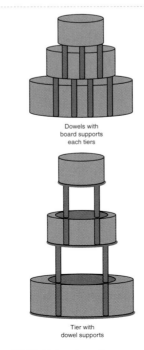

Dowels with
board supports
each tiers

Tier with
dowell supports

Figure 19-14 Using dowells.

Figure 19-15 Simple tiers can be added using inverted wine glasses.

Figure 19-16 Add garlands.

Figure 19-17 Borders.

Figure 19-18 Flowers.

DECORATING

Once the cake set-up is organized, the decorating can begin.

- Add garlands, spacing evenly around cake (Figure 19-16).
- Add borders. Borders should be placed on the outside edge of each cake layer (Figure 19-17).
- Add flowers. Flowers or other decorative accoutrements are added, and the decorating is finished (Figure 19-18).

When planning wedding and anniversary cake decorations and lettering, keep them simple but elegant.

Pricing Wedding Cakes

Consider the following before you determine the price of a wedding cake:

- What are other bakeries in your area charging for a similar cake? You don't want to be too high or too low compared with your competition.
- What are the demographics of your bakery? Are you located in a busy metropolitan city or a suburb or a small town? If the area is affluent, you will be able to charge more for your cake.
- Are you including delivery and set-up fees with the order?
- What are your labor costs? The biggest expense involved in producing a wedding cake is the labor cost because only skilled decorators can be trusted for such important work.
- What is the cost of the food? The food costs for wedding cakes can be quite substantial. Often, unique ingredients such as gold leafing or out-of-season fruit are used and must be absorbed by the price of the cake. You can charge more for unique cakes. You must know exactly what it costs to produce the cake.

Typical prices for wedding cakes range from $1.00 per portion all the way up to $15.00 and beyond. Again, it depends on the factors discussed earlier. Let's look at an example.

Figure 19-19 Baker assembles wedding cake layers at the reception site.

Figure 19-20 For wedding or anniversary cakes, simple design elements are often best. Be careful not to clutter the cake with too much detail.

Figure 19-21 Special anniversary celebrations, such as a 50th anniversary, warrant the need for a cake. Customers often request a smaller version of their original wedding cake.

A white wedding cake with raspberry filling and buttercream frosting will serve 80 people. You have already determined that in your community the going rate is around $5.00 per slice. $5.00 × 80 portions = $400. The food cost is $38.00. As long as you use sound production techniques to keep your labor costs reasonable, it is easy to see that the wedding cake business can be lucrative.

Transportation Considerations

Who will transport the cake? How far is it from the kitchen or bakery to the location of the reception? For longer distances, the cake must be packed in travel-safe packages and then assembled on site. Make sure that the cake is shaded from the sun during the drive.

Most bakers prefer to assemble the cake at the reception site (Figure 19-19). In some cases, the tiers can be assembled in the bakery and the finished cake carefully transported in a large box with foam padding underneath to hold it in place during the drive. Either way, transporting a wedding cake taxes the nerves of most bakers or pastry chefs.

CHEF'S TIP: *Always have a repair kit with frosting, bags, tips, and a spatula for last-minute touch-ups.*

ANNIVERSARY CAKES

A smaller version of a wedding cake is often served for special anniversaries. This type of cake generally has more color than a wedding cake. In the accompanying photos, note how the colors are repeated (Figures 19-20 and 19-21). The darkest color should be used for the inscription.

PROFILE

Anil Rohira
Corporate Pastry Chef
Albert Uster Imports, *Gaithersburg, MD*

Anil was born in India and graduated from Bombay University with a degree in hospitality management. During a 6-week exchange at a five-star hotel, he discovered pastry. "When I saw the huge kitchen full of busy chefs, all dressed in their whites, icing cakes, filling éclairs, building Christmas showpieces and making yule logs, the site overwhelmed me," he says. He went on to study at the CIA.

His first opportunity to work in the United States brought him to The Balsams in New Hampshire. Later, he served as executive pastry chef at the Chevy Chase Club in Washington, D.C. Over the years he has been an active participant in a variety of pastry competitions, often garnering impressive awards. In 2003, Anil led Team USA at the Coupe du Monde (Pastry World Cup) in Lyon, France, and took home the award for Best Sugar Showpiece.

Today, Anil heads the research and development kitchen for Albert Uster Imports in Gaithersburg, Maryland. At this chocolate and pastry import company, Anil uses his unique, creative flair to develop recipes that feature the company's Swiss-imported raw ingredients and convenience products. Through education demonstrations for culinary professionals and other valued customers, he aids the company's efforts to support the industry.

"I have been very blessed with this opportunity. Every day is a new challenge. I feel as though I am the link between the chef in the kitchen and the manufacturer. I constantly stop and think of how I can make life easier for the chefs we serve," Anil says.

When Anil isn't working in the test kitchens or doing demos for customers, he often travels to Europe to research new products or work with manufacturers. "I am lucky to be constantly exposed to new experiences and [sic.] given the opportunity to learn. One lifetime isn't enough to learn it all. My goal is to learn something new each day. The key has always been growth, and that comes from seeking knowledge and passing it on."

SUMMARY

While the wedding cake is the most recognized specialty cake, a host of other creations are included in this category. Many of the original cakes were regional specialties. They combined seasonal fruits and nuts that were available in a particular area. To satisfy the American palette and to utilize local ingredients, substitutions have occurred. Bakers have learned to create their own version of many of the different traditional cakes and tortes.

Roulades are made with only two components: a thin sheet of yellow or chocolate sponge cake that is rolled around a thin layer of filling such as creams, jams, or frostings.

Cheesecake is defined as a cake because of its rich, creamy texture. In reality, it is a form of baked custard. There are many styles and variations of cheesecakes using different types of cheese; the most popular are made of cream cheese garnished with fresh fruit, fruit topping, creams, icings, and so on.

The first step in creating a wedding cake is to determine the size and number of layers required to serve the anticipated number of guests. Wedding cakes range from traditional styles decorated with buttercream flowers and borders to modern cakes that feature pulled sugar, rolled fondant, and pastillage.

Unit Review Questions

SHORT ANSWER

1. The modern wedding cake likely descends from which culture's early celebrations?

2. What is nesselrode?

3. Define the term "torte."

4. Explain how a roulade is made.

5. There are many styles and variations of cheesecake, utilizing a variety of different types of cheese. However, the most popular type of cheese used in making cheesecakes is _____.

6. Outline the three-day procedure for making a wedding cake.

MULTIPLE CHOICE AND MATCHING

7. The cheesecake is actually a form of
   a. baked custard.
   b. sponge cake.
   c. chiffon cake.
   d. stirred custard.

8. How many servings will an 18-in. square cake yield?
   a. 56
   b. 64
   c. 77
   d. 81

9. When calculating the yield of a round cake, you first calculate the yield of a square cake, then subtract
   a. 2.
   b. 4.
   c. 6.
   d. 8.

10. Which combination of round cakes will serve 200 guests?
    a. 10", 12", 14"
    b. 12", 14", 16"
    c. 10", 12", 14", 16"
    d. 12", 14", 16", 18"

pastries
and desserts

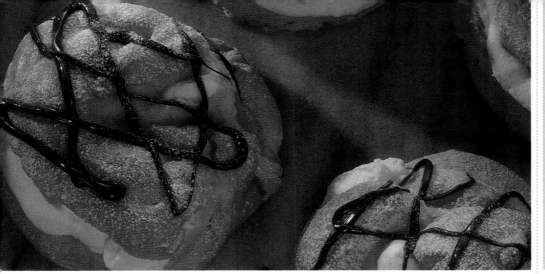

"Mention pastry to diners and most conjure up images of buttery dough baked to crisp, flaky perfection and filled or layered with rich cream, ripe fruit, or smooth custard. Mention pastry to novice chefs and most conjure up images of sophisticated, complex, and intimidating work. Although the diners are correct, the novice chefs are not."

Labensky & Hause, *On Cooking*

KEY TERMS and CONCEPTS

broadcast

dock

ricotta

semolina

LEARNING Objectives

After you have finished reading this unit, you should be able to:

- **Define** old-world, traditional pastries

- **Describe** the components of a plated dessert

- **Create** plated desserts with pies, tarts, cakes, and tortes

- **Make** a variety of individual pastries using several different types of dough, batter, and pastes

PASTRIES ARE INDIVIDUAL UNITS MADE FROM DOUGH, batter, pastes, or individual portions of a completed cake, torte, or pie. When they are plated and garnished, they are referred to as desserts in restaurants, banquets, and homes. A sauce, cream, or baked garnish can be added to plated desserts. Plating allows the individual to combine several components to achieve a combination of different tastes and textures. Warm apple pie ala mode is an early example of a plated dessert; the warm apple is balanced with the cold ice cream, and the creamy texture of the ice cream is balanced with the flaky pie crust. Today's plated desserts maintain a balance of taste and texture by combining opposite components, such as soft and crisp; lean and rich; warm and cold; sweet and tart.

SFOGLIATELLE

The sfogliatelle is an old-world Neapolitan dish. This delicate, delicious pastry is shaped like a clam shell and filled with a creamy semolina and ricotta filling. **Semolina** is another name for durum wheat flour, and **ricotta** is a type of Italian soft cheese. This pastry is very labor-intense and requires the dough to be rested and chilled well before serving. Mary Ann

Espisito, author of *Ciao Italia*, describes sfogliatelle as the "pastry of the nobles" because it was made for noble families during the Renaissance.

The dough that makes up the sfogliatelle is an ancient form of puff pastry dough. Several steps are required to form the layers of fat and dough. This dough was originally crafted by hand; today we can reduce labor intensity with the use of a dough sheeter. The French pastry chef Jean Pierre LeMasion suggests using puff pastry dough to replace the original method of making the sfogliatelle dough; both methods will be presented in this unit.

Lamination Method

Divide the dough into three equal pieces; pass one piece through the dough sheeter, each time reducing the rollers by 25 percent until you reach the lowest setting on the dough sheeter. Smear the top of the dough with the roll-in mixture, creating a very thin layer; be very careful not to tear the dough. Roll the sheeted dough into a cylinder shape (reserve approximately 6 oz of the roll-in mixture to use later) (Figure 20-1). Leave 4 inches of dough to seam the second and third pieces after they have been rolled. Seam the layers together by pressing one layer on top of another and reducing its thickness to a single layer. The completed roll should be 16 inches (500 cm) wide and 3 1/2 inches (90 cm) thick.

Cover with plastic wrap and chill overnight. Save the remaining roll-in at room temperature; this will be used for the final make-up.

Make-Up

1. Place the filling in a pastry bag with a 1-inch (25-cm) opening; no tip is required. Set aside for use in Step 5.
2. Cut 1/4-inch (6-cm) disks from the roll produced from the lamination method (Figure 20-2).
3. Flatten the disk with your palms, pushing from the center out. Lubricate the baker's bench and your hands with the extra roll-in mixture.

sfogliatelle dough (traditional) *Yield: 2 lb 9 1/2 oz (1,170 g)*

Ingredients	Lb	Oz	Metric	Procedures
Bread flour	1	8	680 g	Place all ingredients in a bowl; mix with a dough hook to form a smooth, stiff dough. If the dough is too soft after 5 minutes of mixing, add more flour.
Water, cold	1		450 g	
Egg whites		1	30 g	
Salt		1/4	7 g	
Cream of tartar		1/4	7 g	
ROLL-IN				
Lard	1		450 g	Remove the dough from the mixer and pass it through a dough sheeter; reduce the dough by 50 percent and refold for 10 to 12 passes. Blend all roll-in ingredients together with a paddle attachment at slow speed to form a stiff paste. Spread the roll-in mixture onto the rolled-out dough before rolling it into a cyclinder. Shape the rounded dough into a cylinder approximately 12 inches (300 cm) long. Refrigerate for at least 2 hours; it may be refrigerated longer.
Butter		8	230 g	
Bread flour		2	60 g	

NUTRITIONAL INFORMATION PER 1½ OZ (40 G) SERVING: Per 89 Calories; trace Fat (4.2% calories from fat); 3 g Protein; 18 g Carbohydrate; trace Dietary Fiber; 0 mg Cholesterol; 101 mg Sodium. Exchanges: 1 Grain (Starch); 0 Lean Meat; 0 Fruit.

Roll-in Yield: 1 lb 10 oz (740 g)
NUTRITIONAL INFORMATION PER 1/2 OZ (10 G) SERVING (for roll-in only): 114 Calories; 12 g Fat (96.6% calories from fat); trace Protein; 1 g Carbohydrate; trace Dietary Fiber; 18 mg Cholesterol; 36 mg Sodium. Exchanges: 0 Grain (Starch); 2 1/2 Fat.

Figure 20-1 Rolled dough.

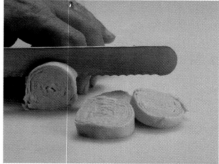

Figure 20-2 Slice into dishes.

4. Form the shell by placing the disk over your thumbs; place your first and second fingers on the outside of the disk, pushing the layers of dough gently to form the cone-shaped shell (Figure 20-3).
5. Place the formed shell in one hand and, with your other hand, fill the shell with the filling using the pastry bag (Figure 20-4). Fill the cavity of the cone-shaped shell completely.

sfogliatelle filling   *Yield: 7 lb 1/2 oz (3,190 g)*

Ingredients	Lb	Oz	Metric	Procedures
Water	1		450 g	Bring the water to a boil; add the semolina and cook until the water is completely absorbed, stirring constantly. Chill to 60°F (16°C).
Semolina	1		450 g	
Pastry ricotta	3		1,360 g	Add the pastry ricotta, sugar, eggs, flavorings, and orange peel. Chill overnight.
Sugar		12	340 g	
Eggs		12	340 g	
Cinnamon oil (6 drops)				
Orange blossom water		1/2	15 g	
Candied orange peel		8	230 g	

NUTRITIONAL INFORMATION PER 4 OZ (110 g) SERVING: 231 Calories; 8 g Fat (29.3% calories from fat); 9 g Protein; 32 g Carbohydrate; 1 g Dietary Fiber; 69 mg Cholesterol; 63 mg Sodium. Exchanges: 1 Grain (Starch); 1 Lean Meat; 1 Fat; 1 1/2 Other Carbohydrates.
NOTE: If pastry ricotta (sometimes called impastata) is not available, you may use ricotta cheese, but you will have to drain the excess liquid from it before using. To drain the ricotta, place in a cheese cloth and squeeze out the excess liquid. Weigh the ricotta after the liquid has been removed.

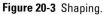

Figure 20-3 Shaping.

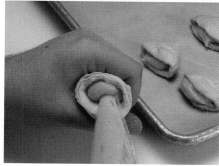

Figure 20-4 Adding the filling.

6. Place the finished shells on sheet pans and freeze them; this will improve the baking process to help define the layers and relax the dough.

Baking and Serving the Sfogliatelle

Place the frozen pastries on a parchment-lined sheet pan, bake at 390°F (200°C) for approximately 30 minutes, and remove when they are golden-brown. Sfogliatelle is best served warm; it may be reheated one time at

Figure 20-28 The traditional Napoleon, when sliced, is rectangular in shape, whereas the Italian-style Napoleon is square.

ITALIAN-STYLE NAPOLEON

1. Trim the edge of the baked puff pastry sheet and cut in half; save the trimmings for the top.
2. Place a thin layer of pastry cream (Unit 11) on the bottom half and top with a sponge cake (Unit 15) layer 1/2-inch thick.
3. Soak the sponge cake layer with rum syrup and cover with pastry cream; place the second half on top.
4. Heat the raspberry jam and spread on top; cover with crumbled puff pastry dough trimmings.
5. Dust with confectionary sugar. Cut servings 2 1/2 by 3 inches (60 cm × 80 cm). The yield will be 20 servings (Figure 20-28).

ROULADE

The French word "roulade" describes a variety of pastries made by filling thin sponge cake sheets with jams and creams, rolling them, and topping them with frostings and nut garnishes. In Unit 15 we introduced the techniques of making a roulade. In this section we are using roulade as a pastry. You can make many variations by changing the flavor, coating, and garnish.

Basic Method

1. Spread the filling evenly over sponge cake (see Unit 15 for formulas); roll up in jellyroll fashion. Chill until firm. (Typical fillings used in roulades include jams, jellies, icings, pastry cream, whipped cream, and fudges.)
2. Cover the outside of the roulade with your choice of coatings, such as powdered sugar dusting or frosting.
3. If desired, roll in chopped nuts or shredded coconut before chilling and slicing. Chill and slice when firm (Figure 20-29).

Figure 20-29 Chocolate roulade sliced and ready for service.

STONE FRUIT TARTS

The stone fruit tart is a favorite late-summer pastry. It can be made with peaches, plums, or nectarines. The stone fruit is baked on a short dough crust that is layered with cake crumbs. After baking, the tart is glazed with apricot coating and served with a dollop of sweetened, whipped heavy cream.

Method of Assembly

1. Line the tart pan with short dough (see Unit 12 for short dough formula) and let it rest in the refrigerator for 15 minutes to prevent shrinkage.
2. Place a thin layer of cake crumbs on the top of the dough to absorb the juice from the fruit.
3. Remove the stone (pit) from the plum or nectarine by cutting the fruit in half vertically from top to bottom; slice into 1/4-inch (6-cm) pieces. To peel the peaches, place them in boiling water for 1 minute, then dip them in cold water. The skins will slip right off the fruit. Plums and nectarines are not peeled.
4. Shingle the sliced fruit on top of the cake crumbs overlapping 1/4 inch (Figure 20-30).
5. Fill the center with chopped fruit.
6. Sprinkle with sugar.
7. Bake 45 minutes at 350°F (180°C).
8. Glaze with a prepared fruit coating (Figure 20-31).
9. Serve warm with sweetened, whipped heavy cream or vanilla ice cream.

CHEF'S TIP: *There are many uses for the trimmings from cake layers. One example was described in the stone fruit tarts recipe. Cake trimmings can also be used as an extender when you make fillings or as a garnish for cakes.*

Plated Desserts

This book has been designed to serve as an entry-level text. As students complete the book, they should be able to combine their newly developed

Figure 20-30 Shingled fruit.

Figure 20-31 Glazed stone fruit tart.

skills to create plated desserts, similar to those produced by pastry chefs at hotels, clubs, and restaurants. When cakes, pies, and pastries are combined with the sauces, creams, and custards discussed in earlier units, along with a few garnishes, beautiful plated desserts will result (Figures 20-32 to 20-34).

Additional Formulas

The following dessert formulas appear in Appendix G, *The Workbench:*

Strudel dough

Cannoli shells

Savarin syrup

Fruit-filled savarin

Hazelnut torte

Apple cream cheese torte

Swiss sugar kuchen

Chocolate sabayon

Almond horn

Figure 20-32 This dessert presentation includes a honeyed pear with berries and mousse.

Figure 20-33 A slice of key lime pie topped with whipped cream and served with strawberry slices and garnished with drops of sweet sauces.

Figure 20-34 A slender slice of pear tart garnished with a simple, yet elegant, chocolate drizzle.

PROFILE

Vincent Termini, Jr.
Pastry Chef, General Manager
Termini Bros. Pasticceria *(three locations in Philadelphia, Pa., and one in N.J.)*

As young children, Vincent Termini, Jr., and his brother could often be found standing on upside-down milk crates, helping their father and grandfather at the family-owned Italian bakery. Today, the two brothers work side-by-side the way their grandfather and his brother did. As young boys, they would have never dreamed that one day they would be appearing on numerous television shows or quoted in food and business magazines as the general managers of the bakery. Just recently, the bakery's cannolis were featured in an episode of the Food Network's "The Best of"

Vincent Termini, Jr. and his brother.

show. "I guess that's one of the benefits of owning your own business; you get media exposure. That's great, but more importantly, I love watching our business grow. To start with an idea, develop a plan and implement it is truly rewarding," says Termini.

Termini Bros. isn't just an ordinary bakery; it's like stepping back in time to an old world Sicilian-style pastry shop. "My grandfather and his brother started the business in 1921, after having apprenticed in Sicily. They came to America, 'the land of opportunity' and started baking traditional Italian-style pastries. Their bakery first serviced the local Italian population. My father brought the business to another level during his generation of management by opening the satellite retail locations. He still works with us almost every day and says that he loves to see his father's dream become a reality as we continue to grow the business. Today we have customers from all over the country," shares Termini.

In recent years, the Termini brothers have expanded the business to include a booming wholesale business and a mail order business. The original retail bakery has now grown to four outlets.

Termini attended the CIA, where he was exposed to different mediums and appreciated the opportunity he was given to go see a variety of bakers in their own shops. He says, "I always learned something from every shop I visited. I also spent five months doing an internship under the executive pastry chef for Marriott Worldwide. There I learned how to combine volume and quality." Today he spends up to 70 hours a week at work and says with a chuckle that he works eight days a week. "If you're not willing to put in the hours, you won't succeed in this business. It's hard work, but very rewarding. I love it; that's why I keep doing it. If only my grandfather was around to see what we have done with this business. I think he would be very proud," says Termini.

SUMMARY

Pastries are individual units made of dough, batter, or pastes, or individual portions of a completed cake, torte, or pie. When they are plated and garnished, they are referred to as a dessert. A sauce, cream, or baked garnish can be added to plated pastries. Plating allows the baker to combine several components to achieve a combination of different tastes and textures. A plated dessert should maintain a balance of taste and texture by combining opposite components, such as soft and crisp; lean and rich; warm and cold; sweet and tart.

Sfogliatelles are pastries shaped like a clam shell and filled with a creamy semolina ricotta filling. The cannoli is a traditional Italian pastry; the shell is tender, light, and crispy. Cannolis are filled with an airy mixture of creamy ricotta filling.

You can make a variety of pastries such as cream puffs or éclairs by piping cream puff paste (pâte à choux) into differently formed shells and filling them with a selection of creams and fruits. These treats are topped off with fondant ganache or a dusting of confectionary sugar. Short dough shells filled with a combination of fruits and creams become fruit tarts, and make quick and simple dessert menu items. Strudel is a German pastry in which sweet or savory fillings are rolled in thin sheets or stretched dough. Babas and savarins are basically rich yeast dough baked in forms and soaked in rum or liquor-flavored syrups.

Puff pastry dough can be used to create a host of light, buttery, flaky desserts including the Napoleon. Roulades are made with sponge cake and filled with jams and creams. You can make many variations by changing the flavor, coating, or garnish. Stone fruit tarts are popular in late summer and early fall when peaches, plums, and nectarines are plentiful. After baking, the tart is glazed with apricot coating and served with a dollop of whipped cream.

Unit Review Questions
SHORT ANSWER

1. Define the term "broadcast" as it relates to the bakeshop.
2. What does the term "dock" mean?
3. The dough used to make sfogliatelle is similar to _____.
4. When using ricotta in place of pastry ricotta (sometimes called impastata), what extra step should be taken?
5. Describe the basic preparation of cannolis.
6. Another name for pâte à choux is _____.
7. Describe how the steps in preparing cream puffs and éclairs are similar and how they are different.
8. How does tart dough differ from pie dough?
9. Describe the basic preparation for fruit tartlets.
10. What is a strudel?
11. Describe babas and savarins.
12. Explain how to prepare a traditional Napoleon.
13. Describe the basic preparation of a roulade.
14. Describe the basic preparation of a stone fruit tart.

MULTIPLE CHOICE AND MATCHING

15. Semolina is derived from
    a. wheat.
    b. corn.
    c. rye.
    d. rice.
16. Cannoli dough is cooked by which method?
    a. baking
    b. sautéing
    c. deep frying
    d. pan frying
17. Cream-filled pastries have a shelf-life of
    a. 1 hour.
    b. 1 day.
    c. 3 days.
    d. 1 week.
18. A common substitution for strudel dough is
    a. short dough.
    b. sweet dough.
    c. bread dough.
    d. phyllo dough.
19. Which of the following preparations is *not* made from puff pastry dough?
    a. cream horns
    b. Napoleons
    c. swans
    d. cream slices

career opportunities
in baking

Unit 21 presents the certification options available for those wanting to enhance their careers. The unit also introduces the student to associations and professional organizations as well as to various trade publications that can serve as valuable resources to them in the future.

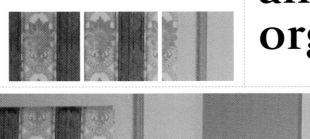

certification
and professional
organizations

A gathering of Certified Master Bakers, Market Basket, Chicago.

"Baking as a business or profession has never been confined to the making of bread alone—that is to say, bread in everyday use. A baker we take to mean is a person who bakes and prepares any farinaceous substance intended for human food. Therefore, baking not only includes loaf-bread baking, biscuit baking, fancy-bread baking, but also pastry-making and confectionery. It is common for all these branches to be practiced by the same person, and it is therefore fitting that they should all be treated in a work of this kind."

Robert Wells, *The Bread and Biscuit Baker's Guidebook*,
Published in 1890

KEY TERMS and
CONCEPTS

LEARNING Objectives

After you have finished reading this unit, you should be able to:

- **Evaluate** career opportunities in baking

- **Discuss** entrepreneurial opportunities in baking

- **Explain** the importance of certification and its requirements

- **Obtain** information from trade associations and federations

- **Recognize** the trade magazines and publications that will keep your knowledge current

accreditation

business plan

certification

product line

IT HAS BEEN SAID THAT, "LOST OPPORTUNITIES NEVER return." The dictionary defines opportunity as "a favorable opening." In this unit we will explore the many paths that one can take to a rewarding career that allows the individual the opportunity to maximize his or her knowledge, skills, talent, and passion as a professional in the baking industry. From baker, pastry cook, assistant pastry chef, baking and pastry arts research assistant, test kitchen worker, to pastry chef or baking entrepreneur, the opportunities abound. Employment may be found in hotels, clubs, restaurants, resorts, and cruise ships, as well as retail and wholesale bakeries and food manufacturers.

CHEFS, BAKERS, AND PASTRY CHEFS

How are chefs, bakers, and pastry chefs different?

The following explanation comes from the publication *On Becoming a Professional Chef* by the American Culinary Federation, Michael Baskette, CEC, CCE, AAC, Editor, and used here with permission.

Cooking professionals, and ultimately chefs, also must develop a basic knowledge of baking principles in order to become a true asset to the food-service industry. Some operations are too small to hire baking and pastry professionals, and the chef must prepare some in-house breads, biscuits, and/or pies. Large operations may employ a pastry professional; if so, it is the chef's job to supervise this individual and evaluate his or her work. The more cooking chefs know about baking and pastry, the more successful they will be overall (Figure 21-1).

Bakery products often play a significant role in cooking applications. Examples of baking products used in cooking include the dough used for making some pates and quiche, fresh Yorkshire pudding for roasted meats, and the pâte à choux pastry for hors d'oeuvres and appetizers. Cooks often are expected to make these products themselves. Fritters, crepes, soufflés, pancakes, batters, and savory custards also may be a cook's responsibility to prepare. Additionally, chefs should understand the fundamentals of making yeast breads, laminated dough (croissant, Danish and puff pastry), cookies, basic cakes, icings, and pies. In a production environment, any person can be asked to help prepare some of these basic items and/or the products derived from them. Skilled chefs must know how dough works; what happens to yeast when it is fed; the relationships among sugar, fat, and flavorings in making cakes, frostings, and fillings; and at what temperatures to bake pies, cookies, and breads.

The sets of required knowledge and competencies for baking and pastry professionals are slightly different than those for cooking professionals. While pastry professionals and bakery production professionals are considered two separate career paths, there is a great deal of crossover between the two disciplines. For example, cooking professionals should know how to make restaurant-style desserts like soufflés, crepes, and sabayon (a pastry sauce made on top of the stove in a double boiler using egg yolks, cream, and flavorings). In addition to basic baking skills, pastry professionals need experience and training in chocolate work; advanced decorating techniques; marzipan (paste made from ground almonds) modeling; candy, ice cream, and other frozen dessert production; and centerpiece decorating. Pastry chefs also should know how to prepare a great variety of tortes and cakes, including classic desserts such as the Sacher torte (a rich, dark chocolate cake layered with apricot jam and coated with melted chocolate), the Black Forest torte (a chocolate cake flavored with

Figure 21-1 A pastry chef fills puff pastry swans while working on board a cruise ship.

kirsch, sour cherries, and sweetened whipped cream), and traditional wedding cakes.

Individuals who want to become pastry chefs have to acquire the higher technical skills associated with finely detailed pastry work. This basic knowledge should include learning to identify and use all the ingredients and equipment found in bakeshops; properly scaling and measuring dry and liquid ingredients; and producing yeast breads, quick breads, laminated dough, choux paste (cream puff dough), meringues, cookies, pies, tarts, cobblers, custards, puddings, dessert sauces, and basic cakes, icings, and fillings.

Nutritional baking is another area of concentration the modern pastry chef is expected to study. Pastry professionals alter recipes and create new ones to ensure compliance with nutritional guidelines in baked products. People generally do not think of desserts when they are talking about nutrition or healthful eating, but there are ways to create desserts that have fewer calories, less fat, and more fiber. For example, when pastry chefs use fresh fruit in their creations, they can add vitamins, minerals, and other healthful nutrients to cakes, biscuits, and other simple prepared desserts.

These are just the general categories of skills and knowledge required of modern chefs. The higher up the career ladder a culinarian climbs, the more details, knowledge, and proficiency he or she must have to meet the greater challenges.

Job Classifications

In 1977, General John D. McLaughlin, Dr. Lewis J. Minor, and Chef Louis Szathmary, Ph.D., led an ACF team of association presidents and its director, L. Edwin Brown, to petition the U.S. Department of Labor to reclassify the title of chef under the *Dictionary of Official Titles* from Services (jobs such as maids, household cooks, and butlers) to Professional, Technical and Management. This change of status moves the job classification of chef to a professional level.

This reclassification also means that individuals in this profession are expected to pursue continuing education credits, training in critical subjects, certification, and apprenticeships.

Apprenticeships

To answer these new needs, the ACF developed an apprenticeship program through a grant from the U.S. Department of Labor that provided training in hand skills as well as a formal educational component for budding culinarians. The ACF apprenticeship program replicated the rigorous on-the-job training of the European model and included an academic component to cover the basics of sanitation, nutrition, and cooking and baking science. It soon became a solid model for promising culinarians who could not, or would not, attend formal culinary schools and colleges. Apprenticeships allowed students to work and go to school at the same time, offering a financial benefit as well as the opportunity to apply their lessons directly to real experiences in working production kitchens.

PROFESSIONAL ORGANIZATIONS

Professional networking is the best way for cooks or chefs to stay current with industry trends and to find progressive employment opportunities as they climb the professional career ladder. One of the best ways to begin is

Complete Estimated Costs

Equipment, tools, and merchandising supplies	$_____
Rental reserve money: 6 months plus security	$_____
Cost of opening inventory for supplies	$_____
Total amount of capital required	$_____

LEARNING ACTIVITY 21-1

Consider the Following

Write a brief statement of your business plan objectives. Address the following questions and add any additional information that will help you achieve your goals:

1. What will be special about your business?

2. What market do you intend to serve? What is the total market? What is your expected share?

3. How can you serve the market better than your competition?

4. How will you find appropriate employees?

5. How do you plan to advertise your business?

LEARNING ACTIVITY 21-2

Contact the Small Business Administration (SBA) for advice on how to raise the capital needed to start a business. SBA's volunteer professionals can also teach you about securing bank loans and creating a partnership or corporation as well as a host of other useful information.

Additional Information

Appendix C gives a list of U.S. Baking and Pastry Arts Educational Programs. Appendix D lists professional association and commodity boards as well as websites of interest.

PROFILE

Bernard Reynolds
Executive Vice President
Retailer's Bakery Association, *Laurel, MD*

The Retailer's Bakery Association, known to most in the industry as the RBA, is a nonprofit trade association that primarily represents retail bakers. "This organization is informational in nature. We strive to provide education and training that will help our members grow their businesses," says Reynolds. As the senior chief paid officer for the RBA, Reynolds is responsible for the administration of the association. He spends most of his time managing the association's staff, and working with the board of directors, the executive committee, and the volunteers. He also is responsible for seeing that the association is always moving in the right direction and meeting its budget and goals. "I love this industry. On a daily basis I get to rub shoulders with some of the most hard-working and creative individuals in the country. Bakers are enormously good people. Many of them look to our organization for advice and technical information. It is very rewarding to help them with their questions and problems," says Reynolds.

He offers the following advice for young people who may be considering a career in the baking industry: "Studies show that those who belong to a professional association are more successful and positive than those who don't. So consider joining the trade association that best reflects what you are doing. Retail bakers can easily feel all alone. Belonging to an association gives them support and helps them to keep up on the latest trends, techniques, and equipment. I also encourage young people to develop an insatiable appetite to learn. Continually seek out opportunities for more training. Stay open to new ideas. Visit other bakeries, keep your eyes open. Remember that a bakery owner is in business first. So learn all you can about running a business. Decorating cakes is only a little of what you will be required to do when you own your own business," says Reynolds.

SUMMARY

The sets of required knowledge and competencies for baking and pastry professionals are slightly different than those for cooking professionals. Cooking professionals should know how to make restaurant-style desserts. Pastry professionals need experience and training in chocolate work; advanced decorating techniques; marzipan modeling; preparation of candy, ice cream, and other frozen desserts, as well as centerpiece decorating. Pastry chefs should also know how to prepare a great variety of tortes and cakes.

There are a number of organizations that provide certification to the bakery and pastry professional. The American Culinary Federation (ACF) offers certification for Certified Pastry Culinarians, Certified Working Pastry Chefs, Certified Executive Pastry Chef, as well as the Certified Master Pastry Chef designation. Each level demands competence in a number of areas as demonstrated through written and practical exams. The Retailer's Bakery Association has developed certifications for the following: Certified Journey Baker, Certified Baker, Certified Decorator, and the Certified Master Baker. The process includes written and demonstrative testing.

There are a number of professional organizations from which to choose, depending on the scope and direction the culinarian wishes to pursue, including general professional cooking organizations, specialized organizations, and organizations for food managers, restaurant owners, and operators. There are also organizations for research chefs who focus on the science of cooking and baking and organizations that focus solely on baking.

Even chefs at the top of their careers understand and appreciate the need for continuing education. Attendance at foodservice conferences and conventions is one of the best forums in which to continue one's training and to meet other professionals. There are continuing education classes on the Internet and through many culinary schools. Those who wish to become an entrepreneur must start with a business plan by determining what kind of business they want to open. Business plans will help you think through the venture to be sure you have considered all of your options. They are also needed to convince potential lenders and investors that you are in control of the project and that their money will be safe with you. A well-executed business plan also serves as an operating guide as you turn your ideas into a viable business.

Unit Review Questions

SHORT ANSWER

1. Define the term "certification."
2. List some reasons why it is beneficial for chefs to develop a basic knowledge of baking principles.

3. Indicate the full name for the following ACF levels of certification.

CC _____

CPC _____

CSC _____

CWPC _____

CCDC _____

CEC _____

CCE _____

CMC _____

4. Which levels of ACF certification require the successful completion of a series of written and practical exams?

5. Indicate the full name for the following professional organizations.

ACF _____

RBA _____

IFSEA _____

NRA _____

RCA _____

CMA _____

APCA _____

6. Why is continuing education important in the foodservice industry?

7. List and describe the three main types of bakery businesses.

8. Outline the purposes of a business plan.

MULTIPLE CHOICE AND MATCHING

9. Currently, there are _____ ACF levels of professional certifications for cooks and chefs.

    a. 8

    b. 9

    c. 10

    d. 13

10. Which is *not* a certification designation of the Retailer's Bakery Association?

    a. Certified Apprentice Baker

    b. Certified Decorator

    c. Certified Baker

    d. Certified Master Baker

helpful charts

Metric Conversion Math

To Change	To	Multiply by
ounces (oz)	grams (g)	28.35
pounds (lb)	kilograms (kg)	2.21
teaspoons (tsp)	milliliters (mL)	5
tablespoon (tbsp)	milliliters (mL)	15
fluid ounces (fl oz)	milliliters (mL)	28.35
cups	liters (l)	.226
pints (pt)	liters (l)	−.453
quarts (qt)	liters (l)	.907
gallons (gal)	liters (l)	3.62

Additional Metric Conversions

Fahrenheit to Celsius	Subtract 32 from the Fahrenheit figure, multiply by 5, then divide by 9 to get the Celsius figure
Celsius to Fahrenheit	Multiply Celsius figure by 9, divide by 5, then add 32 to get the Fahrenheit figure
Inches to centimeters	Multiply inch figure by 2.54 to get number of centimeters
Centimeters to inches	Multiply centimeter figure by .39 to get number of inches

DECIMAL EQUIVALENTS

The American pound is in base 16 and the metric system is in base 10. In base 16, 16 units equal one and in base 10, 10 units equal one. This chart will help you to convert ounces to a decimal when changing yields with a calculator. For example, let's say you need to double a recipe that calls for 13 3/4 oz of milk. Using this chart, find the decimal equivalent for 13 3/4 oz, which is .8594 lb, and type that into the calculator. Then multiply that decimal by two. (.8594 × 2 = 1.7188. You have 1 pound and .7188. Now find .7188 on the chart, and convert it back to ounces .7188 = 11 1/2 oz.) So, you will need 1 lb 11 1/2 oz of milk in the doubled recipe.

Decimal Equivalent Conversions

1 oz = .0625 lb	6 oz = .3750 lb	11 oz = .6875 lb
1 1/4 oz = .0781 lb	6 1/4 oz = .3906 lb	11 1/4 oz = .7031 lb
1 1/2 oz = .0938 lb	6 1/2 oz = .4063 lb	11 1/2 oz = .7188 lb
1 3/4 oz = .1094 lb	6 3/4 oz = .4219 lb	11 3/4 oz = .7344 lb
2 oz = .1250 lb	7 oz = .4375 lb	12 oz = .7500 lb
2 1/4 oz = .1406 lb	7 1/4 oz = .4375 lb	12 1/4 oz = .7656 lb
2 1/2 oz = .1563 lb	7 1/2 oz = .4688 lb	12 1/2 oz = .7813 lb
2 3/4 oz = .1719 lb	7 3/4 oz = .4844 lb	12 3/4 oz = .7969 lb
3 oz = .1875 lb	8 oz = .5000 lb	13 oz = .8125 lb
3 1/4 oz = .2031 lb	8 1/4 oz = .5156 lb	13 1/4 oz = .8281 lb
3 1/2 oz = .2188 lb	8 1/2 oz = .5313 lb	13 1/2 oz = .8438 lb
3 3/4 oz = .2344 lb	8 3/4 oz = .5469 lb	13 3/4 oz = .8594 lb
4 oz = .2500 lb	9 oz = .5625 lb	14 oz = .8750 lb
4 1/4 oz = .2656 lb	9 1/4 oz = .5781 lb	14 1/4 oz = .8906 lb
4 1/2 oz = .2813 lb	9 1/2 oz = .5938 lb	14 1/2 oz = .9063 lb
4 3/4 oz = .2969 lb	9 3/4 oz = .6094 lb	14 3/4 oz = .9219 lb
5 oz = .3125 lb	10 oz = .6250 lb	15 oz = .9375 lb
5 1/4 oz = .3281 lb	10 1/4 oz = .6406 lb	15 1/4 oz = .9531 lb
5 1/2 oz = .3438 lb	10 1/2 oz = .6563 lb	15 1/2 oz = .9688 lb
5 3/4 oz = .3594 lb	10 3/4 oz = .6719 lb	15 3/4 oz = .9844 lb
		16 oz = 1 lb

Range Oven Temperatures

Fahrenheit	Celsius	Description
300°	150°	Slow
325°	160°	Slow–moderate
350°	180°	Moderate
375°	190°	Quick–moderate
400°	200°	Moderately hot
425°	220°	Hot
450°	230°	Hot

Oven temperatures vary, so it is wise to do a test run on common baked goods and then determine how long it will take an item to bake at certain temperatures. Record your findings so that you will have a permanent record. See blank chart on next page.

Suggested Oven Temperatures
(keep a chart for each oven)

Product	Time	Temperature	Product	Time	Temperature
Bread & Buns			**Cakes**		
White			Angel food		
All rye			Brownies		
Wheat			Jelly roll		
French			Boston crème		
Vienna, Italian			Honey crème		
Cinnamon bread			Pound cake		
Golden Indian			7" Layers		
Oat bran bread			8" Layers		
Crunchy Muesli Bread			10" Layers		
Bialy bread			1/4 sheet		
Bialy rolls			1/2 sheet		
Hard rolls			Full sheet		
Hamburger rolls			Crumb cakes		
Weiner buns					
Potato dinner rolls			Cupcakes		
Tea dinner rolls					
Hoagies & kaisers			Cookies		
Steak buns					
Oat bran buns			Muffins		
Oat bran rolls					
Rye buns			Pies		
Rye rolls					
Wheat buns			Quick breads		
Wheat rolls					
Pizza dough					
Sweet Dough			**Danish**		
Old-fashioned cinnamon bread			Snails, twists		
Caramel rolls			Crispies, flips		
Pecan clusters			Danish cut offs		
Sweet dough coffee cake			Danish coffee cake		

Temperature Conversions

Fahrenheit	Celsius (Metric)
−10°	23° (freezer temperature)
0°	18°
32°	0° (water will freeze)
50°	10°
68°	20° (room temperature)
100°	38°
150°	66°
205°	96° (water simmers)
212°	100° (water boils)
300°	149°
325°	163°
350°	177° (baking temperature)
375°	191°
400°	204° (hot oven)
425°	218°
450°	232° (very hot oven)
475°	246°
500°	260° (broiling)

Weights of Common Bakery Ingredients

Ingredient	Weight
2 cups butter or shortening	average 1 pound (454 g)
4 cups sifted, all-purpose flour	average 1 pound (454 g)
2 cups granulated sugar	average 1 pound (454 g)
2 1/2 cups powdered sugar	average 1 pound (454 g)
3 1/2 cups confectioners' sugar	average 1 pound (454 g)
2 1/4 cups brown sugar, firmly packed	average 1 pound (454 g)
3 1/2 cups whole wheat flour	average 1 pound (454 g)
3 cups cornmeal	average 1 pound (454 g)
9 large eggs	average 1 pound (454 g)
1 square baker's chocolate	average 1 ounce (28 g)
1 cup molasses	average 11 ounces (312 g)
2 tablespoons butter	average 1 ounce (28 g)
4 tablespoons flour	average 1 ounce (28 g)

More Weights of Common Ingredients

Item	Amount	Pounds	Ounces
Eggs, whole (1 pint)	10 each	1 lb	
Egg whites (1 pint)	16 each	1 lb	
Egg yolks (1 pint)	25 each	1 lb	
Buttermilk	1 quart	2 lb	
Fruit juice	1 quart	2 lb	
Glucose	1 quart	2 lb	14 oz
Heavy cream	1 quart	2 lb	
Honey	1 quart	2 lb	12 oz
Malt syrup	1 quart	2 lb	15 oz
Milk	1 quart	2 lb	
Molasses	1 quart	2 lb	14 oz
Oil, vegetable	1 quart	2 lb	
Water	1 quart	2 lb	
Apples, sliced (6 oz each)	3 cups	1 lb	
Bananas, sliced	2 1/2 cups	1 lb	
Bananas, crushed	1 cup		14 oz
Berries, cleaned	3 1/2 cups	1 lb	
Coconut, long thread	1 cup		2 oz
Coconut, macaroon	1 cup		2 5/8 oz
Coconut, moist	1 cup		3 oz
Dates, pitted	1 cup		6 oz
Figs	1 cup		7 oz
Lemon rind	4 tbsp.		1 oz
Pineapple, crushed	1 cup		8 oz
Prunes, pitted	1 cup		7 oz
Nuts, chopped	1 cup		3 3/4 oz
Nuts, sliced	1 cup		4 oz
Nuts, ground	1 cup		4 oz
Nuts, shelled	1 cup		4 oz
Raisins	1 cup		6 oz
Butter	1 cup		7 1/2 oz
Lard	1 cup		7 3/4 oz
Vegetable shortening	1 cup		6 3/4 oz

HIGH-ALTITUDE BAKING

If you live in an area of high altitude, you must give special consideration to the amount of leavening you use. Less baking powder will be required because of the decrease in air pressure. At ordinary altitudes, the amount of baking powder is from 1 to 5 percent, based on flour weight. Too much baking powder will produce a cake that is coarse-grained. Too little baking powder will result in a dense cake that has a tendency to pull away from the pan corners during baking. Experiment to determine the exact amount of baking powder you need in the higher-altitude ranges; however, the following is a good guideline.

High-Altitude Conversions

Feet Above Sea Level	Baking Powder Ounces Per Pound of Flour (45 g)
0–3,000	3/4 oz (20 g)
3,001–6,000	1/2 oz (15 g)
6,001–10,000	1/4 oz (10 g)
Above 10,000	1/8 oz (5 g)

You must also consider other changes in cake ingredients, baking time, and temperature to get the best results. Emulsified shortening will give better results than butter because it has a higher water tolerance. Increase baking temperature 5 degrees for each 3,000 feet above sea level. In extremely high altitudes, the baking time is lengthened slightly because of slower heat penetration. The rule of thumb is to lengthen the baking time 10 percent for every 5,000 feet.

TEMPERATURE AND YEAST ACTIVITY

The following chart will help you to understand how temperature affects yeast activity and leavening.

Temperature	Yeast Activity
20 to 30°F (−7 to 1°C)	No yeast activity; the dough is frozen
40 to 50°F (4 to 10°C)	Very little yeast activity
50 to 60°F (10 to 16°C)	Activity starts to accelerate
70 to 80°F (21 to 27°C)	Activity at this temperature is best for conditioning and flavor development of the dough
90 to 100°F (32 to 38°C)	Ideal temperature for leavening activity in proof box
100 to 130°F (38 to 54°C)	Very active in the oven (When the product reaches this temperature range, it causes oven spring to become active.)
130 to 140°F (54 to 60°C)	Yeast activity ends and coagulation begins

All of the formulas in this book call for the use of wet yeast. When you are using active dry or instant active yeast, refer to this chart. The ratio is 100 percent wet yeast to 40 percent active dry yeast to 33 percent instant active dry yeast along with the added water. Measure as carefully as possible to approximate the measurements shown in this chart.

Yeast Conversions

Wet Yeast	Active Dry Yeast	Instant Active Dry Yeast
3 oz (90 g)	1.2 oz (36 g) + 1.8 oz (54 g) water	1 oz (30 g) + 2 oz (60 g) water
6 oz (180 g)	2.4 oz (72 g) + 3.6 oz (108 g) water	2 oz (60 g) + 4 oz (120 g) water
9 oz (270 g)	3.6 oz (108 g)+ 5.4 oz (162 g) water	3 oz (90 g) + 3.6 oz (180 g) water
12 oz (360 g)	4.8 oz (144 g) + 7.2 oz (216 g) water	4 oz (120 g) + 8 oz (240 g) water
16 oz (480 g)	6.4 oz (192 g) + 9.6 oz (288 g) water	5.3 oz (158 g)+ 10.72 oz (322 g) water
1 lb 8 oz (720 g)	9.6 oz (288 g) + 14.4 oz (432 g) water	7.92 oz (238 g)+ 16.08 oz (482 g) water

appendix

B

pan care

USE AND CARE OF BAKING PANS IN FOODSERVICE OPERATIONS

By Bill McCoy, Chicago Metallic–THE BAKEWARE COMPANY. Reproduced with the permission of Bill McCoy and Chicago Metallic—the BAKEWARE COMPANY

After the foodservice operator purchases the required pans and places them into operation, it is important that proper care be given to the pans, in order to maximize their usable life. Pan life can be prolonged with a preventative maintenance program designed for each particular pan. The key to success of any foodservice baking pan maintenance program is that management must first develop a philosophy about the care of pans, establish a definitive pan-care training program, and insist that all associated with the use of the pans follow the designed program.

Pan Exposure—Bakery pans should never be exposed to water, humidity, condensation, or cold temperature.

Use Warm Pans—Warm pans eliminate the moisture of condensation on pans. This procedure also enables the glaze to release better and even helps to prevent pan corrosion due to contact with sticky dough. Warm pans also shorten proofing times and reduce the amount of lubrication that is necessary. Using warm baking pans will also give the baker greater control of baked product uniformity. In short, many bakers will tell you that warmed or preheated pans help produce better quality baked products.

Pan Storage—Pans should always be stored in a warm, dry area of the facility, far away from the dish machine or pot and pan sinks. Pans should be protected against moisture and humidity, drafts, windows, and doors. Pans should not be stored in a cool or cold place in order to avoid possible moisture condensation on their return to the kitchen. Pans can be stacked on a pan truck, pan dolly, or pan carrier and rolled into a convenient storage area. Always store pans upside down. Pans should never be stacked wet. Allow pans to completely dry in a warm oven, if storing pans immediately after contact with moisture of any type.

Depanning—Bakery pans should not be used for storage of baked products. All baked products should be depanned as soon as possible after removal from the oven. If baked products are allowed to cool in the pan, steam from the product will penetrate the glaze and may cause glaze lifting, premature glaze failure, and/or corrosion damage to the surface of the pan.

Pan Cleaning—Do not use metal utensils, harsh cleansers, highly alkaline or highly acidic chemicals, scouring pads, or any other abrasive cleaning aid that could damage the glaze. Use of abrasive cleaning methods such as scratching and scouring may cause glaze lifting, premature glaze failure, and/or corrosion damage to the surface of the pan. Do not soak pans in water. Do not wash pans in automatic dishwashers. Clean pans as you go; usually just wiping still-warm pans with a dry soft cloth is all that is necessary. Sometimes it may help to apply a little pan lubricant to the towel first. Avoid pan washing whenever possible. If absolutely necessary, wash pans with a soft towel and a mild soap and water solution. Lightly rinse but thoroughly towel dry all pans immediately. Cross-stack pans in a warm oven and allow them to thoroughly dry, especially if pans are immersed. **Immediately after washing, re-season pans with pan lubricant and bake the empty pan in the oven for five to six minutes at 350°F.** Pan Straightening—Bakery pans should be kept as straight as possible. Operators should inspect and straighten pans periodically to prevent them from becoming severely damaged. Severely damaged pans are a safety hazard and should be replaced.

PAN COATINGS

All commercial pan companies use the same source of *silicon release coating* (usually just called *glaze*) for their pans. This silicon is the only release coating that, when cured, meets the FDA provision of 21 CFR 175.400 for repeated food contact use when used as continuous coating on metal surfaces. The release coating's primary purpose in baking is to provide lubricant-free or reduced-lubricant product bakes, depending on the amount of fat or sugar in the baked product.

New pans should release the baked good with a minimum of "crumb" left in the pan. As the glaze gradually wears out, the operator can use a little more lubricant a little more often and extend the pan's remaining glaze life. Eventually, the glaze will wear completely off and will cease to be effective. At this point the operator must weigh the additional labor costs and oil costs of having to fully lubricate the pan for each bake cycle, against the costs and down time of sending the pans to a pan "reglazing" company for cleaning and reglazing. If he/she chooses to reglaze, his/her pans will come back clean and shiny, looking and baking as good as when new. By having pans reglazed regularly, a foodservice operator can keep the baking pan investment paying off for many years, reducing each pan's average "cost per bake." The cheapest baking pan is often the one that lasts the longest!

According to one manufacturer of this type of silicon release coating, "the life of [the] glaze coating is dependent upon the use and the abuse the coating receives." The manufacturer goes on to suggest that several factors, including proper glaze application, will affect the life of the glaze. These include "higher [bakery] use temperatures," noting that "at 600°F, only a few hours will degrade the coating," "constant exposure to certain chemical solvents **or high moisture,**" "in bakery release applications, the use of some oils at elevated temperatures will degrade the coating," and, "high-sugar-content food will shorten the life of the coating." Learning how to interpret these cautions is covered later, in the USE and CARE section.

Most baking pans must be "seasoned" before their first product bake, whether they are glazed or not. This is accomplished by applying a pan lubricant or spray to the baking surfaces of the pan and then allowing the pan to be heated to 350°F (without product in the pan), for a period of about five or six minutes. This step can be repeated as needed. These days, most pans are purchased with a silicon release coating to help reduce the amount of pan lubrication that might be needed. Glazing is almost always the best option for bakers. A freshly glazed surface and proper pan lubrication will serve the foodservice baker well, by eliminating non-sellable or non-usable baked goods [stickers] and, therefore, keeping the overall costs of the bakery department in line. The operator's food vendors can make specific recommendations as to which pan lubricant to use. Try to avoid any lubricant or spray that lists "water" as an ingredient.

The use of other types of "non-stick" coatings on baking pans is primarily limited to the use of coated household-weight pans designed for light duty use at home. DuPont's Teflon® coating is one notable exception that, when applied to sheet pans, has been used successfully in foodservice, but only for limited cooking and baking operations. One thing to remember in the future when choosing between "non-stick" coatings on bakeware, even on household-weight baking pans, is that it is usually better to choose a coating that has been applied to coiled sheets of metal ("coil-coated") *before manufacturing into pans*, than to choose a coating that has been painted on after the pan has been manufactured. Because coil-coated non-stick finishes are applied by machines specifically designed for the optimal coating result, non-stick coatings applied in this way will adhere more tenaciously to the underlying metal, and will last measurably longer than the post-manufacturing application of non-stick finishes.

Unfortunately, despite coating manufacturers' success with other types of foodservice products, most applied coatings will ultimately scratch, peel, or flake off bakery pans, and thus will lose their effectiveness as a bakery release coating. It is almost prohibitively expensive to have this type of coating reapplied, due as much to the methods of removing the old coating, as much as the inherently higher coating costs. Therefore, the use of these types of applied coatings is not recommended in either commercial or foodservice baking operations.

Some new PTFE-type proprietary coating processes have been developed and used in automated wholesale bakeries producing specific hamburger bun or roll products, but have not found general acceptance in other baking product segments. PTFE coatings don't work well with high-sugar bakery products, they have a shorter working life than is desirable, and, at current price levels, they add too much of a premium to the cost of pans. DuPont's Teflon® is one brand name of PTFE coatings.

REGLAZING BAKING PANS

There are many pan reglazing facilities located in the United States and Canada. Pan reglazing plants are geared to the wholesale baking industry's need for a fast pan cleaning and reglazing cycle. Reglazing plant managers are accustomed to the demands of their wholesale bakery customers to return multiple thousands of reglazed baking pans to the bakery almost immediately after reglazing, sometimes with the pans still warm from curing ovens!

This is because wholesale bakery plant managers and engineers monitor their pans' glaze life very carefully, product by product, and plan their reglazing needs according to the expected glaze life of their pans. Experienced foodservice bakers must learn to do the same thing, after first getting to know the requirements of their local reglazing company and the expected glaze life for their particular bakery products.

educational programs

The following schools offer baking and pastry arts programs. Both the ACF and RBA shared with us much of this information. We apologize to any school that we inadvertently overlooked.

SECONDARY PROGRAMS

Arizona
East Valley Institute of Technology
Mesa, Ariz.
480.461.4132

Arkansas
North Pulaski High School
Jacksonville, Ark.
479.241.2260

California
Advanced Culinary Arts School CSD
San Francisco, Calif.
415.277.2389

Ramona High School
Ramona, Calif.

School of Culinary Services
San Bernardino, Calif.
888.435.3915

Serrano High School
Phelan, Calif.
760.868.2503

West Valley Occupational Center
Woodland Hills, Calif.
818.346.3540

Colorado
Emily Griffith Opportunity School
Denver, Colo.
303.575.4814

Connecticut
Bullard-Haven Regional Vocational
Technical School
Bridgeport, Conn.
203.382.8405

Ella Grasso Regional Technical High School
Groton, Conn.
www.ctttech.org
860.448.0220

Howell Cheney R.L.T.S
Manchester, Conn.
860.649.5396

Morse School Center for Culinary Arts
Cromwell, Conn.
860.613.3350

Platt Regional Vocational Technical School
Milford, Conn.
203.783.5339

Florida
Atlantic Technical Center
Coconut Creek, Fla.
954.977.2000

Interlachen High School
Interlachen, Fla.
904.684.2116

McFatter Vocational Technical Center
Davie, Fla.
954.382.6543

North Technical Education Center
Riviera Beach, Fla.
561.881.4600

Palatka High School
Palatka, Fla.
904.329.0577

Pinellas Technical Center
Clearwater, Fla.
727.538.7167

Robert Morgan Vo-Tech
Miami, Fla.
305.253.9920

Sheridan Technical Center
Hollywood, Fla.
954.985.3262

Southeast High School
Bradenton, Fla.
813.741.3370

Withlacoochee Technical Institute
Inverness, Fla.
352.726.2430

Georgia
Atlanta Area Technical School
Atlanta, Ga.
404.756.3727

Atlanta Job Corps Center
Atlanta, Ga.
404.794.9512

Augusta Technical Institute
Augusta, Ga.
706.771.4083

Marietta High School
Marietta, Ga.
770.428.2631

Illinois
Area Career Center
La Salle, Ill.
815.223.1010

Chicago Public Schools
Chicago, Ill.
773.553.2470

Corliss High School
Chicago, Ill.
773.535.5115

Dawson Technical Institute
Chicago, Ill.
773.451.2053

Fenger High School
Chicago, Ill.
773.535.5430

Indian Valley Vocational Center
Sandwich, Ill.
815.786.9873

Manley High School
Chicago, Ill.
773.534.6900

Oak Park & River Forest High School
Oak Park, Ill.
708.383.0700

Red Bud High School
Red Bud, Ill.
618.282.3826

Richards High School
Chicago, Ill.
773.535.4945

Indiana
Anthis Career Center
Fort Wayne, Ind.
219.425.7667

Central 9 Career Center
Greenwood, Ind.
317.888.4401

Elkhart Area Career Center
Elkhart, Ind.
219.262.5880

Hammond Area Career Center
Hammond, Ind.
219.933.2428

Heartland Career Center
Wabash, Ind.
219.563.7481

Iowa
Assumption High School
Davenport, Iowa
319.326.5313

Denison Job Corps Center
Denison, Iowa
712.263.4192

Maine
Bath Regional Vocational Center
Bath, Maine
207.443.8257

Maryland
Carroll County Career
Westminster, Md.
410.751.3669

Center for Applied Technology
Severn, Md.
410.969.3100

Charles County Career & Technology Center
Pomfret, Md.
301.934.9061

Merganthaller High School
Baltimore, Md.
410.396.6495

Parkside High School
Salisbury, Md.
410.546.3155

Washington County Technical High School
Hagerstown, Md.
301.766.8057

Massachusetts
Cape Cod Regional Vocational Technical
High School
Harwich, Mass.
508.432.4500

Essex Agricultural and Technical Institute
Danvers, Mass.
978.774.0050

Joseph P. Keefe Technical School
Framingham, Mass.
508.879.5400

Leominster Center for Technical Education
Leominster, Mass.
978.534.7735

Minuteman Regional Vocational Technical
School
Lexington, Mass.
www.minuteman.org
781.863.1254

Montachusett Vocational Technical High
School
Fitchburg, Mass.
978.345.9200

North Shore Technical High School
Middleton, Mass.
978.762.0001

Plymouth South Regional High School
Plymouth, Mass.
508.224.7512

Southeastern Regional Vocational
Technical High School
South Easton, Mass.
508.238.4371

South Shore Vocational Technical High
School
Hanover, Mass.
781.878.8822

Tigers Pride Westfield Vocational Technical
High School
Westfield, Mass.
431.572.6533

Upper Cape Cod Regional Vocational
Technical High School
Wareham, Mass.
508.295.1320

WJ Dean Technical High School
Holyoke, Mass.
413.534.2071

Worcester Vocational High School
Worcester, Mass.
508.799.1964

Michigan
Allegan County Area Tech Ed Center
Allegan, Mich.
616.673.3121

Careerline Tech Center
Holland, Mich.
616.738.8950

Oakland Technical Center
Pontiac, Mich.
947.451.2724

St. Clair Technical
Port Huron, Mich.
810.364.8990

Missouri

Franklin Technology Center
Joplin, Mo.
417.625.5260

Poplar Bluff Tech. Career Ctr.
Poplar Bluff, Mo.
573.785.7751

Saline County Career Center
Marshall, Mo.
660.886.6958

Southwest Area Career Center
Monett, Mo.
417.235.7022

Nebraska

Omaha Career Center
Omaha, Neb.
402.557.3700

Nevada

Area Technical Trade Center
N. Las Vegas, Nev.
702.799.8300

Glenn Hare Occupational Center
Reno, Nev.
702.333.5377

Southern Nevada Vocational Technical
Center
Las Vegas, Nev.
702.799.7545

New Hampshire

Manchester School of Technology
Manchester, N.H.
603.624.6490

Milford High School
Milford, N.H.
203.673.4201

White Mountains Regional High School
Whitefield, N.H.
603.837.2528

New Jersey

Atlantic County Vocational Technical
School
Mays Landing, N.J.
609.625.2249

Bergen County Academies
Hackensack, N.J.
201.343.6000

Burlington County Institute of Technology
(Medford Campus)
Medford, N.J.
609.654.0200

Camden County Area Vo-Tech
Sicklerville, N.J.
609.767.7000

Gloucester County Institute of Technology
Sewell, N.J.
609.468.1445

Hackensack Technical Institute
Hackensack, N.J.
201.343.6000

Middlesex County Vo-Tech High School
Piscataway, N.J.
732.985.0717

Monmouth County Career Center
Freehold, N.J.
732.431.3773

Somerset County Vo-Tech
Bridgewater, N.J.
908.526.8900

Union County Vo-Tech
Scotch Plains, N.J.
908.889.2935

Woodbridge Vocational High School
Woodbridge, N.J.
732.634.5858

New Mexico

Albuquerque Technical Vocational Institute
Albuquerque, N.M.
505.224.3730

New York

Abrookin Vocational Technical Center
Albany, N.Y.
518.438.2503

Eastern Suffolk BOCES
Oakdale, N.Y.
631.244.5800

Erie IBOCES
Cheektowago, N.Y.
716.632.6680

Herkimen County BOCES
Herkimen, N.Y.
315.867.2000

Hewes Educational Center
Ashville, N.Y.
716.763.1801

North Franklin Education Center
Malone, N.Y.
518.483.5230

OCM BOCES
Syracuse, N.Y.
315.433.2635

Orleans Niagara BOCES
Medina, N.Y.
800.836.7510

Questar III
Hudson, N.Y.
518.828.4157

Park West High School (Formerly Food &
Maritime Trades High School)
New York, N.Y.
212.262.5861

Rockland BOCES
West Nyack, N.Y.
914.627.4700

SCT Technical Education & Career Center
Elmira, N.Y.
607.739.3581

Saratoga Vo-Tec Myer's BOCES
Saratoga Springs, N.Y.
518.581.3600

Saunders Trades & Technical High School
Yonkers, N.Y.
914.376.8151

Southern Adirondack Education Center
Hudson Falls, N.Y.
518.746.3460

W.D. Ormsby Vocational Center
East Aurora, N.Y.
716.652.8250

Wayne Area Vocational Center
Williamson, N.Y.
315.589.2625

WeMoCo Vocational Trades Center
Spencerport, N.Y.
800.352.2471

Wilson Technological Center
Dix Hills, N.Y.
516.667.6000

Ohio

Akron North High School
Akron, Ohio
330.434.0114

Greene County Career Center
Xenia, Ohio
937.372.6941

Mahoning County Joint Vocational School
Canfield, Ohio
330.533.6871

Shaker Heights Middle School
Shaker Heights, Ohio
216.295.4102

Oklahoma

Indian Meridian Vocational Technical
School
Stillwater, Okla.
405.377.3333

Southern Oklahoma Technology Center
Ardmore, Okla.
580.223.2070

Oregon

Sisters High School
Sisters, Ore.
541.549.4045

Pennsylvania

Berks Career and Technology Center
East Campus
Oley, Pa.
610.987.6201

Bucks County Technical School
Fairless Hills, Pa.
215.949.1700

Center for Technical Studies
Central Montgomery County
Norristown, Pa.
610.277.2301

Connelley Skill Learning Center
Pittsburgh, Pa.
412.338.3700

Dobbins Technical School
Philadelphia, Pa.
215.227.4421

Edward Bok A.V.T.S.
Philadelphia, Pa.
215.952.6200

Franklin County Career & Technology
Center
Chambersburg, Pa.
717.263.9033

Hiram Andrews Center
Johnstown, Pa.
814.225.8386

Lancaster County Career & Technology
Center
Hummelstown, Pa.
717.653.3000

Lebanon County Career & Technology
Center
Lebanon, Pa.
717.273.8551

Lehigh County Vocational Technical
School
Schnecksville, Pa.
610.799.1309

North Montco Technical Center
Lansdale, Pa.
215.368.1177

Reading Muhlenberg Area Vocational
Technical School
Reading, Pa.
610.921.7331

Somerset County Technology Center
Somerset, Pa.
814.443.3651

South Vocational Technical High School
Pittsburgh, Pa.
412.488.5184

Rhode Island

Chariho Career Technical School
Wood River Junction, R.I.
401.364.6869

Davies Career & Technical High School
Lincoln, R.I.
401.728.1500

Warwick Area Career Center
Warwick, R.I.
401.737.3300

Tennessee

Glencliff High School
Nashville, Tenn.
615.333.5092

Texas

Brownfield High School
Brownfield, Texas
806.637.2591

Utah

DATC-Davies Area Technical Center
Kaysville, Utah
801.593.2339

Ogden Weber Applied Technology Center
Ogden, Utah
801.627.8423

Virginia

Charlottesville-Albemarle Technical
Education Center
Charlottesville, Va.
804.973.4461

Louisa County High School
Mineral, Va.
540.894.5436

Spotsylvania Vocational Center
Spotsylvania, Va.
540.898.2655

Washington

Auburn High School
Auburn, Wash.
253.931.4719

West Virginia

Monongolia County Technical Education
Center
Morgantown, W.Va.
304.291.9240

Wisconsin

Marshall High School
Marshall, Wis.
608.655.3461

POST-SECONDARY PROGRAMS

(An asterisk identifies the post-secondary schools that are currently accredited by the ACF and have baking and pastry arts programs.)

Alabama

Culinard, The Culinary Institute of Virginia College
Birmingham, Ala.
www.culinard.com
205.802.1200

*James H. Faulkner State Community College
Gulf Shores, Ala.
www.faulkner.cc.al.us
800.231.3752

Alaska

*Alaska Vocational Technical Center
Seward, Alaska
www.eed.state.ak.us/avtec
907.224.3322

Arizona

The Art Institute of Phoenix
Phoenix, Ariz.
www.aipx.edu
800.474.2479

Maricopa Skill Center
Phoenix, Ariz.
www.gwc.maricopa.edu
602.238.4300

Scottsdale Community College
Scottsdale, Ariz.
www.wc.maricopa.edu
602.423.6241

*Scottsdale Culinary Institute
Scottsdale, Ariz.
www.wcichefs.com
800.848.2433

California

American River College
Sacramento, Calif.
www.arc.losrios.cc.ca.us
916.484.8526

Bakersfield College
Bakersfield, Calif.
805.395.4564

*California Culinary Academy
San Francisco, Calif.
www.baychef.com
800.BAYCHEF

California School of Culinary Arts
Pasadena, Calif.
www.calchef.com
626.403.8490

Cerritos College
Norwalk, Calif.
www.cerritos.edu
562.860.2451

*Columbia College
Sonara, Calif.
www.columbia.yosemite.cc.ca.us
209.588.5135

Contra Costa College
San Pablo, Calif.
www.contracosta.cc.ca.us
510.235.7800

The Culinary Institute of America
St. Helena, Calif.
www.ciachef.edu
800.333.9242

Diablo Valley College
Pleasant Hill, Calif.
www.dvc.edu
925.685.1230

Institute of Technology
Roseville, Calif.
916.797.6337

Laney College
Oakland, Calif.
www.laney.peralta.cc.ca.us
510.464.3407

Long Beach City College
Long Beach, Calif.
www.lbcc.cc.ca.us
562.938.4502

*Los Angeles Trade Technical College
Los Angeles, Calif.
www.lattc.cc.ca.us
213.744.9482

National Culinary and Bakery School
La Mesa, Calif.
www.nationalschools.com
619.461.2800

New School of Cooking
Culver City, Calif.
www.newschoolofcooking.com
310.842.9702

Northern California Baking School
Chico, Calif.
530.879.3746

Opportunities Industrialization Center
(West)
Menlo Park, Calif.
www.oicw.org
650.462.6322

Orange Coast College
Costa Mesa, Calif.
www.orangecoastcollege.com
714.432.5835

Richardson Researches, Inc.
Confectionery School
Hayward, Calif.
www.richres.com
510.785.1350

Riverside Community College
Riverside, Calif.
714.684.3240

San Francisco Baking Institute
South San Francisco, Calif.
www.sfbi.com
650.589.5784

San Joaquin Delta College
Stockton, Calif.
www.deltacollege.org
209.954.5582

Santa Barbara City College
Santa Barbara, Calif.
www.sbcc.net
805.865.0581

Southern California School of Culinary Arts
So. Pasadena, Calif.
626.403.8490

Tante Marie's Cooking School
San Francisco, Calif.
www.tantemarie.com
415.788.6699

Westlake Culinary Institute
Westlake Village, Calif.
www.letsgetcookin.com
818.991.3940

Colorado

Culinary School of the Rockies
Boulder, Colo.
www.culinaryschoolrockies.com
303.494.7988

Johnson & Wales University
Denver, Colo.
www.jwu.edu
303.256.9338

Pikes Peak Community College
Colorado Springs, Colo.
www.ppcc.ccoes.edu
719.540.7371

The Art Institute of Colorado
Denver, Colo.
www.aic.artinstitutes.edu
800.275.2420

Connecticut

Center for Culinary Arts
Cromwell, Conn.
www.centerforculinaryarts.com
860.613.3350

Connecticut Culinary Institute
Farmington, Conn.
www.ctculinary.com
860.677.7869

Florida

The Art Institute of Fort Lauderdale
Ft. Lauderdale, Fla.
www.artinstitute.edu
800.275.7603

Capital Culinary Academy of Keiser
College
Tallahassee, Fla.
www.capitalculinaryinstitute.com
850.906.9494

Capital Culinary Academy of Keiser
College
Melbourne, Fla.
www.capitalculinaryinstitute.com
312.255.2255

Florida Community College at Jacksonville
Jacksonville, Fla.
www.fccj.cc.fl.us
904.766.6652

*Florida Culinary Institute
West Palm Beach, Fla.
www.floridaculinary.com
561.668.2001

Gulf Coast Community College
Panama City, Fla.
www.gc.cc.fl.us
850.872.3850

Johnson & Wales University, North Miami
North Miami, Fla.
www.jwu.edu
800.232.2433

Orlando Culinary Academy (Le Cordon Bleu)
Orlando, Fla.
www.culinary-school.us/orlando
407.888.4000

Pensacola Junior College
Pensacola, Fla.
www.pjc.cc.fl.us
850.484.1159

Pinellas Technical Educational Center
St. Petersburg, Fla.
www.ptecclw.pinellas.k12.fl.us
727.893.2500

The Southeast Institute of the Culinary Arts
St. Augustine, Fla.
904.829.1061

Georgia

*The Art Institute of Atlanta
Atlanta, Ga.
www.aia.aii.edu
800.275.4242

Chattahoochee Technical College
Marietta, Ga.
www.chattcollege.com
770.509.6305

Hawaii

*Kapiolani Community College
Honolulu, Hawaii
www.hawaii.edu
808.734.9466

Kauai Community College
Lihue, Hawaii
www.kauaicc.hawaii.edu
808.245.8265

*Maui Community College
Kahului, Hawaii
www.hawaii.edu
808.984.3225

Idaho

Boise State University
Boise, ID
www.idbsu.edu
208.426.1532

BYU Idaho
Rexburg, ID
www.byui.edu
208.356.1338

Illinois

College of DuPage
Glen Ellyn, Ill.
www.cod.edu
630.942.2720

College of Lake County
Grayslake, Ill.
www.clc.cc.il.us
847.543.2823

Cooking Academy of Chicago
Chicago, Ill.
www.cookingacad.com
773.478.9840

*Cooking & Hospitality Institute of Chicago (Le Cordon Bleu)
Chicago, Ill.
www.chicnet.org
312.944.2725

Dawson Technical Institute
Chicago, Ill.
773.451.2053

Elgin Community College
Elgin, Ill.
www.elgin.cc.il.us
847.214.7461

French Pastry School, Inc.
Chicago, Ill.
www.frenchpastryschool.com
312.726.2419

The Illinois Institute of Art
Chicago, Ill.
www.ilia.aii.edu
800.351.3450

Joliet Junior College
Joliet, Ill.
815.729.9020

Kendall College
Evanston, Ill.
www.kendall.edu
847.866.1304

Lexington College
Chicago, Ill.
773.779.3800

Moraine Valley Community College
Palos Hills, Ill.
www.moraine.cc.il.us
708.974.5320

William Rainey Harper College
Palatine, Ill.
847.925.6874

Wilton School of Cake Decorating &
Confectionary Art
Woodridge, Ill.
www.wilton.com
630.963.7100

Indiana
*Ivy Tech State College (Central)
Indianapolis, Ind.
www.ivy.tec.in.us
317.921.4312

Ivy Tech State College (Ft. Wayne)
Fort Wayne, Ind.
www.ivy.tec.in.us
219.480.4240

Ivy Tech State College (Northwest)
Gary, Ind.
www.ivy.tec.in.us
219.981.4445

McDowell Adult Ed Center
Columbus, Ind.
812.376.4451

Vincennes University
Vincennes, Ind.
www.vinu.edu
812.888.5828

Iowa
Eastern Iowa Community College
Davenport, Iowa
319.236.0142

Indian Hills Community College
Ottumwa, Iowa
www.ihcc.cc.ia.us
641.683.5198

Kirkwood Community College
Cedar Rapids, Iowa
www.kirkwood.cc.ia.us
319.398.5411

Kansas
American Institute of Baking
Manhattan, Kan.
www.aibonline.org
785.537.4750

Kansas State University
Manhattan, Kan.
www.ksu.edu
785.532.4065

Kentucky
Elizabethtown Technical College
Elizabethtown, Ky.
270.766.5133

Jefferson Community College
Louisville, Ky.
www.jctc.kctcs.net
502.584.0181

*Sullivan University Baking Department
Louisville, Ky.
www.sullivan.edu
502.456.6504

Louisiana
Culinary Institute of New Orleans
New Orleans, La.
www.ci-no.com
504.525.2433

Delgado Community College
New Orleans, La.
www.dcc.edu
504.483.4476

Louisiana Technical College
Jefferson Campus
Metaric, La.
www.brti.tec.la.us
504.736.7081

Louisiana Technical College
Lafayette Campus
Lafayette, La.
www.brti.tec.la.us
318.262.5962

Louisiana Technical College
Sowela Campus
Lake Charles, La.
www.brti.tec.la.us
337.491.2640

Sclafani's Cooking School
Matairie, La.
www.sclafanicookingschool.com
504.833.7861

Maine

Washington County Technical College
Calais, Maine
www.wctc.org
207.454.2144

Maryland

Anne Arundel Community College
Arnold, Md.
www.aacc.cc.md.us
410.777.2707

Baltimore International College
Baltimore, Md.
www.bic.edu
410.752.4710

International School of Confectionary Arts
Gaithersburg, Md.
www.notterschool.com
301.963.9077

L'Academie de Cuisine, Inc.
Gaithersburg, Md.
www.lacademie.com
301.670.8670

Massachusetts

Bristol Community College
Fall River, Mass.
www.bristol.mass.edu
508.678.2811

Holyoke Community College
Holyoke, Mass.
www.hcc.mass.edu
413.552.2408

International Institute of Culinary Arts
Fall River, Mass.
www.iica.com
508.675.9305

Newbury College
Brookline, Mass.
www.newbury.edu
617.730.7161

North Shore Community College
Danvers, Mass.
www.nscc.mass.edu
978.762.4000

Michigan

Gogebic Community College
Ironwood, Mich.
906.932.4231

*Grand Rapids Community College
Grand Rapids, Mich.
www.grcc.cc.mi.us
616.234.3690

Henry Ford Community College
Dearborn, Mich.
www.henryford.cc.mi.us
313.845.6390

Macomb Community College
Clinton Township, Mich.
www.macomb.cc.mi.us
810.286.2023

Mott Community College
Flint, Mich.
www.mcc.edu
810.232.7845

Northwestern Michigan College
Traverse City, Mich.
www.nmc.edu
616.922.1197

Oakland Community College
Framington Hills, Mich.
www.occ.cc.mi.us
947.471.7770

Schoolcraft College
Livonia, Mich.
www.schoolcraft.edu
734.462.4423

Siena Heights College
Adrian, Mich.
www.sienaheights.edu
517.264.7635

*Washtenaw Community College
Ann Arbor, Mich.
www.washtenaw.cc.mi.us
734.973.3601

Minnesota

Anoka-Hennepin Technical College
Anoka, Minn.
www.ank.tec.mn.us
612.576.4884

The Art Institutes International Minnesota
Minneapolis, Minn.
www.aii.edu
612.332.3361

Dakota County Technical College
Rosemount, Minn.
651.423.8536

Hennepin Technical College
Plymouth, Minn.
www.htc.mnscu.edu
612.550.2116

Le Cordon Bleu at Brown College
Mendota Heights, Minn.
www.browncollege-info.org
800.627.6966

St. Paul Technical College
St. Paul, MN
www.saintpaul.edu
651.846.1493

South Central Technical College
North Mankato, Minn.
www.sctc.mnscu.edu
507.389.7229

Mississippi

Hinds Community College
Pearl, Miss.
www.hinds.cc.ms.us
800.446.3722

Missouri

Ozarks Technical Community College
Springfield, Mo.
417.895.7282

*St. Louis Community College
St. Louis, Mo.
www.stlcc.cc.mo.us
314-539-5000

Nebraska

*Metropolitan Community College
Omaha, Neb.
www.mccneb.edu
800.228.9553

Nevada

*Truckee Meadows Community College
Reno, Nev.
www.tmcc.edu
775.674.7917

New Hampshire

New Hampshire College Culinary Institute
Manchester, N.H.
603.644.3128

Thompson School of Applied Science
University of New Hampshire
Durham, N.H.
603.862.1025

New Jersey

Atlantic Community College
Mays Landing, N.J.
www.atlantic.edu
609.343.5009

Brookdale Community College
Lincroft, N.J.
201.224.2836

Hudson County Community College
Jersey City, N.J.
www.hudson.cc.nj.us
201.714.2193

Mercer County Community College
Trenton, N.J.
www.mccc.edu
609.586.4800

New Mexico

Albuquerque Technical Vocational Institute
Community College
Albuquerque, N.M.
www.tvi.cc.nm.us
505.224.3755

New York

Adirondack Community College
Queensbury, N.Y.
www.suny.edu
518.743.2264

*The Art Institute of New York City
New York, N.Y.
www.nyrs.artinstitutes.edu
212.226.5500

Culinary Academy of Long Island
Westbury, N.Y.
516.876.8888

The Culinary Institute of America
Hyde Park, N.Y.
www.ciachef.edu
845.451.1716

Erie Community College
Buffalo, N.Y.
www.ecc.edu
716.851.1135

The French Culinary Institute
New York, N.Y.
www.frenchculinary.com
212.219.8890

The Institute of Culinary Education
New York, N.Y.
www.newyorkculinary.com
800.522.4610

Institute of Culinary Education (Formerly
Peter Kump)
New York, N.Y.
www.iceculinary.com
212.847.0757

Mohawk Valley Community College
Rome, N.Y.
www.mvcc.edu
315.339.3470

New School University
New York, N.Y.
www.newschool.edu
212.255.4141

New York City Technical College
Brooklyn, N.Y.
www.nycic.cuny.edu
718.260.5630

New York Restaurant School
New York, N.Y.
212.226.5500

Niagara County Community College
Sanborn, N.Y.
www.sunyniagara.cc.ny.us
716.731.3271

NYIT Culinary Arts Center
Central Islip, N.Y.
www.nyit.edu
518.746.3409

NYIT Culinary Program
Old Westbury, N.Y.
www.nyit.edu
516.348.7675

Paul Smith's College
Paul Smiths, N.Y.
www.paulsmiths.edu
518.327.6227

Schenectady County Community College
Schenectady, N.Y.
www.sunysccc.edu
581.381.1366

SUNY Cobleskill State College
Cobleskill, N.Y.
www.cobleskill.edu
518.234.5425

SUNY College at Alfred
Wellsville, N.Y.
www.alfredstate.edu
800.4ALFRED

North Carolina

Asheville Buncombe Technical
Community College
Asheville, N.C.
www.asheville.cc.ne.us
828.254.1921

Cape Fear Community College
Wilmington, N.C.
www.capefear.cc.nc.us
910.251.5960

Central Piedmont Community College
Charlotte, N.C.
www.cpcc.cc.nc.us
704.330.6721

Johnson & Wales University
Charlotte, N.C.
www.jwu.edu
704.207.9577

South Piedmont Community College
Monroe, N.C.
www.southpiedmont.org
704.289.8588

Wake Technical Community College
Raleigh, N.C.
www.wake.tec.nc.us
919.662.3417

Wilkes Community College
Wilkesboror, N.C.
www.wilkes.cc.ne.us
336.838.6141

Ohio

Cincinnati State Technical & Community
College
Cincinnati, Ohio
www.cinstate.cc.oh.us
513.569.1663

Columbus State Community College
Columbus, Ohio
www.cscc.edu
614.227.2579

Cuyahoga Community College
Cleveland, Ohio
www.tri-c.cc.oh.us
216.987.4082

Great Oaks Institute of Technology and
Career Development
Cincinnati, Ohio
513.771.8840

*Hocking College
Nelsonville, Ohio
740.753.3531

International Culinary Arts and Sciences
Institute
Chesterland, Ohio
www.icasi.net
440.729.7340

Sinclair Community College
Dayton, Ohio
www.sinclair.edu
937.512.5197

The Western Reserve School of Cooking
Hudson, Ohio
www.wrsoc.com
330.650.1665

Oklahoma

Oklahoma State University
Okmulgee, Okla.
www.osu-okmulgee.edu
918.293.5030

Pioneer Technical Center
Ponca City, Okla.
www.pioneertech.org
580.762.8336

Oregon

International School of Baking
Bend, Ore.
www.schoolofbaking.com
541.389.8553

Lane Community College
Eugene, Ore.
www.lanecc.edu
503.747.4501

Western Culinary Institute Le Cordon Bleu
Portland, Ore.
www.westernculinary.com
800.666.0312

Pennsylvania

The Art Institute of Philadelphia
Philadelphia, Pa.
www.aiph.artinstitutes.edu
800.275.2474

Bucks County Community College
Newtown, Pa.
www.bucks.edu
215.968.8241

Community College of Philadelphia
Philadelphia, Pa.
www.ccp.cc.pa.us
610.277.2301

Harrisburg Area Community College
Harrisburg, Pa.
www.hacc.edu
717.780.2674

International Culinary Academy Le
Cordon Bleu
Pittsburgh, Pa.
www.iup.edu
800.438.6424

*Pennsylvania College of Technology
Williamsport, Pa.
www.pct.edu
570.326.3761

*Pennsylvania Culinary Institute
Pittsburgh, Pa.
www.paculinary.com
800.432.2433

The Restaurant School at Walnut College
Philadelphia, Pa.
www.therestaurantschool.com
215.222.4200

*Westmoreland County Community
College
Youngwood, Pa.
www.westmoreland.cc.pa.us
724.925.4254

Yorktown Business Institute
York, Pa.
www.yorkchef.com
800.840.1004

Rhode Island

Johnson & Wales University
Providence, R.I.
www.jwu.edu
800.342.5598

South Carolina

Horry-Georgetown Technical College
Conway, S.C.
www.gvltec.edu
843.347.3186

Johnson & Wales University
Charleston, S.C.
www.jwu.edu
800.868.1522

Trident Technical College
Charleston, S.C.
www.trident.tec.sc.us
843.722.5542

Tennessee

State Technical Institute at Memphis
Memphis, Tenn.
www.xap.com
901.383.4637

Texas

Alain and Marie LeNotre Culinary Institute
Houston, Texas
www.lenotre-alain-marie.com
713.692.0077

The Art Institute of Dallas
Dallas, Texas
www.aid.artinstitutes.edu
800.275.4243

The Art Institute of Houston
Houston, Texas
www.aihartinstitutes.edu
800.275.4244

Central Texas College
Killeen, Texas
www.ctcd.cc.tx.us
800.792.3348

Culinary Academy of Austin
Austin, Texas
www.chefs.home.texas.net
512.451.5743

*Del Mar College
Corpus Christi, Texas
www.delmar.edu
361.698.1734

*El Centro College
Dallas, Texas
214.860.2202

Galveston College
Galveston, Texas
www.gc.edu
409.763.6551

Houston Community College
Houston, Texas
www.hccs.cc.tx.us
713.630.7246

St. Philip's College
San Antonio, Texas
www.accd.edu
210.531.3315

Texas Culinary Academy
Austin, Texas
www.lechef.org
888.5LE.CHEF

Utah

Dixie College
Saint George, Utah
801.673.4811

Salt Lake Community College
Salt Lake City, Utah
www.slcc.edu
801.957.4643

Utah Valley State College
Orem, Utah
www.uvsc.edu
801.222.8000

Vermont

New England Culinary Institute
Montpelier, Vt.
www.neculinary.com
800.223.6324

Virginia

The Art Institute of Washington
Arlington, Va.
www.aiw.artinstitutes.edu
877.303.3771

Johnson & Wales University
Norfolk, Va.
www.jwu.edu
757.853.3508

Stratford College
Falls Church, Va.
www.stratford.edu
703.821.8570

Washington

The Art Institute of Seattle
Seattle, Wash.
www.ais.edu
206.448.6600

Bellingham Technical College
Bellingham, Wash.
www.belltc.ctc.edu
509.466.2602

Clark College Culinary Arts
Vancouver, Wash.
www.clark.edu
360.992.2156

*Lake Washington Technical College
Kirkland, Wash.
www.lwtc.ctc.edu
425.739.8349

Olympic College
Bremerton, Wash.
www.oc.ctc.edu
360.478.4576

Renton Technical College
Renton, Wash.
www.renton-tc.ctc.edu
425.235.2352

*Seattle Central Community College
Seattle, Wash.
www.seattleculinary.com
206.587.5424

South Puget Sound Community College
Olympia, Wash.
www.spscc.ctc.edu
360.754.7711

*South Seattle Community College
Seattle, Wash.
www.chefschool.com
206.764.5344

Spokane Community College
Spokane, Wash.
www.scc.spokane.cc.wa.us
509.533.7346

Washington, D.C.

Stonecrest Home Arts, Inc.
Washington D.C.
202.244.5698

*Stratford University
Washington D.C.
www.stratford.edu
800.444.0804

Wisconsin

Blackhawk Technical College
Janesville, Wis.
www.blackhawk/tec.wi.us
608.757.7696

Chippewa Valley Technical College
Eau Claire, Wis.
www.chippewa.tec.wi.us
715.833.6360

Fox Valley Technical College
Appleton, Wis.
www.foxvalleytech.com
920.735.2277

*Madison Area Technical College
Madison, Wis.
www.madison.tec.wi.us
608.246.6007

Milwaukee Area Technical College
Milwaukee, Wis.
www.milwaukee.tec.wi.us
414.297.6860

Moraine Park Technical College
Fond du Lac, Wis.
www.moraine.tec.wi.us
800.472.4554

Nicolet Area Technical College
Rhinelander, Wis.
www.nicolet.tec.wi.us
715.365.4649

appendix D

resources

BAKING AND PASTRY PERIODICALS

American Cake Decorating Magazine

Art Culinaire
Culinaire, Inc. 973.993.5500

Bakery Food Industry

Baking & Snack

Equipment Solutions Magazine

Baking Buyer

Baking Management Magazine

Bakery Net (online bakery resource)
www.bakery-net.com

Food Arts
M. Shanken Communications

Food Engineering Magazine
BNP Media

Food Quality Magazine
Publisher Carpe Diem

Milling and Baking News

Modern Baking

Prepared Foods
BNP Media

Restaurants and Institutions
Reed Business Information

Snack Food & Wholesale Bakery Magazine

WEBSITES OF INTEREST

American Culinary Federation
www.acfchefs.org

American Institute of Baking
www.aibonline.org

American Society of Baking
www.asbe.org

Bakery Net
www.bakery-net.com

Baking Management Magazine
www.bakery-net.com

BEMA (an International Association
  Serving Baking and Food Industries)
www.bema.org

Careers in the Baking Industry
www.careersinfood.com

Grocery Manufacturers Association
www.gmabrands.com

International Food Information Council
  Foundation
www.ific.org

International Foodservice Executives
  Association
www.ifsea.com

Milling & Baking News
www.bakingbusiness.com

National Restaurant Association
www.restaurant.org

Research Chefs Association
www.culinology.com

Retail Baker's Association
www.rbanet.com

Snack Food & Wholesale Bakery Magazine
www.snackandbakery.com

U.S. Pastry Competition Website
www.pastrychampionship.com

Wheat Foods Counsel
www.wheatfoods.org

Women Chefs & Restaurateurs
www.womenchefs.org

PROFESSIONAL ASSOCIATIONS AND COMMODITY BOARDS

The following is a list of associations and commodity boards pertaining to the baking industry. This is by no means a comprehensive list, but rather a collection of some of the associations and commodity boards to which we have become acquainted. These websites are full of useful information as well as recipes.

Almond Board of California
www.almondsarein.com

American Bakers Association
www.americanbakers.org

American Butter Institute
www.butterinstitute.org

American Culinary Federation
www.acfchefs.org

American Dietetic Association
www.eatright.org

American Egg Board
www.aeb.org

American Frozen Food Institute
www.affi.com

American Institute of Baking
www.aibonline.org

American Peanut Council
www.peanutsusa.com

American Peanut Research & Education Society
www.apres.okstate.edu

American Pie Council
www.piecouncil.org

American Society of Baking
www.asbe.org

American Spice Trade Association
www.astaspice.org

American Sugar Alliance
www.sugaralliance.org

American Wholesale Marketers Association
www.awmanet.org

Association for Dressings & Sauces
www.dressing-sauces.org

Bakery Engineering and Manufacturing Association
www.bema.org

Baking Industry Sanitation Standards Committee (BISSC)
www.bissc.org

The Bread Bakers Guild of America
www.bbga.org

California Cling Peach Advisory Board
www.calclingpeach.com

California Date Administrative Committee
www.datesaregreat.com

California Dried Plum Board
www.californiadriedplums.org

California Fig Advisory Board
www.californiafigs.com

California Pistachio Commission
www.pistachios.org

California Strawberry Commission
www.calstrawberry.com

Cherry Marketing Institute Inc.
www.cherrymkt.org

Chocolate Manufacturers Association of the USA
www.chocolateusa.org

Cranberry Institute
www.cranberryinstitute.org

Flavor & Extract Manufacturers Association
www.femaflavor.org

Florida Strawberry Growers Association
www.straw-berry.org

Food Ingredient Distributors Association
www.fidassoc.com

Food Institute
www.foodinstitute.com

Food Marketing Institute
www.fmi.org

Food Processors Institute
www.fpi-food.org

Georgia Pecan Commission
www.georgiapecans.org

Hazelnut Marketing Board
www.oregonhazelnuts.org

Independent Bakers Association
www.mindspring.com-independent baker

In-Flight Food Service Association
www.ifsanet.com

Institute of Food Technologists
www.ift.org

Institute of Shortening & Edible Oils, Inc.
www.iseo.org

International Association of Color
    Manufacturers
www.iacmcolor.org

International Association of Culinary
    Professionals
www.iacp.com

International Association of Food Industry
    Suppliers
www.iafis.org

International Banana Association
www.eatmorebananas.com

International Cake Exploration Societé
www.ices.org

International Dairy-Deli-Bakery
    Association
www.iddba.org

International Food Information Council
www.ific.org

International Foodservice Manufacturers
    Association
www.ifmaworld.com

International Ice Cream Association
www.idfa.org

International Jelly & Preserve Association
www.idfa.org

International Maple Syrup Institute
www.internationalmaplesyrupinstitute.com

Kosher Foods Distributors Association
www.specialtyfoods.org

National Association of Fruits, Flavors &
    Syrups
www.naffs.org

National Cherry Growers and Industries
    Foundation
www.nationalcherries.com

National Confectioners Association
www.candyusa.org

National Cottonseed Products Association
www.cottonseed.com

National Frozen & Refrigerated Foods
    Association
www.nafraweb.org

National Honey Board
www.nhb.org

National Institute of Oilseed Products
www.oilseed.org

National Restaurant Association
www.restaurant.org

National Sunflower Association
www.sunflowernsash.com

North American Millers' Association
www.namamillers.org

Oregon Hazelnut Marketing Board
www.oregonhazelnuts.org

Oregon Raspberry and Blackberry
    Commission
www.oregon-berries.com

Organic Trade Association
www.ota.com

Peanut Advisory Board
www.peanutbutterlovers.com

The Peanut Institute, Inc.
www.peanut-institute.org

Pear Bureau Northwest
www.usapears.com

Private Label Manufacturers Association
www.plma.com

Raisin Administrative Committee
www.raisins.org

Refrigerated Foods Association
www.refrigeratedfoods.org

Research Chefs Association
www.culinology.com

Salt Institute
www.saltinstitute.org

Snack Food Association
www.sfa.org

The Sugar Association
www.sugar.org

Texas Pecan Growers Association
www.tpga.org

U.S. Pastry Competition
www.pastrychampionship.com

The Vinegar Institute
www.versatilevinegar.org

Walnut Marketing Board
www.walnut.org

Washington State Apple Commission
www.bestapples.com

Wheat Foods Council
www.wheatfoods.org

Wild Blueberry Association of North
   America
www.wildblueberries.com

Women Chefs & Restaurateurs
www.womenchefs.org

egg tips

appendix

E

CARTON DATES

Egg cartons from USDA-inspected plants must display a Julian date—the date the eggs were packed. They may also carry an expiration date beyond which the eggs should not be sold. In USDA-inspected plants, this date cannot exceed 30 days after the pack date. It may be less than 30 days through choice of the packer or quantity purchaser such as your local supermarket chain. Plants not under USDA inspection are governed by laws of their states.

FRESHNESS

How recently an egg was laid has a bearing on its freshness but is only one of many factors. The temperature at which it is held, the humidity, and the handling all play their part. These variables are so important that a one-week-old egg, held under ideal conditions, can be fresher than an egg left at room temperature for one day. The ideal conditions are temperatures that do not go above 40°F (4°C) and a relative humidity of 70 to 80 percent.

Proper handling means prompt gathering, washing, and oiling of the eggs within a few hours after laying. Most commercially produced eggs reach supermarkets within a few days of leaving the laying house. If the market and the buyer handle them properly, they will still be fresh when they reach the table.

It is not true that you can judge an egg's freshness by placing it in salt water. A carefully controlled brine test is sometimes used to judge shell thickness of eggs for hatching purposes but has no application to the freshness of table eggs.

How important is "freshness"? As an egg ages, the white becomes thinner and the yolk becomes flatter. These changes do not have any great effect on the nutritional quality of the egg or its functional cooking properties in recipes. Appearance may be affected, though. When poached or fried, the fresher the egg, the more it will hold its shape rather than spread out in the pan. On the other hand, if you hard-cook eggs that are at least a week old, you will find them easier to peel after cooking and cooling than fresher eggs.

494

GRADING

Classification is determined by interior and exterior quality and designated by letters—AA, A, and B. In many egg-packing plants, the USDA provides a grading service for shell eggs. Its official grade shield certifies that the eggs have been graded under federal supervision according to USDA standards and regulations. The grading service is not mandatory. Other eggs are packed under state regulations, which must meet or exceed federal standards.

In the grading process, eggs are examined for both interior and exterior quality and are sorted according to weight (size). Grade quality and size are not related to one another. In descending order of quality, grades are AA, A, and B. There is no difference in nutritive value among the different grades.

Because production and marketing methods have become very efficient, eggs move so rapidly from laying house to market that you will find very little difference in quality between grades AA and A. Although grade B eggs are just as wholesome to eat, they rate lower in appearance when broken out. Almost no grade B eggs find their way to the retail supermarket. Some go to institutional egg users such as bakeries or foodservice operations, but most go to large manufacturers for use in egg products.

CHEF'S TIP: *Although eggs of any size can be used for frying, scrambling, cooking in the shell, or poaching, most recipes for baked dishes such as custards and cakes are based on the use of large eggs. However, the professional baker will crack the eggs, run through a chinois, and use by weight.*

Kept under proper refrigeration at 45 °F or below (7 °C or below), eggs will retain their quality for several weeks. Do not freeze eggs. Cool temperatures slow or stop the growth of most bacteria. Eggs should be stored in their original packaging materials to prevent the loss of moisture. Store eggs away from foods such as fish, onions, apples, and cabbage as eggs can absorb strong odors.

mold prevention

With the high humidity and high temperatures that prevail during summer months, baked goods mold more readily and can cause considerable difficulty and, in many instances, loss of business. To better understand mold and its control, you should study the following carefully.

Mold is a plant growth whose spores are carried about in the air. Like dust, the spores settle everywhere. Whenever these spores fall upon fertile soil (chiefly moisture and warmth), they germinate and start to grow, forming roots, stock, and flowers, just as plants in the garden. Mold can develop and prosper in dark places as well as in sunlight.

There are three common types of mold that attack bread: *Aspergillus* or "brush mold," which is green, brown, or black; *Penicilium* or "pencil mold," which is green or blue; and *Rhizopus* or "whisker mold," which is grey-black to black.

The development of mold is relatively easy to prevent and can be overcome through normally reasonable care.

1. Cleanliness is the number 1 rule. Keep the shop, including machines, floors, walls, ceilings, proof boxes, and bread coolers, tidy, as clean as possible, and free from dust. Wash with a solution of calcium or sodium hypochlorite—there are a number of commercial products available. Follow instructions carefully.

2. Keep stale and moldy bread out of the shop. This is a serious source of infection. Dispose of stale goods as quickly as possible.

3. Ventilation and sunlight both discourage molds, which thrive best in dark, damp places.

4. Bake products thoroughly. A well-baked, crusty loaf is less apt to mold.

5. Cool products carefully and thoroughly. Do not cool where dust-laden drafts from the outside can reach the bread. Do not hurry the cooling process. The inside of the loaf should not exceed 90°F (32°C) when slicing and wrapping are started. Avoid bread storage in steamy, humid rooms.

6. Use less of those materials or agents in the bread that attract moisture and those that often, with wrapped bread, produce a condition between the crust and the wrapper that is referred to as "sweating."

7. Store wrapping paper in a mold-free and cool environment. Eliminate dust and insects. Both are mold spore carriers of the worst form.

8. Keep racks, conveyors, slicers (never clean machine by slicing a stale loaf), trucks, bread boxes, and showcases clean and free of dust and stale crumbs. Follow suggestions outlined in number 1.

9. Eliminate rubbish—any rubbish pile, no matter how small, is an active mold "factory."

10. Keep your ingredient storeroom clean, dry, and well ventilated.

11. Include in your dough one of the accepted mold and rope inhibitors. Baking temperatures kill mold spores, but the infection occurs after baking; this is both a preventative and a cure.

the workbench: applying what you have learned

"The least of learning is done in the classroom."

Thomas Merton (1915–1968)

The Workbench is an editorial feature of the *Modern Baking* magazine (Associate publisher, Edward Lee; executive editor, Heather Brown). For a number of years, Noble Masi served as the editor of the magazine's "*Workbench*" baker-to-baker question section. Each month questions came from across the United States. He answered the questions based on his own personal experience and knowledge as well as research he conducted at the Conrad Hilton Library Culinary Institute of America Hyde Park, N.Y. It is with permission of *Modern Baking* that we reproduce a number of the questions he answered while serving as the editor of this column.

As students move into the workplace, they will encounter some of the same problems or dilemmas mentioned here and many others as well. No matter how well you have mastered your work in the classroom, questions and problems will arise once you are working in the industry. A baker must always continue to learn.

One of the unique advantages of this trade is the support network that exists. When problems arise at work, a baker can turn to a number of individuals and professional associations to get answers to his or her questions. We offer this appendix as an attempt to give the students some true-to-life situations and solutions and to show that there are general corrections that can be made to solve any baking problem.

INGREDIENTS

Q: What is molasses? And what is the difference between sulfured and unsulfured molasses?

C.M., Cape Cod, Mass.

A: Molasses is the syrup obtained when sugarcane is processed into sugar. Molasses has a unique flavor that has not been successfully duplicated in artificial form. Sulfured molasses is treated with sulfur dioxide to deepen the color of the molasses. This also changes the pH level of the molasses.

Q: We would like to use more honey in our products. Do you have some guidelines for using honey to add flavor or replace sugar in baked goods?

R.T., Pleasant Valley, N.Y.

A: Honey is a popular sweetener. It adds a subtle flavor to breads and cakes. Honey blends well with all spice combinations. In cream-type cakes, replace 20 percent of the sugar with honey. In breads and rolls, use honey at 5 percent of flour weight. For a practical product rich in honey, try this honey cake formula.

honey cake *Yield: 9 lb 1 oz (4,110 g); eight loaves*

Ingredients	Lb	Oz	Metric	Procedures
Sugar	1		450 g	Combine. Mix at second speed of 3-speed mixer for 10 minutes.
Baking soda		1	30 g	
Honey	3		1,360 g	
Vegetable oil		8	230 g	Add. Mix at second speed for 10 minutes.
Whole eggs	1		450 g	
Rye flour, sifted	2	8	1,140 g	Add. Mix at second speed for 5 minutes.
Water	1		450 g	Add. Mix at second speed for 5 minutes. Prepare eight loaf pans. Pour l lb 2 oz (510 g) of batter in each pan. Bake at 300°F (150°C) for 1 hour.

NUTRITIONAL INFORMATION PER 2 OZ (60 G) SERVING: 174 Calories; 4 g Fat (19.8% calories from fat); 2 g Protein; 34 g Carbohydrate; 1 g Dietary Fiber; 24 mg Cholesterol; 116 mg Sodium. Exchanges: 1 Grain (Starch); 0 Lean Meat; 1/2 Fat; 1 1/2 Other Carbohydrates.

Q: Can you please tell me which preservative I can use in pies, cakes, and cookies to give them a longer shelf-life?

J.W., Harvey, Ill.

A: A small amount of invert sugar added to cakes and cookies will produce moist baked goods and preserve flavor longer. To determine how much invert sugar to add, figure 10 percent of the sugar weight for batter cakes, 5 percent for sponge cakes, and 1 to 3 percent for cookies.

YEAST-LEAVENED DOUGH

Q: The crust on our French bread pulls away from the top, large holes develop, and the sides split. Our troubles seem to coincide with the purchase of a new mixer and bread divider. Could this be the cause of our problems?

W.T., Austin, Texas

A: If the crusts are pulling away from the top, I would guess your dough may be too stiff or had insufficient proofing time. Also check to see that your proof box settings are at 90°F (32°C) and 80 percent humidity.

Holes in your breads can result from overmixing your dough or from the molding process. Both may be related to your new equipment, but both can easily be corrected. First, keep a closer eye on the mixing time. Your new mixer may be mixing the dough faster than your old mixer. If this is the case, simply reduce mixing times.

Make certain that the compression plates are set tight enough during molding so that sufficient gas is expelled. If not molded sufficiently tight, pockets of gas will remain in the dough and create holes. Molded loaves should have a very smooth surface. A smooth surface will provide a uniform skin, which facilitates uniform expansion of carbon dioxide to the interior of the loaf during proofing. This also will prevent bursting on the sides.

Q: During the past several months, I have received several requests for salt-rising bread. Do you have such a formula?

K.O., Seattle, Wash.

A: I used this formula when working in Miami during the early 1960s. Salt-rising bread sales decreased in the 1970s and 1980s, but this item is now enjoying renewed demand.

salt-rising bread   Yield: 25 lb 5 oz (11,480 g); about 22 loaves

Ingredients	Lb	Oz	Metric	Procedures
SPONGE				
Skim milk	3		1,360 g	Bring to a boil. Cool in a crock to 100°F (38°C).
Salt-rising yeast		8	230 g	Add. Cover and place in a warm area for 9 to 12 hours.
Bread flour	5		2,270 g	Combine and stir well. Add to sponge and let rest for 1 to 1 1/2 hours.
Water 115°F (45°C)	3		1,360 g	
DOUGH				
Water	3		1,360 g	Combine with sponge. Mix with a dough hook at low speed for 8 to 10 minutes until smooth. Let rest for 15 minutes.
Salt		3	90 g	Scale 1 lb 2 oz (510 g) of dough per loaf. Mold, pan, and allow dough to proof for about 30 minutes until double in size. Bake at 370°F (188°C) for 40 to 45 minutes. Cool on a wire rack.
Sugar		5	140 g	
Shortening		5	140 g	
Bread flour	10		4,540 g	

NUTRITIONAL INFORMATION PER 2 OZ (60 G) SERVING: 136 Calories; 1 g Fat (8.9% calories from fat); 5 g Protein; 26 g Carbohydrate; trace Dietary Fiber; trace Cholesterol; 168 mg Sodium. Exchanges: 1 1/2 Grain (Starch); 0 Lean Meat; 0 Nonfat Milk; 0 Fat; 0 Other Carbohydrates.

Q: We recently attended a bakers' convention in Dusseldorf, Germany, and were amazed at the bread displays. We would like to make some centerpieces for display. Do you have a formula?

R.H., Seattle, Wash.

A: There are several dough options, such as noodle dough or lean dough containing no yeast, that are used to make display bread. I have obtained great results with this formula:

display dough   *Yield: 16 lb 14 oz (7,660 g)*

Ingredients	Lb	Oz	Metric	Procedures
White rye flour	10		4,540 g	Combine ingredients.
Water	5		2,260 g	To darken the dough, add to each pound of light dough: 2 oz (60 g) dark rye flour and 1 oz (30 g) caramel color.
Cookie or short dough (no baking powder)	1	8	680 g	
Salt		5	140 g	
Vinegar		1	30 g	

NUTRITIONAL INFORMATION PER 2 OZ (60 G) SERVING: 141 Calories; 2 g Fat (10.1% calories from fat); 3 g Protein; 29 g Carbohydrate; 1 g Dietary Fiber; 1 mg Cholesterol; 419 mg Sodium. Exchanges: 1 1/2 Grain (Starch); 1/2 Fat; 0 Other Carbohydrates

Q: I grew up in Brooklyn, N.Y., and remember that we would enjoy a crusty, horn-type roll that had a dusting of caraway and coarse salt. Do you know this product and its formula?

L.D., Woodlawn, Tenn.

A: I believe that this product is known as a caraway salt horn. This roll is made from lean dough. The shaping and baking of this roll contribute to its flavor. Lean dough has poor keeping qualities, so the rolls must be baked and eaten within 4 to 6 hours. This is probably why these rolls are difficult to find.

lean dough for caraway salt horns
Yield: 9 lb 1 oz (4,120 g); six dozen horns

Ingredients	Lb	Oz	Metric	Procedures
Yeast		4	110 g	Dissolve yeast in water.
Water	3		1,360 g	
Bleached flour	2	9	1,160 g	Add remaining ingredients. Mix at first speed of 3-speed mixer for 3 minutes. Check consistency. Continue mixing at second speed for 8 minutes.
Hi-gluten flour	2	10	1,190 g	
Egg whites		4	110 g	Mix dough and allow to ferment for 40 minutes. Punch down dough and divide into 4-lb 8-oz (2,040-g) pieces. Divide into 2 oz (60 g) pieces and dust with rye flour.
Shortening		3	90 g	Allow to rest for 20 minutes. Roll out and cut pieces into pennant-shaped triangles. Roll up from base to form a horn. Wash with water, dust with caraway and coarse salt.
Salt		2	60 g	Bake at 400°F (200°C) for 15 to 18 minutes.

NUTRITIONAL INFORMATION PER 1 HORN SERVING: 119 Calories; 2 g Fat (15.3% calories from fat); 4 g Protein; 21 g Carbohydrate; 1 g Dietary Fiber; trace Cholesterol; 398 mg Sodium. Exchanges: 1 1/2 Grain (Starch); 0 Lean Meat; 1/2 Fat.

Q: We produce a three-grain bread using rye, wheat, and oats. The gluten does not develop, and the dough is very dry. What's going on?

K.S., Anaheim, Calif.

A: When using whole grains, soak them overnight in cold water. You also can boil grains; use an amount of water that is equal to the weight of the grain. Bring the water to a boil; then add the grain. Remove grain from heat, let cool, and then add to the dough during the mixing stage.

Q: I plan to make onion rolls and wonder if dehydrated onions would work well.

E.P., Denver, Colo.

A: Dehydrated onions should work fine, but be sure to soak them for a sufficient time in water to ensure they are fully hydrated. If you fail to do this, the onions will absorb the moisture from the dough, which will cause an inferior product.

Q: I want to improve the quality of our soft rolls. Unfortunately, the only flour that we have to use is hotel and restaurant flour. Any suggestions?

E.U., Albany, N.Y.

A: Hotel and restaurant flour contains less protein. If you add 1 oz of egg white for each pound of liquid you add to your flour, your dough will have more strength. This also will help to develop your dough at a slow speed.

For consistent, high-quality rolls, I suggest that you use a bread flour, which contains more protein.

Q: We have received many requests for panettone at our bakery. Could you please give us a recipe for this item and also tell us where it originated?

P.J., San Antonio, Texas

A: Panettone was introduced in Milan, Italy, about 1490 by a young baking assistant who fell in love with the baker's daughter. Trying to make an impression on her father, the assistant, named Toni, created this special bread and called it "Pan de Toni." This specialty item became a symbol of Milan and later of Italy. Bake this bread in round pans that are at least 5 inches tall. Scale 1 1/2 lbs of dough per pan.

panettone *Yield: 27 lb 15 oz (12,680 g)*

Ingredients	Lb	Oz	Metric	Procedures
SPONGE				
Warm water	1		450 g	Mix using the sponge method.
Yeast		4	110 g	
Hi-gluten flour	2	4	1,020 g	
Sugar	2	4	1,020 g	Cream together until smooth.
Butter	2		900 g	
Rum flavor		1 1/2	40 g	
Eggs, whole	2		900 g	
Egg yolks	1		450 g	
Milk powder		6	170 g	
Salt		3	90 g	
Lemon flavor		1	30 g	
Orange flavor		1	30 g	
Vanilla		2	60 g	
Water, warm	2		900 g	Dissolve yeast in water. Add flour and sponge. Mix until dough cleans sides of mixing bowl.
Yeast		4	110 g	
Hi-gluten flour	7	12	3,520 g	
Citron, dried	3		1,360 g	Add citron and raisins. Bake at 340°F (170°C).
Raisins	3	4	1,470 g	

NUTRITIONAL INFORMATION PER 2 OZ (60 G) SERVING: 176 Calories; 5 g Fat (24.8% calories from fat); 4 g Protein; 29 g Carbohydrate; 1 g Dietary Fiber; 50 mg Cholesterol; 192 mg Sodium. Exchanges: 1 Grain (Starch); 0 Lean Meat; 1/2 Fruit; 0 Nonfat Milk; 1 Fat; 1/2 Other Carbohydrates.

Q: Do you have a good Russian bread formula that you could send me? My community has a large number of Russian immigrants. Several of my Russian customers said that they miss their type of bread and that my bread doesn't compare.

B.J., Vallejo, Calif.

A: That's not surprising. My Russian students (all eight of them) said the same thing to me, so I had them help me develop this Russian bread formula. Here is what we came up with:

Black Russian bread   *Yield: 25 lb (11,300 g)*

Ingredients	Lb	Oz	Metric	Procedures
Hi-gluten flour	5	6	2,440 g	Place all ingredients into mixing bowl and mix to full development. Dough temperature off mixer should be about 82°F (28°C). Ferment dough for about 1.5 hours. Scale 2 lb (900 g) units; let rest 20 minutes, then mold into loaf shape or round shape. Proof on cornmeal-dusted boards and bake on 400°F (200°C) hearth for 30 to 35 minutes.
Rye flour	3		1,360 g	
Whole-wheat flour	4	2	1,870 g	
Potato flour		4	115 g	
Cornmeal (cooked)	4	2	1,880 g	
Butter		4	110 g	
Caraway seeds		2	60 g	
Caramel color	1	2	510 g	
Dark molasses	1	8	1,130 g	
Yeast		10	280 g	
Water	4	8	2,040 g	

NUTRITIONAL INFORMATION PER 2 OZ (60 G) SERVING: 154 Calories; 1 g Fat (6.8% calories from fat); 5 g Protein; 32 g Carbohydrate; 3 g Dietary Fiber; 1 mg Cholesterol; 9 mg Sodium. Exchanges: 2 Grain (Starch); 0 Lean Meat; 0 Vegetable; 0 Fat; 0 Other Carbohydrates.

cooked cornmeal   *Yield: 4 lbs 2 oz (1,870 g)*

Ingredients	Lb	Oz	Metric	Procedures
Cornmeal		12	340 g	Bring water to a boil, add cornmeal and salt; cook until mass thickens. Refrigerate before using.
Salt		2	60 g	
Water	3	4	1,470 g	

Q: In a previous issue of *Modern Baking,* you answered a question about signature breads and how to research them. Do you have a base formula for hearth bread that you would share?

A.L., Tampa, Fla.

A: Here is a base formula using baker's percentages of ingredients that process an open-textured loaf with an incomparable flavor. Remember that under-baked bread will taste starchy while thoroughly baked bread tastes sweet and clean. You may add various other ingredients as you develop your formula.

basic hearth bread

Percentage	Ingredient	Procedures
100	Unbleached flour	Use straight dough mixing method. With mixing time about 8 minutes in low speed, dough consistency should be medium-strong. Dough temperature off the mixer should be about 70°F (21°C). The first fermentation should be about 60 minutes at 77°F (25°C). Then shape, proof, and bake. A long fermentation is critical for great flavor and quality.
62 (approx.)	Water	
2	Salt	
1.8	Yeast	

From this base, variations could include:

- Replace up to 20 percent of the flour with rye, whole wheat, or triticale flour.
- Replace up to 5 percent of flour with corn or oat flour or meal.
- Replace up to 5 percent of flour with nut meal. Allow longer fermentation and baking time to fully develop flavor.

Q: We are expanding our bread line and will soon begin production of whole grain and multi-grain breads. How do you handle these grains?

R.M., Plymouth, Mass.

A: When a large quantity or large-sized grains are to be used in bread dough, it is best to first "soak" the grains before incorporating them into the final dough mixture. Whole grains tend to deprive the dough of moisture and also damage the developing gluten network. Good results can be achieved as long as a "soaker" is produced first. A soaker can be produced in one of two ways—hot or cold. A hot soaker is best when you are pressed for time. A cold soaker must be made at least a day before you make the bread. For a cold soaker, incorporate the grains and liquid. Slightly cover the grains with the liquid. Allow grains to soak overnight. To produce a hot soaker, first boil the liquid. Then incorporate the grains, and cook the mixture for 5 minutes over low heat. After cooking, the hot soaker should cool for approximately one hour before use.

Soakers Offer Many Benefits

1. Soften the grains
2. Hydrate the grains
3. Create a smoother final dough yield
4. Cause less gluten deterioration
5. Encourage the beginnings of enzymatic activity
6. Help form stronger gluten (when cracked or flaked whole wheat is soaked, the gluten proteins are drawn to the surface during the soaking).

Q: I have been asked to make spelt bread for my customers who are allergic to wheat flour. I came across several formulas for spelt bread that substitute the spelt flour for the wheat flour. Can you tell me the difference between the two flours?

P.F., Pittsburgh, Pa.

A: Spelt has many names; the ancient Romans knew it as "farrum," Italians call it "faro," Germans know it as "dinkle." The protein content in spelt flour is from 10 to 25 percent greater than that of the common varieties of commercial wheat. Spelt is unique because of its genetic make-up and nutritional profile.

Spelt is really good for you. It has high water solubility, so the nutrients are easily absorbed by the body. It contains special carbohydrates, which stimulate the body's immune system. It also is a superb fiber source and contains large amounts of B-complex vitamins. Spelt flour can be substituted for whole wheat in breads, cookies, cakes, and muffins. Whenever you use it, reduce the water 15 to 25 percent and reduce the mixing time 4 to 4 1/2 minutes.

I know of a baker who formulated one of the most popular breads in the Pacific Northwest. He called it "Paulsbo Bread" after his hometown and said he got the recipe from the Bible: "Take wheat and barley, beans and lentils, millet and spelt; put them in a storage jar and use them to make bread for yourself." (Ezekiel 4:9)

Q: Now that natural grain breads are becoming more popular, I'd appreciate a formula for a multi-grain bread that contains nuts, fruits, and oats.

W.N., Lubbock, Texas

A: There's no question that the popularity of whole-grain breads has increased. This particular formula should meet your needs.

multi-grain bread
Yield: 16 lb 2 oz (7,320 g); eight 2-lb (900 g) loaves

Ingredients	Lb	Oz	Metric	Procedures
Instant yeast		1	30 g	Combine in 60-qt. bowl. Dissolve with hand whisk.
Water	4	8	2,040 g	
Whole-wheat flour	5		2,270 g	Attach dough hook. Add ingredients to above; mix at second speed of a 3-speed mixer for 12 to 14 minutes or until dough is elastic and cleans side of bowl.
Bread flour	2	8	1,140 g	
Milk powder (high heat)		8	230 g	
Honey (dark amber)		6	170 g	
All-purpose shortening		8	230 g	
Salt		2	60 g	
Sunflower seeds		8	230 g	Add to above; mix at second speed for 2 minutes or until well distributed.
Raisins		12	340 g	Allow dough about 1 1/2 hours floor time. Take dough to bench and scale into 2-lb (900 g) pieces. Mold and roll dough onto pan filled with oats; then deposit dough into standard-sized bread pans. Proof for a short time, then bake at 325°F (160°C) in a radiant heat oven for 25 to 30 minutes or until done.
Chopped walnuts		12	340 g	
Rolled oats		9	260 g	

NUTRITIONAL INFORMATION PER 2 OZ (60 G) SERVING: 162 Calories; 5 g Fat (27.8% calories from fat); 5 g Protein; 25 g Carbohydrate; 3 g Dietary Fiber; 2 mg Cholesterol; 179 mg Sodium. Exchanges: 1 1/2 Grain (Starch); 0 Lean Meat; 0 Fruit; 0 Nonfat Milk; 1 Fat; 0 Other Carbohydrates.

Q: I have little experience making such bread varieties as pumpernickel and rye. Can you provide a brief description of each of these bread varieties?

B.K., Raleigh, N.C.

A: Pumpernickel bread is a dark, tough, and close-textured loaf. It's made from crushed or ground whole rye kernels and contains varying amounts of wheat flour. Pumpernickel breads may be leavened with yeast or by using sourdoughs. Many times pumpernickel is baked in sandwich pans and is heavily textured.

For rye breads, rye and wheat flours are combined, which produces a bread with a more uniform texture, lighter color, and milder flavor than pumpernickel. Because rye flour contains little if any gluten, hard wheat flour is almost always added. Caramel coloring and caraway seeds often are added to rye bread dough.

Rye bread can be made using the sourdough method, which involves the use of a small amount of old dough in which lactic-acid-producing bacteria have developed to create leavening and flavor. These microorganisms ferment some of the carbohydrates in the fresh dough, producing characteristic sour tastes and odors. Standard yeast also may be used to leaven rye breads.

Q: I make a variety of bread doughs that require fermentation and punching down. It seems that every dough ferments at a different rate, and I literally guess at when I should punch down the dough. Is there a technique that's more precise?

L.T., Seattle, Wash.

A: The fermentation time for your dough will vary depending on formulation and environmental conditions. The only way to make the proper determinations is to test the dough occasionally during fermentation. To determine if the dough is ready, gently insert your fingers into the top of the dough. The dough should neither collapse nor spring back, but should sink slightly around the depression when the proper fermentation stage has been reached. If the indentation tends to spring back, the dough is not ready for punching. If the dough falls rapidly, the proper time for punching has passed; in this case, the dough should be made up as soon as possible. With practice, you should be able to easily tell when your dough is ready to punch down.

Q: We would like to discontinue using bromated flour. What effect do bromates have on dough? How would not using them affect our products?

N.B., Dallas, Texas

A: Bromates stimulate yeast enzyme activity, liberate oxygen, and soften gluten to promote elasticity. Also, bromates' oxidizing agents buffer the action of protease. Using bromated flour increases loaf volume. During baking, it acts as a maturing agent. Bakers in European countries that do not allow the use of bromated flour substitute ascorbic acid to achieve similar effects.

Q: We would like to produce a light, flavorful rye bread. What do you recommend as a percentage of rye flour to use?

J.W., St. Louis, Mo.

A: To maintain the lightness in your rye bread, use 40 percent rye and 50 percent clear or hi-gluten flour. To develop more flavor, use a strong sour and an additional ounce of onion juice and 1 oz of caraway tea* for every 5 lb (2,270 g) of rye flour.

*Caraway tea: Boil 4 oz of caraway seeds and 1 pint of water. Strain.

Q: During a recent trip to Germany, we enjoyed Bavarian soft pretzels. Do you have a formula for this type of pretzel?

E.U., Quincy, Ill.

A: Here is a good soft pretzel dough formula. These pretzels are dipped in a mild solution of sodium hydroxide before baking.

soft pretzel dough *Yield: 8 lb (3,630 g)*

Ingredients	Lb	Oz	Metric	Procedures
Water	2		900 g	Combine. Mix until dough develops, about 6 minutes. Ferment 1 hour.
Buttermilk		8	230 g	Divide dough into 4-lb (1,810 g) units, and then divide each unit into 36 pieces. Roll each piece into a thin, 12-inch-long (300 cm) rope; taper ends. Fold each piece into a pretzel shape. Place pieces on a heavily greased frying screen. Dry proof for 30 to 45 minutes. Use a razor to cut a thin line on top of each pretzel. Dip pretzels into sodium hydroxide solution and dust with a salt. For smaller quantities, such as four dozen, the sodium hydroxide may be sprayed on the pretzels. Bake pretzels at 450°F (230°C) for 15 to 17 minutes.
Hi-gluten flour	5		2,250 g	
Yeast		3	90 g	
Sugar		1/2	10 g	
Malt		1/2	10 g	
Oil		2	60 g	
Salt		2	60 g	

NUTRITIONAL INFORMATION PER 2 OZ (60 G) SERVING: 142 Calories; 2 g Fat (10.1% calories from fat); 5 g Protein; 27 g Carbohydrate; trace Dietary Fiber; trace Cholesterol; 349 mg Sodium. Exchanges: 2 Grain (Starch); 0 Lean Meat; 0 Nonfat Milk; 0 Fat; 0 Other Carbohydrates

PIES/TARTS

Q: I've recently begun making fresh fruit flans and tarts for my customers, but the crusts become very soft after only a short time. Can you explain why this might be occurring?

E.P., Denver, Colo.

A: The problem with your shells becoming soft during refrigeration can't be completely eliminated, but it can be significantly reduced if you follow these steps. First, make certain that your short paste formula is lean in sugar and liquid and not overly aerated. Bake flan shells and tarts for as long as possible without burning them. This will yield crisp shells that contain the least amount of residual moisture.

After cooling, brush the insides of the shells with melted chocolate and allow to set. This step will form a moisture barrier and significantly slow migration of moisture between the fruit and the shell.

Q: We would like to produce a two-crust lemon pie. This pie, iced with chocolate fondant, is very popular in the Boston area. Would you have a good formula for this item?

E.K., Boston, Mass.

A: To make this pie, use your favorite formula to prepare the crusts. Then prepare the following lemon filling.

lemon pie filling Yield: 6 lb (2,720 g); four 10-inch (250 cm) pies

Ingredients	Lb	Oz	Metric	Procedures
Water	2	12	1,250 g	Bring to a boil.
Sugar	2		900 g	
Shortening		2	60 g	
Cornstarch		6	170 g	Mix together and add to above. Cook until clear. Allow to cool.
Lemon juice		8	230 g	Prepare filling. Line four 10-inch (250 cm) pie pans with pie pastry and pour in 1 lb 8 oz (680 g) of filling per pan.
Egg yolks		4	110 g	Top with upper crust and bake at 425°F (220°C) for 30 minutes.

NUTRITIONAL INFORMATION PER 4 OZ (110 G) SERVING: (pie filling only): 214 Calories; 4 g Fat (15.8% calories from fat); 1 g Protein; 45 g Carbohydrate; trace Dietary Fiber; 61 mg Cholesterol; 5 mg Sodium. Exchanges: 1/2 Grain(Starch); 0 Lean Meat; 0 Fruit; 1/2 Fat; 2 1/2 Other Carbohydrates.

Q: My grandmother used to make an Italian cheese pie during the holidays. Do you have a formula for this item?

R.E., Reading, Pa.

A: This formula will satisfy your search and, if made with skim milk, is low in fat.

Italian cheese pie Yield: 8 lb 14 oz (4,020 g); six pies

Ingredients	Lb	Oz	Metric	Procedures
Sugar	1	4	560 g	Combine at first speed of 3-speed mixer.
Butter		5	140 g	
Cornstarch		5	140 g	
Eggs		8	230 g	Add slowly.
Ricotta cheese	4	8	2,040 g	Fold in by hand.
Milk	2		900 g	Fill unbaked 10-inch (250 cm) pie shells 2/3 full. Bake at 400°F (200°C) until filling is set, about 30 minutes. After the pie has cooled, top with lemon, cherry, or pineapple.

NUTRITIONAL INFORMATION PER 2 OZ (60 G) SERVING: 115 Calories; 6 g Fat (47.0% calories from fat); 4 g Protein; 11 g Carbohydrate; trace Dietary Fiber; 32 mg Cholesterol; 51 mg Sodium. Exchanges: 0 Grain (Starch); 1/2 Lean Meat; 0 Nonfat Milk; 1 Fat; 1/2 Other Carbohydrates.

Q: I want to make our own mincemeat pie filling for the upcoming
holiday season. Do you have a good formula?

P.K., Rolling Meadows, Ill.

A: Here is an old-fashioned formula of mine.

mincemeat   *Yield: 100 lbs 9 oz (45,500 g)*

Ingredients	Lb	Oz	Metric	Procedures
Sugar	30		13,610 g	Combine; boil until mixture reaches a syrup consistency. Remove from heat.
Cider vinegar	2		900 g	
Water	2		900 g	
Apples, cored, coarsely chopped	40		18,000 g	Combine; mix thoroughly.
Raisins	15		6,800 g	
Citron, lemon and orange peel, chopped	4		1,810 g	
Cinnamon		10	280 g	
Ground cloves		3	90 g	
Nutmeg		2	60 g	
Ground suet	5		2,270 g	
Jamaica dark rum	1	9 1/2	720 g	Add with prepared syrup; mix until thoroughly incorporated. Use as desired. Mincemeat will keep for a considerable amount of time if stored properly; store in covered glass or plastic containers at a temperature less than 80°F (27°C). Baldwin and New York State Greening are the best apples to use.

NUTRITIONAL INFORMATION PER 4 OZ (110 G) SERVING (filling only): 270 Calories; 6 g Fat (19.3% calories from fat); 1 g Protein; 56 g Carbohydrate; 2 g Dietary Fiber; 5 mg Cholesterol; 3 mg Sodium. Exchanges: 0 Grain(Starch); 1 1/2 Fruit; 1 Fat; 2 1/2 Other Carbohydrates.

Q: Could you describe the different types of meringues and their uses?
Also, which would you recommend for meringue-topped pies?

A.C., Orlando, Fla.

A: There are three types of meringue; each has its own characteristics, uses, and production methods.

- Cold meringue is referred to as common meringue. It is used as a leavener in cakes and fillings.
- Warm meringue is referred to as Swiss meringue. To make this product, egg whites are heated with sugar to 110°F (40°C). This is the type recommended for meringue-topped pies.
- Cooked meringue is known as Italian meringue. A sugar syrup is cooked to 230°F (110°C) and added to beaten egg whites to make this version. This is a very stable meringue and is used for baked Alaska, icings, and meringue and meringue shells.

NOTE: I have found that rubbing a lemon inside the clean mixing bowl used to whip egg whites helps condition the whites.

Q: I offer an apple crumb pie that my customers find difficult to neatly slice. Any suggestions?

S.R., Wilkes, N.C.

A: For an apple crumb pie, I find it is better to dice the apples into 1/2-inch cubes rather than slice them. You also may add some cake flour or cornstarch to your sugar and spice mixture to thicken the filling; add 1 oz (30 g) of cake flour or cornstarch per 2 lb (900 g) of mixture.

Q: After several days of refrigeration, our pie fillings separate. What causes this, and can we do something to prevent this from occurring?

V.N., St. Louis, Mo.

A: Acid present in sugar and in some fruits probably is the cause of your separation problem. Switch to modified starch to correct this problem. You also may freeze fillings containing modified starch.

Q: Our fruit pie fillings separate after being refrigerated for two days. We have tried to correct the problem by increasing their amount of starch, but this makes them gummy. Can you suggest a solution?

A.C., Orlando, Fla.

A: Although regular cornstarch has strong thickening properties, it produces a gel that is cloudy and opaque. Switch to a modified, waxy maize starch; this starch will produce a gel that is clear, viscous, and cohesive. Waxy maize starch is made from a special type of corn that has cross-linked starch molecules and is more resistant to breakdown.

Q: We currently sell a German chocolate cake that has a coconut pecan topping. Do you have a formula for a German chocolate pie?

R.M., Syracuse, N.Y.

A: Here is the formula you requested.

German chocolate pie *Yield: 19 lb 13 oz (8,990 g); 11 10-inch (250 cm) pies*

Ingredients	Lb	Oz	Metric	Procedures
Sweet chocolate	2	8	1,130 g	Combine. Melt in a heavy saucepan over low heat.
Butter	1	4	560 g	
Sweetened condensed milk	8	12	3,860 g	Add. Combine.
Eggs	2	8	1,130 g	Add.
Very warm water	2	8	1,130 g	
Vanilla		1	30 g	
Salt		1	30 g	
TOPPING				
Chopped pecans	1	4	560 g	Combine in separate bowl.
Flaked coconut		15	430 g	Prepare eleven 10-inch (250 cm) pie shells. Pour 1 lb 8 oz (680 g) batter per shell. Top each pie with 3 1/2 oz (100 g) of topping. Bake at 375°F (190°C) for 35 to 40 minutes.

NUTRITIONAL INFORMATION PER 2 OZ (60 G) SERVING: 188 Calories; 11 g Fat (52.4% calories from fat); 3 g Protein; 20 g Carbohydrate; 1 g Dietary Fiber; 42 mg Cholesterol; 146 mg Sodium. Exchanges: 0 Grain (Starch); 0 Lean Meat; 0 Fruit; 2 Fat; 1 Other Carbohydrates.

COOKIES/BISCOTTI

Q: I would like to make a chewy raisin cookie for our back-to-school promotion. Can you provide a good formula?

G.M., Reno, Nev.

A: I'm sure you will find that this hermit cookie bar will become very popular.

hermits   *Yield: 14 lb 1 oz (6,380 g)*

Ingredients	Lb	Oz	Metric	Procedures
Sugar	3		1,360 g	Cream together.
Shortening	1		450 g	
Butter		8	230 g	
Molasses		12	340 g	
Salt		3/4	20 g	
Allspice		1/2	10 g	
Cinnamon		1/2	10 g	
Eggs	1		450 g	Add gradually.
Water		10	280 g	Add gradually.
Baking soda		1 1/2	40 g	Sift together. Add to mixture. Mix until smooth.
Cake flour	5		2,250 g	
Raisins	2		900 g	Mix in. Scale dough out into 12-oz (340 g) units. Roll out each piece into four 2-inch (50 cm) wide strips and place on parchment-lined sheet pans the width of the pan. Press down lightly. Bake at 380°F (190°C) until done. When bars have cooled, glaze with thin fondant and cut into desired portions.

NUTRITIONAL INFORMATION PER 2 OZ (60 G) SERVING: 207 Calories; 6 g Fat (26.5% calories from fat); 2 g Protein; 36 g Carbohydrate; 1 g Dietary Fiber; 19 mg Cholesterol; 200 mg Sodium. Exchanges: 1 Grain (Starch); 0 Lean Meat; 1/2 Fruit; 1 Fat; 1 Other Carbohydrates.

Q: Can you explain the creaming method of mixing?

J.R., Plano, Texas

A: The creaming method primarily is used for preparing cookie dough and cake batter with a flour content equal to or greater than the sugar content. Combining, or creaming, the fat and sugar together incorporates air into the mixture; in the oven, this air expands to help leaven the product. Here are the basic steps of the creaming method:

1. Place the room-temperature fat in a mixer bowl. Using a paddle attachment, beat the fat until smooth and creamy.
2. Add the sugar and mix at medium speed until light and fluffy.
3. Add the eggs gradually, mixing after each addition to ensure all is absorbed.

4. Add the sifted dry ingredients alternately with the liquid, mixing lightly after each addition. Scrape down the bowl frequently to ensure even mixing.

Q: I am looking for formulas for rum balls and vanilla wafers. Do you have any you can share?

M.N., Miami, Fla.

A: Rum balls were developed to utilize cake trimmings or stale cake. Mix the cake with a fruit jam to moisten the crumbs, then add rum to taste. Mold into 3/4-oz (20 g) balls and enrobe with chocolate. Rum balls also can be coated with vanilla wafer crumbs. Here is a formula for vanilla wafers:

vanilla wafers   Yield: 11 lb 3 oz (5,080 g); about 14 dozen wafers

Ingredients	Lb	Oz	Metric	Procedures
Sugar	3		1,360 g	Combine. Mix at second speed of a 3-speed mixer until smooth.
Salt		1	30 g	
Nonfat dry milk		4	110 g	
Butter		12	340 g	
Shortening		11	310 g	
Honey		4	110 g	
Baking soda		1/2	10 g	
Eggs, whole		12	340 g	Add eggs in two stages; beat well after each addition.
*Ammonium bicarbonate		1/4	10 g	Dissolve ammonium bicarbonate in water. Combine with flavorings; add alternately with flour. Mix at first speed until smooth.
Water	1	8	680 g	Using a pastry bag fitted with a plan tube, pipe dough into nickel-sized round drops on parchment-lined pans; space drops about 1 1/2 inches (40 cm) apart. If desired, top with chocolate sprinkles or finely chopped or ground nuts. Bake at 375°F (190°F) until done, about 7 minutes.
Vanilla		1	30 g	
Lemon rind, freshly grated		1	30 g	
Cake flour, sifted	3	12	1,700 g	

NUTRITIONAL INFORMATION PER 2 OZ (60 G) SERVING: 201 Calories; 7 g Fat (31.6% calories from fat); 2 g Protein; 32 g Carbohydrate; trace Dietary Fiber; 22 mg Cholesterol; 227 mg Sodium. Exchanges: 1 Grain (Starch); 0 Lean Meat; 0 Fruit; 0 Nonfat Milk; 1 1/2 Fat; 1 Other Carbohydrates
*If ammonium bicarbonate (also known as bicarbonate of ammonia) is not available, substitute 1/2 oz (10 g) baking powder and sift in with cake flour.

Q: We have several cookie formulas that use bicarbonate of ammonia. Could you explain what it is and where to purchase this product?

T.M., Madison, Wis.

A: You may substitute baking powder for bicarbonate of ammonia and get good results. Bicarbonate of ammonia, or salt of hartshorn, is one of the oldest "chemical" leavens. It was actually in use for many centuries before modern baking powder was developed in the middle of the nineteenth century.

The original hartshorn, as its name implies, was ground from deer antler and used primarily in Scandinavian countries. Today, hartshorn is difficult to find, although there is a chemical version of the original, better known as "baker's ammonia," available from some pharmaceutical and bakery supply companies.

Dough that contains hartshorn produces a strong smell of ammonia when it is in the oven; the ammonia dissipates completely during the baking process, leaving no aftertaste or odor. Its unique action makes extremely crisp cookies and crackers.

Q: Do you have a formula for sugar-free cookies that actually taste good?

C.K., Schiller Park, Ill.

A: I've had good luck with this cookie.

sugar-free spritz cookie
Yield: 15 lb 6 oz (6,970 g); 20 dozen 3/4 oz (20 g) cookies

Ingredients	Lb	Oz	Metric	Procedures
Cake flour	1		450 g	Sift. Blend well.
Bread flour	2		900 g	
Sugar substitute suitable for baking	(Use enough to replace 2 lb. sugar, see directions on label.)			
Salt		1	30 g	
Butter	3		1,360 g	Add, cream lightly, scraping sides often.
Shortening	3		1,360 g	
Egg whites	2		900 g	Add egg whites and vanilla in four stages at medium speed in 3-minute intervals.
Vanilla		1	30 g	
Bread flour	4		1,810 g	Sift together, fold in lightly, do not overmix. Pipe out cookies onto a pan and bake for 12 minutes in 375°F (190°C) oven. Cookies may be garnished with dietetic jam or nuts.
Baking powder		1/4	10 g	

NUTRITIONAL INFORMATION PER 2 OZ (60 G) SERVING: 109 Calories; 2 g Fat (14.0% calories from fat); 3 g Protein; 20 g Carbohydrate; trace Dietary Fiber; 2 mg Cholesterol; 106 mg Sodium. Exchanges: 1 1/2 Grain (Starch); 0 Lean Meat; 1/2 Fat; 0 Other Carbohydrates.

Q: I'm not happy with my biscotti recipe. I've enclosed my recipe and would appreciate it if you could review it or perhaps provide a new one.

W.U., Mayfield, Ky.

A: I have received many requests for biscotti formulas. Here are formulas for two different types of biscotti. One is mixed using the foam method and does not contain butter or shortening; it produces a very light biscotti. To market its lightness, I call it almond angel biscotti. The second variety, double chocolate devil, is made with butter, cocoa, and chocolate chips. Both varieties have their place in the market.

almond angel biscotti *Yield: 11 lb 12 oz (5,329 g)*

Ingredients	Lb	Oz	Metric	Procedures
Eggs	3		1,360 g	Combine. Heat to 110°F. Whip 5 minutes at third speed of a 3-speed mixer, then 10 minutes at second speed.
Sugar	3		1,360 g	
Baking powder		2	60 g	
Honey		2	60 g	
Bread flour	5		2,270 g	Fold in flour, nuts, and almond extract. Portion batter with a pastry bag. Pipe 2-inch (50 cm) bar columns across the width of a baking pan; pipe five bars to a pan. Bake at 380°F (190°C) for about 20 minutes. When cool, slice bars into 1/2-inch (10 cm) pieces. Turn bars on sides and toast until golden-brown.
Crushed almonds		8	230 g	
Almond extract		1/2	10 g	

NUTRITIONAL INFORMATION PER 2 OZ (60 G) SERVING: 179 Calories; 3 g Fat (14.6% calories from fat); 5 g Protein; 33 g Carbohydrate; trace Dietary Fiber; 52 mg Cholesterol; 80 mg Sodium. Exchanges: 1 Grain (Starch); 1/2 Lean Meat; 1/2 Fat; 1 Other Carbohydrates.

double chocolate devil biscotti *Yield: 9 lb 1 oz (4,110 g)*

Ingredients	Lb	Oz	Metric	Procedures
Sugar	2	8	1,130 g	Combine sugar and cocoa.
Cocoa		8	230 g	
Butter, softened	1		450 g	Add softened butter; cream until light. Add eggs slowly.
Eggs	1		450 g	
Pastry flour	2	8	1,130 g	Add the remaining ingredients in order shown. Scale batter into 12-oz (340 g) units. Shape batter into bars across width of baking pan. Bake at 325°F (160°C) for 30 minutes; let cool. Slice bars 1/4-inch (6 cm) thick and toast.
Sliced almonds		10	280 g	
Chocolate chips		12	340 g	
Baking powder		2 1/2	70 g	

NUTRITIONAL INFORMATION PER 2 OZ (60 G) SERVING: 225 Calories; 10 g Fat (36.8% calories from fat); 4 g Protein; 34 g Carbohydrate; 2 g Dietary Fiber; 37 mg Cholesterol; 165 mg Sodium. Exchanges: 1 Grain (Starch); 0 Lean Meat; 2 Fat; 1 1/2 Other Carbohydrates.

Q: When we place our cookie dough on baking sheets, it spreads excessively. How can we alter our formula to prevent this spreading?

P.K., Arlington Heights, Ill.

A: Try using 6X sugar in your cookie dough. The smaller crystalline structure of this sugar will allow your cookies to set faster and spread less.

Q: I need a formula for raspberry linzer cookies. I've tried several formulas but have yet to find one I like.

B.P., Eighty Four, Pa.

A: Here's a formula you should like. The leavening for this dough is baking ammonia, which can be purchased from your bakery ingredient distributor.

linzer cookie dough   *Yield: 24 lb 4 oz (11,000 g); 16 dozen 2-oz cookies*

Ingredients	Lb	Oz	Metric	Procedures
Butter	4	8	2,040 g	Place in 60-qt. mixer with a paddle attachment and cream at second speed on a 3-speed mixer for 3 minutes. Scrape down.
Granulated sugar	4	8	2,040 g	
Baking ammonia		3/4	20 g	Dissolve baking ammonia in cold water; set aside.
Water		6	170 g	
Whole eggs	2		900 g	Add to butter and sugar mixture, along with water ammonia mixture. Mix at second speed for 5 minutes. Scrape down.
Cocoa		6	170 g	
Cinnamon		4	110 g	
Ground cloves		2	60 g	
Lemon zest		1	30 g	
Cake flour	7	4	3,290 g	Add last and mix at first speed for 2 minutes or until flour clears. Place on sheet pan and refrigerate overnight. After refrigerating, roll out dough to about 1/4-inch (6 cm) thickness and cut out with a round cookie cutter. Place on parchment paper-lined sheet pans and brush tops lightly with egg wash. Fill a pastry bag with an oven-proof raspberry filling and deposit a small amount of filling in the center of each cookie. Bake at 350°F (180°C) between 15 and 20 minutes or until done. Formula will yield about 16 dozen 2-oz (60 g) cookies.
Ground filberts, roasted	4	12	2,150 g	

NUTRITIONAL INFORMATION PER ONE 2-OZ COOKIE SERVING (excluding raspberry filling): 223 Calories; 13 g Fat (49.5% calories from fat); 3 g Protein; 26 g Carbohydrate; 1 g Dietary Fiber; 40 mg Cholesterol; 125 mg Sodium. Exchanges: 1 Grain (Starch); 0 Lean Meat; 0 Fruit; 2 1/2 Fat; 1/2 Other Carbohydrates.

QUICK BREADS AND DOUGHNUTS

Q: Our customers often ask us if we make sugar-free breads and breads that do not contain yeast. Do you have any recipes for these types of breads?

K.K., Oceanside, Calif.

A: Several quick breads can be produced without using yeast and sugar. Here are two formulas:

cornbread *Yield: 8 lb 1 oz (3,660 g)*

Ingredients	Lb	Oz	Metric	Procedures
Canned corn puree		8	230 g	Mix together.
Sugar-free applesauce		8	230 g	
Cornmeal		12	340 g	
Cake flour	2	6	1,080 g	Sift together. Add to above. Mix at second speed of 3-speed mixer for 1 minute.
Milk powder		4	110 g	
Salt		1	30 g	
Baking powder		2	60 g	
Shortening		12	340 g	Add. Mix at second speed for 3 minutes.
Water	2		900 g	Combine and add in three stages.
Eggs, whole		12	340 g	Mix at first speed until blended. Bake this cornbread in a sheet pan, a skillet, or corn stick forms. Bake at 365°F (190°C) until done.

NUTRITIONAL INFORMATION PER 2 OZ (60 G) SERVING: 145 Calories; 6 g Fat (39.7% calories from fat); 3 g Protein; 19 g Carbohydrate; 1 g Dietary Fiber; 21 mg Cholesterol; 285 mg Sodium. Exchanges: 1 Grain (Starch); 0 Lean Meat; 0 Fruit; 0 Nonfat Milk; 1 Fat; 0 Other Carbohydrates.

potato buttermilk quick bread   *Yield: 12 lb 6 oz (5,610 g); 11 loaves*

Ingredients	Lb	Oz	Metric	Procedures
Bread flour	3		1,360 g	Combine. Mix at second speed for 3-speed mixer for 2 minutes.
Pastry flour	3		1,360 g	
Salt		1 1/2	40 g	
Baking powder		8	230 g	
Butter, softened	1		450 g	Add. Mix at second speed for 2 minutes.
Mashed potatoes		12	340 g	
Eggs, whole	1		450 g	Combine. Add and mix at first speed for 5 minutes.
Buttermilk	3		1,360 g	Scale into 1 lb 2 oz (510 g) loaves; round loaves. Wash loaves with milk and dust with rye flour. Create a lattice design on the tops of the loaves using a dough knife. Bake loaves on cornmeal-dusted pans at 360°F (180°C) for about 20 minutes.

NUTRITIONAL INFORMATION PER 2 OZ (60 G) SERVING: 148 Calories; 5 g Fat (28.5% calories from fat); 4 g Protein; 22 g Carbohydrate; trace Dietary Fiber; 27 mg Cholesterol; 475 mg Sodium. Exchanges: 1 1/2 Grain (Starch); 0 Lean Meat; 0 Nonfat Milk; 1 Fat; 0 Other Carbohydrates.

Q: Our bakery makes frozen, raw scones. After a couple of weeks in the freezer, they fail to rise very high when they are baked. Can you explain why this might be occurring?

Q.T., Denver, Colo.

A: One possible cause is that you may be allowing your scones to sit too long before freezing them. When baking powder is exposed to warm temperatures, moisture decomposition occurs, which reduces the powder's lifting power.

Make certain that your dough comes from your mixer as cold as possible and that the made-up product is frozen as soon as possible. You also may want to begin using a baking powder formulated to release very little gas when it is exposed to moisture. I suggest you contact your local bakery ingredient distributor for more information.

Q: Our company recently installed an automated doughnut fryer. To date, we've had problems with cracks forming inside the circle. What might be causing this?

E.N., Charlotte, N.C.

A: Frequently you will find that a hard ridge of dough forms around the cutter die. As the dough begins falling, it tears the inside of the circle, which will grow into cracks during frying. The easiest solution is to occasionally splash the cutter with frying fat to prevent build-up.

Q: Our bakery supplies many bed and breakfast inns, and we have received requests for fresh-baked English muffins. Can you give us a formula?

K.S., Erie, Pa.

A: While English muffins are best baked on a flat grill or skillet, I have obtained good results using a pan that is used to make hamburger buns. This pan has 24 indentations in it. Lightly coat the pan with shortening and dust with cornmeal prior to adding dough.

English muffins   Yield: 5 lb 4 oz (2,380 g); 24 3 1/2 oz (100 g) muffins

Ingredients	Lb	Oz	Metric	Procedures
Milk	1		450 g	Bring ingredients to a boil in a medium saucepan.
Water	1		450 g	
Sugar		2	60 g	
Salt		1	30 g	
Margarine		4	110 g	Stir in margarine. Let mixture cool to between 110°F and 115°F (43°C and 46°C).
Eggs		4	110 g	Combine using a paddle attachment. Gradually beat in the liquid until smooth and a loose, sticky consistency. Cover with plastic wrap and refrigerate overnight.
Yeast		1	30 g	
Bread flour	2	8	1,130 g	Stir down dough with a rubber spatula to release air; the dough should be sticky and elastic. Cut into small pieces with a sharp knife. Fill each pan indentation with about 3/4 oz (110 g) of dough. Cover pan loosely and let rise in a draft-free area until doubled in size, about 45 minutes. Sprinkle the tops with cornmeal. Bake muffins in the lower third of the oven at 400°F (200°C) for about 25 minutes or until lightly browned. Let cool on baking sheets on a rack for 15 minutes.

NUTRITIONAL INFORMATION PER ONE 3 1/2 OZ (100 G) SERVING: 235 Calories; 6 g Fat (22.0% calories from fat); 7 g Protein; 38 g Carbohydrate; trace Dietary Fiber; 20 mg Cholesterol; 519 mg Sodium. Exchanges: 2 1/2 Grain (Starch); 0 Lean Meat; 0 Nonfat Milk; 1 Fat; 0 Other Carbohydrates

Q: I am looking for a simple, good-tasting, yeast-raised doughnut formula. Do you have a formula that you could suggest?

K.J., Des Plaines, Ill.

A: Here is one of my favorite yeast-raised doughnut formulas.

yeast-raised doughnuts *Yield: 16 lb 9 oz (7,510 g)*

Ingredients	Lb	Oz	Metric	Procedures
Water	4		1,810 g	Combine all ingredients, using straight-dough mixing method.
Yeast		12	340 g	
Bread flour	5		2,270 g	
Pastry flour	3		1,360 g	
Baking powder		2	60 g	
Sugar		8	230 g	
Salt		2	60 g	
Nutmeg		1/2	10 g	
Milk powder		8	230 g	
Emulsified shortening	1	8	680 g	
Eggs, whole	1		450 g	

NUTRITIONAL INFORMATION PER 2 OZ (60 G) SERVING: 172 Calories; 6 g Fat (33.5% calories from fat); 5 g Protein; 24 g Carbohydrate; 1 g Dietary Fiber; 14 mg Cholesterol; 223 mg Sodium. Exchanges: 1 1/2 Grain (Starch); 0 Lean Meat; 0 Nonfat Milk; 1 Fat; 0 Other Carbohydrates.

Q: What type of shortening or oil would you recommend for frying doughnuts?

J.T., McKeesport, Pa.

A: I recommend a hard fat with high melting point, around 115°F (46°C) to 120°F (49°C), and a high smoke point, about 400°F (204°C). A hard fat will solidify at room temperature, sealing the doughnut and providing a good base for sugars or glazes.

CAKES

Q: I was given the following formula for chocolate sponge cake. The cake had good volume but poor color and flavor and was very dry. I adjusted the formula by adding 1 lb (450 g) of cocoa, 2 lb (900 g) of water, 4 oz (110 g) of corn syrup, and reduced the amount of eggs to 14 lb (6,350 g). The cake now is slightly more moist and darker in color but has less volume. I'm still not happy with this cake. I've included my original formula for your review.

Ingredients	Lb	Oz	Metric
Cake flour	8		3,630 g
Baking powder		8	230 g
Chocolate fudge base	2		900 g
Whole eggs	16		7,260 g

B.D., Dana, Ind.

A: There are several problems with your formula. Not only is it totally unbalanced, it fails to include any sugar. Sugar not only adds flavor but provides and retains moisture. Adding corn syrup is a step in the right direction. I recommend making some wholesale changes. To begin, add 8 lb (3,630 g) granulated sugar; replace the fudge base with 2 lb (900 g) cocoa; delete the baking powder; decrease cake flour by 2 lb (900 g); and reduce the amount of eggs by 4 lb (1,810 g). Additionally, fold in 1 lb (450 g) butter along with flour. These changes will make your formula perfect!

   If you are ever put in this position again, here are the basic rules of formula balance for sponge cakes:

■ The combined weights of flour and eggs should exceed the combined weights of sugar and liquids other than whole eggs. This would include either water or milk.

■ The amount of sugar should equal or slightly exceed the amount of eggs.

■ The weight of either the sugar or the eggs should exceed the weight of the flour.

■ The combined weights of the liquid in water, milk, or eggs should exceed the weight of the sugar by a ratio of 1.5 to 1.

Q: Is there a ratio for determining how much cake batter to place in a cake pan? We have been making cakes shaped like numbers and animals, so it's hard to judge the right amount.

J.M., Cape Cod, Mass.

A: Fill the cake pan with water to the midway mark. Weigh the water. The weight of the water is equal to the weight of the batter required.

Q: Our customers frequently request low-fat bakery items. Would you have a high-quality angel food cake formula?

T.R., Bar Harbor, Maine

A: Merchandise this angel food cake with strawberries or other fruit as a delicious, low-fat dessert.

angel food cake
Yield: 4 lb 14 oz (2,210 g); five 8-inch (200 cm) cakes

Ingredients	Lb	Oz	Metric	Procedures
Egg whites	2		900 g	Combine. Beat at high speed for 5 minutes.
Vanilla, to taste				
Sugar	1		450 g	Combine. Add gradually to egg whites. Beat at high speed until soft peaks form.
Cream of tartar		1/4	10 g	
Salt		1/4	10 g	
Sugar	1		450 g	Sift together. Carefully fold by hand into egg whites. Prepare five 8-inch baking pans. Scale 15 oz (430 g) of batter into pans. Bake at 350°F (180°C) for 35 to 40 minutes or until cakes spring back when touched. Remove from oven, turn pans over on racks, and allow to cool before removing from pan.
Cake flour		13	370 g	

NUTRITIONAL INFORMATION PER 2 OZ (60 G) SERVING: 138 Calories; trace Fat (0.5% calories from fat); 3 g Protein; 31 g Carbohydrate; trace Dietary Fiber; 0 mg Cholesterol; 109 mg Sodium. Exchanges: 1/2 Grain (Starch); 1/2 Lean Meat; 0 Fruit; 1 1/2 Other Carbohydrates.

Q: We have been given a formula for a high-ratio cake that is mixed to a specific gravity of .775. Can you explain "specific gravity"?

A.M., Newburg, Vt.

A: Specific gravity is the ratio between a volume of batter and an equal amount of water. Flour distributors can supply a specific gravity cup to measure this relationship. A specific gravity cup will weigh 10 oz (280 g) when full of water. If this cup weighs 9 oz (260 g) when filled with batter, that batter has a specific gravity of .09; batter weighing 11 oz (310 g) will have a specific gravity of 1.1. Products made using specific gravity specifications are more uniform because the temperature of the ingredients, the mixing speed, and the mixing time all affect the aeration of batters. You should cream ingredients until you obtain the correct specific gravity for your formula.

Q: I'm looking to add carrot cake to my production line. Do you have a great recipe for this item?

J.K., Omaha, Neb.

A: This traditional formula will have customers asking for more.

carrot cake   *Yield: 13 lbs 9 oz (6,150 g)*

Ingredients	Lb	Oz	Metric	Procedures
Sugar	1	5	600 g	Combine. Mix at low speed for 3 minutes.
Light-brown sugar	1	5	600 g	
Vegetable oil	3		1,360 g	
Eggs	2		900 g	
Cake flour	2	7	1,110 g	Sift together and add. Mix at low speed for 3 minutes.
Baking powder		1 1/2	40 g	
Baking soda		1	30 g	
Raisins		12	340 g	Add. Mix at medium speed for 5 minutes.
Chopped walnuts		12	340 g	
Grated carrots	1	12	800 g	
Cinnamon		1/2	10 g	Rub together. Add to above. Mix at medium speed for 3 minutes.
Cloves		1/3	10 g	Fill cake pans halfway with batter. Bake at 360°F (180°C) for 25 minutes per pound of batter in pan. Yield will vary depending on the size of pan used.
Salt		1/2	10 g	

NUTRITIONAL INFORMATION PER 2 OZ (60 G) SERVING: 231 Calories; 15 g Fat (57.4% calories from fat); 3 g Protein; 23 g Carbohydrate; 1 g Dietary Fiber; 30 mg Cholesterol; 177 mg Sodium. Exchanges: 1/2 Grain (Starch); 0 Lean Meat; 0 Vegetable; 0 Fruit; 3 Fat; 1/2 Other Carbohydrates.

Q: Could you please define the terms *cake, torte, tart,* and *gateau?*

N.C., Bangor, Maine

A: *Cake* generally refers to sweet baked products made from batter containing flour, butter, milk, and flavorings. Although the eggs act as a leavener, other leavening action can be supplied by baking powder or baking soda.

Torte is a German word that refers to a rich cake made with little or no flour, instead containing ground nuts or breadcrumbs, eggs, sugar, and flavorings. Tortes usually have several layers and are filled with such products as buttercream or jam.

Tart refers to a pie-like product with a shallow pastry shell and no top crust. Fillings can be either savory, such as meat or cheese, or sweet, such as fruit or custard.

Gateau is simply the French word for cake.

Q: Our bakery is located in apple country. We would like to add an apple cake to our selection of apple pies and pastries. Would you have such a formula?

T.M., New Paltz, N.Y.

A: This delicious apple cake can be made with Rome Beauty, Cortland, Winesap, or York Imperial apples.

apple cake   *Yield: 11 lb 3 oz (5,080 g); eight 8-inch (200 cm) cakes*

Ingredients	Lb	Oz	Metric	Procedures
Sugar	2	8	1,130 g	Combine. Cream at medium speed for 8 minutes.
Butter		12	340 g	
Salt		1/2	10 g	
Mace		1/2	10 g	
Cinnamon		1/2	10 g	
Eggs	1		450 g	Add in two stages. Mix at medium speed for 5 minutes.
Milk	1		450 g	
Baking soda		1	30 g	Sift together; add alternately with milk.
Cake flour	2	12	1,250 g	
Baking powder		1	30 g	
Apples, diced	3		1,360 g	Fold in by hand. Scale 1 lb 6 oz (620 g) batter per 8-inch pan. Bake at 360°F (180°C) for 35 to 40 minutes.

NUTRITIONAL INFORMATION PER 2 OZ (60 G) SERVING: 145 Calories; 4 g Fat (23.8% calories from fat); 2 g Protein; 26 g Carbohydrate; trace Dietary Fiber; 27 mg Cholesterol; 223 mg Sodium. Exchanges: 1 Grain (Starch); 0 Lean Meat; 0 Fruit; 0 Nonfat Milk; 1/2 Fat; 1 Other Carbohydrates.

Q: Please provide a formula for an all-butter sour cream pound cake. Also, can you tell me why pound cakes fall in the middle during and after baking?

D.C., Jacksonville, Fla.

A: Pound cake will fall in the middle if it is disturbed during the first 15 minutes of baking, if the oven is too hot, or if the meringue is not properly distributed. I think this formula will suit your needs.

sour cream pound cake
Yield: 28 lbs 11 oz (13,000 g); about 26 loaves

Ingredients	Lb	Oz	Metric	Procedures
Butter, room temperature	3	8	1,590 g	Combine. Mix with paddle attachment until blended.
Sugar	10	8	4,760 g	
Sour cream	4	8	2,040 g	Add. Mix at first speed until smooth.
Eggs	2	2	970 g	Add. Mix at second speed until blended.
Vanilla	6	1	30 g	Add. Combine.
Cake flour, sifted	2		2,720 g	Add. Mix at second speed until batter is smooth.
Egg whites	8		900 g	Whip with whip attachment until stiff peaks develop. Fold in by hand. Scale 17 1/2 oz (500 g) per loaf. Bake at 330°F (170°C) for about 20 minutes.

NUTRITIONAL INFORMATION PER 2 OZ (60 G) SERVING: 199 Calories; 8 g Fat (35.3% calories from fat); 2 g Protein; 30 g Carbohydrate; trace Dietary Fiber; 34 mg Cholesterol; 73 mg Sodium. Exchanges: 1/2 Grain (Starch); 0 Lean Meat; 0 Nonfat Milk; 1 1/2 Fat; 1 1/2 Other Carbohydrates.

Q: We haven't been happy with the white cake we're currently making; it's too dry. Could you please run a formula that produces very moist white cake?

R.H., Virginia Beach, Va

A: This formula should give excellent results:

hi-ratio white cake
Yield: 24 lb 6 oz (11,000 g); about 16 10-in. (250 cm) cakes

Ingredients	Lb	Oz	Metric	Procedures
Cake flour	6		2,720 g	Combine. Using a paddle attachment, mix at second speed of 3-speed mixer for 4 minutes, scraping bowl frequently.
Butter	1	6	620 g	
Emulsified shortening	1	6	620 g	
Sugar	7		3,180 g	
Salt		3	90 g	
Baking powder		6	170 g	
Milk	2		900 g	Combine. Add in three stages, mixing well after each addition. Line bottoms with parchment paper and grease sides of 16 10-inch (250 cm) round cake pans. Scale 1 lb 8 oz (680 g) of batter into each pan. Bake at 350°F (180°C) for 35 to 40 minutes or until cake springs back when touched lightly in center.
Vanilla extract		1	30 g	
Egg whites	3		1,360 g	
Eggs	1		450 g	

NUTRITIONAL INFORMATION PER 2 OZ (60 G) SERVING: 334 Calories; 12 g Fat (32.2% calories from fat); 5 g Protein; 52 g Carbohydrate; trace Dietary Fiber; 31 mg Cholesterol; 575 mg Sodium. Exchanges: 1 1/2 Grain (Starch); 0 Lean Meat; 0 Nonfat Milk; 2 1/2 Fat; 2 Other Carbohydrates.

Q: We have tried several formulas for rum cake and have not been satisfied with the results. We are looking to produce a cake that will retain a firm texture even after absorbing the rum syrup.

P.R., Chicago, Ill.

A: I have used the following formula for many years. It has a fine texture and good absorption qualities. Enjoy!

rum cake *Yield: 13 lb (5,870 g); nine 24 oz (680 g) cakes*

Ingredients	Lb	Oz	Metric	Procedures
Shortening	2		900 g	Combine; cream until light.
Sugar	3	8	1,590 g	
Salt		1	30 g	
Orange zest		1/2	10 g	
Lemon zest		1/2	10 g	
Egg yolks	1	6	620 g	Add slowly; cream until light.
Eggs	1	6	620 g	
Cake flour	3		1,360 g	Sift together.
Baking powder		1 1/2	40 g	
Milk	1	8	680 g	Add alternately with flour. Mix until smooth. Grease and flour nine, 8-inch tube pans. Scale 1 lb 8 oz (680 g) batter per pan. Bake at 360°F (180°C) for 40 to 45 minutes. Invert pans and allow cakes to cool. Dip cooled cakes in rum syrup, drain on screens, then dust with confectioners' sugar.

NUTRITIONAL INFORMATION PER 2 OZ (60 G) SERVING: 217 Calories; 11 g Fat (47.0% calories from fat); 3 g Protein; 26 g Carbohydrate; trace Dietary Fiber; 99 mg Cholesterol; 162 mg Sodium. Exchanges: 1/2 Grain (Starch); 0 Lean Meat; 0 Fruit; 0 Nonfat Milk; 2 Fat; 1 Other Carbohydrates.

Q: We are considering adding wedding cakes to our catering line. We are looking for a formula that would produce a moist chocolate cake with a fine grain. Any suggestions?

G.S., Atlanta, Ga.

A: This formula will help you create wonderful chocolate wedding cakes.

hi-ratio chocolate cake
Yield: 13 lb 7 oz (6,100 g); nine 10-inch (250 cm) cakes or four half-sheet cakes

Ingredients	Lb	Oz	Metric	Procedures
Cake flour	2		900 g	Combine. Mix at medium speed for 5 minutes.
Emulsified shortening	1	6	620 g	
Sugar	3		1,360 g	Add. Mix for 5 minutes.
Cake flour		8	230 g	
Salt		1 1/4	35 g	
Baking powder		2	60 g	
Baking soda		3/4	20 g	
Cocoa powder		9	260 g	
Milk	1	14	850 g	
Invert sugar		1	30 g	
Eggs	1	14	850 g	Add slowly; mix 3 minutes.
Milk	1	14	850 g	Add in three stages. Mix for 2 minutes.
Vanilla		1	30 g	Grease sides and paper bottoms of baking pans. Scale 1 lb 8 oz (680 g) of batter per each 10-inch pan or 3 lb (1,360 g) for each half-sheet cake. Bake at 350°F (180°C) for 35 to 40 minutes or until cake springs back when touched lightly in center.

NUTRITIONAL INFORMATION PER 2 OZ (60 G) SERVING: 165 Calories; 7 g Fat (39.0% calories from fat); 3 g Protein; 23 g Carbohydrate; 1 g Dietary Fiber; 31 mg Cholesterol; 254 mg Sodium. Exchanges: 1/2 Grain (Starch); 0 Lean Meat; 0 Nonfat Milk; 1 1/2 Fat; 1 Other Carbohydrates.

Q: Is it possible to make hi-ratio cakes using butter? I've heard different opinions and am interested in trying this if possible.

W.Y., Boise, Idaho

A: Hi-ratio cakes require a special shortening due to their high liquid content. If you use butter, you will need to increase the amount of butter by 10 percent. Another alternative is to use a high-grade margarine that contains soybean oil and a high level of lecithin; use it at the same percentage as you would the shortening.

Q: I have many customers on sugar-restricted diets. Can you tell me which sweeteners I can use to replace sugar in cakes and pastry?

W.W., Hooma, La.

A: Many sugar replacements are available, such as saccharin. For most pastry dough, you may generally use 1 oz (30 g) of replacement for 1 lb (450 g) sugar, depending on the replacement. However, in batter-type formulas, sugar contributes moisture and bulk. I would suggest substituting apple puree for sugar in a hi-ratio cake. In the following formula, the use of apple puree reduced the sugar content by as much as 50 percent.

reduced-sugar apple purée cake
Yield: 12 lb 3 oz (5,530 g); eight 10-inch (250 cm) cakes

Ingredients	Lb	Oz	Metric	Procedures
Cake flour	3		1,360 g	Cream together at medium speed with paddle attachment for 3 to 5 minutes.
Emulsified shortening	1	6	620 g	
Baking powder		3	90 g	
Salt		1	30 g	
Apple puree	3	8	1,590 g	Add in order shown. Mix at low speed until blended, about 12 minutes.
Vanilla		1	30 g	
Milk	2		900 g	
Egg whites	1	8	680 g	
Eggs		8	230 g	Scale 1 lb 8 oz (680 g) of batter per 10-inch pan. Bake at 350°F (180°C) for 35 to 40 minutes or until cakes spring back when touched lightly in center.

NUTRITIONAL INFORMATION PER 2 OZ (60 G) SERVING: 131 Calories; 7 g Fat (49.0% calories from fat); 2 g Protein; 14 g Carbohydrate; trace Dietary Fiber; 10 mg Cholesterol; 225 mg Sodium. Exchanges: 1 Grain (Starch); 0 Lean Meat; 0 Fruit; 0 Nonfat Milk; 1 1/2 Fat; 0 Other Carbohydrates.

ICINGS/FROSTINGS

Q: I tasted the best French buttercream at a local store. Do you have a favorite formula?

C.H., Stow, Ohio

A: You should be pleased with the results of this formula.

French buttercream   *Yield: 5 lb 8 oz (2,490 g)*

Ingredients	Lb	Oz	Metric	Procedures
Sugar	2		900 g	Combine sugar and water. Bring to a boil. Wash sides of saucepan with water to incorporate sugar crystals in syrup and cook to 240°F (116°C).
Water		8	230 g	
Egg yolks		12	340 g	Whip egg yolks to a lemon color. Add cooked sugar to egg yolks while mixing at second speed. Whip until cool.
Butter, soft	2	8	1,130 g	Mix in softened butter and vanilla. Refrigerate when not using.
Vanilla		1/2	150 g	

NUTRITIONAL INFORMATION PER 2 OZ (60 G) SERVING: 293 Calories; 23 g Fat (70.1% calories from fat); 2 g Protein; 21 g Carbohydrate; 0 g Dietary Fiber; 155 mg Cholesterol; 217 mg Sodium. Exchanges: 0 Lean Meat; 4 1/2 Fat; 1 1/2 Other Carbohydrates.

Q: We have been having difficulty with our chocolate fondant when we ice cupcakes and éclairs. The product develops a dull, hard finish. We blend 2 oz (60 g) of bitter chocolate with each pound of fondant and heat the mixture until it is soft; we also add some syrup sometimes. Can you tell us what is wrong?

W.K., Naperville, Ill.

A: To properly ice cupcakes and éclairs with fondant, heat the fondant to between 95°F and 105°F (35°C to 41°C). This will allow the fondant to crystallize and produce a glossy finish. Fondant at a temperature lower than 95°F (35°C) will not crystallize, while fondant higher than 105°F (41°C) will dry hard and with a dull finish. Remember to always heat fondant in a double boiler and never exceed 120°F (50°C).

Q: I've had an ongoing problem with my scratch fudge icing. Can you explain why my icing is too light in color and develops white spots?

D.S., Mobile, Ala.

A: Light-colored icing most often results from overwhipping. When icing is overmixed, air is incorporated, resulting in a light color. Other possibilities are the inclusion of gum or starch stabilizers and the use of milk solids.

The white spots most likely are "fat bloom." This is a result of overheating icing during preparation. Simply lowering temperatures should resolve this problem.

Q: How do you make white and dark chocolate fondant?

R.M., Lorena, Texas

A: To make chocolate fondant, add 1 oz (30 g) of chocolate liquor (or unsweetened chocolate) to each pound (450 g) of fondant. Adjust the consistency of the fondant with simple syrup or corn syrup and temper

2. Place flour on top and let hydrate for 30 minutes.

3. Dissolve the yeast in remaining water; do not allow yeast to sit more than 15 minutes.

4. Never add yeast to a salt solution as salt will inhibit the yeast activity.

5. Mix until flour is thoroughly incorporated and add shortening.

6. Adjust dough consistency; flour absorption is variable and affected by temperature of liquid.

7. Mix dough to develop the gluten, test by stretching.

SPONGE DOUGH MIXING METHOD

Water Temperature

In figuring the water temperature for sponge dough, follow the same method used for the straight dough method, except multiply the desired dough temperature by four.

Example (Sponge Dough Method)

Add the following temperatures:

Sponge (fermented)	82°F (28°C)
Room	80°F (27°C)
Flour	71°F (22°C)
Friction	20°F (−7°C)
	253°F (123°C)

Desired dough temperature is 80°F (27°C).

$4 \times 80 = 320 - 253 = 67°F (19°C)$ for the desired water temperature.

Mixing (Sponge Dough Method)

1. Dissolve yeast in 50 percent of the water. Add 30 percent of the flour mix to spongy consistency and let ferment for 45 minutes.

2. Follow steps 3 to 7 on the straight dough method using the remaining water.

ADDITIONAL METHODS

There are three basic foaming methods that can be used for mixing sponge cakes. They are the cold foaming method, the warm foaming method, and the separation foaming method. Most formulas will designate which mixing method is preferred. In general, the foaming method whips the eggs and the sugar together prior to the flour being added.

CREAMING

Place sugar, butter or shortening, salt, and spices in a mixing bowl and cream together. Ingredients must be at room temperature to cream properly. Add eggs slowly and fold in sifted flour; be careful not to overmix.

BLENDING

Place all the ingredients in a mixing bowl and mix until all are smoothly blended. Allow 2 to 3 minutes at low speed for mixing to be complete. There are six basic methods for shaping these mixtures, which give the different types of cookies their names.

forms

Copy this worksheet and use it whenever a change in yield is necessary.

Form for Changing Yield: Original Formula					New Yields		
% Ratio	Ingredients	Lb	Oz	Metric	Lb	Oz	Metric

Use this form to calculate the cost of your formulas.

Formula and Cost Form

Product _____   Date _____

Source _____

Method of Mixing and Comments	Ingredients Used in Order of Mixing	Weight of Ingredients Lb	Weight of Ingredients Oz	Unit Cost	Extended Material Costs

Block letters Capital

A B C D E F

G H I J K L

M N O P Q

R S T U V

W U X Y Z

556

Cursive #1 letters — CAPITAL

A B C D E F

G H I I J K

L M M N O P

Q R S T U V

W X Y Z

Block letters lower case

a b c d e f g h i

j k l m n o p q r

s t u v w x y z

1 2 3 4 5 6 7

8 9 0 "&?!$"

bibliography and recommended reading

BREADS

Beard, James. *Beard on Bread*. New York: Alfred Knopf, 1980.

Dunwoody Institute. *Bread and Rolls*. Minneapolis, Minn. (No copyright.)

General Mills. *Specialty Breads*. Revised, 1948.

Hamelman, Jeffrey. *Bread*. Hoboken, N.J.: John Wiley & Sons, 2004.

CAKES AND PASTRY

Desaulniers, Marcel. *Desserts to Die For*. New York: Simon & Schuster, 1995.

Dunwoody Institute. *Cakes & Pastries*. Minneapolis, Minn. (No copyright.)

Friberg, Bo. *The Professional Pastry Chef*, 4th ed. New York: John Wiley & Sons, 2002.

General Mills. *Quality Cakes*. Minneapolis, Minn. 1949.

Hopkins, Dennis M. *Simple But Effective Cake Decorating*. Chicago, Ill.: Clissold, 1925.

Maglieri, Nick. *Nick Maglieri's Perfect Pastry*. New York: Macmillan, 1989.

Yard, Sherry. *The Secrets of Baking*. Boston, Mass.: Houghton Mifflin, 2003.

CHOCOLATE

Coe, Sophie D., and Michael D. Coe. *The True History of Chocolate*. New York: Thames and Hudson, 1996.

Desaulniers, Marcel. *Death By Chocolate*. New York: Simon & Schuster, 1997.

Desaulniers, Marcel. *Death By Chocolate Cake*. New York: Harper Collins, 2000.

Presilla, Maricel. *The New Taste of Chocolate: A Cultural and Natural History of Cacao with Recipes*. Berkeley, Calif.: Ten Speed Press, 2001.

GENERAL BAKING

Amendola, Joseph. *The Baker's Manual*, 2nd ed. New York: Ahreans, 1960.

Culinary Institute of America. *Baking and Pastry*. Hoboken, N.J.: John Wiley & Sons, 2004.

Dooveen, K. Camille Den. *The Master Baker and His Work*. Boston: Simonds Co., 1928.

Fannie Farmer, *The Boston Cooking School Cookbook*. Boston: Little, Brown and Company, 1918.

Fleishmann Company. *A Treatise on Baking*, 2nd ed. New York: Fleishmann Co., 1928.

General Mills. *Product Control Box*. Minneapolis: General Mills, 1955.

Retail Baker's Association. *RBA Workshop Book*. Laurel, Md.: RBA, 1981.

Labensky, Sarah R., with Eddy Van Damme, Priscilla Martel, and Klaus Tenbergen. *On Baking*. Upper Saddle River, N.J.: Prentice Hall, 2005.

Sultan, William J. *Practical Baking*, 3rd ed. Westport, Conn.: AVI, 1983.

Sultan, William J. *Modern Pastry Chef*. Westport, Conn.: AVI, 1997.

GENERAL INDUSTRY

Chon, Kye Sung, and Raymond T. Sparrowe. *Welcome to Hospitality*, Albany, N.Y.: Thompson Learning, 2000.

Cooper, Ann. *A Women's Place is in the Kitchen: The Evolution of Women Chefs*. Stamford, Conn.: Thomson, 1997.

Culinary Institute of America. *The Professional Pastry Chef*, 6th ed. Van Nostrand Reinhold, 1996.

Dornenburg, Andrew, and Karen Page. *The New American Chef*. Hoboken, N.J.: John Wiley & Sons, 2003.

Kittler, Pamela Goyan, and Kathryn P. Sucher. *Cultural Foods*, 3rd ed. Belmont, Calif.: Wadsworth Division, Thompson, 2001.

Labensky, Sarah R., and Alan M. Hause. *On Cooking*, 2nd ed. Upper Saddle River, N.J.: Prentice Hall, 1999.

Mintz, Sidney W. *Sweetness and Power: The Place of Sugar in Modern History*. New York: Viking Press, 1995.

FOOD SAFETY

International Life Sciences Institute. *A Simple Guide to Understanding and Applying the Hazard Analysis Critical Control Point Concept*. Washington, D.C.: ILSI Press, 1993.

Loken, Joan K. *The HACCP Food Safety Manual*. New York: John Wiley & Sons, 1995.

Marriott, Norman G. *Principles of Food Sanitation*, 4th ed. Gaithersburg, Md.: Aspen Publishing, 1999.

McSwane, David, Nancy Rue, and Richard Linton. *Essentials of Food Safety and Sanitation*, updated 2nd ed. Upper Saddle River, N.J.: Prentice Hall, 2002.

National Assessment Institute. *Handbook for Safe Food Service Management*, 2nd ed. Upper Saddle River, N.J.: Prentice Hall, 1998.

National Restaurant Association Educational Foundation. *SerSave Coursebook*. New York: John Wiley & Sons, 2001.

FOOD SCIENCE

Campbell, Ada Marie, Marjorie Porter Penfield, and Ruth M. Griswold. *The Experimental Study of Food*. 2nd ed. Mass.: Houghton Mifflin, 1962.

Charley, Helen, and Connie Weaver Merrill. *Foods: A Scientific Approach*, 3rd ed. Upper Saddle River, N.J.: Prentice Hall, 1998.

Hoseney, R. Carl. *Principles of Cereal Science & Technology*, 2nd ed. St. Paul, Minn.: American Assn. of Cereal Chemists, 1994.

McGee, Harold. *On Food and Cooking*. New York: Scribner, 1984.

Pyler, E.J. *Baking Science & Technology*. Chicago: Siebel, 1973.

Schunemann, Claus, and Gunther Treu. *Baking: The Art & Science*. Calgary: Baker's Tech, 1986.

INGREDIENTS

Feinstein, Andrew Hale, and John W. Stefanelli. *Purchasing*. New York: John Wiley & Sons, 2002.

Kurlansky, Mark. *Salt*. New York: Penguin Books, 2002.

Zuckerman, Larry. *Potato*. North Point Press, New York: 1998.

NUTRITION

Baskette, Michael, and Eleanor Mainella. *The Art of Nutritional Cooking*, 2nd ed. Upper Saddle River, N.J.: Prentice Hall, 1999.

Berkoff, Nancy. *Nutrition for the Culinary Arts.* Upper Saddle River, N.J.: Prentice Hall, 2004.

Culinary Institute of America. *Techniques of Healthy Cooking.* USA and Canada: New York: John Wiley & Sons, 2000.

Eagen, Maureen, and Susan Davis Allen. *Healthful Quantity Baking.* New York: John Wiley & Sons, 1992.

REFERENCE

Bickel, Walter. *Hering's Dictionary of Classical and Modern Cookery*, 13th English ed. London: Virtue, 1994.

Chalmers, Irena. *The Great Food Almanac: A Feast of Facts From A to Z.* San Francisco: Collins, 1994.

Fortin, Jacques. *The Visual Food Encyclopedia.* Montreal: John Wiley & Sons, 1996.

General Mills. *Rye Dictionary*, Minneapolis, Minn. 1936.

Hill, Julia. *Culinary Math.* Hoboken, N.J.: John Wiley & Sons, 2004.

Labensky, Steven, Gaye G. Ingram, and Sarah R. Labensky. *Webster's New World Dictionary of Culinary Arts*, 2nd ed. Upper Saddle River, N.J.: Prentice Hall, 2001.

Riley, Elizabeth. *The Chef's Companion.* New York: John Wiley & Sons, 2003.

glossary

The following definitions apply to some of the words that are commonly used in the baking industry. You need not memorize them, but make yourself familiar with their meanings. When a word has more than one definition, the term that applies to baking is given here.

A

absorption—taking in, or capture, by molecular action; in baking, the property of flour to absorb and hold liquid

accreditation—verification of a standard as established by a trade organization

acid alkaline reaction—the process of dissolving alkaline in water, which produces carbon dioxide gas with the introduction of an acid

acidity—sourness; tartness; a condition indicating excess fermentation in yeast dough

add-mix—additional flavoring unit of one or more ingredients added to a basic mix to change appearance and taste (see *mix*)

aeration—treatment of dough or batter by charging with air or gas (such as carbon dioxide) to produce a volume increase

agar-agar—gelatinous seaweed product used for bacteria culture or in making decorating jelly or gumdrops

albumen—egg white

almond—nut (kernel or seed) of a small tree similar to peach

almond paste—almonds ground to paste, with sugar as a preservative

almond sponge—cake batter containing almond paste

almond tart—tart with an egg white and almond paste filling

amaretto—almond-flavored liqueur

amylopectin—basic component of a starch granule; has better pasting properties than amylase

amylose—basic component of a starch granule; these larger granules absorb more liquid than amlopectin

angel food—fine white cake without shortening made of egg white, sugar, flavoring, and flour, baked in a tube pan

angel food tin—round loaf pan having a center tube

angelique (angelica)—candied leaf stalks of an aromatic plant; used for decorating

anise drops—small cookies flavored with anise oil or seed

anise oil—flavoring made from anise seed, a plant of the celery family

apricot glacé—jam-like product of boiled apricots and sugar

ash—powdery, incombustible residue left after burning glacé

average flour value—values composed of four factors: color of flour, loaves per barrel, size of loaf, and quality of bread as applied to any given shipment of flour

B

baba—cake made of leavened dough steeped in liqueur syrup

bacteria—numerous microscopic organisms; various species are involved in fermentation and spoilage

bain-marie—French word for water bath

bake—to cook by dry heat in a closed place, as an oven

baked Alaska—ice cream dessert and sponge cake dessert that has been encased with meringue and baked until meringue is golden-brown

baker's balance beam scale—device with two balanced platforms used to measure dry ingredients

baker's bench—work table made of laminated wood; provides a surface for dough rolling and shaping

baker's chocolate—unsweetened block of high-quality chocolate

baker's pantry—basic ingredients used in baking

bakery—baker's shop or place where goods are made and/or sold

baking or bicarbonate of soda—sodium salt of carbonic acid; has the ability to combine with acid to produce carbon dioxide; alkaline in nature

baking powder—chemical leavening agent composed of soda, dry acid, and usually cornstarch to absorb air moisture; when wet, carbon dioxide (a gas) is given off to raise the batter

balance beam scale—apparatus used to weigh dry ingredients; uses two balanced platforms and a graduated bar; also used to weigh dough and cake batter

balloon whip—a hand-held whip using thinner "piano wire"; is more effective than whips with thicker wire at creating the small bubbles of air in the cream that give whipped cream its structure

banneton—French woven basket used during the fermentation stage of breadmaking

barrel—flat-ended, wooden, somewhat cylindrical container with bulging sides; the measure of what a standard size barrel contains: 31 1/2 gallons of liquid or 296 lb of flour

bars—cookies made in oblong shapes

base—a mixture of dry ingredients, often without characterizing flavors, to which other dry and wet ingredients may be added in varying proportions to create a range of different products

batter—pourable mixture of combined ingredients such as flour, sugar, eggs, shortening, milk, etc.

Bavarian cream—custard sauce thickened with gelatin and whipped cream

beignets—éclair paste that is cut into squares, deep-fried, and then dusted with powdered sugar

bench—baker's work table, usually made of hardwood, on which the make-up takes place

bench scraper—flat metal about 5 or 6 inches long with a wood handle; used to cut yeast dough into pieces and to scrape the wood bench

bench time—amount of time a yeast raised dough is allowed to sit or relax on the bench prior to make-up

berliner—round, jelly-filled doughnut containing a prize and typically served on New Year's day

biscuit—small roll made with yeast dough; small round bread stuff made of dough raised with baking powder; kind of crisp or hard bread, thin and flat, made without leavening

bittersweet chocolate—also known as semisweet; prepared by blending a minimum of 35 percent chocolate liqueur with varying amounts of sweeteners and cocoa butter

blanch—to plunge food briefly into boiling water and then into cold water to stop the cooking process

bleeding—term applied to dough that has been cut and left unsealed at the cut, thus permitting the escape of air and gas

blend—mixture of two or more flavorings or grades of flour

bloom—method to hydrate gelatin by placing it in cold water and stirring

blooms—pale, light streaks and blotches that appear on the surface of chocolate that has gotten too hot

boil—to bubble, emitting vapor, when heat is applied; boiling temperature for water is considered at 212°F (100°C) at ordinary altitudes but varies with other liquids

boiled icing—made by boiling sugar and water to thread stage (238°F or 114°C), then adding it to beaten egg whites and confectionary sugar

bolting—sifting of ground grain to remove the bran

bombe—bomb-shaped dessert consisting of mousse or ice cream with mousse

Boston brown bread—dark, sweet bread (not yeast raised) containing, among the ingredients, cornmeal and molasses; steamed and not baked

Boston cream pie—rich, creamy dessert made from a combination of yellow cake, custard, and chocolate glaze

bouchees—bite-sized hors d'oeuvres made out of puff pastry shells

bowl knife—spatula or flexible, dull-edged knife used to scrape batter or dough from bowl sides

bowl scraper—plastic scraper used to scrape the side of the mixing bowl so as to remove the unmixed product so it will mix smoothly

bran—skin or outer covering of the wheat berry removed during milling

bran muffin—sweet muffin containing a large percentage of bran

brandy—alcoholic liquor distilled from wine

bread—accepted term for food of flour, sugar, shortening, salt, and liquid made light by the action of yeast

bread dough—uncooked mass of ingredients used to make bread

bread faults—deviations from standards of perfection used to determine wrong factors in the process of production of bread

bread schedule—list of exact periods of dough fermentation; also shows time needed for completing the baking process

bread scoring—analysis of finished loaf to determine quality

bread shop order—form sent to shop foreman giving amount of bread needed for production during or by a given time

brioche—sweet yeast bread usually shaped like a fat muffin with a little cap on top; most often served at breakfast

broadcast—act of distributing (spraying) dry ingredients by hand

bromate—a dough conditioner that improves the volume of yeast dough

bundt pan—tube cake pan with fluted sides

buns—small cakes of bread dough, sometimes slightly sweetened or flavored

butter—fat obtained by churning sweet or sour cream

buttercream—creamed or whipped frosting used to enrobe and decorate cakes and pastries

butter horns—basic sweet dough cut and shaped like horns

butterscotch—flavor produced by the use of butter and brown sugar

butter sponge—sponge-cake type batter to which shortening is added and used for torten and French pastry

butter stars—cookies made by pressing rich dough through star tube

C

cacao—evergreen tree native to tropical America from which chocolate is obtained

cake—leavened and shortened sweet product containing flour, sugar, salt, egg, milk, liquid, flavoring, shortening, and leavening agent

cake doughnut—a doughnut that is leavened with baking powder (not yeast); it is made like a cake batter and dropped by a depositing machine into the frying oil

cake faults—deviations from standards of perfection for the type

cake flour—finely milled, soft wheat flour

cake machine—machine with vertical agitators operating at different speeds used for mixing cake ingredients

cake stand—plastic or metal frame used to separate a tiered cake

cake tester—rigid steel wire with a loop handle that takes the guesswork out of bake times for the baker; simply insert the tester into a cake or quick bread during baking; if batter sticks to the tester, the cake is not done baking; if nothing sticks to the wire, the cake or quick bread is done

cane sugar—sweet carbohydrate obtained from sugar cane

cannoli—Italian pastry made in the shape of a tube, deep fried, and traditionally filled with sweetened ricotta cheese

caramel buns—sweet dough pieces baked in a sugared pan

caramel icing—cooked icing of brown sugar, shortening, and milk

caramelization—a browning of sugar when the surface temperature of baked goods reaches 300°F (150°C)

caramelized sugar—dry sugar heated, with constant stirring, until it melts and darkens in color; used for flavoring and coloring caramel sugar—cane sugar boiled to a certain density, then cooled and pulled for use in decorating

caraway seeds—small, light-brown seeds that have a flavor similar to a blend of dill and anise; commonly used in rye bread and other German, British, and European dishes

carbohydrates—sugar and starches derived chiefly from vegetable sources, that contain set amounts of carbon, hydrogen, and oxygen according to the kind of carbohydrate

carbonated ammonia—leavening agent made of ammonia and carbonic acid

carbon dioxide—colorless, tasteless, edible gas obtained during fermentation or from combination of soda and acid

cardamon—seed of an East Indian spice plant; used for flavoring

casein—principal nitrogenous, or protein, part of milk

certification—person's skill level certified by a trade organization rather than by the government

charlotte—dessert made in a mold that has been lined with ladyfingers and filled with custard and gelatin cream

cheesecake—cake made of sweet or short dough base with a filling of combined cheese, eggs, and milk

cheese torte—rich cheese mixture baked in a shell of combined crumbs, sugar, and butter

cherries jubiliee—dessert that consists of cherries flamed tableside with sugar and Kirsch (cherry brandy) spooned over vanilla ice cream

chiffon—sponge cake leavened with beaten egg whites

chinois—a cone-shaped strainer with very fine, mesh holes used for straining sauces and stocks

chocolate—sweetened, edible product processed from cacao; may contain flavorings, added cocoa butter, and milk

chocolate liqueur—finely ground nib, or meat, of the cacao bean, technically not yet chocolate; also referred to as unsweetened or baking chocolate (when warm, the liquor is fluid; when cold, it solidifies)

chocolate snaps—fairly crisp drop cookies flavored with chocolate

chou paste—another name for éclair paste

cinnamon—aromatic bark of certain trees of the laurel family; ground and used as a spice flavoring

citron—sweetened rind of a fruit

clear flour—flour made from middlings after patent flour is taken

coagulation—transformation of the proteins in a liquid to a solid state

cobbler—dessert made with fruit and rich biscuit dough placed on top of the fruit

cocoa—powder made from chocolate minus most of its cocoa butter

cocoa butter—naturally occurring fat in cacao beans, essential to the manufacturing of eating chocolate

coconut—inside meat of the coconut, shredded or grated

coffee cake—sweet bread in various shapes, with filling and topping

colors—shades produced by use of vegetable dyes; flour colors.

compote—fruit stewed or cooked in syrup

compound—in the baking industry, certain mixtures of fats and oils

compound/coating—typically a blend of sugar, cocoa powder, and/or chocolate liqueur and vegetable (vegetable oil is substituted for cocoa butter; known as a confectionary product)

conching—process in which heavy rollers plow back and forth through the liquid chocolate, kneading it to smooth out its texture and round out its flavor

condensed milk—whole milk from which part of the water has been taken and to which sugar has been added

congealing point—temperature at which a liquid becomes solid

convection oven—oven in which heat is spread through fans that rotate in both directions; this air movement speeds the cooking process by increasing the heat transfer to the food and bakes 15 percent faster than nonconvection ovens

cornet—cornucopia-shaped (horn-shaped) container of paper or cloth used for tubing soft dough, frosting, etc.

corn flour—coarse flour ground from corn; finer than meal

cornmeal—granular form of corn; somewhat coarser than corn flour corn muffin—sweet muffin containing corn flour or meal

cottage cheese—drained curd of soured cow's milk

coulis—thin, puréed sauce made of fruit and often used to garnish plated desserts

coupe—fruit-topped ice cream sundae

couverture—highly refined chocolate that has a higher cocoa butter content than eating or baking chocolate

cream—fat part of cow's milk; a thickened, cooked mass of sugar, egg, milk, and a thickener; used for pies and fillings

cream cheese—drained curd of soured cream, pressed

creaming—process of beating sugar and shortening

cream pies—one-crust pies having cream filling, topped with whipped cream or meringue

cream puffs—baked puffs of cream puff dough (choux paste) that are hollow; usually filled with whipped cream or a cream

cream rolls—puff paste rolled and baked in spiral shape, then filled with whipped cream or marshmallow

crème—also known as creams; are made of whipped cream or whipped egg whites and used to create dessert fillings such as crème anglaise or Bavarian cream

crème anglaise—a light vanilla sauce or thick custard made from milk, vanilla bean, egg yolks, and sugar

crème brulee—baked custard dessert topped with a burnt sugar topping

crème chantilly—vanilla-flavored whipped cream

crème de menthe—green flavoring of light mint taste

crème fraiche—heavy cream that has soured and thickened to the consistency of yogurt

crepes—thin, unleavened griddlecake made with egg batter filled with sweet or savory ingredients and rolled before serving

crescent rolls—hard, crusted rolls shaped into crescents, often with seeds on top

critical control points—the times in the food-handling process when you can prevent, eliminate, or reduce a hazard

croissant—crescent-shaped roll made from a rich, laminated dough

cross contamination—the transfer of harmful, foodborne microorganisms from one source to another

crown—protrusion of a muffin or quick bread above the pan line

cruller—long, twisted baking powder doughnut

crumb—the internal features of a baked good

crust—caramelized outer covering of a baked good

crystallization—when sucrose returns to its crystallized state

culinary—the art of cookery

cupcakes—small cakes of layer cake batter baked in muffin pans

curacao—orange-flavored liqueur

currant—acidulous berry of a shrub; usually used dried

custard—sweetened mixture of eggs and milk that is baked or cooked over hot water

cutting or "cut"—process of adding butter or shortening to dry ingredients; can be accomplished by using on/off turns with the standard mixer until the dough resembles coarse meal

D

danger zone—temperature range that may allow the growth of harmful foodborne microorganisms, which can cause customers to become sick

Danish pastry—flaky yeast dough having butter rolled into it

date—fruit of a species of palm; very sweet

date filling—cooked blend of dates, water, and sugar

deck—shelf in a bread oven

deck oven—type of oven with stationary shelves and arranged on individually heated levels; also called a peel oven

decorating tips—metal or plastic tip in which the frosting passes through, creating various designs

decoration—fancy designs or ornamentation

depositing—dropping into place such as depositing cookies onto a pan, muffin batter, icing on a cake to decorate

detection of flour—manner in which poor flour is contrasted with a good flour to show the former has been bleached

determination of ash—finding of the ash content of flour

determination of flour color—comparison of flour samples to show how they approach color standards

develop—process of mixing dough to a point where the mass is properly mixed; the proteins are hydrated and the gluten is stretched and relaxed; a dough's development can be judged to the point at which it pulls away from the sides of the mixing bowl

dextrin—soluble, gummy substance formed from starch by the action of heat, ferments, etc., having characteristic properties

dextrose—sugar of vegetables (except beets); less sweet than cane or beet sugar and more simple in structure, chemically speaking

diastase—enzyme possessing the power to convert starches into dextrin and maltrose (a simple sugar)

dissolve—liquefy or carry in suspension in liquid

divider—machine used to cut dough automatically into a required size

dock—a standard term for venting the dough with a fork or knife, breaking the surface to allow steam to escape

dough—thick, uncooked mass of combined ingredients for bread, rolls, cookies, etc.; usually applied to bread

dough conditioner—emulsifiers and enzymes added to dough to improve the development of the gluten or to soften the dough for faster mixing and fermentation

dough hook—attachment for a vertical mixer that is used for mixing dough; a metal hook that resembles a crooked letter "C"

doughnut—round cake, usually with center hole, made of yeast or baking powder dough and cooked in hot deep fat

doughnut kettle—large kettle used for frying doughnuts

doughnut screens—screens used to lift doughnuts from fat or for keeping them under the fat surface during cooking

doughnut sticks—wooden sticks for turning doughnuts while cooking

dough rollers—also called sheeters; equipment used in bakeshops that produce a high volume of laminated dough; with two sets of rollers, this machine applies pressure to both sides of the dough evenly

dough room—special room in which bread dough is mixed

dough room record—sheet of paper showing the time and losses of dough going through different stages (bread dough)

dough sheet—paper showing the formulas for a day's doughs

dough temperature—temperature of dough at different stages

dough time cards—cards usually punched with a time clock at different stages of dough processing

dropped—cookie made using a scoop or spoon to form and shape

drops—small globules of liquid that will drip instead of flow from spoon or container; a form of cookie

dry fruit—fruit from which moisture has been removed by drying

dry milk—milk from which water has been removed by drying

dry yeast—dehydrated form of yeast

durum wheat—hard wheat with a high protein content often used in making pasta

dusting—distributing a film of flour on pans or work bench

dusting flour—flour spread on work bench to prevent sticking

E

éclair—long, thin shell of same paste as cream puffs

éclair paste—also known as pâté à choux; used for making éclairs and cream puffs

emulsification—the suspension of a liquid and fat created by agitation, temperature, or the addition of an acid while agitating

emulsify—combine together, such as water and fat

emulsions—flavorful oils used in baking that have been mixed with water and vegetable gums

English brandy snaps—spicy cookies, very small and flat

enrobing—to cover a cake with icing or frosting

enzyme—minute substance produced by living organisms; has the power to bring about changes in organic materials

essential oils—pure oils extracted from fruits, nuts, or spices and used as a flavoring

evaporated milk—unsweetened, canned milk from which water has been removed before canning

expansion of dough—stage of dough production when the most air has been assimilated

extract—essence of fruits or spices used as flavoring

F

fat absorption—property of fried foods, such as doughnuts, that causes some of the frying fat to remain in the product; the type of fat used may affect the flavor of the finished product

fat bloom—white cast and soft texture that is the result of poor tempering or exposure of the chocolate to high temperatures; while visually undesirable, the product is safe to eat

fat filter—machine used to clean frying shortening

fats—term used for butter, lard, shortening, oil, or margarine

FDA food code—federal code of established practices for safe processing, purchasing, receiving, storing, cooking, and serving of food

ferment—substance, such as yeast, that produces fermentation

fermentation—chemical changes of an organic compound due to action of living organisms (as yeast) producing the formation of the leavening gas, carbon dioxide

fermentation period—time a dough is allowed to rest after mixing to increase in bulk

feuilletees—French puff pastry boxes that are filled with sweet or savory ingredients

fig—pear-shaped fruit of the fig tree

filberts—cultivated hazelnuts

filbert rolls—jelly-roll-type cake with roasted filberts in filling and batter

fillings—sweet creams, jams, etc. placed between baked layers, in cake rolls, or shaped into yeast-raised goods

finger roll—bun about 3 inches long and 1 inch wide

firing—process of heating an oven with fuel

flambé—food that is served flaming; liquor is ignited and the alcohol burns off but the flavor remains

flavor—extract, emulsion, or spice used to produce a pleasant taste; the taste of a finished product

flavoring compounds—concentrated essence of a spice or a fruit used to enhance the taste of baked goods

flax—grain, also known as linseed, that is rich in omega-3 fatty acids

fleurons—crescent-shaped puff pastry often used as a garnish

floor time—also referred to as fermentation time; the amount of time the yeast dough is to set prior to being taken to the bench

flour—finely ground meal of grain (wheat, rye, etc.)

flour scales—large platform scales used to show weight of flour when delivered and when used to detect losses by shrinkage

fluff—mass of beaten egg white and crushed fruit

fluid milk—the whole milk product normally served for beverage purposes and utilized in the preparation of certain foods

foam—mass of beaten egg and sugar, as in sponge cake, before adding flour

fold—method of lapping dough over on itself after it reaches right fermentation, as in making yeast-raised sweet goods

fold-over—also known as punching; action taken to release carbon dioxide and alcohol from the dough

fondant—icing of boiled sugar and water, without egg white

fondant slab—marble slab on which fondant is worked until creamy

fork—pronged utensil, usually of metal

formula—a recipe giving ingredients, amounts to be used, and method of combining them

foundation—reinforced base on which an oven or machine rests

frangipane—sweet almond and egg filling used in a variety of pastry recipes

French bread—unsweetened, crusty bread baked in a narrow strip and containing very little shortening

French knife—long knife with pointed blade used in cutting cakes, dough, and nuts

friancises—small pastry served after a meal, such as a petit four

friction factor—process of mixing that creates heat from friction against the bowl and dough hook; since dough is sensitive to heat it must be mixed at a specific temperature; the friction factor must be taken into account to make the dough come out at the specified temperature

fritter—doughnut made from cream puff paste and fried in hot deep fat; fruit-filled drops of heavy cake batter fried in deep fat

fructose—a natural invert sugar; found in honey

fruit cake—loaf containing large amounts of dried fruits and nuts with only enough batter to bind the fruit together

frying—cooking in hot deep fat

fuel—anything that is burned to produce heat

fuse—plug with a piece of metal of low melting point that is placed in an electric circuit to break the current when the load is too heavy, thus preventing fires from hot wire

G

ganache—smooth cream made from mixing chocolate and boiled cream

garnish—edible trimming or embellishment to enhance the flavor or visual appeal of food

garnishing bag—similar to a cornet and equipped with fancy tips

gastronomy—the art and science of good eating

gateau—French term for torte

gelatin—odorless, tasteless, colorless thickener that is dissolved in warm water and forms a jelly consistency when cooled

gelatinization of starch—formation of jelly-like substance when moistened starch is cooked

gelato—soft and silky Italian style of ice cream

genoise or genois—rich, light cake that is similar in texture to sponge cake and made from flour, sugar, eggs, vanilla, and butter

germ—part of seed (such as in grain) from which the new plant grows; microorganism

ginger—spicy root of a tropical plant used for flavoring

glacage—using a broiler or salamander to brown a food

glace—sugar so treated as to look like ice

glaze—application of a thin icing that will become shiny upon cooling

glazing screens—screen where doughnuts are iced and dried after frying

gliadin—part of the gluten that gives it elasticity

glucose—simple sugar made by action of acid on starch (corn syrup)

gluten—protein part of flour that gives structure to bakery products by enabling flour to expand around air or gas and to hold the texture so formed; the determining quality factor

glutenin—the part of gluten that gives it strength

gougere—savory hors d'oeuvre paste flavored with herbs or cheeses

gourmet—a person devoted to good food and drink

grading—separating middlings of wheat according to size

graham flour—unbolted wheat meal

graham muffin—sweet muffin with graham flour as main ingredient

greasing—spreading a film of fat on a surface

gum arabic—gum obtained from species of acacia trees

gum paste—white modeling substance of gum tragacanth or gelatin and sugar plus water

gums—extracts from vegetables that have the ability to suspend oil and water mixtures

gum tragacanth—gum used to give firmness

H

hamburger rolls—soft, round bun about 4 inches in diameter

hardness of water—indication of mineral salts in greater amount than is found in soft water

hazard analysis critical control points—also known as HACCP; the system used to maintain sanitary and safe conditions in all types of food service operations; focuses on the flow of food through the facility

hazelnut—edible nut, has a hard, smooth brown shell; also called filbert

hearth—heated baking surface or floor of an oven

herb—plant whose leaves, stems, seeds, or flowers is used as flavoring

holland rusk—toast of yeast biscuits rich in milk, eggs, etc.

homemade bread—plain-topped bread rolled in flour before panning or that is baked in household-type bread pans

homogenized milk—milk subjected to a mechanical process wherein the fat globules are reduced in size and a cream layer will not form on the product during storage

honey—sweet syrup substance made by bees from flower nectar

horn of plenty—cornucopia-shaped cookie or bread dough made with gum paste or buttercream trimming

horseshoes—Danish or puff pastry shaped like horseshoes

hot cross buns—yeast-raised buns with cross cut on top that is usually filled with plain frosting

humidity—amount of moisture in the air

hush puppy—made popular in southern states; a deep-fried cornmeal dumpling, often served with fish

hydrate—absorption of water by flour to form gluten

hydrogenated oil—oil treated with hydrogen to give a type of shortening

hygrometer—instrument to determine the degree of humidity

I

ice—frost or put on an icing or frosting; frozen water

icebox—type of cookie dough that is refrigerated prior to cutting and baking

icing—also known as frosting; decorative coating used as a filling or covering for baked goods

infection—presence of injurious microorganisms

infuse—to let sit in a liquid in order to extract the flavor

ingredients—food materials blended to give palatable products

ingredients room—separate room where ingredients are stored

inventory—itemized list of goods and equipment on hand, together with the estimated worth or cost

invertion—process in which an acid mixes with a carbohydrate and changes sucrose to dextrose and levalose

invert sugar—simple sugar; combination of dextrose and levulose

IQF—individual quick frozen

J

jam—gel made from fruit pulp and sugar, stiffened by the action of the sugar on the pectin in the fruit

jelly—stiffened combination of fruit juice and sugar, stiffened by the action of the sugar on the pectin in the fruit

jelly-roll pan—rectangular pan with 1-inch deep sides used to make sheet cakes or sponge cakes for jelly rolls

jelly wreath—rolled ring of basic sweet dough containing jelly

K

kaiser roll—large round yeast roll made with five folds and named after the five-pointed crown worn by the Kaiser in Germany; often used for sandwiches

kernel paste—mass of ground apricot kernels and sugar

kimmelwick—hard roll that originated in Buffalo, N.Y., and topped with caraway seeds and salt

kisses—meringue confection of egg whites and sugar baked slowly

knead—process of mixing and working dough into a pliable mass; it can be accomplished by using a mixer with a dough hook or by hand folding the dough in half, turning one quarter, folding in half, etc.

kuchen—German cake made with yeast

L

lactose—sugar of cow's milk

lady Baltimore cake—rich, white layer cake with fruit and nut filling and white icing

lady finger—light, delicate sponge cake that is shaped into long, fat "fingers"; used in making desserts such as tiramisu

laminated dough—dough that contains over 30 percent shortening and up to 10 percent sugar (puff pastry, Danish, and croissants) and follows a rolled-in procedure with multiple layers

lamination—process used to create light, fluffy baked goods such as croissants; made by laying dough and fat (butter) with multiple layers

lard—rendered hog fat

lattice—open design made by crossing or interlocking strips of dough and frostings

lean dough—dough that contains less than 10 percent shortening and sugar (French bread or Italian-style loaf)

leavening—raising or lightening by air, steam, or gas (carbon dioxide)

leavening agent—ingredient(s) used to introduce carbon dioxide, like yeast, baking powder, or soda plus sour milk

lecithin—emulsifier found in egg yolks and soy beans

leipziger stollen—rich coffee cake with a great deal of fruit

levulose—simple sugar found in honey and fruits

liaison—go between; mixing method used to bring opposites together, such as light and heavy or cold and hot

licensing—government requirement for teaching of a trade

linzer—pastries named for a city in Austria famous for its hazelnut and raspberry delicacies

liqueur—sweet alcoholic beverage made by mixing or redistilling spirits with fruits, flowers, herbs, or spices

liquid measures—container used to measure ingredient by volume

loaf bread—bread baked in pans

loaf cake—cake baked in bread pan or similar deep container

M

macaroon paste—combination of almond and kernel paste

macaroons—small cookies of nut paste (like almond), sugar, and egg white

madeleines—shell-shaped sponge cakes

make-up—method of mixing ingredients or handling of dough

malt extract—syrupy liquid obtained from malt mash

maltose—a simple sugar obtained from fermented barley; used as a yeast food in dough

mandoline—hand-operated slicing device

maple flavoring—extract of maple sugar or a syrup so flavored

maraschino—cordial distilled from Maraca cherry juice

maraschino cherries—artificially colored white cherries in maraschino

marble cake—cake of two or three colored batters partially mixed

marmalade—jelly made of unpeeled citrus fruit

marquise—frozen, mousse-type dessert

marzipan—almond paste used for modeling, masking, and torten

marshmallow—white confection of meringue-like consistency

marjolaine—dessert made of sponge cake, custard cream, buttercream, and cake crumbs

mascarpone cheese—rich Italian cream cheese used in tiramisu and other desserts

masking—act of covering with icing or frosting or such

meal—coarsely ground grain; unbolted wheat flour

measuring—apportioning ingredients by volume or weight; ascertaining dimensions, capacities, or weight

measuring cup—standardized cup marked with fractions of a cup used for accurate measure

measuring spoons—standardized spoons in a variety of sizes used for accurate measure

melba sauce—raspberry and currant jelly made into a sauce

melting point—temperature at which a solid (fat) will melt

meringue—white, frothy mass of beaten egg white and sugar

metric system—system of weights and measures based on multiple units of 10; used in the baking industry chiefly for flour analysis

middlings—coarse particles of ground wheat made during rolling of the grain in flour mills

milk—fluid secreted by the mammary glands of mammals; the white, opaque fluid squeezed from the udder of a cow

milk bread—white bread in which all liquid is milk or contains not less that 8.8 parts (by weight) of milk solids for each 100 parts of flour (by weight); this is a federal standard that is rigidly enforced

milk chocolate—composed of cocoa mass, sugar, and cocoa butter with the addition of a minimum of 14 percent milk solid

milk solids—all of cow's milk except the water

millet—high-protein cereal grain

milling—the process of turning grain into flour or meal

mincemeat—combination filling of fruit, spices, beef, and suet

mise en place—French term given to the organization of a work area

mix—combined ingredients of a batter or dough

mixing—blending of ingredients

mixing bowl—concave, hemispherical container for mixing

mocha—flavor combination of coffee and cream

moisture—water held in or appearing on a substance

molasses—light- to dark-brown syrup obtained in making cane sugar

mold infection—casual introduction of foreign, deleterious microscopic organisms of vegetable nature

moulder or molder—machine that shapes dough pieces for various shapes

mousse—light dessert consisting of whipped cream, egg yolks, boiled sugar, and flavoring

mousseline—egg-sugar base to which lightly whipped cream is added

muffins—small, light quick bread baked in muffin pans

mushrooms—Schaum torte confections in mushroom shapes

N

napoleon—baked good made with numerous sheets of puff pastry and filled with pastry cream

nappe—a sauce that reaches the consistency to coat the back of a spoon

neopolitan ice cream—three-layered ice cream; traditionally the layers are strawberry, chocolate, and vanilla ice cream

neopolitans—puff pastry slices filled with cream and frosted

nesselrode—consists of cream-enriched custard mixed with chestnut purée, candied fruits, currants, raisins, and maraschino liqueur; often frozen or made into a pie or dessert sauce

nibs—meat of the cacao bean; the fundamental item from which chocolate is made (these dark, rich bits remain when the shells detach from the beans after they have been roasted)

nougat—confection made with sugar or honey, roasted nuts, and sometimes candied fruit; usually made with egg whites or caramelized sugar

nut—edible seed

O

oatmeal—meal made by grinding oats

oil—type of fat that remains a liquid at room temperature

one-mix—cake mixing method that combines all ingredients and beats them at one time

oven spring—rapid rise of yeast goods during the first phase of baking; a time when the yeast is very active

P

paddle—attachment for a vertical mixer that is used for creaming and blending; typically made of metal and is similar to a flat spatula

pain—French word for bread

pandowdy—deep-dish apple dessert covered by a rich crust

panettone—sweet Italian sweet bread filled with candied fruits, anise seeds, and nuts and served during the Christmas season

pan glaze—spray used to season baking pans and forms

pans (tins)—variously shaped metal containers used for cooking and baking parchment paper—heavy, grease-resistant paper used to line cake pans and baking sheets

parfait—dessert served in tall, slender glasses and layered with ice cream or mousse and sauce or whipped cream

parker house rolls—folded buns of fairly rich dough

pasteurized milk—milk exposed to a specific heat treatment for a prescribed time to destroy the majority of the microorganisms present

pastillage—paste made of sugar, cornstarch, and gelatin; often molded into shapes

pastry bag—cone-shaped bag with two open ends; the small, pointed end may be fitted with a decorative tip; the filling is spooned into the larger end; when the bag is squeezed, the fillings are forced out of the bad

pastry brush—small brush used for applying glazes to baked goods

pastry cream—custard made with egg yolks, sugar, and milk and thickened with starch

pastry wheel—tool similar to a pizza cutter; used to cut dough into different-sized pieces

pâte à choux—also called éclair paste; used for making éclairs or cream puffs

pâte à glacer—chocolate coating made with vegetable oils; made to retain its shine

pâte brisée—flaky dough used for pie shells

pâte fermente—leftover dough from the previous day

patent flour—fine meal of ground spring wheat

patissier—French word for pastry chef

pazekè—type of popular Polish rich doughnut filled with prune filling served on Fat Tuesday in preparation of Lent

pectin—carbohydrate found in fruits and vegetables

peel—long-handled wooden or metal implement used to remove bakery products from oven hearths or shevles

petit fours—miniature frosted cakes

pH factor—the percentage of acidity or alkalinity found in a substance

pie—dessert with pastry bottom, fruit or cream filling, and meringue, whipped cream, or pastry top

pignoli—pine nuts

pine nuts—high-fat nuts that come from a variety of pine trees

piping gel—gel made from water, corn syrup, and vegetable gum used for piping designs and inscriptions

plain tube decorating—decorations made with plain round tube

pliable—condition of fat that allows it to be sheeted without breaking

poached—to simmer below the boiling point in liquid

poppy seeds—tiny seeds that are slate blue in color and have nut-like taste; often used topically on breads and rolls

pot de crème—custard baked and served in a small cup

pound cake—fine-textured cake made of flour, butter, vanilla, and eggs and flavored with lemon or vanilla

praline—paste made from sugar, almonds, and other nuts; can also be the term used for caramelized nuts

preservative—ingredients added to a product to inhibit organisms that cause spoilage

production yield—identifies the size of formula needed to fulfill an order

profiteroles—small, round pastry made from éclair paste

proofer—also called a proof box; a box or cabinet equipped with shelves; it also permits the introduction of heat and steam; used for fermenting dough

proofing period—time during which dough rises

pudding—thick custard made with eggs, milk, sugar, and flavorings

puff paste—rich pastry with rolled butter and special shortening for added flakiness

puff pastry—rich, delicate pastry consisting of many layers

pumpernickel—coarsely ground rye flour or the name of a type of rye bread made with this type of flour

pumpernickel meal—meal ground from rye flour

punch—see *fold*

punching—process whereby fermentation gas is expelled out and redistributed through the dough; it is accomplished by folding the dough onto itself several times until the mass feels tight

purée—food that has been mashed to a fine pulp

Q

quiche—savory tart filled with custard and savory ingredients

quick bread—bread leavened with chemical leavenors such as baking soda or baking powder

quinoa—seeds that can be used as a grain or ground into a flour

R

rack oven—type of oven heated by heating elements and circulating air; racks may revolve within the chamber, depending on the manufacturer

raisins—dried sweet grapes, either dark or bleached

ramekin—individual baking dish

ratio—the balance of the ingredients within a formula (or recipe)

reach-in—retarder, refrigerator, or freezer with shallow shelves, making products accessible from the outside door

recede—in the warm foaming method, eggs whipped until they reach their full volume; continue whipping at high speed until they drop or recede in volume

recipe—a formula used for creating a certain food or beverage

reel oven—reel oven or rotary oven; moderate in size with a pan capacity of 12 to 36 pans; the pans are placed on shelves that rotate like a Ferris wheel

retarder—refrigerator box designed specifically to accommodate fermented sweet dough

rich dough—dough that contains more than 10 percent shortening and sugar but less than 30 percent (American sandwich loaf)

ricotta—cooked whey from cows' milk, sometimes enriched with milk or cream

roasting—cooking or heating process using high-temperature dry heat, which fully develops the chocolate flavor of cocoa beans

rocks—small, rough-surfaced cookies resembling stone shapes

rolling pin—smooth-surfaced wooden piece for rolling dough

rolls—soft breads, sometimes called buns; hard-crusted pieces of lean dough

rope—spoiling bacterial growth in bread formed during production

rotary oven—rotary or reel oven; moderate in size with a pan capacity of 12 to 36 pans; the pans are placed on shelves that rotate like a Ferris wheel

rotary rack convection oven—used in hotel foodservice operations where a large volume of single products are baked at one time

roulade—sponge cake that is filled and rolled

rounding—shaping of dough pieces to seal ends and prevent bleeding

royal icing—decorative frosting of cooked sugar and egg white

S

sabayon—custard sauce made with eggs, sugar, and wine

salt—sodium chloride; used for flavor and dough control

sanitizing—process that destroys disease-causing organisms that may be present on equipment, even after cleaning

saturation—absorption to the limit of capacity

savarin—rich yeast cake soaked with rum syrup and often filled with pastry cream

savory—salty to the taste, not sweet

scald—to heat a liquid to just below boiling; tiny bubbles form on the sides of the pan

scale—instrument used for weighing

scaling—apportioning batter or dough according to unit weight

schedule—shop form designating amount and types of goods to be made and hour when needed

scone—small biscuit made with cream and eggs; cut into diamonds or bars and generally baked in an oven

score—to make shallow cuts on the surface of a food before cooking or baking

scoring—judging finished goods according to points of favor

seasoning—adding pan glaze or shortening to a pan prior to use; baked goods will brown better and release easier if pan is seasoned

semifreddi—frozen desserts including those that are mousses, soufflés, marquise, and Neapolitans

semi-sweet chocolate—chocolate that generally contains more sugar than bittersweet chocolate

semolina—also known as durum wheat; hard wheat with a high protein content often used in making pasta

separate—to keep apart as in egg whites and egg yolks; to come apart as in pie fillings

sesame seeds—oval-shaped seed that has a nutty flavor when roasted

sequence—the order in which the ingredients should be added in a formula

sfgolia—thin sheet of pasta dough that can be cut into shapes

sfogliatelle—old-world Neapolitan delicate pastry shaped like a clam shell and filled with a creamy semolina ricotta filling

sheeter—also called dough rollers; equipment used in bakeshops that produce a high volume of laminated dough: with two sets of rollers, this machine applies pressure to both sides of the dough evenly

shelf-life—the length of time a product can sit on the store shelf before it is considered no longer fresh and is unsaleable

sherbet—frozen dessert made of fruit juice or fruit purée and milk; may contain eggs

shoo fly pie—wet bottom molasses pie with German and Pennsylvania Dutch background

short breads—type of cookie traditionally made of one part sugar, two parts butter, and three parts flour

shortening—fat or oil used to tenderize flour products

shrink—undefined product loss from expected yield; caused by inaccurate scaling, pilferage, etc.

sifting—passing through fine sieve for perfect blending and to remove foreign or oversized particles

simmer—maintaining a temperature just below the boiling point

simple sugar—syrup made from sugar and water and used in a variety of frostings, sauces, and desserts

slurry—a thick liquid formed when yeast or starch is dissolved in water

small-deck oven—often called a pizza oven; used in retail operations because it affords the baker multiple temperature options and uses limited floor space

snaps—small cookies that run flat during baking

soda bread—a flat, round bread made with baking soda and buttermilk

soft peaks—to beat egg whites or whipping cream to the stage where the mixture forms soft, rounded peaks when the beaters are removed

solidifying point—temperature at which a fluid changes to a solid

sorbet—well-flavored, semi-frozen ice

souffle—very light baked or steamed pudding or dessert

sour—a ferment containing acid-producing bacteria; creates sour flavor in the dough

specific gravity—weight of a liquid compared to the weight of equal amounts of water

spelt—grain that has many names; the ancient Romans knew it as "farrum," Italians call it "faro," Germans know it as "dinkle"; can be milled into flour

spices—aromatic, dry vegetable substances used for flavoring

spiral mixers—conventional mechanical batch mixer that has a rotating set of arms and a rotation bowl

sponge cake—light, rich cake made light from beaten egg whites

sponge dough method—method for mixing dough; a *sponge* is first set by using about one-half of the flour, about four-sevenths of the water, and all the yeast and incorporating all other ingredients in a second operation sometime later when the dough is made

spoon bread—bread traditionally made with cornmeal, eggs, milk, and butter

springform pan—round pan with high, straight sides that expands with the aid of a clamp; the bottom of the pan is removable; often used to make cheesecakes

spritz—act of depositing cookies by means of a pastry bag

spun sugar—dark, caramelized sugar that is used to create hair-like threads

stabilizers—ingredients such as eggs and flour that bind liquids and become firm during baking

stollen—German, rich yeast bread containing raisins, citron, and chopped nutmeats

starches—complex carbohydrates that are from plants; often used as a thickening agent

steam—vapor formed and given off from heated liquid

stiff peaks—egg whites that are beaten until they leave a firm peak when the beaters are lifted above the mixture

stir—mixing method that blends ingredients by hand

straight dough mixing—method for mixing dough in which all of the ingredients are incorporated in one long process of mixing and kneading

straight flour—flour containing all of the wheat berry except the bran and feeds; termed 100 percent extraction flour

streusel—topping for baked goods made with fat, flour, sugar, nuts, and spices

strudel—pastry made of fruit or cheese rolled in thin sheets of dough and baked

style—mode of expression or execution

"swab the deck"—a term given to the oven attendant before steam injection ovens were available

syrup—mixture of equal parts of sugar and water that is often flavored with fruits or spices

T

tare—when a baker's balance beam scale is counterbalanced it is tared

tart—pastry with heavy fruit filling or cream

tartlet—single-serving size of tart

tea rolls—small, sweet buns

temperature—degree of heat or cold; it is a major factor for controlling the quality of baked goods; each formula has a suggested number of degrees in which it should be baked

tempering—adjusting temperature of ingredients to a certain degree that is generally achieved by heating or cooling and mixing or stirring

tenderizers—ingredients such as sugar, fat, oil, and liquids that provide moisture and tenderness or softness to the grain and texture of the baked good

testing—trying a cake or bread at the oven for doneness; checking product or ingredients for quality according to a set method

texture—interior grain or structure of a baked product as shown by a cut surface; the feeling of a substance under the fingers

thermometer—instrument for measuring heat and cold

time—amount of minutes needed to develop each step in a formula

tiramisu—classic Italian dessert made with sponge cake or lady fingers dipped in espresso and marsala, rum, or Kahlua, mascarpone cheese, grated chocolate, and sometimes whipped cream

toque—white hat worn by chefs

torte—European term for rich, round layered cake

torten—large, fancy cakes enriched with creams, marzipan, etc.

trifle—English dessert consisting of sponge cake that has been soaked in rum, sherry, or brandy and topped with layers of jam, custard, and whipped cream

troughs—large, rather shallow, containers, usually on wheels; used for holding large masses of rising dough

truffle—rich chocolate candies

tubing—pressing a substance through a decorating or other type of tube

turntable—round, revolving platform used for rotating the cake when filling, frosting, and decorating

tutti frutti—confection or filling made of a fruit mixture

U

unsaturated fats—fats that remain liquid at room temperature

V

vanilla bean—long, bean-like fruit; seeds are used as flavoring

vanillin—vanilla flavoring

vegetable colors—liquids or pastes of vegetable nature used for coloring

vertical mixer—conventional mechanical batch mixer that has a stationary bowl and several attachments that rotate and move around the inside of the bowl

Vienna bread—hearth bread with heavy, crisp crust; sometimes finished with a seed topping

vou-au-vent—individual-sized puff pastry; often filled with savory ingredients

W

walk-in—retarder, refrigerator, or freezer that a person can walk into and that holds large quantities of product

wash—liquid brushed on the surface of an unbaked product (may be water, milk, starch solution, thin syrup, or egg)

water bath—also called a bain marie; cooking technique that places container into a large, shallow pan of water that surrounds the food with a gentle heat; can be used in the oven or on top of the stove

whip—to beat to a froth; an instrument consisting of strong wire held together by a handle and used for whipping; also the name for an attachment for a vertical mixer; the whip is used for aeration of egg foams and creams and resembles the head of a giant egg beater

white chocolate—mixture of cocoa butter, sugar, milk solids, lecithin, and vanilla

whole wheat—flour created from entire hulled wheat kernel or components added after it was milled

Y

yeast—microscopic fungus (plant) that reproduces by budding; causes fermentation and the giving off of carbon dioxide

yeast-raised doughnut—doughnut leavened with yeast that is raised on the bench and cut into ring-type doughnuts, long johns, or bismarks

yield—amount of product produced by a formula

Z

zest—outer covering of the rind of citrus fruit

zwieback—toast made of rich coffee cake that has been twice-baked (*zwie* is German for "two")

index

credits

© Dorling Kindersley; page 110, 2nd from top: Richard Embery; page 110, 3rd from top: Richard Embery; page 110, 3rd from bottom: Richard Embery; page 110, 2nd from bottom: Richard Embery; page 110, bottom: Richard Embery; page 111, top: Richard Embery; page 111, 2nd from top: Labensky, Sarah R., Van Damme, Eddy, Martel, Priscilla, and Tenbergen, Klaus (2005). *On Baking*. Upper Saddle River, NJ: Pearson Prentice Hall. page 26, 2nd from top; page 111, 3rd from top: Labensky, Sarah R., Van Damme, Eddy, Martel, Priscilla, and Tenbergen, Klaus (2005). *On Baking*. Upper Saddle River, NJ: Pearson Prentice Hall. page 26, 3rd from top; page 111, 4th from top: Labensky, Sarah R., Van Damme, Eddy, Martel, Priscilla, and Tenbergen, Klaus (2005). *On Baking*. Upper Saddle River, NJ: Pearson Prentice Hall. page 25, bottom; page 111, 5th from top: Clive Streeter and Patrick McLeavy © Dorling Kindersley; page 111, 4th from bottom: Richard Embery; page 111, 3rd from bottom: Richard Embery; page 111, 2nd from bottom: Ian O'Leary © Dorling Kindersley; page 111, bottom: Richard Embery; page 112: Noble Masi.

Unit 7

Unit 7 Opener: Richard Embery; 7-1: Richard Embery, Pearson Education/PH College; 7-2: Richard Embery; 7-7: Labensky, Sarah R., Van Damme, Eddy, Martel, Priscilla, and Tenbergen, Klaus (2005). *On Baking*. Upper Saddle River, NJ: Pearson Prentice Hall. Page 27, middle of page; 7-9: Richard Embery; page 133: Courtesy of Jackie Scott; page 134: Used with permission of William Reynolds.

Unit 8

Section 4 Opener: Ian O'Leary © Dorling Kindersley; Unit 8 Opener: Ian O'Leary © Dorling Kindersley; 8-1: Ian O'Leary © Dorling Kindersley; 8-2: Richard Embery; 8-3: Richard Embery; 8-4: Richard Embery; 8-5: Richard Embery; 8-6: Richard Embery; 8-7: Richard Embery; 8-8: Richard Embery; 8-9: Richard Embery; 8-10: Richard Embery; 8-11: Richard Embery; 8-12: Richard Embery; 8-13: Richard Embery; 8-14: Richard Embery; 8-15: Richard Embery; 8-16: Richard Embery; 8-17: Ian O'Leary © Dorling Kindersley; 8-18: Richard Embery; 8-19: Richard Embery; 8-20: Richard Embery.

Unit 9

Unit 9 Opener: Mitch Hrdlicka, Getty Images, Inc.—Photodisc; 9-1: Richard Embery; page 160, top: Richard Embery; page 160, 2nd from top: Richard Embery; page 160, 2nd from bottom: Richard Embery; page 160, bottom: Richard Embery; page 161, bottom: Ian O'Leary © Dorling Kindersley; page 161, top: Ian O'Leary © Dorling Kindersley; page 161, middle: Ian O'Leary © Dorling Kindersley; page 161, 2nd from bottom: Richard Embery; page 162, bottom left: Kevin Sanchez, Getty Images, Inc.—PhotoDisc; page 162, top: Ian O'Leary © Dorling Kindersley; page 162, 2nd from top: Ian O'Leary © Dorling Kindersley; page 162, bottom right: Ian O'Leary © Dorling Kindersley; page 163, top: Richard Embery; page 163, 2nd from top: Richard Embery; page 163, 2nd from bottom: Richard Embery; page 163, bottom: Richard Embery; page 164, bottom left: Richard Embery; page 164, top: Richard Embery; page 164, middle: Richard Embery; page 164, bottom right: Richard Embery; page 165, bottom left: Paul Bricknell © Dorling Kindersley; page 165, top: Ian O'Leary © Dorling Kindersley; page 165, 2nd from top: Ian O'Leary © Dorling Kindersley; page 165, 3rd from top: Ian O'Leary © Dorling Kindersley; page 165, 2nd from bottom: Jerry Young © Dorling Kindersley; page 165, bottom: Jerry Young © Dorling Kindersley; page 166, top: Richard Embery; page 166, bottom: Richard Embery; page 167, top: Richard Embery; page 167, bottom: Roger Phillips © Dorling Kindersley; page 168, top: Richard Embery; page 168, bottom: MARK CARLETON/PHOTOGROUP, Getty Images, Inc.—Taxi; page 169, top: © Dorling Kindersley; page 169, bottom: © Dorling Kindersley; page 170, top: Mitch Hrdlicka, Getty Images, Inc.—Photodisc; page 170, bottom: Stephen Oliver © Dorling Kindersley; page 171,

top: Richard Embery; page 171, bottom: Getty Images, Inc.—PhotoDisc; page 172, top: Ian O'Leary © Dorling Kindersley; page 172, bottom: © Dorling Kindersley; page 173: Richard Embery, Pearson Education/PH College; page 174: Richard Embery, Pearson Education/PH College; 9-2: Ian O'Leary © Dorling Kindersley; page 177, top: Photo courtesy of Paul Smith; page 177, bottom: Photo courtesy of Daniel J. Matt.

Unit 10

Section 5 Openers: Allen Polansky, The Stock Connection; Gould, David, Getty Images Inc.— Image Bank; Unit 10 Opener: Allan Rosenberg, Getty Images, Inc.—PhotoDisc; 10-1: Richard Embery; 10-5: Richard Embery; page 190, top: Richard Embery; page 190, middle: Richard Embery; page 190, bottom: Richard Embery; page 191, top: Richard Embery; page 191, 2nd from top: Richard Embery; page 191, 2nd from bottom: Richard Embery; page 191, bottom: Paul Webster, Getty Images Inc.—Stone Allstock; 10-6: Richard Embery; page 193, top: Richard Embery, Pearson Education/PH College; page 193, 2nd from top: Richard Embery, Pearson Education/PH College; page 193, 3rd from top: Richard Embery, Pearson Education/PH College; page 193, 2nd from bottom: Richard Embery, Pearson Education/PH College; page 193, bottom: Richard Embery, Pearson Education/PH College; 10-8: Richard Embery; 10-9: Richard Embery; 10-10: Richard Embery; 10-11: Richard Embery; 10-12: Richard Embery; 10-13: Richard Embery; 10-14: Richard Embery; 10-15: Richard Embery; 10-16: Richard Embery; 10-17: Richard Embery; page 197, top: Richard Embery; page 197, bottom: Dave King © Dorling Kindersley; page 198, top:Richard Embery; page 198, bottom: Richard Embery;10-18: Richard Embery; page 199, bottom: Richard Embery; 10-19: Richard Embery; 10-20: Richard Embery; 10-21: Richard Embery; 10-22: Richard Embery; 10-23: Richard Embery; 10-24: Richard Embery; 10-25: Richard Embery; 10-26: Dave King, Dorling Kindersley Media Library; page 202, top: Labensky, Sarah R., Van Damme, Eddy, Martel, Priscilla, and Tenbergen, Klaus (2005). *On Baking*. Upper Saddle River, NJ: Pearson Prentice Hall. page 286, top; page 202, 2nd from top: Richard Embery, Pearson Education/PH College; page 202, 3rd from top: Labensky, Sarah R., Van Damme, Eddy, Martel, Priscilla, and Tenbergen, Klaus (2005). *On Baking*. Upper Saddle River, NJ: Pearson Prentice Hall. page 286, bottom left; page 202, 2nd from bottom: Richard Embery, Pearson Education/PH College; page 202, bottom: Labensky, Sarah R., Van Damme, Eddy, Martel, Priscilla, and Tenbergen, Klaus (2005). On Baking. Upper Saddle River, NJ: Pearson Prentice Hall. page 286, bottom right; page 204, top: Used with permission of Marshall Faye; page 204, bottom: Used with permission of Dominick Simone.

Unit 11

Section 6 Opener: Unidentified, Dorling Kindersley Media Library; Unit 11 Opener: David Murray and Jules Selmes © Dorling Kindersley; 11-1: Richard Embery; 11-2: Richard Embery; 11-3: Richard Embery; 11-4: Richard Embery; 11-5: Richard Embery; 11-6: Richard Embery; page 218, top: Richard Embery; page 218, 2nd from top: Richard Embery, Pearson Education/PH College; page 218, 2nd from bottom: David Murray and Jules Selmes © Dorling Kindersley; page 218, bottom: Richard Embery; page 219, top: Richard Embery; page 219, 2nd from top: Richard Embery; page 219, 3rd from bottom: Richard Embery; page 219,2nd from bottom: Richard Embery; page 219, bottom: Berit Myrekrok, Getty Images—Digital Vision; page 221, top: Richard Embery; page 221, bottom: Richard Embery, Pearson Education/PH College; page 222: © Dorling Kindersley; page 223, top: Richard Embery; page 223, bottom: Richard Embery; page 225, top: Martin Brigdale © Dorling Kindersley; page 225, bottom: Richard Embery; page 226, top: Steve Adams, Creative Eye/MIRA.com; page 226, bottom: Richard Embery; page 227, top: Richard Embery; page 227, middle: Richard Embery, Pearson Education/PH College; page 227, bottom: Richard Embery, Pearson Education/PH College; page 228: Jerry Young © Dorling

Kindersley; page 229, top: David Murray © Dorling Kindersley; page 229, bottom: Richard Embery; page 230: Martin Brigdale © Dorling Kindersley; page 231, top: James Jackson © Dorling Kindersley; page 232, top: Richard Embery; page 232, 2nd from top: Richard Embery; page 232, 2nd from bottom: Richard Embery; page 232, bottom: Richard Embery; page 233, top: Richard Embery; page 233, 2nd from top: Richard Embery; page 233, 3rd from top: Richard Embery; page 233, 2nd from bottom: Richard Embery; page 233, bottom: © Dorling Kindersley; page 234, top: Jerry Young © Dorling Kindersley; page 234, bottom: Richard Embery; page 235: Noble Masi.

Unit 12

Unit 12 Opener: Bruna Stude, Omni-Photo Communications, Inc;. page 240, top: Richard Embery; page 240, middle: Richard Embery; page 240, bottom: Richard Embery; page 241: Felicia Martinez, PhotoEdit Inc.; page 242: Richard Embery; 12-1: Richard Embery; 12-2: Richard Embery; 12-3: Richard Embery; 12-4: Richard Embery; 12-5: Richard Embery; page 244: Richard Embery; page 245, top: Richard Embery; page 245, 2nd from top: Richard Embery; page 245, 3rd from top: Richard Embery; page 245, 3rd from bottom: Richard Embery; page 245, 2nd from bottom: Richard Embery; page 245, bottom: Richard Embery; page 246: Richard Embery; page 247, top: Richard Embery; page 247, bottom: Richard Embery; page 249, top: Corbis Digital Stock; 12-8: Richard Embery, Pearson Education/PH College; 12-9: Richard Embery, Pearson Education/PH College; 12-10: Richard Embery, Pearson Education/PH College; 12-11: Richard Embery, Pearson Education/PH College; 12-12: Richard Embery, Pearson Education/PH College; 12-13: Richard Embery, Pearson Education/PH College; 12-14: © Dorling Kindersley; page 251: Richard Embery; 12-15: Richard Embery, Pearson Education/PH College; 12-16: Richard Embery, Pearson Education/PH College; page 253, bottom: Richard Embery, Pearson Education/PH College; page 254, top: Richard Embery; page 254, bottom: Richard Embery; page 255, top: Richard Embery; page 255, bottom: Used with permission of Janet Lightizer; page 256: Used with permission of Terry Wagner.

Unit 13

Section 7 Opener: Richard Embery; Unit 13 Opener: Richard Embery; 13-1: Richard Embery; 13-2: Richard Embery; 13-3: Richard Embery; 13-4: Courtesy of Culinary Institute of America; 13-5: David Murray © Dorling Kindersley; page 265, top: Richard Embery; page 265, 2nd from top: Richard Embery; page 265, 2nd from bottom: Richard Embery; page 265, bottom: Richard Embery; page 266: Richard Embery; page 267: © Burazin/Masterfile Stock Image Library; 13-15: EyeWire Collection, Getty Images—Photodisc; 13-16: Richard Embery; page 270, top: Richard Embery; page 270, 2nd from top: Richard Embery; page 270, 2nd from bottom: Richard Embery; page 270, bottom: Richard Embery, Pearson Education/PH College; page 271, top: Richard Embery, Pearson Education/PH College; page 271, bottom: Richard Embery; page 272, top: Richard Embery; 13-17: Richard Embery; 13-18: Richard Embery; 13-19: Richard Embery; page 273: Richard Embery, Pearson Education/PH College; page 274, middle: Richard Embery; 13-20: Richard Embery; page 274, top: C Squared Studios, Getty Images, Inc.—Photodisc; page 275: Getty Images, Inc.- Photodisc; page 276: Richard Embery; page 277: KLEIN, MATTHEW, Photo Researchers, Inc.; page 278, top: Richard Embery; page 278, bottom: Richard Embery; page 279, left: Richard Embery; page 279, right: Richard Embery; page 280: Getty Images, Inc.—PhotoDisc; 13-21: Richard Embery; 13-22: Richard Embery; page 282: Used with permission of Wally Amos; page 283: Used with permission of Tina Powers.

Unit 14

Section 8 Opener: Richard Embery; Unit 14 Opener: KLEIN, MATTHEW, Photo Researchers, Inc.;page 292, bottom: David Murray © Dorling Kindersley; page 292,

top: Richard Embery; page 292, 2nd from top: Richard Embery; page 292, 2nd from bottom: Richard Embery; 14-1: Russ Lappa, Prentice Hall School Division; 14-2: Dave King © Dorling Kindersley; 14-3: Ian O'Leary © Dorling Kindersley; page 293, bottom: Ian O'Leary © Dorling Kindersley; 14-4: Ian O'Leary © Dorling Kindersley; 14-5: Richard Embery; page 295, top: Richard Embery; page 295, middle: Richard Embery; page 295, bottom: Richard Embery; page 296: Richard Embery, Pearson Education/PH College; page 297: Courtesy of Dorling Kindersley; page 298: David Murray and Jules Selmes © Dorling Kindersley; page 299, top: David Murray and Jules Selmes © Dorling Kindersley; page 299, middle: Richard Embery; 14-6: Jerry Young © Dorling Kindersley; page 300, top: Jerry Young © Dorling Kindersley; page 300, middle: Jerry Young © Dorling Kindersley; page 300, bottom: Jerry Young © Dorling Kindersley; page 301: Andy Crawford © Dorling Kindersley; page 302: Richard Embery; 14-7: Reprinted with permission of John Folse; page 304: Richard Embery; page 305, top: Photo courtesy of Tom Gumpel; page 305, bottom: Photo courtesy of Katherine R. Perrotti.

Unit 15

Unit 15 Opener: Richard Embery; 15-1: Richard Embery; 15-2: Richard Embery, Pearson Education/PH College; 15-3: Dave King © Dorling Kindersley; 15-4: Richard Embery; 15-5: JONELLE WEAVER, Getty Images, Inc.—Taxi; page 316, bottom: Russ Lappa, Prentice Hall School Division; 15-6: Richard Embery; 15-7: Richard Embery; page 318, top: Richard Embery; page 318, middle: Richard Embery; page 318, bottom: David Murray and Jules Selmes © Dorling Kindersley; page 319, top: Courtesy of Pearson Education; page 319, 2nd from top: Courtesy of Dorling Kindersley; page 319 2nd from bottom: © Dorling Kindersley; page 319, bottom: Courtesy of Dorling Kindersley; 15-8: Richard Embery; page 321, top: © Dorling Kindersley; page 321, bottom: Dave King © Dorling Kindersley; 15-9: Dave King © Dorling Kindersley; 15-10: Richard Embery; page 323: Richard Embery; page 324, top: Richard Embery, Pearson Education/PH College; page 324, 2nd from top: Richard Embery; page 324, 3rd from top: Richard Embery; page 324, 2nd from bottom: Richard Embery, Pearson Education/PH College; page 324, bottom: Dave King © Dorling Kindersley; page 325, top: Jerry Young © Dorling Kindersley; page 325, bottom: Richard Embery; 15-11: Richard Embery; page 327, top: Richard Embery; page 327, middle: Richard Embery; page 327, bottom: Richard Embery; page 328, top: © Dorling Kindersley; page 328, bottom: FoodPix/Getty Images, Inc.; 15-12: Richard Embery; page 329, bottom: Richard Embery, Pearson Education/PH College; page 330: Richard Embery; page 332: Noble Masi.

Unit 16

Section 9 Opener: Richard Embery; Unit 16 Opener: Richard Embery; 16-1: Richard Embery; 16-2: Richard Embery; page 341: Richard Embery; page 342: Labensky, Sarah R., Van Damme, Eddy, Martel, Priscilla, and Tenbergen, Klaus (2005). On Baking. Upper Saddle River, NJ: Pearson Prentice Hall. page 361; 16-4: © Dorling Kindersley; 16-5: Richard Embery, Pearson Education/PH College; page 344: Richard Embery; page 345: Richard Embery, Pearson Education/PH College; page 346: Richard Embery; 16-6: Richard Embery; 16-7: Richard Embery; 16-8: Richard Embery; page 347, bottom: Richard Embery; page 348, top: Labensky, Sarah R., Van Damme, Eddy, Martel, Priscilla, and Tenbergen, Klaus (2005). On Baking. Upper Saddle River, NJ: Pearson Prentice Hall. page 358; page 348, bottom: Richard Embery; 16-9: Richard Embery; 16-10: Richard Embery; page 349, bottom: Richard Embery; page 350: Richard Embery; 16-11: Roger Phillips © Dorling Kindersley; 16-12: Roger Phillips © Dorling Kindersley; page 351: Photo courtesy of Stephen James; page 352: Photo courtesy of Andrew Come.

Unit 17

Unit 17 Opener: Pearson Education/PH College; 17-1: Walter H. Hodge, Peter Arnold, Inc.; 17-2: James V. Elmore, Peter Arnold, Inc.; 17-3: Fotos & Photos, Index Stock Imagery, Inc.; 17-4: Dave King © Dorling Kindersley; 17-5: Richard Embery, Pearson Education/PH College; 17-6: James Jackson © Dorling Kindersley; 17-7: Dave King © Dorling Kindersley; 17-8: Dave King © Dorling Kindersley; 17-9: Richard Embery; 17-10: Richard Embery; 17-11: Richard Embery; 17-12: Richard Embery; 17-13: Ian O'Leary © Dorling Kindersley; page 365: Richard Embery, Pearson Education/PH College; 17-15: Richard Embery, Pearson Education/PH College; page 366, top: Ian O'Leary © Dorling Kindersley; page 366, middle: David Murray and Jules Selmes © Dorling Kindersley; page 366, bottom: Richard Embery; page 367, top: Richard Embery; page 368: © Dorling Kindersley; 17-16: Richard Embery, Pearson Education/PH College; 17-17: Richard Embery, Pearson Education/PH College; 17-18: Richard Embery, Pearson Education/PH College; 17-19: Richard Embery; 17-20: Richard Embery, Pearson Education/PH College; page 370, left: Richard Embery, Pearson Education/PH College; page 370, right: Richard Embery, Pearson Education/PH College; page 371, top: Frank LaBua, Pearson Education/PH College; 17-21: Richard Embery; 17-22: John Kelly, Getty Images Inc.—Stone Allstock; page 372: Used with permission of Joseph Decker.

Unit 18

Section 10 Opener: Richard Embery; Unit 18 Opener: Rene Sheret/Stone/Getty Images; 18-1: Richard Embery; 18-2: Richard Embery; 18-3: Richard Embery; 18-4: Richard Embery; 18-5: Dave King © Dorling Kindersley; 18-6: Richard Embery; 18-7: Richard Embery; 18-8: Richard Embery; 18-9: Richard Embery; 18-10: JONELLE WEAVER, Getty Images, Inc.—Taxi; 18-11: Richard Embery; 18-12: Richard Embery; 18-13: Richard Embery; 18-14: Richard Embery; 18-15: Richard Embery; 18-16: Richard Embery; 18-17: Richard Embery; 18-18: Richard Embery; 18-19: Richard Embery; 18-20: Richard Embery; 18-21: Richard Embery; 18-22: Richard Embery; 18-23: Richard Embery; 18-24: Richard Embery; 18-25: Richard Embery; 18-27: Richard Embery; 18-28: Richard Embery; 18-29: Richard Embery; 18-30: Richard Embery; 18-31: Richard Embery; 18-32: Richard Embery; 18-33: Richard Embery; 18-34: Richard Embery; 18-35: Richard Embery; 18-36: Richard Embery; 18-37: Richard Embery; 18-38: Richard Embery; 18-39: Richard Embery; 18-40: Richard Embery; 18-41: Richard Embery; 18-42: Richard Embery; 18-43: Richard Embery; 18-44: Richard Embery; 18-45: Richard Embery; 18-46: Richard Embery; 18-47: Richard Embery; 18-48: Richard Embery; 18-49: Richard Embery; 18-50: Richard Embery; 18-51: Richard Embery; 18-52: Richard Embery; page 393: Noble Masi; page 394: Photo courtesy of Sue Martin.

Unit 19

Unit 19 Opener: Richard Embery; page 400: Richard Embery; page 401, top: Richard Embery; page 401, bottom: Richard Embery; page 402, top: Richard Embery; page 402, bottom: Richard Embery; 19-1: Richard Embery; 19-2: Richard Embery; 19-3: Richard Embery; 19-4: Stockbyte; page 404, top: © Dorling Kindersley; page 404, bottom: Richard Embery; page 405: Richard Embery; page 406: Richard Embery; page 407: Richard Embery; 19-5: Richard Embery; 19-6: David Murray © Dorling Kindersley; page 408: Richard Embery; page 409: Richard Embery; page 410, left: Richard Embery, Pearson Education/PH College; page 410, right: David Murray © Dorling Kindersley; page 411: Richard Embery; 19-7: Noble Masi; 19-8: Noble Masi; 19-9: Noble Masi; 19-10: Noble Masi; 19-11: Richard Embery; 19-12: Richard Embery; 19-13: Richard Embery; 19-15: Richard Embery; 19-16: Richard Embery; 19-17: Richard Embery; 19-18: Richard Embery; 19-19: Courtesy of PhotoEdit; 19-20:

Richard Embery; 19-21: Richard Embery; 19-22: Richard Embery; page 416: Used with permission of Anil Rohira.

Unit 20

Unit 20 Opener: © Dorling Kindersley; page 422: Richard Embery; 20-1: Richard Embery; 20-2: Richard Embery; 20-3: Richard Embery; 20-4: Richard Embery; page 423: Richard Embery; 20-5: Richard Embery; page 424: Richard Embery; 20-6: Richard Embery; 20-7: Richard Embery; 20-8: Richard Embery; 20-9: Richard Embery; page 425: Richard Embery; 20-10: David Murray © Dorling Kindersley; 20-11: Dave King © Dorling Kindersley; 20-12: Labensky, Sarah R., Van Damme, Eddy, Martel, Priscilla, and Tenbergen, Klaus (2005). *On Baking.* Upper Saddle River, NJ: Pearson Prentice Hall. page 286, bottom right; 20-13: Richard Embery, Pearson Education/PH College; 20-14: Richard Embery, Pearson Education/PH College; 20-15: Labensky, Sarah R., Van Damme, Eddy, Martel, Priscilla, and Tenbergen, Klaus (2005). *On Baking.* Upper Saddle River, NJ: Pearson Prentice Hall. page 260, left photo; 20-16: Labensky, Sarah R., Van Damme, Eddy, Martel, Priscilla, and Tenbergen, Klaus (2005). *On Baking.* Upper Saddle River, NJ: Pearson Prentice Hall. page 260, right photo; page 428: Richard Embery; 20-17: Richard Embery; page 429, top: Richard Embery; page 429, bottom: Richard Embery; 20-18: David Murray © Dorling Kindersley; 20-19: David Murray © Dorling Kindersley; 20-20: David Murray © Dorling Kindersley; 20-21: Getty Images, Inc.—PhotoDisc; 20-22: Richard Embery; 20-23: Richard Embery; page 432, top: Richard Embery; page 432, bottom: Richard Embery; 20-24: Richard Embery; 20-25: Richard Embery; 20-26: Richard Embery; 20-27: Richard Embery; 20-28: Richard Embery; 20-29: Ian O'Leary © Dorling Kindersley; 20-30: Richard Embery; 20-31: Richard Embery; 20-32: PETER JOHNSON, Photolibrary.Com; 20-33: Jeffrey Greenberg, Photo Researchers, Inc.; 20-34: Allen Polansky, The Stock Connection; page 437: Used with the permission of Vincent Termini, Jr.

Unit 21:

Section 11 Opener: SuperStock, Inc.; Unit 21 Opener: Photo courtesy of *Modern Baking;* 21-01: Jeff Greenberg, Omni-Photo Communications, Inc.; 21-2: Photo used with permission of the American Culinary Federation; 21-3: Photo used with permission of the Retail Bakers of America; 21-4: Rene Sheret, Getty Images Inc.—Stone Allstock; 21-5: Dufault,Kent, Index Stock Imagery, Inc.; 21-5: Richard Embery; 21-6: Photo used with permission of the International Association of Culinary Professionals; 21-7: Photo used with permission of the International Food Service Executives Association; 21-8: Photo used with permission of National Restaurant Association; 21-9: Photo courtesy of the *National Culinary Review;* 21-10: Photo courtesy of *Chef* magazine; 21-11: Used with permission of Nation's Restaurant News; 21-12: Photo courtesy of *Modern Baking;* 21-13: Richard Hutchings, PhotoEdit Inc.; 21-15: STEVE SMITH, Getty Images, Inc.—Taxi; 21-16: Ron Sherman, Creative Eye/MIRA.com; 21-17: Bill Aron, PhotoEdit Inc.; 21-18: Bill Aron, PhotoEdit Inc.; page 459: Used with permission of Bernard Reynolds.

Front Matter

page v: Richard Embery; page vii: Courtesy of Red Star Yeast & Products (Division of Universal Foods Corp.) Milwaukee, Wisconsin; page xiiii: Dave King © Dorling Kindersley; page xvii: Allen Polansky, The Stock Connection; page xxiii: Francis G. Sheehan, Photo Researchers, Inc.; page xxv: Mel Winer, The Stock Connection; page xxxii: Ian O'Leary © Dorling Kindersley.

End Matter

page 463, 470, 473, 490, 494, 496, 498, 552, 554, 556: Izzy Schwartz, Getty Images, Inc.—Photodisc, page 559: Steve Adams, Creative Eye/MIRA.com; page 562: Courtesy of Dorling Kindersley; pages 578, 592: Simon Smith © Dorling Kindersley